UNWARRANTED INTRUSIONS

The Case against Government Intervention in the Marketplace

Martin Fridson

WILEY

John Wiley & Sons, Inc.

Published by John Wiley & Sons, Inc., Hoboken, New Jersey.
Published simultaneously in Canada.

For general information on our other products and services or for technical support, please contact our Customer Care Department within the United States at (800) 762-2974, outside the United States at (317) 572-3993 or fax (317) 572-4002.

Wiley also publishes its books in a variety of electronic formats. Some content that appears in print may not be available in electronic books. For more information about Wiley products, visit our web site at www.wiley.com.

Library of Congess Cataloging-in-Publication Data:

Fridson, Martin
  Unwarranted intrusions : the case against government intervention in the marketplace / Martin Fridson.
      p. cm.
    ISBN-13 978-0-471-68713-9 (cloth)
    ISBN-10 0-471-68713-8 (cloth)
  1. Industrial policy—United States.   2. Trade regulation—United States.   3. Restraint of trade—United States.   4. Intervention (Federal government)—United States.   5. Economics—Political aspects—United States.   6. United States—Politics and government—2001–ᅠ I. Title.
    HD3616.U47F747 2006
    338.6′0480973—dc22
                                                                          2005035953

Printed in the United States of America.

10 9 8 7 6 5 4 3 2 1

This book is dedicated to Margot Sisman,
my unfailing source of challenging ideas, sound advice,
and invaluable encouragement.

Contents

III. Telling It Like It Isn't

Preface

The seeds of this book were planted in 1999 when I joined a public affairs chat room with some investment research colleagues. Although the subject matter had always interested me, participating in the discussion required me to follow events more closely than in the past. As I studied politicians' statements, I was struck by the extent to which they consisted of elementary economic fallacies.

Members of administrations past and present quarreled over credit and blame for inconsequential changes in gross domestic product and the Consumer Price Index. They presumed a degree of control over short-term trends that no respectable economist would uphold. The claims that government officials made on behalf of savings incentives could easily be refuted with material found in introductory economics textbooks. Serious research had long since demolished the arguments that politicians hauled out to defend subsidies for everything from ethanol production to athletic stadiums.

As time went on, I realized that these gaps between rhetoric and reality could provide the material for an important book. The nation was paying a huge price for politicians' defiance of basic laws of economics. Dissecting the taxpayer-financed follies might help to refocus voters from superficial to fundamental issues.

Happily, government's unjustified market intervention was a subject I felt well equipped to tackle. My previous books addressed fallacies that I had observed in the course of three decades in investment research. As a periodic guest columnist for *Barron's* "Economic Beat," I could comment with authority about the world beyond stocks and bonds. Finally, my experience in historical writing would help me explain how past political follies evolved into present-day grotesqueries.

My enthusiasm for the project was fueled by the ferocious rhetoric leading up to the 2004 election. The accusations of lying exchanged by the two major parties were harsh, even by the appalling standard of past presidential campaigns. Fierce partisanship characterized almost all private and public conversations about the campaign. A few observers condemned Democrats and Republicans alike for the tone of the debate, but hardly anybody criticized the preposterous economic theories emanating from both camps. I saw an opportunity to fill a gap by showing that articles of faith shared by the two major parties were rejected by economists at all points on the ideological spectrum.

Politicians remained badly in need of debunking after the 2004 elections, and they will surely persist in their economic fallacies for many years to come. Left to their own devices, they will keep the electorate focused on personalities. Elected officials will spout noble-sounding rationales for legislation expressly designed to benefit selected interest groups at a huge, hidden cost to the general population. Without prodding, they will probably never concede that programs supposedly intended to reduce income disparities sometimes achieve the opposite result.

I hope to help voters shift the terms of the debate. Reminding politicians of the proper aims of government necessitates a willingness to question every program and regulation. Businesspeople must take an honest look at tax incentives for locating corporate facilities, just as aesthetes must confront dubious justifications for arts subsidies. Everybody must be prepared to reconsider even such basic assumptions as the wisdom of outlawing payola. *Unwarranted Intrusions* is not geared to making readers comfortable with their existing beliefs.

Writing a book entails many lonely hours, but I was blessed with superb moral support. Pamela van Giessen of John Wiley & Sons helped immeasurably in giving shape to my basic concept. Many others assisted by challenging my thinking or steering me toward useful information. They are not responsible for the opinions expressed in the book, but for their friendship and in some cases strenuous disagreement, I thank Alberto Baider, Richard Bookstaber, Reuven Brenner, Oren Cohen,

Matthew Crakes, Michael Edelman, Michael Enmon, Edward Galanek, David Kelley, Jonathan Laurence, Kenneth Pollock, Donald Prutzman, Greg Rosenbaum, Jonathan Savas, Ben Stein, William Stepp, and Laurence Tarini. Jennifer MacDonald and Pam Blackmon provided outstanding editorial support. In addition, I am grateful to my children Arielle and Daniel, along with my wife, Elaine Sisman, for their thoughtful and candid feedback. Finally, my brother Howard gave me uniquely effective encouragement.

MARTIN FRIDSON

New York, New York
April 2006

1

The Politics of Market Intervention

In an ideal democracy, the winning strategy in the competition for votes would be delivery of efficient, corruption-free government. The most capable candidates would rise to the positions of greatest responsibility. They would concentrate on updating and upgrading the services that government is best equipped to provide, including law enforcement and national defense.

At election time, the incumbents would make their case for staying in office. Focusing on such items as budget management and the updating of laws in our changing world, they would present an honest account of their performance. Meanwhile, the challengers would offer specific plans for doing the job better. Voters would then have a sound basis for either re-electing or replacing the incumbents.

Office seekers inevitably discover a much easier way to get elected and reelected: They buy the votes of special interest groups by favoring them with unwarranted intrusions in the marketplace. Politicians learn that they can move up the ladder faster with a kind word and a subsidy than with a kind word alone. Best of all, they don't even have to spend their own money.

The corrupt practice examined in this book is far more insidious than simply handing out cash at the polls. It is the perfectly legal, outright purchase of political power with taxpayers' money under the guise of building a coalition.

A BIPARTISAN EFFORT

The ideological brand names *conservative* and *liberal* reveal little about any particular politician's willingness to inject government into the marketplace. On the campaign trail, candidates differentiate themselves by attacking one another's positions on noneconomic hot-button issues such as abortion and school prayer. But once in office, they uniformly settle down to the real business of rewarding their backers by making the playing field less level.

Democrats and Republicans are like-minded on this matter. They diverge only in the particular constituencies that they shower with favors at the taxpayers' expense. Furthermore, the shrewdest benefit seekers work both sides of the street. That way, they ensure that they will get to feed at the trough no matter which party triumphs.

Businesspeople are among the most enthusiastic participants in this charade. Although they grumble about government's high cost and intrusiveness, they don't refuse to truck with politicians who perpetuate their power through billion-dollar giveaways. The business leaders are too intent on lobbying for their own subsidies, which in their minds are always uniquely justified.

Naturally, the captains of industry plead their case in the name of objectives more politically correct than profit maximization. If they claim to be primarily interested in creating jobs, that ploy conveniently enables them to enlist labor unions in their schemes. Creating affordable housing and encouraging Americans to save are other subterfuges that facilitate their masquerade as champions of the little people.

A REASONABLE STANDARD

With the complicity of both the right and the left, abetted by the combined forces of labor and capital, the election-through-subsidization scheme threatens to expand to infinity. To prevent the handouts from bankrupting the nation, the political system is forced to devise some objective test for subsidies. Politicians of all stripes and interest groups of every description must agree on a standard for determining whether a proposed government intervention in the marketplace is warranted.

Here, at last, is some good news. Economists have hit on a suitable criterion. The simple rule is to leave economic activity to the market, except where the market fails. *Failure* means that goods and services do not wind up being allocated efficiently.

This principle is not a matter of significant controversy among economists. Although they vary in their political opinions, economists broadly agree about the benefits of a properly functioning market. Both liberal and conservative economists believe that people's free decisions to buy and sell generally lead to optimal employment of resources, provided information is readily accessible and barriers to competition are low. There is a consensus that unimpeded markets tend to satisfy consumers' wants and allocate scarce goods equitably. And an efficient economy is a prosperous economy that opens doors to individuals who hope to improve their circumstances.

Even in boom times, some workers can't find employment, and it is appropriate for government to provide income to them. Direct income support is likewise necessary for individuals with disabilities that limit their capacity to support themselves through participation in the labor market. But when the market is putting resources to their best use, government can't improve conditions by injecting itself into the process. Dictating prices, subsidizing one segment of market participants, or creating regulations won't make anyone better off, except at the cost of making someone else worse off. Government intervention in the economy is appropriate only when, for whatever reason, the market fails to produce an optimal outcome.

A common example is the need for government to channel resources into education. By creating a skilled and productive workforce, education benefits not only its direct recipients, but also society at large. The nation would allocate less than the optimal amount to education if the level of investment was determined solely by individuals' personal demand for it.

Economists aren't alone in recognizing market failure as a fair criterion for deciding when government should take matters into its own hands. Politicians, from conservative to liberal, also accept the idea—at least in theory. They are sensitive to voters' suspicions that a costly new program might have no legitimate purpose. Accordingly, when elected officials concoct some new subsidy or regulation, they feel obliged to defend it on the grounds that leaving people to the mercy of the marketplace has resulted in an economic injustice.

In practice, politicians often concoct the program first and only afterward find a supposed market failure to justify it. Sometimes, to their chagrin, their initial so-called market failure gets completely discredited. This forces them to dream up a new one.

But even though politicians play games with market failures, they don't publicly dispute the underlying principle. As a result, the real debate focuses on how frequently markets fail. The more failures that occur, the more subsidies the legislators can justify. More subsidies mean more opportunities to buy votes. Consequently, politicians are predisposed to see market failures all over the place.

MYTHICAL MARKET FAILURES

There are some economists who reinforce the politicians' bias toward lending credence to every alleged market failure. These true believers perceive that government is uniquely effective in curing social problems and therefore ought to be as large as possible. A centerpiece of their case is the New Deal's reining in of unrestrained financial markets. That series of reforms, they are mistakenly convinced, ended for all time the scourge of bank runs and stock market crashes. Imbued with faith in the benefits of government intrusion, these prointervention economists are eager to proclaim additional market failures.

Economists who yearn for a bigger and more active government promote their cause in the court of public opinion. As they seek to win over voters, most of whom have only a rudimentary understanding of economics, the prointerventionists avoid deadly dull statistics. Instead, they rely on persuasive stories.

Two particularly popular tales of market failure involve subjects familiar to most voters: Betamax and the QWERTY keyboard. According to the first story, clever marketing caused a manifestly superior video recording technology to lose out to an inferior one—Video Home System (VHS). The second story is about a scientifically designed typewriter and computer keyboard that has failed to replace the silly setup named for the letters in the upper left-hand corner. According to this tale, the highly inefficient QWERTY system has survived only because it got there first.

To politicians, whose self-interest lies in adopting the interventionists' viewpoint, the conclusion is clear: The market can't even get these comparatively trivial things right. Surely, then, the market needs the helping hand of government on more vital matters such as savings rates and the level of homeownership.

Diehard advocates of increased government intrusion are unfazed that their pet stories have been thoroughly debunked. Economists Stan Liebowitz, of the University of Texas at Dallas, and Stephen E. Margolis, of North Carolina State University, overturned the verdict of market failure in both cases during the 1990s.[1]

Liebowitz and Margolis showed that the minor technical differences between the Betamax and VHS systems were of interest only to professional video editors (who, by the way, continued using the Betamax system). The difference that mattered in the much larger consumer market was the length of recording time that the competing systems offered. Consumers had a choice between a compact cassette with a short running time and a bulky cassette with a long running time. Under fair competitive conditions, consumers chose VHS, because unlike Betamax, it ran long enough to record football games and feature-length movies.

As for QWERTY's rival, the Dvorak keyboard, no reliable ergonomic evidence supports the claims for its superiority. Although a 1943 study by the U.S. Navy concluded that typists achieved greater speed with the Dvorak keyboard, the study's data failed to truly support the conclusion. Neither was the case for replacing QWERTY upheld by a subsequent General Services Administration study. Liebowitz and Margolis uncovered a likely explanation for the navy's apparent bias in favor of the Dvorak system: At the time of its study, the navy's top time-and-motion expert was Lieutenant-Commander August Dvorak, who owned the patent on the eponymous keyboard.

These findings are a caution to anyone wishing to determine the true frequency of market failures. An investigation of the interventionists' showcase examples heightens skepticism about the wisdom of government intrusion. Similar inquiries call into question countless other rationales for subsidies and regulations.

For politicians, however, objective intellectual inquiry is beside the point. Debunking traditional justifications for market intervention reduces government officials' capacity to buy votes with taxpayers' money and to maintain the appearance of "doing something." Once the country starts down that road, candidates could wind up having to run on their records of actual achievement, rather than on their ability to secure unfair advantages for their supporters.

PLAN OF ATTACK

Making a persuasive case that the government's intrusion in the market-place is largely unwarranted represents no small undertaking. Subsidies in areas such as housing and agriculture are solidly entrenched sacred cows. It is so hard to imagine life without these intrusions that many readers will find the arguments against them highly counterintuitive. Utter disbelief will likely greet any questioning of the wisdom of constraints on record industry payola and short selling in the stock market.

But the provocativeness of the subject matter should open people's minds to the possibility that a more market-based economy would be a more equitable economy. Encouraging that sort of outside-the-box thinking is this book's ambitious, yet realistic objective. The intention isn't to dissect every major example of government intervention, but instead to examine some egregious examples and highlight the common threads.

Part I in this book, "A Nation of Subsidies," focuses on government meddling in forms ranging from trade protection, to publicly financed athletic stadiums, to subsidies for the arts. Some of these outrages represent hugely inefficient allocations of resources, whereas the adverse economic effects of others are comparatively minor. The pattern is accommodation of special interests masked by false claims of lofty public purposes. On close examination, society's disadvantaged frequently become more, rather than less disadvantaged as a result of tampering with markets.

Part II, "Restraint of Trade," deals with unwarranted intrusions into ordinary commercial activities. Unable to restrain themselves, politicians unnecessarily stick their noses into apartment rentals, banks' strategies for recovering the cost of operating automatic teller machines (ATMs), and even audience ratings for television programs. Whatever market failure the elected officials claim to be redressing, the market havoc they create is generally worse.

Government interventions in the market cause immense economic harm, yet that's not necessarily a reason for voters to reject them. In a democracy, the people are just as entitled to approve a bad program as a good one. But in a perfect world, politicians would at least describe their proposals honestly. Chances are, the voters would do a creditable job of spotting the clunkers and giving them thumbs-down.

Part III, "Telling It Like It Isn't," shows just how far the system is from perfection. From the exaggeration of their impact on the nation's economic performance to their long record of phony campaign finance reform, politicians have proven themselves masters of false advertising.

Finally, the Epilogue poses the question, "Can This Mess Be Fixed?" Without giving away the ending, suffice it to say that I undertook this project in hopes of actually making a difference. Although that is an ambitious goal, nothing is impossible, even when the government is involved. But if the world is to change, the first step is to change people's minds.

I

A NATION OF
SUBSIDIES

2

Here They Come to Save the Day!

Americans take it for granted that saving is a good thing. After all, that is what our parents told us repeatedly when we were growing up. But perhaps because they transmitted this truth in a negative way, we conclude that however much Americans are saving, it isn't good enough. Trust politicians to wrap themselves in a cause that everyone already embraces. Hardly an election goes by without new schemes being advanced to encourage people to do what's good for them by saving more money.

Candidates for the 2004 presidential nominations proposed a wide variety of plans for increasing Americans' savings rate. Republican incumbent George W. Bush favored a "lifetime savings account" and a "retirement savings account" that would provide tax-free income for people's nest eggs. On the Democratic side, North Carolina Senator John Edwards advocated federal subsidies for lower-income families only. Connecticut Senator Joseph Lieberman wanted to give tax credits to banks for matching the funds of low-income families setting up their first bank accounts.

The candidates' solutions differed, but they all agreed that the nation's low and declining savings rate was a serious problem. In 2002, Americans saved a mere 3.7 percent of disposable personal income, down from 7.1 percent a decade earlier.[1] It followed, at least in the candidates' minds, that the United States was at risk of economically underperforming more savings-and-investment-oriented countries.

Republicans and Democrats alike acknowledged that existing tax incentives had prevented the savings gap from growing even larger. But now, they all agreed, Individual Retirement Accounts (IRAs) and 401(k)s needed to be supplemented. The candidates parted company on only one question: Whose proposed incentives would do the best job of inducing Americans to put aside more cash for a rainy day?

Voters who aspire to be well-informed must remember that politicians' rhetoric represents a separate reality. In the time-space continuum where the rest of us reside, there is no clear, simple relationship between tax incentives and the savings rate. Economists are not sure that Americans have saved one penny more than they would have if IRAs and 401(k) plans had never been invented. Neither do they unanimously believe that Americans' alleged aversion to saving constitutes a crisis.

Accordingly, it is pointless to discuss the relative merits of different candidates' savings schemes. The more pertinent question is whether new tax incentives of any sort will have a positive effect. It is even possible that additional savings subsidies would do more harm than good.

POTENTIALLY PERVERSE INCENTIVES

An optimistic interpretation of the data is that although government savings subsidies do no good, at least they don't cause people to save *less*. The reason that tax incentives may not boost the national savings rate is that people may respond solely by shifting their existing savings from non-tax-favored to tax-favored vehicles. Former Federal Reserve Chairman Paul Volcker observes, "If you give people a tax-exempt way to save, they will choose the tax-exempt way instead of the taxable way, but it doesn't seem to do much for the overall savings rate."[2]

Even if tax incentives don't *decrease* the savings rate, that doesn't necessarily mean they are harmless. As Greg Mankiw, who chaired the White House Council of Economic Advisers (CEA) under Bush, notes in his elementary economics textbook, "It is an undeniable fact that high-income households save a greater fraction of their income than low-income households."[3] Therefore, the average high-income household receives a bigger tax reduction from Uncle Sam, in the guise of a savings incentive, than the average low-income household. The net effect is that low earners subsidize high earners to do something they were probably planning to do anyway—save part of their income.

Mankiw points out another way that tax incentives can backfire. One public policy objective commonly invoked in defense of savings subsidies is the promotion of business investment and, by extension, economic growth. Because cutting taxes for savers reduces government revenues, which can produce (or magnify) a budget deficit, the government must borrow to make up its cash shortfall. That sops up some of savers' capital, making less available for business investment.

It is not good enough for a tax incentive merely to generate new savings. The incentive must generate more savings than the Treasury loses through tax breaks. If not, the program defeats the stated purpose of promoting economic growth by stimulating investment.

The even worse possibility is that a savings subsidy will backfire completely by reducing savings. By lowering taxes on the income that people's savings generate, a new incentive program raises their net investment return. As a result, it takes fewer dollars of savings today to accumulate a targeted amount of wealth at retirement.

Although we can't rule out the possibility that savings incentives actually do some good, serious research on the subject hardly presents a resounding affirmation. Consider the following conclusions of three sets of experts:

> [W]e find a strong effect of savings incentives on the allocation of saving and wealth, but little or no effect on the level.[4]

> Different analyses, even when applied to the same data, can lead to different conclusions. All methods have limitations. *In our judgment, however, the weight of the evidence,* based on the many approaches we have used, as well as our evaluation of other methods, provides strong support for the view that the bulk of IRA and 401(k) contributions are net additions to saving.[5] [Italics added.]

> Given more than a decade of data on the impact of targeted savings incentives on saving behavior, it is somewhat surprising that economists still disagree on the fundamental question of whether such incentives work. One reason why disagreements remain is that economists are just beginning to realize how little is understood about consumption and saving behavior, and in particular about the wide variation in saving behavior among people who are of similar age, education, and income.[6]

To recapitulate, one study finds that people gladly switch their savings from non-tax-subsidized to tax-subsidized vehicles to make more wealth available at retirement, but balk at reducing their consumption to achieve the same effect. Another offers a heavily qualified opinion that tax incentives do add to savings. A third concludes that we really don't know how people decide how much to save. That being so, how can we possibly predict whether a particular tax program will induce them to save more?

WHO SHOULD KNOW BETTER?

Based on the research, it is far from certain that the billions expended on tax incentives generate incremental savings. Reasonable people might nevertheless support yet another new savings program on the chance that it *might* do some good. As a minimum condition, though, they would probably want assurance that the savings shortfall was a problem that truly needed solving. The evidence doesn't inspire strong confidence on that point.

A tantalizing hint of high-level doubt about the reality of the savings crisis was tucked away on the inside pages of the *Financial Times* on November 6, 2003. The salmon-colored business daily characterized Council of Economic Advisers Chairman Greg Mankiw as saying that "he believed that national saving was too low." Mankiw conceded that it was risky to encourage savings at a time when continued economic recovery depended on vigorous consumer spending. Nevertheless, "in the longer term, he said, the rationale for increasing savings in the United States was clear."[7]

It should be noted that the last sentence was a paraphrase of the CEA chief's actual words. In direct quotation, he sounded much less emphatic. "In the longer term," said Mankiw, "there are a lot of economists who argue that the national saving rate is too low."[8] Elsewhere in the interview, the former Harvard professor didn't hesitate to state on his own authority that unemployment was too high. When asked whether savings were too low, however, he fell back on the opinions of "a lot of economists." By implication, there were also a lot of economists who were not convinced.

Why was Mankiw apparently reluctant to say straight out that the savings rate was unsatisfactory? Only Mankiw can answer that question. But if the head of the Council of Economic Advisers entertained doubts about the fundamental rationale for the president's proposed new savings incentives, it would have been impolitic for him to say so. Citing other unnamed economists was a way to avoid identifying himself as a skeptic.

If Mankiw, in fact, questioned whether the U.S. savings rate was genuinely inadequate, he had good reason. At the time, it was hard to find signs that the economy was suffering as a result of Americans' supposed profligacy. Perhaps the savings rate was low only from the perspective of financial services companies with a natural interest in seeing it higher.

AN EVER-RECEDING CRISIS

At the beginning of the 1990s, the Federal Reserve Bank of New York published a study highlighting a 10-year drop in the savings rate.[9] It warned of the consequences—erosion in the nation's growth potential and increased indebtedness to foreigners. The authors conceded, however, that so far, no disaster had accompanied the decline in the savings rate. On the contrary, during the 1980s, the United States enjoyed the postwar period's longest peacetime expansion.

In September 1998, alarms really started to go off as the savings rate dipped to −0.2 percent. It was the first negative number ever in the Commerce Department's monthly statistics dating back to 1959. (According to the quarterly data available for earlier years, savings hadn't fallen below zero since 1933.) Still, the chickens refused to come home to roost.

The widespread angst over savings partly reflected fears that business would be unable to invest sufficient capital in productivity-enhancing innovations. But to Federal Reserve Bank of Boston chief economist Lynn Brown, commenting in early 1998, business investment was a lesser problem than many observers made it out to be. Brown wasn't convinced that increased business investment would generate much of a payoff in productivity gains. Already, National Association of Manufacturers chief economist Gordon Richards was predicting that the annual increase in productivity, which had averaged about 1 percent during the 1980s, would step up to 1.65 percent through 2005.[10] One reason to be optimistic was a late-1980s pickup in key measures of technological advance, such as new patents.

Over the next few years, as politicians continued to trumpet the need for increased savings, productivity surprised economists on the upside. As measured by nonfarm output per hour, the annual increase in productivity had averaged 1.97 percent between 1990 and 1999. Over the next 5 years, the average rate of improvement jumped to 3.28 percent.[11] Like every statistical series, productivity measures have quirks. But even if the 1999 to 2004 figures were somehow overstated, nobody was suggesting that productivity had stagnated as a result of inadequate savings.

If the feared day of reckoning somehow never seems to arrive, then just possibly, the level of savings isn't so dismal after all. It is meaningless to argue that the savings rate is too low, just because it is below some arbitrarily determined threshold (or, alternatively, lower than in some arbitrarily chosen earlier period). To make their case, proponents of savings incentives must document the harm that is arising from the present, supposedly too low, rate.

A BASIC PROBLEM

A fundamental difficulty in determining whether the savings rate is too low involves pinning down what the rate is in the first place. Conceptually, savings are what is left over after taxes and consumption have been deducted from income. Certain "consumption" expenditures, however, give rise to enduring wealth. Therefore, some economists consider the acquisition of consumer durable goods, such as automobiles and major appliances, to be a form of saving. The personal savings rate reported in the Federal Reserve System's Flow of Funds Accounts incorporates this idea.

The version of the personal savings rate more frequently cited in the press is produced by the Commerce Department's Bureau of Economic Analysis (BEA). The BEA calculation begins with personal income. This includes wages, salaries, and fringe benefits, as well as income from rents, dividends, and interest. Savings consist of what remains after taxes, individuals' contributions to social insurance (programs such as Social Security and Medicare), and personal outlays for items such as food, shelter, clothing, and interest on consumer debt. The savings rate equals savings divided by *disposable* personal income. Disposable personal income, in turn, consists of personal income minus taxes and individuals' contributions to social insurance programs.

Based on this definition, consider the effect of a rise in stock, bond, and real estate prices. First off, the size of people's retirement savings increases. Suppose that in response, they step up their spending, but by only a small fraction of the growth in the value of their homes and investment portfolios. The net effect is that people are more financially secure than before the rise in asset values. According to the BEA, however, they are saving *less* than in the past. The reason is that the BEA's definition of personal income includes income earned from stocks, bonds, and rental properties, but not capital gains on the same assets.[12]

As a practical illustration of the BEA's concept of savings, suppose that over a period of years you save $100,000 and invest it in mutual funds. After a few excellent years in the stock market, your nest egg has increased to $150,000. Feeling pleased with your thrift and your good fortune, you decide to splurge by spending $5,000 of this year's salary on a special vacation trip. Your view of the matter is that your savings have increased by $50,000, but according to the BEA definition, you have contributed to the nation's declining savings rate.

Those who lament the supposedly inadequate U.S. savings rate commonly chastise Americans for forsaking the sturdy pioneer virtues of their forebears. Consider, though, that investors who strike it rich in the stock market have the choice of selling out and squandering their profits. If they resist the temptation, the BEA gives them no credit for saving. Somehow, the talk of profligacy seems off base.

Certainly, carrying this argument too far poses a risk. During the stock market boom of the late 1990s, a substantial portion of the period's investment gains, which made the savings rate appear to be understated, disappeared when stocks nosedived between 2000 and 2002. If economists had adjusted the BEA calculation throughout the late 1990s by adding capital gains to the denominator, they would have *overstated* the savings rate.

Still, overlooking the fairly reliable long-run increases in the value of real estate and securities creates too pessimistic a picture of Americans' saving habits. People don't ignore the impact of investment gains on their retirement security, even if the government statisticians do. Neither does it escape people's notice when the Dow Jones Industrial Average (DJIA) stops going up, as it did in 2000 after quadrupling over the preceding decade. With their accumulated wealth no longer increasing through stock market gains, Americans did the responsible thing; they began to save more. The BEA savings rate bottomed out at −0.2 percent in October 2001 and remained in the 1.5 percent to 3.0 percent range throughout 2002 and 2003.[13] By late 2003, it appeared that the allegedly profligate Americans might even overtake the famously frugal Japanese.[14] In 2004 and 2005, with housing prices rising strongly, the savings rate once again slackened.

The key point is that determining whether Americans are saving too little isn't solely a matter of determining whether any harm has resulted. To some extent, the dispute is a disagreement over what to count as savings.

WHO'S AFRAID OF THE BIG, BAD SAVINGS GAP?

Considering that the evidence of an inadequate savings rate is ambiguous, many pronouncements on the subject sound remarkably emphatic. In 1997, U.S. Treasury Secretary Robert Rubin declared, "Our savings rate is far too low in this country. The rate is equivalent to 4.2 percent of GDP, the lowest by far of the G-7 countries, and lower than many developing countries. Increasing that rate has been a high priority for President Clinton."[15] In 1999, Jack Bobo, former national president of the Association of Insurance and Financial Advisors, decried the "lottery mentality" of a culture that "glamorizes consumption." The only reason the United States had avoided the inevitable misery of a country that saves too little, said Bobo, was that the thrifty Japanese and Germans were providing American businesses the necessary capital for expansion.[16] In 2001, Robert C. Pozen, vice chairman of Fidelity Investments, echoed Rubin by pointing out how low the U.S. savings rate was compared with other industrialized countries. Pozen urged Congress to enact previously rejected pension legislation aimed at boosting savings.[17]

The common thread in these cautionary statements was the speaker's financial interest in seeing savings rise. Both the life insurance companies represented by Bobo and money management companies such as Fidelity would benefit if tax-subsidized programs succeeded in stimulating growth in personal savings and investment. Even Treasury Secretary Rubin made his remarks in the context of promoting the sale of savings bonds. Not only was the savings rate too low, according to Rubin, but the government had to increase the proportion of Americans who owned savings bonds, because "more savings means more investment and greater productivity."[18] Incidentally, savings bonds provide the government with comparatively low-interest-cost financing.

Weighing in as well from the public sector was Representative Earl Pomeroy (D-ND). The author of the Savings Are Vital to Everyone's Retirement (SAVER) Act, Pomeroy warned a 1998 gathering of retirement experts that lower-paid workers' inability to save for old age was making them increasingly dependent on programs such as Social Security that the government had bungled. By some inscrutable logic, Pomeroy concluded that the solution was more government intervention. He expressed his hope that Congress would adopt a proposal to facilitate the provision of pension plans by small employers.[19]

Unlike the spokespeople for the insurance and money management industries, Representative Pomeroy had no direct financial interest in a higher savings rate. But he was intimately acquainted with the financial services industry's views on the matter. Prior to entering Congress, Pomeroy was elected State Insurance Commissioner of North Dakota. In that capacity, he served as president of the National Association of Insurance Commissioners. With that background, it is not surprising that the largest political action committee (PAC) contributions to his 2002 reelection campaign came from the Finance/Insurance/Real Estate sector. Insurance companies and trade groups dominated that category. They anted up $213,087, dwarfing the contributions of such economic powerhouses as the National Potato Council ($1,500) and the National Turkey Federation ($500).[20]

Indeed, vested interests are a recurring theme in the story of savings subsidies. As journalist Charles Lane commented after Congress added several bells and whistles to traditional IRAs to create Roth IRAs, the biggest winners were "financial services firms, estate planners, accountants, and everyone else who makes a living advising people how to keep the government away from their money."[21] Lane noted that the thrust of financial services companies' Roth IRA marketing programs was not to sign up new IRA savers. Rather, the industry focused on shifting the existing $1.3 trillion cache of IRA assets into the more lucrative Roth variety. Once again, the government's ostensible goal of enlarging the nation's pool of savings appeared elusive.

Even the critics of subsidized savings programs, in some cases, have their own financial axes to grind. Donald B. Trone, an investment counseling industry representative on the Employee Retirement Income Security Act (ERISA) Advisory Council, has excoriated 401(k) plans. Many companies that instituted 401(k)s, he says, have phased out other kinds of retirement plans. The implication is that total savings have not increased. As a remedy, Trone advocates a mandatory savings plan, modeled on Australia's, in which employers contribute a stated percentage of workers' salaries to individual retirement accounts. A key political obstacle to this eminently sensible plan in the United States, says Trone, is that it would eliminate jobs in the vast industry that has sprung up to support 401(k)s. But he omits mentioning the silver lining: Instituting Australian-style individual retirement accounts would create massive new assets for Trone and his fellow investment counselors to manage. (Trone does have the presence of mind to recite the financial services industry's mantra: "[W]orkers . . . aren't saving enough.")[22]

THE BOTTOM LINE

It is neither illegal nor unusual to support legislation that benefits one's industry or political backers. Nor is there necessarily any reason to question the sincerity of executives and legislators who lament Americans' poor savings habits. For financial services industry stalwarts, the conviction that savings are too low is a necessary belief. They cannot lobby effectively for their economic interests if they doubt the need for increased thrift, whatever the evidence may indicate.

To those who hope to form an objective opinion, however, evidence is paramount. The threshold of proof should be high for such individuals, given the considerable uncertainty about whether savings incentives really work. It is hard to conclude, based on recent history, that market forces fail to provide the economy with a satisfactory level of savings.

Yes, the United States has depended on overseas savers to fund its productivity-enhancing investments. If foreigners were to curtail their purchases of American securities, however, prices of those securities might just drop far enough to entice Americans to step up their own savings and investments. And yes, under present arrangements, many Americans will retire with fewer assets than they'll need for their golden years. But that problem won't be solved by siphoning money out of the Treasury to reward people who are saving anyway.

All in all, voters can spend their time better than in analyzing the differences in candidates' schemes to boost the savings rate. The larger issue is that any one of the plans could backfire by steering the economy away from its natural and optimal savings rate. For investors, the best advice is to be a bit skeptical about the perennial warnings of economic lethargy that will result from the nation's abysmally low savings rate. Anyone who heeded those warnings in the past proved to be far too bearish on America.

3

Be It Ever So Deductible

If you drive a car, the government leaves it up to you to decide whether to own a vehicle or lease it. There is no presumption among politicians or voters that you would be better off owning than leasing. No elaborate federal bureaucracy exists to ensure that you fulfill the American dream of automobile ownership.

This isn't to say that public policy stands entirely aloof from the subject of transportation. The government's main objective in that sphere is to ensure access. People who lack transportation may be unable to participate in the workforce or secure basic amenities. There is also an ongoing political debate about the optimal mix of transportation methods: private cars versus public transit. But if driving turns out to be the right solution for you, the government stays away from the question of who should hold the title to your car.

When it comes to another basic need—housing—it's a different story altogether. Elected officials don't limit themselves to guaranteeing the availability of basic shelter through public housing programs for low-income families. Instead, politicians insist on people owning their homes instead of renting them.

Toward that end, the government promotes homeownership through substantial financial incentives. Interest costs on home mortgages, unlike rental payments, are deductible from income taxes. Homeowners can also deduct property taxes. Additionally, mammoth housing-oriented government-sponsored entities receive benefits that lower their financing costs.

Underlying the government's extensive intervention in the housing market is the conviction that when it comes to homeownership, more is better. This is an article of faith among politicians of both major parties. If the proportion of Americans who own their homes is anything less than 100 percent, every elected official has a bounden duty to boost the ratio. In contrast, the percentage of drivers who own, rather than lease, their cars is a statistic of interest primarily to marketing and finance departments within the auto industry.

Refreshingly, there is a more plausible market-failure-based argument for homeownership subsidies than for many other government interventions. There is significant evidence that people have a greater stake in their communities when they own, rather than rent. Consequently, they may participate more actively in local organizations and increase neighborhood stability. That, in turn, may benefit other homeowners by raising property values.

The larger the percentage of families who own their homes, the more widespread these desirable outcomes presumably will be. On that basis, the government can justify engineering a higher homeownership rate than the marketplace would produce without help. The only caveat is that the government must avoid throwing more money into the effort than the associated benefits warrant.

Politicians can never be relied on to stop when they have done enough. That is like hoping that kudzu[1] will stop proliferating once it fulfills its original purposes of stabilizing the soil and providing forage. The problem with homeownership incentives is that aspiring homeowners are not the only beneficiaries. The federal dollars also find their way into the pockets of homebuilders and the management and shareholders of the Federal National Mortgage Association (Fannie Mae) and the Federal Home Loan Mortgage Association (Freddie Mac). These politically powerful interest groups are not the ones who pay the price if the government overshoots the mark. They are consequently keen to see tax dollars pumped into homeownership incentives without limit.

DON'T EVEN THINK ABOUT IT

Most sacred of all the homeownership sacred cows is the deductibility of mortgage interest. In 1963, Democratic President John Kennedy's administration proposed limiting deductions for home mortgage interest, along with all other personal deductions. The real estate industry's intense lobbying of Congress induced the administration to back off before the idea even made it as far as public hearings. In 1969, Republican Housing and Urban Development Secretary George Romney discarded a prepared speech and proposed repealing homeowner deductions. The revenue generated by this change in the tax code, he suggested, could be used to address the problems of the slums. Richard Nixon's administration promptly rejected the idea, and Romney soon fell into line. During the debate over tax reform in 1984, Republican President Ronald Reagan told the National Association of Realtors that everything was on the table, including the homeowner deduction. Just one day later, bowing to an onslaught by real estate industry lobbyists, Reagan backed off and affirmed his support of the mortgage deduction.[2]

Over the next two years, Reagan challenged Congress to enact the most sweeping overhaul of the tax system in generations. It was a tall order. Arrayed against the proposed reform were entire industries built on uneconomical tax shelters. In addition, the mighty farm lobby opposed the legislation. Manufacturers stood to lose benefits previously conferred by the Investment Tax Credit.

Despite the gargantuan political obstacles, Republicans and Democrats for once declared their determination to stand up to the vested interests. Looking beyond the demands of their local constituencies and political contributors, elected officials saw that the existing hodgepodge of loopholes and preferences was stifling economic growth.

Illinois Representative Lynn Martin hailed the proposal saying it would remove six million of the working poor from the tax rolls altogether. "But common wisdom says they probably won't vote for me, a Republican, anyway."[3] On the other hand, his district contained natural opponents of the bill, including farmers, machine tool manufacturers, a steel mill, and an automobile plant. Nevertheless, Martin said that he had to support the bill, lest the special interests achieve a final and permanent victory.

Even with this extraordinary display of statesmanship, the mortgage deduction was too sacred a cow to do away with entirely. Instead, the legislators made the eminently reasonable proposal that a household should be allowed to deduct mortgage interest on only one residence. Surely, no one would argue with a straight face that giving the average family a piece of the American Dream necessitated tax incentives on the purchase of a vacation house. Reagan's proposed tax overhaul called on a wide spectrum of individuals and industries to give up ill-conceived tax breaks for the greater good. In a nation where some families couldn't afford one home, equity surely demanded a sacrifice by taxpayers wealthy enough to afford two.

Out of principled stands by scores of members of Congress emerged the monumental Tax Reform Act of 1986. The bill's chief author, Democratic House Ways and Means Committee Chairman Dan Rostenkowski, wiped away tears as colleagues congratulated him on his long-shot legislative victory over the hosts of entrenched interests. To President Reagan, the new order in tax policy represented nothing less than a second American Revolution.

But thanks to the tenacity of the real estate industry lobbyists, mortgage deductibility for second homes survived the revolution. The advocates of equitable taxation made a small dent by abolishing deductibility for houses number three, four, and beyond. The following year, Congress even managed to place a $1 million ceiling on the amount of mortgage principal eligible for the interest deduction. But by flexing their muscles on vacation houses, the National Association of Realtors, the National Association of Home Builders, and the Mortgage Bankers Association sent a clear message to future reformers: Any questioning of the basic mortgage deduction was completely off limits.

During the early 1990s, several proposals emerged to rein in the mortgage deduction. The Congressional Budget Office (CBO) suggested lowering the ceiling on mortgage principal eligible for the deduction from $1 million to $300,000. The CBO also recommended eliminating the deduction for second homes and capping mortgage interest deductions at $12,000 for a single return and $20,000 for a joint return. Politicians ranging from former Democratic Senator Paul Tsongas and former Republican Senator Warren Rudman to Independent presidential candidate Ross Perot endorsed a limitation on the mortgage deduction as a budget-balancing measure.[4] In testimony to the enduring clout of the real estate lobbyists, the proposals went nowhere.

ILLOGICAL DEDUCTION

Notwithstanding the real estate industry's consistent success in smothering curtailment of the mortgage interest deduction, it would be an exaggeration to describe realtors and homebuilders as all-powerful. Their lobbyists are able to cow presidents and cabinet officials only because a large portion of the electorate buys their story. Popular devotion to the mortgage deduction springs from two distinct sources. Some voters consider the tax preference sacrosanct because they don't understand its economic effect. Others defend it precisely because they understand what a phenomenally good deal it is.

The first step in framing the issue for voters is to pin down the mortgage deduction's economic impact. Defenders of the tax preference vehemently object to characterizing it as a subsidy. The government, they argue, isn't giving homeowners anything that doesn't already belong to them. After all, people have earned their income. A decision by the government to extract a smaller percentage of it in taxes can hardly be described as providing a subsidy.

Leaving aside the semantics, the granting of a mortgage deduction alters people's economic behavior and redistributes after-tax income. Those are the effects that subsidies generally produce. So it is fair to say that the mortgage deduction walks like a duck and quacks like a duck, even though it is technically a bird of a slightly different feather.

While the quibbling about terminology goes on, the ardent supporters of mortgage deductibility quack loudly about the American Dream. This noise diverts people from recognizing that like any other fiscal measure, this tax preference has a two-sided impact. The purported benefits have offsetting drawbacks.

A major drawback is that the mortgage deduction confers its biggest benefits on those who need them least. All other things being equal, a family that buys a million-dollar home with a $750,000 mortgage receives 10 times as much back in taxes as a family that buys a $100,000 home with a $75,000 mortgage. In all probability, the family that receives the bigger tax break has something like 10 times the income and 10 times the cash available for a down payment as the family that gets the smaller deduction.

Actually, this understates the disparity. For one thing, taxpayers don't benefit from mortgage deductibility unless they itemize their tax returns. Lower-income households instead tend to take the standard deduction. In that case, they are no better off from a tax standpoint than their peers who rent. In the second place, high earners are subject to higher marginal tax rates than low earners. Therefore, a dollar of mortgage interest generates a bigger tax saving for a high earner than for a low earner.

Beleaguered taxpayers are inclined to suppose that none of this matters. It is all coming out of the government's pocket, so why begrudge high-income folks a little extra relief? In reality, Uncle Sam has no money except what it extracts from the taxpayers. If high earners get a bigger share of tax savings, somebody must pick up the balance. The most likely victims are low earners who are less able to take advantage of the mortgage deduction.

A common rejoinder is that the government should spend less and then everyone would pay less in taxes. That, however, is a separate discussion. As long as the federal budget is greater than zero, tax preferences will redistribute the burden among taxpayers. Under the current arrangement, the more money you make, the greater the amount you can avoid paying by owning a home.

From a fiscal viewpoint, the government earmarks a chunk of its revenues for homeownership incentives and distributes it disproportionately to those with the smallest need. This is a curious result for a tax preference that is sold with images of young families struggling to grab onto the middle class by their fingernails. But the mortgage deduction's defenders have good reason to portray it as a helping hand for the working class. If mortgage deductibility didn't already exist, but was being proposed honestly to voters, low-to-average-income voters would hardly be likely to endorse a plan that runs directly counter to the progressive principle of the federal income tax.

The unfavorable distributional impact of mortgage deductibility might be palatable if it were offset by clear-cut benefits. Alas, it is not even certain that homeownership rates are higher than they would be without the tax preference. In 2002, the *Economist* compiled homeownership data from 13 countries. The table showed rates between 60 percent and 70 percent for (from highest to lowest) Australia, the United States, and Canada. Australia and Canada have no mortgage deduction in their tax codes.[5]

It is neither radical nor outside the mainstream of economic thought to maintain that there is only a loose connection between mortgage deductibility and homeownership. The idea has long been accepted by economists, including those who might seem predisposed to read a closer link into the data. As far back as 1993, at a conference sponsored by the Federal National Mortgage Association, economists from the major housing industry organizations conceded that abolishing the mortgage deduction would have no major impact on home purchasing.[6]

All in all, the mortgage deduction is a highly inefficient way of disbursing government funds to make the American Dream more widely available.

ANOTHER HOLE IN THE BOAT

To make matters worse, there is a second large source of leakage in the system. Housing-oriented government-sponsored entities (GSEs) receive vast taxpayer-supported benefits. Just as less than 100 percent of the energy injected into a lightbulb emerges as light, the GSEs convert only a part of the government's largess into assistance for families that could not otherwise afford to purchase homes.

The transmission is handled by two shareholder-owned GSEs, the Federal National Mortgage Association (FNMA or Fannie Mae) and Federal Home Loan Mortgage Corporation (FHLMC or Freddie Mac). These two entities can borrow at lower interest rates than other privately owned financial institutions because of an implicit federal guarantee of their debt. Uncle Sam doesn't officially stand behind the GSEs' obligations, but there is a widespread assumption among investors that the government would bail them out if they ever became insolvent.

To a naive observer, it might appear that the implicit guarantee costs taxpayers nothing. Indeed, as long as FNMA and FHLMC stay current on their obligations, they draw no dollars out of the Treasury. But the federal government's borrowing cost is a function of its ability to meet its liabilities. The liabilities include both actual cash commitments and certain contingent liabilities. Among those contingent liabilities is the possibility of one day being called on to bail out the housing-oriented GSEs.

Fannie and Freddie capitalize on their borrowing cost advantage by investing in mortgages originated by banks, purchasing mortgage-related securities, and providing credit guarantees on mortgage-backed securities. (On a separate track, the Federal Home Loan Bank System makes collateralized loans to member institutions. These include commercial banks, thrifts, credit unions, and insurance companies.)

In establishing FNMA and FHLMC, Congress intended that they would pass along the taxpayer-interest subsidy. Homeownership, the legislators hoped, would consequently become a reality for families that could not otherwise afford it. As profit-making ventures, however, Fannie Mae and Freddie Mac have an economic incentive to capture part of the value of the subsidies.

MEASURING THE LEAKAGE

How much of the taxpayer-financed incentive actually gets diverted in this way? In 1996, the Congressional Budget Office (CBO) estimated that Fannie Mae and Freddie Mac were retaining one-third of the value of the subsidies.[7] At the time, the CBO estimated the subsidies' total value to be $6.5 billion a year. Five years later, the CBO updated its findings and concluded the two GSEs were retaining 37 percent of subsidies by then worth $10.6 billion annually.[8] By 2003, according to the CBO, the estimated annual value of the subsidies had escalated to $23 billion.[9]

This is not a simple analysis. The only direct way to measure the value of the subsidies would be on the basis of dollars actually forked over to Fannie Mae and Freddie Mac by the federal government. But Uncle Sam will never have to pony up cash unless the GSEs someday fail on their obligations. Analysts have to fall back on an estimation technique. They calculate the value of the subsidies as:

> The annual interest that Fannie Mae and Freddie Mac would pay if they lacked an implicit government guarantee of their debt minus Fannie Mae and Freddie Mac's actual annual interest expense

Estimating the GSEs' interest expense absent the guarantee requires an assumption about the degree of credit risk that investors would attribute to their debt under those conditions. It is impossible to be precise about this sort of thing, but Fannie and Freddie's cost savings are sizable under any reasonable assumption.

Several studies have argued that the CBO's analysis substantially overstates the amount by which taxpayer subsidies enrich FNMA and FHLMC shareholders instead of boosting homeownership.[10] But another approach to the issue corroborates the view that not all the dollars are flowing through to home purchasers. Fannie Mae and Freddie Mac are far more profitable than financial institutions that lack similar support for their borrowing. In 2000, the return on shareholders' equity was 25.6 percent for Fannie Mae and 22.8 percent for Freddie Mac. The combined return for all commercial banks insured by the Federal Deposit Insurance Commission was only 14 percent.[11]

Some portion of the difference may represent the effect of superior management. But whatever is not accounted for by brilliant and inspiring leadership is a strong indication that the GSEs pass along to homeowners something less than 100 percent of their taxpayer-financed benefits. It seems likely that part of the wealth transfer is getting intercepted by the GSEs' shareholders.

Another government-created benefit that FNMA and FHLMC capture for themselves is a quasi-monopoly in the purchase of conventional mortgages. The CBO estimates that the two GSEs have a 71 percent market share in fixed-rate mortgages that conform to their standards for purchase.[12] With such limited competition for the loans, the GSEs need not pass along all their interest rate subsidies. All they have to do is keep home purchasers' interest rates low enough to discourage unsubsidized, would-be competitors from bidding for the mortgages.

A HELPING HAND FOR THE AFFLUENT

The operations of FNMA and FHLMC diverge in another important way from the entities' ostensible public purpose. Of the taxpayer-financed incentives that flow through to home purchasers, a disproportionate amount goes to the upper half of Americans by income. *FM Watch,* published by a trade group coalition that monitors the GSEs, calculates that more than five times as much of the FNMA and FHLMC subsidies get passed along to households with above-median income than to households with below-median incomes.[13]

This lopsided distribution undercuts the GSEs' contention that they buy upper-income homeowners' mortgages solely to earn profits with which they can subsidize lower-income borrowers.[14] The reality is that Fannie Mae and Freddie Mac have drifted far from their original mission. Congress created them, in 1938 and 1970, respectively, to encourage banks to lend to low-income households by agreeing to buy those mortgages from the banks. In place of that vision, we have a system whereby families who can afford to own their homes subsidize one another. Shareholder-owned enterprises siphon off part of the subsidy and to boot, the government extracts administrative costs. Had politicians ever proposed this cockamamy idea to the electorate, the voters surely would have hooted it down.

In 1989, Congress made technical-sounding, yet profound changes in the rules under which FNMA and FHLMC operated. The new setup permitted the GSEs to customize securities to the differing risk preferences of different types of investors. In addition, bank regulators allowed mutual funds and pension funds to classify Fannie Mae's debt as a low-risk asset.

These modifications greatly enhanced the investment appeal of FNMA and FHLMC stock. The GSEs raised vast amounts of new capital and began buying mortgages on a dramatically increased scale. In a decade, their holdings of mortgage debt swelled from $1 trillion to $4 trillion. Their share of the conventional (fixed-interest-rate) mortgage market doubled.[15]

Along the way, Fannie Mae and Freddie Mac shifted away from their traditional emphasis on mortgages for low-priced homes. Middle- and upper-middle-class homeowners were increasingly the beneficiaries of whatever government subsidies remained after the GSE shareholders took their cut. The public purpose behind FNMA and FHLMC's government support became more and more difficult to discern.

Despite erosion of the rationale for their government subsidies, Fannie Mae and Freddie Mac succeeded for years in fending off attempts to end their privileged status. Their boards of directors were sprinkled with ex-White House aides, defeated candidates, and former government officials appointed by presidents of both parties. Appointees included former Senator Dennis DeConcini (D-AZ) and from the ranks of Bill Clinton's political operatives, Rahm Emmanuel, Harold Ickes, Jack Quinn, and Eli Segal. Republican George W. Bush named his one-time Yale classmate Victor Ashe; regional reelection campaign director Molly H. Bordanaro; David J. Gribbin III, a longtime associate of Dick Cheney; and Michelle Engler, the wife of former Michigan governor John Engler.[16] Some directors moved on to become well-paid lobbyists for the GSEs.

Over the years, FNMA's executive ranks were likewise peppered with political operatives. They included former Clinton administration Budget Director Franklin Raines and Deputy Attorney General Jamie Gorelick, as well as Frederick V. Malek, who was part owner of the Texas Rangers baseball team along with George W. Bush.

The GSEs' politically connected all-stars delivered. At a Christmas party in 1998, a Fannie Mae official heard that the Clinton administration was thinking about terminating the company's exemption from Securities and Exchange Commission fees for registering securities. Quickly, FNMA recalled key executives from their Christmas vacations and mobilized dozens of mayors, housing industry lobbyists, and members of Congress to call the White House. Their message, implausible though it might sound, was that requiring Fannie Mae to pay registration fees, just like any other public company, would harm low- and middle-income homeowners. Before even going public with the idea, the White House abandoned the proposal.[17]

In 2003, the seemingly omnipotent GSEs turned out to have a major vulnerability in the form of questionable accounting practices. Soon, the mortgage giants were under scrutiny by the Justice Department and the Securities and Exchange Commission. Freddie Mac's chairman, president, and chief financial officer were fired or resigned.[18] Late in 2004, Fannie Mae ousted chief executive officer (CEO) Franklin Raines, who had been mentioned as a candidate for Treasury Secretary under Democratic presidential hopeful John Kerry.[19] The GSEs' image of political invincibility, if not exactly shattered, had suffered a crack.

Reputable authorities came out in favor of clipping the wings of FHLMC and FNMA. Federal Reserve Chairman Alan Greenspan proposed limiting the size of their mortgage portfolios to $100 billion or $200 billion each. Former Fannie Mae president James E. Murray went so far as to advocate abolishing Fannie and Freddie's authority to borrow $2.25 billion from the U.S. Treasury, which is a key support for their favorable interest rates.[20]

Abolishing the GSEs was too radical a notion for politicians to contemplate. In 2005, Congress tussled over legislation to restructure the regulation of Fannie Mae and Freddie Mac. Inevitably, the spirit of reform got mired in the lawmakers' horse trading. Among the Bush administration's objections to the House of Representatives version was that in the middle of a scandal-driven effort to clip the GSEs' wings, House members were proposing to expand their mortgage purchasing authority beyond the basic mission of assisting low-income and first-time homebuyers.[21]

HOW MUCH COMMUNITY SPIRIT DO TAXPAYERS GET FOR THEIR MONEY?

Between mortgage deductibility and subsidies to Fannie Mae and Freddie Mac, taxpayers foot a huge bill for homeownership incentives. But the mere fact that the dollars are big doesn't necessarily mean that the outlay is excessive. The social benefits that they buy might be even bigger.

As former Illinois Senator Charles Percy put it in a less gender-sensitive era:

> For a man who owns his own home acquires with it a new dignity. He begins to take pride in conserving and improving it for his children. He becomes a more steadfast and concerned citizen of the community.[22]

Good citizenship strengthens neighborhoods. That boosts home values, which represent an important form of personal saving. But if the matter is left entirely to the market, many individuals won't wind up with strong stakes in their neighborhoods. Either they will fail to accumulate enough cash for a down payment or else they will earn too little to qualify for a mortgage. The government, it is argued, should lower the bar to enable otherwise unqualified applicants to obtain home loans. Otherwise, their communities will never enjoy the benefits of their heightened involvement.

Unlike the rationales presented for many other government interventions, this story of market failure has considerable empirical support. Researchers have documented a positive relationship between home-ownership rates and neighborhood stability. Because such effects can be quantified, it is possible to determine whether taxpayers are getting as much community spirit as they are paying for. Based on the evidence, it appears they are not.

A 1996 review of research on the subject[23] revealed a strong and consistent tendency of homeowners to stay put in their neighborhoods. The authors, from the University of North Carolina at Chapel Hill (UNC) and Research Triangle Institute, reported that almost all studies found homeowners less likely than renters either to be planning a move or to have moved recently. Another set of studies queried people about their attachment to their neighborhoods and found homeowners to be more strongly committed than renters. The UNC/Research Triangle Institute literature review also supported, although not as extensively or as consistently, the proposition that homeowners interact with their neighbors more frequently than renters. In addition, the research consistently showed that homeowners were more likely than landlords to undertake repairs and tended to spend more on those repairs. Finally, several studies characterized homeowners as more prone than renters to participate in local organizations.

Neighborhood stability, commitment, and involvement have a quantifiable economic impact. The authors of the UNC/Research Triangle Institute research review also conducted original analysis of the impact of homeownership rates on property values. They concluded that holding all other factors constant, an increase of one percent in a neighborhood's homeownership rate produced a $1,600 increase in the value of the average single-family home over a 10-year period. (The study's authors focused on moderate-income neighborhoods with an average single-family home value of $42,529 in 1980, the base year of their study.)

Cynics might question the objectivity of this resounding confirmation of society-wide benefits of homeownership. After all, the report was published by the Fannie Mae Foundation, which is probably predisposed to favor its upbeat conclusions. The large number of studies that the authors cite, however, lends credibility to their research. On the whole, there seems little reason to doubt that homeowners make good neighbors. The real question is whether their public spiritedness fully justifies the size of the government's homeownership incentives.

THE PAYBACK ON HOMEOWNERSHIP

How is it possible to answer that question? First, we must calculate the profitability—or rate of return—on investments in both housing and other types of fixed assets. The latter include factories, public buildings, and schools. In this context, the rate of return means the rate before giving effect to the government's intervention through the tax code.

By comparing the unadulterated rates of return, it is possible to determine whether the nation is allocating its capital to best promote the general welfare. If capital is indeed being allocated in an optimal way, rates of return will be equivalent on all different types of investment. This means that a small addition to capital will increase national output by an equivalent amount, whether it is invested in housing or nonhousing assets. In this happy state of affairs, national prosperity always gets the biggest return on investment no matter how an investor chooses to deploy a particular chunk of capital.

Suppose, however, that the rate of return on housing is lower than the rate of return on other investments. That means the invested dollars are not working as hard as they could be to increase national income and wealth. By intervening in the market to shift a bigger piece of the pie into housing, the government is slowing down the growth of the pie.

Calculating the economy-wide rates of return on various categories of investment requires a lot of data collection. But once the numbers are compiled, the calculations are conceptually simple. Each asset category's rate of return is represented by a fraction:

1. *Nonhousing fixed assets.* Most assets in this category are used to produce goods that are sold in markets, generating prices that make it possible to observe their value.

$$\text{Rate of return} = \frac{\left(\begin{array}{c}\text{Market value} \\ \text{of goods} \\ \text{produced}\end{array}\right) - \left(\begin{array}{c}\text{Associated returns} \\ \text{to labor and} \\ \text{other noncapital inputs}\end{array}\right)}{\text{Amount of capital invested}}$$

2. *Rental housing.*

$$\text{Rate of return} = \frac{\text{Market rents generated}}{\text{Amount of capital invested}}$$

3. *Owner-occupied housing.* If you own your home, you are effectively acting as your own landlord. By doing so, you save an amount equivalent to the rent you would otherwise pay for comparable housing. The rental-equivalent amount is imputed to you as your return on the investment in your home.

$$\text{Rate of return} = \frac{\text{Imputed rents}}{\text{Amount of capital invested}}$$

In a pioneering 1987 study,[24] Edwin S. Mills of Princeton University analyzed rates of return using newly available Commerce Department data on the country's total stock of fixed capital. Mills found that the United States was far from the ideal point at which all forms of investment generate equivalent economic benefits. The rate of return on investment in housing, he concluded, was only 55 percent as high as on nonhousing investments. Based on the size of its economy, the United States had too much housing, and economic growth was being penalized as a result.

The magnitude of the growth penalty was substantial. If the rates of return on investment *had* been equivalent in housing and nonhousing, Mills concluded, the United States would have had almost 25 percent less housing, as of 1983. That would have been offset by about 12 percent more nonhousing capital. (At the time, the total stock of nonhousing capital was about twice as great as the total stock of housing capital.) Mills's econometric model indicated that with capital more efficiently allocated, gross national product (GNP) would have been 10 percent higher.[25] This substantial sacrifice in standard of living was hardly a trivial price to pay for policies that artificially diverted investment to housing.

UPDATING THE ANALYSIS

Although the 1987 study showed the United States was undercutting its prosperity by favoring investment in housing, Edwin S. Mills also sounded an optimistic note. He found that over time, the rate-of-return gap between housing and nonhousing capital was narrowing.[26] One reason that the government's intervention in the market was producing less distortion, Mills speculated, was that marginal income tax rates had declined over the preceding decade. He concluded, "The Tax Reform Act of 1986 will reduce average marginal tax rates even more and should further reduce the discrepancy between [housing and nonhousing] returns."[27]

In 1998, Lori L. Taylor of the Federal Reserve Bank of Dallas took an updated look at the economics of investment in housing.[28] She noted that in addition to reducing marginal tax rates, the Tax Reform Act of 1986 included provisions that increased the effective tax rate on rental housing. Also, declining inflation rates had reduced the incentive to invest in housing as a hedge against inflation. All these changes, said Taylor, might have altered the comparative economic benefits of housing and nonhousing investment.

It turned out, however, that the great overhaul of the tax system had made little difference. For both housing and nonhousing investments, the post–1986 rates of return were the same as the rates up to 1986, within a standard statistical margin of error. This meant that investment in housing continued to generate less income and wealth than other uses of capital. In particular, Taylor found that the United States would increase its prosperity if it invested more heavily in high school education and less heavily in housing.

Taylor then turned to certain society-wide benefits of homeownership not captured by her initial rate-of-return analysis. Specifically, she addressed homeowners' greater incentive, vis-à-vis landlords, to maintain their properties and resolve neighborhood problems. In addition, Taylor noted that homeowners' children were less likely than renters' children to become school dropouts or teenage mothers.

These "unmeasured benefits of housing investment," Taylor calculated, would have to exceed $220 billion a year to justify the prevailing level of housing investment. That came to $300 a month for each owner-occupied home. In the absence of such implausibly large unmeasured benefits, wrote Taylor, it remained the case that nonhousing investment would generate more economic growth than housing investment. "Therefore," she concluded, "the evidence suggests that despite substantial reform, the United States continues to overinvest in housing."[29] The remedy, Taylor suggested, would be to cut taxes on nonhousing investment, which would encourage increased allocation of capital to that category. In the context of her scholarly study, it was probably inappropriate to point out that no known politician was about to campaign on a platform of reduced favoritism for homebuyers.

THE BOTTOM LINE

In a perfect world, the full benefit of taxpayer-financed homeownership incentives would flow to homebuyers. Ideally, the beneficiaries would all be people with incomes too low to qualify for mortgages without subsidization. After all, if folks who can afford to buy homes simply subsidize one another's purchases, they are no better off in aggregate. In fact, they are collectively worse off because the government has squandered some of their tax dollars on administering a pointless, circular handoff of cash.

It is easier to imagine how homeownership incentives would work in a perfect world than to achieve that ideal through a government program. Incentives that lower the cost of purchasing a home increase the demand for housing. That means more business for builders and real estate agents. Some of the value of the subsidy is therefore likely to flow to these facilitators. Furthermore, the increased demand for housing produces a windfall for the owners of existing homes. They capture part of the subsidy by boosting their resale prices, making it harder for young families to afford homes.

Politicians don't dwell on the fact that some of the money thrown at homebuyers lands in the pockets of builders and realtors. Certainly, it is unnecessary to point that out to the builders and realtors. Those beneficiaries of the government's generosity make the connection on their own, and they respond with vigorous support for the incentives, expressed through lobbying and campaign contributions.

The indirect beneficiaries' highly effective strategy is to make government support of homeownership a third rail that no politician dares touch. Anyone who objects to excesses in such incentives can expect to be vilified as an enemy of the fundamental right of homeownership. Curiously, homeownership is not mentioned anywhere in the Bill of Rights. But what the proincentives proposition lacks in intellectual honesty, it makes up for in political potency.

4

Protection Racket

Few activities inflate politicians' self-importance as effectively as obstructing international trade. They get to feel like world statesmen, while posing as defenders of their nation's honest laborers. In reality, governmental intrusions into cross-border commerce constitute shabby protection rackets. The trade barriers that public officials erect operate for the benefit of the few at the expense of the many. All that is grand about them is the scale of reductions in world prosperity that result.

There is no shortage of ludicrous stories spawned by trade protection, but the catfish story is as good a place to start as any. Catfish make up a genuinely global order of organisms. They include approximately 54 families, about 400 genera, and roughly 2,500 species. Catfish inhabit all continents except Antarctica; fossil remains of one species, dating back 37 million years, have been found there as well. Catfish are remarkably diverse creatures, ranging in length from one-half inch to 16.5 feet, and inhabiting rivers, streams, estuaries, and coral reefs. Certain catfish can breathe oxygen directly from the atmosphere, and some can even walk on land. Many species are bottom-feeders subsisting mainly on aquatic invertebrates, but others eat plankton, algae, fallen leaves, woody parts of fallen trees, or fish. Members of a predatory African family stun their prey with electric discharges, while those of a certain Asian family lure their victims by wiggling whiskerlike sensory organs.

This extraordinary diversity is a well-established scientific fact, at least according to the authoritative *Encyclopedia of Fishes*.[1] In the view of the United States Congress, on the other hand, catfish include only members of the Ictaluridae family, found mostly in North America. That taxonomic opinion became the law of the land with the enactment of the 2002 farm bill (P.L. 107-71). The measure prohibited any other kind of catfish, such as certain varieties originating in Vietnam, from being marketed as catfish.

During the debate over this landmark legislation, Democratic Representative Mike Ross of Arkansas declared that Vietnamese catfish were "not catfish at all—not even from the same species."[2] The congressman was unimpressed by the scientific establishment's inclusion of 2,500 species under the catfish rubric. Neither, seemingly, did he care that the U.S. Food and Drug Administration regarded the Asian imports as bona fide catfish.[3] In Ross's opinion, the Vietnamese impostor was "no more related to a catfish than a cat is to a cow."[4] Chimed in Hugh Warren, vice president of the Catfish Farmers of America (CFA), "They're from a different species and a different family. It's like trying to equate kangaroo meat with hamburger meat."[5]

How did Congress get into the business of revising the Linnaean system of classifying the creatures of the earth? It all came about through the growing popularity of two types of Vietnamese catfish called *basa* and *tra*. Their mild, pleasant flavor won them favor at seafood and Asian restaurants, resulting in an increase of United States imports of the fish from 575,000 pounds in 1998 to more than 20 million pounds in 2001.[6]

The CFA blamed the increased level of imports for a drop in U.S. catfish prices from $0.69 a pound in January 2001 to around $0.55 a pound in 2002. According to the trade group, American catfish farmers could not make a profit unless the price was above $0.60 a pound. The CFA also attributed a decline in frozen catfish fillet prices to Vietnamese imports.

Less prominent in the CFA's analysis was another possible reason for the downward pressure on catfish prices: overproduction within the United States. Catfish pond acreage increased by 28 percent between 1994 and 2002, according to the U.S. Department of Agriculture.[7] It would not have been unprecedented for farmers to find a sympathetic ear among politicians even if their difficulties were of their own making, as Chapter 5 abundantly documents. Still, pointing the finger at an overseas culprit was a more promising strategy for enlisting political support, even if the facts failed to prove that foreigners were engaging in unfair trade practices.

From the viewpoint of diners with a fondness for catfish, a wider choice of varieties and a potential reduction in restaurant bills constituted clear benefits. Some segments of the government saw a problem, however. There were 13,000 Americans employed in the catfish industry, mainly in Arkansas, Mississippi, and a few additional southern states. They would be disadvantaged if consumers were permitted to express their preferences in a free market.

It made no difference to the politicians that solving the problem through the machinery of trade protection was bound to create other problems. Cracking down on Vietnam's catfish farmers would undermine the U.S. policy of encouraging development of the private sector in that country. Preserving jobs in the U.S. catfish industry would adversely affect the much larger number of Vietnamese catfish industry workers (300,000 to 400,000).[8] This was hardly likely to strengthen the United States' negotiating stance that in the interest of fairness, developing countries should open their markets to U.S. agriculture exports. Neither would a protectionist response benefit the U.S. manufacturers of certain specialized equipment that Vietnam's largest catfish producer uses to make fine ice chips and slice fish skin swiftly.[9]

Republican Senator John McCain of Arizona reported that the U.S. embassy in Vietnam had reviewed reports by U.S.-based experts and met with Vietnamese officials. The embassy concluded that the country's catfish exports were neither subsidized nor a source of injury to the U.S. market. McCain was joined by California Democratic Senator Diane Feinstein, as well as three Republican colleagues, in stating:

> The evidence we have seen indicates clearly that the success of Vietnamese catfish exporters in the United States is due not to dumping or government subsidies, but to the quality of the Vietnamese product and its relatively low cost of production.[10]

U.S. catfish farmers nevertheless implored the Commerce Department to impose protective tariffs as high as 190 percent on the Vietnamese imports. The Commerce Department consequently looked like a paragon of reason and moderation when it slapped on tariffs of 37 percent to 64 percent,[11] based on its contention that Vietnamese producers "made sales to U.S. consumers at less than fair value."[12] In the Mekong Delta, catfish prices crashed and farmers faced ruin. Eager, apparently, to do its part in winning Vietnam over to the free market system, Congress declared that all previous scientific research to the contrary notwithstanding, basa and tra were not really catfish.

THE INS AND OUTS OF OUTSOURCING

Rolling back the frontiers of science is not the only, or even the most common, tactic that politicians employ in granting protection to American industries. Fallacious economic reasoning also plays a vital role. Distorting the facts rounds out the office seekers' arsenal of persuasive techniques.

The success of all these methods depends on the arithmetic of costs and benefits in trade. Corporations and labor unions have strong interests in protecting specific markets and jobs from legitimate competition. It is therefore worth their while to obtain tariff barriers and import quotas by lobbying legislators intensively and doling out campaign contributions. The cost of any individual trade barrier represents a small—and not very visible—portion of the average voter's annual expenditures. Consequently, few voters pay much attention to a particular protective measure, even though protection's overall cost to them is substantial.

To see how these dynamics play out, consider the hullabaloo over outsourcing, which suddenly became a flashpoint of the debate on foreign trade in 2003. Politicians and journalists began spotlighting the relocation of jobs to lower-wage countries, particularly India, by cost-conscious U.S. companies. CNN's Lou Dobbs fingered corporations that he pronounced guilty of "exporting America" by hiring cheap foreign workers in lieu of Americans. During the Democratic presidential primary in South Carolina, billboards sprouted up with the question: "Lost your job to free trade or offshore outsourcing yet?"[13] Candidate John Kerry railed against "Benedict Arnold CEOs [who] send American jobs overseas."[14] His favored approach to preserving American jobs was to outsource President Bush.[15]

Council of Economic Advisers chief Gregory Mankiw's take on the issue was consistent with the principles he espoused in his widely used economics textbook.[16] Outsourcing, he explained, simply represented a new form of international trade. As such, said Mankiw, it was a good thing.

Mankiw did not have to go out on any theoretical limbs to defend outsourcing. He was merely applying the principle of comparative advantage, part of the bedrock of economic thought. Comparative advantage predicts efficiency gains all around when each country concentrates on producing a good or service for which it has a lower opportunity cost of production than other countries. Accordingly, if the United States outsources services that can be provided more cheaply in India, it can direct its own resources to producing the goods and services in which it has a comparative advantage. To borrow an analogy from Adam Smith, an intelligent businessman won't build a house if he can save money by paying someone else to build it for him. The businessman can increase his wealth when he invests the money he saves by hiring a carpenter.

Economists across the political spectrum joined Mankiw in his argument against demonizing outsourcing. Professor Douglas Irwin of Dartmouth, with ties to conservative think tanks such as the Cato Institute and the American Enterprise Institute, noted the benefits of service sector outsourcing to U.S. consumers and exporters. "If a capable radiologist in India can read x-ray pictures at a quarter of the cost of doing so domestically," he wrote, "Important health care services can be delivered at a lower cost to everyone, putting a brake on exploding medical costs."[17] Around the same time, Paul Krugman, once described by *Newsweek* as "an unabashed liberal,"[18] stated that outsourcing was not to blame for the then-prevailing shortfall in jobs in the United States. He warned that if the nation were to turn protectionist the world would become more dangerous.[19] Others who took a similarly benign view of outsourcing included former Clinton administration Labor Secretary Robert Reich, among the Democrats, and former Federal Reserve Chairman Alan Greenspan, among the Republicans.[20]

None of the favorable commentary on outsourcing represented new, radical economic theory. Politicians, on the other hand, recycled old fallacies, ignoring the economic gains realizable from outsourcing. John Kerry accused the incumbent Bush administration of aiming "to export more of our jobs overseas."[21] On the Republican side, Dennis Hastert ignored evidence such as McKinsey Global Institute's estimate that for every dollar the United States spent on outsourcing to India, the country realized $1.12 to $1.14 of benefits.[22] Outsourcing, insisted the Speaker of the House, "can be a problem for American workers and the economy."[23]

Democratic Senator Charles Schumer of New York and former Reagan Administration Assistant Treasury Secretary Paul Craig Roberts went so far as to question whether the long-established arguments for free trade still held.[24] They contended that unlike conditions two centuries earlier, when the British politician and economic theorist David Ricardo first outlined the notion of comparative advantage, the resources used to produce goods ("factors of production") could now move easily across international borders. "Comparative advantage is undermined," Schumer and Roberts wrote, "if the factors of production can relocate to wherever they are most productive; in today's case, to relatively few countries with abundant cheap labor." This statement made little sense. Just as in the past, when trade disputes focused on manufacturing rather than on services, the market's response to cost differentials consisted of moving the work, rather than the factors of production (the workers), across international borders. Even Schumer's fellow liberal, Paul Krugman, chided him for helping "old fallacies about international trade"[25] to make a comeback.

Tellingly, Schumer and Roberts attributed the allegedly altered (and certainly more competitive) global environment to three profound new forces:

1. Political stability that allowed freer flow of capital and technology than in the past.
2. Strong educational systems that were turning out "tens of millions of intelligent, motivated workers,"[26] especially in India and China.
3. Inexpensive, high-bandwidth communications.

Talk about the system being rigged against the United States!

Schumer and Roberts never quite explained why progress in technology and education invalidated Ricardo's ideas. Neither did they offer any remedies, beyond commencing an honest debate about the economy's state and the country's direction. (Presumably, they believed that defenders of the free trade status quo favored a *dishonest* debate on the subject.) By failing even to suggest a solution to the nonexistent problem that they identified, Schumer and Roberts deviated from politicians' customary practice of rushing headlong into enacting a bad solution.

On the whole, however, the response to the outsourcing crisis highlights yet another case of politicians offering a solution for which there is no problem. To begin with, nearly 90 percent of U.S. jobs require geographic proximity, meaning that they cannot be outsourced.[27] As for the jobs that can theoretically be shifted overseas, the movement is concentrated for the most part in standardized tasks such as data entry and Information Technology (IT) support. No significant numbers of more complex and interactive tasks, such as marketing and research are moving overseas. These are higher-value-added activities that command comparatively high wages, notwithstanding the popular image of people losing high-paying jobs and being consigned to flipping burgers for the minimum wage. Contrary examples are newsworthy precisely because they are rare. (In one case, reported in 2004, Microsoft outsourced some higher-skill-level work to Indian software architects.)[28]

What's more, the dire predictions assume that the majority of workers affected by outsourcing will be terminated by their employers, rather than assigned to other jobs. Evidence from the study of large financial firms, however, indicates that fewer than 20 percent of the affected employees lose their jobs. IBM's January 2004 announcement that it would outsource 3,000 IT jobs provided the outsourcing alarmists an attention-grabbing statistic. The same company's plan to expand its domestic payroll by 4,500 was less helpful to their case.[29]

Another example of muddled thinking about outsourcing is the tendency to overlook the United States' gains from *insourcing*. The biggest beneficiary of cross-border movement of jobs, according to the Organization for International Investment, has been the United States. In 2003, amid the sound and fury about American companies locating jobs overseas, Honda increased its U.S. manufacturing by 15 percent. While politicians fretted about white-collar jobs being outsourced, Novartis began moving its global research and development operation from Switzerland to Massachusetts. Even Mexico, the country to which Ross Perot once predicted American jobs would vanish with a great sucking sound, was creating thousands of jobs in the United States through its newfound ability to invest abroad. Ironically, creation of manufacturing jobs through other countries' outsourcing was huge in certain Midwestern states where the cries about exporting jobs were loudest (Ohio had imported 242,000 jobs, and Michigan 244,000).[30]

Outright misrepresentation of the facts further confused the issue. John Kerry introduced legislation to regulate the call center industry, a highly visible outsourcer. In support of his proposal, the Democrats' 2004 presidential nominee cited a projection that 3.3 million white-collar jobs would be lost to outsourcing. The Massachusetts senator's press release noted that the number represented "2 percent of the entire workforce."[31] Omitted from the hoopla was any mention that the 3.3 million figure, drawn from a 2002 study by John McCarthy of Massachusetts-based Forrester Research, was an estimate of job losses though 2015. That equated to just 220,000 a year, or approximately 0.2 percent of the U.S. workforce, a figure far exceeded by projected new job creation on the order of three million annually over the next few years.[32]

Any attempt to link international trade and employment over an extended period was largely a red herring. Between 1960 and 2003, the

United States went from a small trade surplus to a large trade deficit—about 4.5 percent of gross domestic product (GDP). Imports surged from 4 percent to almost 14 percent of GDP, measured on a balance of payments basis. Over that period, the U.S. economy added more than 60 million jobs, far outpacing the growth in population. In short, the United States became substantially more dependent on foreign goods, yet added enough jobs to accommodate the sharply increased participation of women in the workforce.[33]

Outsourcing simply became the scapegoat for job losses that were actually attributable to productivity increases. Economist Joseph Carson of Alliance Capital Management LP found that the decline in U.S. manufacturing jobs between 1995 and 2002 was *not* reflected by an increase in manufacturing jobs in developing countries. Instead, he calculated that 18 million manufacturing jobs were eliminated globally during the period, even though manufacturing output increased. It was not a case of low-wage countries taking manufacturing jobs away from the United States. Rather, restructuring and advancements in technology enabled companies around the world to expand their production with fewer workers. This included manufacturers in countries such as China that were accused of stealing U.S. jobs.

Between 1990 and 2001, the number of American steelworkers plummeted from 169,000 to 88,000, a 48 percent drop. Steel production in the United States, on the other hand, *rose* by 17 percent.[34] The ability to produce more with fewer people was the predominant cause of reduced manufacturing employment, not transfer of jobs overseas. Clamping down on outsourcing was really just a futile attempt to prevent technology from continuing to make the economy more efficient. The politicians lost a chance to stop this insidious trend when they failed to block the invention of the wheel.

CHEATING

Happily, the picture is not entirely bleak for voters who put a premium on rationality and honesty. Most politicians now are reconciled to the notion that free trade benefits American workers and consumers. It would be hard for them to contend otherwise when a survey shows that 93 percent of economists agree with the proposition that tariffs and import quotas usually reduce general economic welfare.[35]

Most politicians probably lack a fully articulated, global perspective on international trade. But they understand the howls of protest that arise from steel appliance manufacturers and their employees when restrictions on imported steel raise their raw material costs, making them less competitive and *harming* the U.S. balance of trade. This visceral grasp of the folly of tariffs and quotas might sound like feeble progress, considering that Ricardo laid out the argument nearly two centuries ago. It would be far more harmful, however, if Congress were filled with unreconstructed protectionists.

In a perfect world, office holders would gear their actions to the insight that it is counterproductive to protect industries in which the United States has no comparative disadvantage. What matters in the real world, however, is what affects votes in a candidate's congressional district or state. The country's general welfare often has a less tangible impact than the parochial interests of an industry with a comparative disadvantage in international trade. When workers see their jobs jeopardized by imports or outsourcing, they embrace candidates who promise to make the threat disappear. As an added attraction, those workers' employers and labor unions lavish campaign contributions on candidates who are willing to say, "To hell with the general welfare."

These forces dictate that the broad, market-generated benefits of free trade must yield to governmental tampering with the market. The parties to the scheme face a public relations problem, however. Protectionism, like racial segregation and imperialism, has long since become a dirty word in U.S. political discourse. The consequence is that candidates must uphold the principle of free trade, even if they are preparing to violate it. The corporations, for their part, must defend the use of government force to cut off low-cost competitors at the knees, while piously proclaiming the virtues of free enterprise. Finally, the labor unions must somehow reconcile their credo of international solidarity among workers with a strategy of wiping out overseas jobs. (Readers should not assume that this dilemma exists only for unions with socialist origins. Samuel Gompers, founder of the comparatively conservative American Federation of Labor, said: "There is an ideal that has been the scope of liberty-loving men and women of all ages and the labor movements of all countries—internationalism.")[36]

As a rule, the players try to avoid charges of hypocrisy by affirming their vigorous support of free trade—as long as everyone "plays by the rules." Loss of American jobs, by their reckoning, shows, ipso facto, that the foreigners are *not* playing fair. In their view, overseas producers are successful only because they underpay their workers and receive government subsidies. That is unfair, goes the standard rhetoric, and it is time for the United States to fight back. "When I'm elected," thunders the candidate, "I'll enforce the trade laws that my opponent has been ignoring."

The cheating argument is certainly more palatable than an outright call for protection. But it falls far short of establishing a bright, white line between the good kind of free trade and the bad variety. For starters, the cost of living is lower in less developed economies than in advanced industrial and postindustrial nations. Therefore, it is natural for wages to be lower in countries that are only beginning to industrialize. Short of capturing foreign employers on video dragooning workers at gunpoint, it is hard to prove that the overseas producers' wages are below the market-clearing level in their countries. As for complaints of subsidies, they are based on judging the accused by the standard of a perfect but nonexistent country, rather than the United States, which has extensive government subsidies of its own.

In separating the advancement of special interests from the rhetorical camouflage, remember that politicians who denounce unfair trade have no real interest in achieving fairness. There are no votes in that. It is much like the position of a lawyer defending a murderer. Ensuring that justice is done is the judge's responsibility; the attorney's job is to get the client acquitted. For the candidate, similarly, success consists of preserving jobs that would disappear (but that would be replaced by others) in a truly free market. Far from pursuing economic efficiency, the politician strives to perpetuate inefficiency. Preserving constituents' jobs is paramount, even though it will throw Americans in other states onto the unemployment rolls.

The point of this discussion is not to render moral judgments. A lawyer has a duty to represent the client vigorously in an adversarial proceeding, even if the client is a hit man for the mob. A politician's first job is to get elected. Regrettably, that task often gets in the way of being a statesman.

Instead of judging the politicians' actions, the objective here is to cut through their doubletalk. Officeholders and candidates loftily speak of trade that is fair as well as free, but their true objective is to promote local and regional interests over the national interest. Among their policy goals, global well-being comes in a distant third.

THE BOUNTY HUNTERS

On the face of it, protectionism represents a generous deal for industries that have sufficient political skill to obtain it. Their profits are higher than they would be under open competition, with consumers picking up the tab through higher prices. As sweet a deal as this is, Congress in 2000 found a way to make it even sweeter.

A measure sponsored by Democratic Senator Robert Byrd of West Virginia decreed that revenues generated by antidumping duties would no longer go to the U.S. Treasury. Instead, the affected businesses would henceforth pocket the cash. To qualify for its share of the loot, the Byrd Amendment decreed, a company must be on record as supporting the antidumping action by the time the International Trade Commission completes its investigation of the antidumping case.

In 2003, the Customs Service distributed $293 million to producers of steel, ball bearings, and other industries. The Congressional Budget Office estimated that over the coming decade, a total of $3.85 billion would be disbursed under the Byrd Amendment. That might represent a mere rounding error in the total federal budget, but payments to individual small businesses could be well worth the effort of applying for them. Antidumping duties on Chinese crawfish generated $9.8 million for Louisiana producers of that delicacy. A single company, Atchafalaya Crawfish Processors in Breaux Bridge, hauled in $1.4 million.[37]

The possibility of a big payday also mobilized shrimp producers, who by one estimate had the potential to collect $180 million a year under the Byrd Amendment.[38] They accused their counterparts in Brazil, China, Ecuador, India, Thailand, and Vietnam of selling frozen shrimp at artificially low prices and beseeched the Commerce Department to impose tariffs ranging from 30 percent to 349 percent.[39] In late 2002, the shrimp companies plastered ports from North Carolina to Texas with flyers urging shrimp fishermen to contribute $100 apiece to raise a $600,000 initial legal fund. The posters noted the possibility of monetary benefits.

The Southern Shrimp Alliance, which filed the antidumping case, denied that the hope of obtaining payments under the Byrd Amendment was a primary motivation for the case. Perhaps so, but the lure of cash, on top of insulation from competition, was an incentive to file trade cases that every import-sensitive industry was bound to notice. By earmarking the revenues of special duties for the supposed victims, Congress assured that industries would work harder than ever to subvert the free market. It was little wonder that the Bush administration advocated the Byrd Amendment's repeal, the World Trade Organization ruled against it, and the Congressional Budget Office declared that it injured both the U.S. economy and American policy goals.

REGRESSIVE PROTECTION

In March 2002, President George W. Bush's administration imposed tariffs of 8 percent to 30 percent on imported steel. Critics called it a blatant attempt to buy votes in Pennsylvania and West Virginia, two steel-producing states that were critical to his reelection hopes. The controversy was heated, but the tariffs lasted only until December 2003. In addition to contrasting starkly with the free trade rhetoric on which Bush campaigned in 2000, the steel duties hurt him in Michigan and Tennessee, two other pivotal states. There, jobs were lost in steel-using industries that became less competitive as the tariffs pushed up steel prices.

The temporary imposition of steel tariffs was a hot, politically charged story that attracted extensive media attention. Journalists took much less interest in the unglamorous story of routine, permanent tariffs in the range of 8 percent to 30 percent on products consumed by low-income families. These levies have created a massively regressive tax system, more by accident than by design.

As Edward Gresser of the Progressive Policy Institute has shown,[40] tariff levels vary widely by type of good. A key determining factor in setting the rates is the aggressiveness with which particular domestic industries seek protection. Tariffs on such goods as semiconductors and chemicals are generally low. American producers of these industrial items generally want to keep foreign markets open, so they accept the quid pro quo of low tariffs on imports.

Similarly, producers of luxury consumer items seldom push for high tariff barriers. They compete largely on the basis of prestige and brand name, rather than price. Therefore, they would gain little from having the Customs Service jack up the prices of their foreign competitors' products.

It is a different story, though, for manufacturers of inexpensive consumer items. The low-income consumers that they target are highly price-sensitive. Stiff tariffs can put imported goods out of reach for this group, creating a tremendous price advantage for domestic producers.

As a result of this divergence in strategies, tariffs are higher on ordinary consumer goods than on luxury items. For drinking glasses valued at less than $0.30 each, the rate is 28.5 percent, but for lead crystal glasses valued at more than $5.00, the rate is only 3 percent. Men's knit shirts made of synthetic fiber have a tariff of 32 percent. For men who can afford silk shirts, on the other hand, the tariff is a mere 0.9 percent.[41]

This topsy-turvy tariff schedule hits low-income households especially hard. The average single-parent family spends nearly $2,000 a year on clothes and shoes. Gresser estimates that as much as one-fifth of that total outlay may represent pumping up of prices through tariffs.[42] (The exact figure varies according to the family's mix of purchases.)

Surely no sane politician has ever explicitly campaigned on a platform of maximizing the tax burden on those who are least able to afford it. The way that the tariff policy works is an outcome that no one desires, generated by a democratic system that is supposed to reflect the will of the majority. It is just one more instance of politicians creating a real problem through their ham-fisted attempts to fix an imagined one.

The problem addressed by high tariffs on low-priced consumer goods is the high per capita income in the United States. It means that an hour of labor fetches a higher price than in less developed countries. The labor market rationally responds to the economic facts by locating low-skilled jobs in low-wage countries, generating benefits for both the United States and other countries through comparative advantage. Politicians, on the other hand, erect trade barriers that hurt both sides.

Worse still, the poor are hurt the most. Not only does the cost of the tariffs fall heaviest on low-income households, but the goods subject to the highest tariffs are generally manufactured in countries with low per capita income. The developed countries of Europe primarily export cars, power equipment, computers, and chemicals to the United States. Tariffs on those goods average just a little over one percent. In contrast, clothing makes up nearly 90 percent of exports to the United States from such countries as Bangladesh, Cambodia, Nepal, and Mongolia. Tariff rates on clothing average more than 14 percent. Poor Nepal pays 60 times the tariff rates on its skirts, scarves, and suits than Ireland pays for selling chemicals, pacemakers, and silicon chips to the United States.[43]

Regrettable as these outcomes are, protectionist politicians might nevertheless justify them on the grounds of saving American jobs in light manufacturing. They would be defending failure, however. Since 1990, employment in the high-tariff industries has fallen by half. The job decline in the manufacture of women's shoes since 1992 has measured 90 percent, even though no shoe tariff has been cut since the 1970s.[44] The U.S. tariff policy on consumer goods amounts to a regressive tax that fails to achieve a dubious goal of impeding the economy's long-run movement toward higher-value-added activities.

THE BOTTOM LINE

The undeclared trade policy of most politicians is to find an imperfect situation and turn it into a definitively bad one. In carrying out this policy, they make themselves ridiculous by mangling the principles of economics and, in the case of American catfish doctrine, biology. Members of Congress offer laughable justifications for paying bounties to industries that bring antidumping cases and for taxing basic consumer goods more heavily than luxury items. The victims of these policies may be forgiven for failing to appreciate the joke.

5

How Are You Going to Keep Them Down on the Farm?

Of all the supposed market failures that politicians strive to fix, probably none has given rise to more outlandish subsidies than the disappearing family farm. Politicians are determined to negate the benefits of the long-run rise in farmers' productivity that has engendered an inevitable rural-to-urban population shift. Like most other unwarranted intrusions, the government's disruption of agricultural markets is accompanied by overblown rhetoric. The bombast plays well to city dwellers. Blinded by a sentimental view of agrarian life, they fail to see how dearly they are paying for economically indefensible programs.

"Our farm policy should be designed to help family farmers in need, not corporate giants," declaimed former Vermont Governor Howard Dean as he campaigned for the Democratic presidential nomination in 2004. Failure to strengthen support for the family farm, he warned, would "mean an end to the middle class in rural America, lower wages and higher poverty for our rural citizens."[1] Ohio Representative Dennis Kucinich, a rival for the Democrats' nod, thundered, "Something's wrong when profits of agribusiness corporations skyrocket, but farmers must find off-farm jobs or sell their farms to survive."[2]

It would be unfair to suggest that politicians talk this way only when they are hustling votes on the campaign trail. Consider what another aspirant to the 2004 Democratic presidential nomination told a gathering of young farmers in 1999: "Every citizen should be concerned with the welfare and survival of young farm families," said North Carolina Senator John Edwards. Sadly, he noted, the prices charged by grocery stores did not reflect the low prices that hog and dairy producers were receiving. "The average consumer pays full retail price, and often has no idea where the meat and produce they are buying comes from."[3]

Outraged by the sorry state of affairs, the Georgia General Assembly highlighted the plight of the family farmer in a joint resolution. The legislators complained that American farmers were forced to compete with meat, oils, peanuts, and textiles produced in low-wage countries with poor living standards. "Whereas our farmers are the backbone of this country," the Assembly declared, "and by reason of international conniving have been forced to move from the farm to the city in large numbers," the President, Secretary of Agriculture, and Congress should give immediate and fair consideration to farmers.[4]

The lawmakers' efforts on behalf of the backbone of the country did not begin with the presidential campaign of 2004. In fact, the elected officials had been at it for quite a while by the time freshman Senator Edwards commiserated with the young farmers of his state in 1999. The resolution just quoted passed the Georgia legislature in 1956.

Four decades later, the issues were much the same and so were the clichés. In 1996, the Georgia House of Representatives commended the state's Future Farmers of America Association by testifying to the effect that "agriculture is the backbone and basic strength of our nation's economy."[5]

The plain fact is that if politicians are determined to block the disappearance of family farms, they are a tad late. Between 1893 and 1982, the proportion of the U.S. population living on farms shrank from 42 percent to 3 percent. Over the same period, the total population more than tripled. The net effect was that the farm population contracted by more than 20 million people.[6] To elaborate on the standard metaphor, the backbone of the nation contracted a severe case of osteoporosis.

MAKING THEMSELVES EXPENDABLE

If we take the established political debate seriously, we are forced to conclude that the farmland depopulation of the twentieth century was a calamity. After all, politicians tell us that the disappearance of family farms undermines the basic strength of the nation's economy. It must follow that the U.S. gross domestic product stagnated throughout the period.

Over here in the real world, the opposite was true. Wealth and living standards have increased dramatically over the past 100 years. The farmland depopulation was anything but a setback. In truth, it was a case of something going terribly right.

According to a favorite song of Farmers Alliance glee clubs around the time of the Populist movement in the 1890s, "The lawyer hands around while the butcher cuts a pound, but the farmer is the man who feeds them all."[7] These words told a bigger truth than the singers realized.

During the nineteenth century, farmers achieved spectacular advances in productivity by adopting new technology. They switched from hand power to horses and began using steel plows and reapers. As the average farmer's output increased substantially beyond the needs of his own family, he was able to feed a larger number of urban lawyers and butchers. This meant that a smaller proportion of the working population was needed to produce farm goods. In the 1790s, farmers represented 90 percent of the U.S. labor force. Fifty years later, the ratio was down to 69 percent. By the 1880s, less than half the workforce was employed in agriculture.[8]

Technological progress accelerated in the twentieth century. Scientists boosted yields by developing disease-resistant plants and breeding more productive farm animals. Horses gave way to tractors. By the 1930s, a single farmer supplied the needs of 9.8 persons in the United States and abroad. The ratio climbed to 15.5 in the 1950s and 129 by the 1990s.[9] By 2000, the Census Bureau estimated the farm population at a touch below 3 million out of a total population of 281 million, or just over 1 percent.[10]

After 200 years, one would think that politicians would get the connection: As technological progress makes the family farm more productive, the number of families it can feed rises and fewer family farms are needed. Evidently, though, politicians don't see the pattern.

The problem isn't poor eyesight. Politicians have 20/20 vision when it comes to seeing that the remaining family farmers can tip elections in localities and states in which they are concentrated. Presidential aspirants recognize that the Iowa caucuses represent an important hurdle on the way to their parties' nominations. What's more, saving family farms sounds good even to voters who are urban to the core. The Jeffersonian tradition

lives on in their souls, upholding virtuous tilling of the soil over evil manufacturing. Playing on these prejudices, elected officials gear their policies
to the lyric of the previously mentioned song, which stresses the banker
and merchant's dependence on the farmer:

> It would put them to the test if the farmer took a rest
> Because the farmer is the one who feeds them all.[11]

Neither Republicans nor Democrats advise the country's surplus
farmers to rest or better yet, switch to careers that offer better rewards in
the contemporary economy. Instead, politicians strive at all costs to keep
farmers working on the land—a policy that runs afoul of the fundamental
laws of economics. If the number of farmers is kept artificially high, too
much food and fiber gets produced. The glut depresses prices to levels that
make farming unprofitable, even for the number of family farms actually
required to supply the country's urban population.

Unlike the "disappearance of the family farm" (in reality, the rational
adjustment of the number of farming units to the current level of productivity), overproduction is a genuine problem. Although it was created
by the politicians' solution to a problem that existed only in their minds,
it is a problem all the same; and politicians see it as their duty to provide
a solution.

Over the decades, as the following pages show, the government has
offered many solutions to the problem of overproduction. The wide variety of approaches is a credit to politicians' creativity. Two themes unite all
the programs, however: They have either compounded the problem or
created new problems. In some cases, they have done both.

SOLUTION 1: PROP UP PRICES

The most straightforward way to balance supply and demand is to rely on
the decisions of buyers and sellers. Chronically low prices for a commodity send a message that it is time to cut back on production. Before long,
the economy is devoting the correct amount of resources to supply the
commodity. Producers and consumers, in short, manage supply pretty
well on their own as long as the market transmits clear price signals.
Only politicians would go to the trouble of finding a way to interfere
with the reception.

They begin with the premise that prices are the problem, not the solution. If the premise is that a decline in the price of a farm product is inherently bad, it follows that putting a floor under the price is an inherently good idea. The flaw in the logic becomes apparent when farmers keep producing a commodity, even if there is no demand for it. Someone has to wind up getting bagged and the taxpayer is generally the most convenient baggee.

To see how far out of hand this sort of thing can get, consider what happened when falling milk prices threatened to bankrupt small dairy farmers during the Great Depression.[12] Congress responded with a "temporary" program of dairy price supports. The scheme was formalized as the *Commodity Credit Corporation,* which bought farmers' surplus milk, butter, and cheese. In addition, Congress instituted "federal milk orders" to prevent milk from being produced in states with low costs and sold in states with higher costs. In time, the plan came to include 31 different federal milk territories. The benefit, as the politicians saw it, was that it prevented out-of-state competitors from putting dairy farmers out of business. Viewed from another angle, the program sustained milk production in regions where conditions for producing milk were unfavorable. That ensured both the misallocation of resources and unnecessarily high prices to consumers. Just to make sure that consumers wouldn't get a break, Congress imposed import controls to prevent competing foreign cheese and butter from putting a lid on prices.

The dairy farmers were no fools. They responded to the guarantee of artificially high prices by endeavoring to produce as much as possible. The farmers expanded their operations, bought cows that were bred for the highest possible milk production, and installed the newest, most efficient equipment available. Because the government's solution ensured that no price drop would ever signal dairy farmers that it was time to cut back production, the surpluses grew and grew. Excess supplies of dairy products piled up in government storage facilities.

In 1981, the government began trying to unload its burden by distributing the surplus cheese, butter, and nonfat dry milk to the poor. But the public servants couldn't give the stuff away fast enough. A decade later, government warehouses were still bulging with 38 million pounds of cheese, 280 million pounds of dry milk, and a whopping 577 million tons of butter.[13]

It would be bad enough if dairy price supports were merely costing taxpayers billions of dollars annually, but the program's cost can also be measured in more loathsome terms. By preventing the price of milk from declining in line with productivity improvements, Uncle Sam has helped to make calcium the nutrient most lacked by the poor. The victims include not only malnourished children, but also elderly sufferers of osteoporosis.[14] In seeking to solve the supposed problem of the disappearing family dairy farm, the government has helped to create a bona fide problem of nutrition.

SOLUTION 2: PAY FARMERS NOT TO PRODUCE

On the face of it, we shouldn't expect the economy to benefit from paying people *not* to do something they are good at (in the case of American farmers—growing food). Over many years, inducing them to refrain from the activity has turned out badly. Politicians, however, have failed to learn this lesson.

During World War I, American farmers expanded their croplands by 40 million acres to meet wartime needs. Along with peace came a retrenchment of world demand for their goods, but no commensurate cutback in production. By the early 1930s, surpluses were swamping rural areas in the United States. Farmers left fruit on the trees to rot, let their cotton go unpicked, and burned their corn.

In May 1933, Congress authorized the New Deal's Agricultural Adjustment Administration (AAA) to address the problem by paying farmers not to produce. Unfortunately, seeds were already sprouting and livestock were already giving birth. The AAA launched a ferocious campaign against the glut. When six million little pigs were consigned to subsidized slaughter, city dwellers squealed with outrage. By order of the AAA, farmers plowed up ten million acres of cotton. This confused the mules, who were accustomed to being beaten for treading on growing cotton. Now they found themselves getting thrashed if they didn't. Notwithstanding the government's efforts, farmers assiduously cultivated the untrampled rows and produced a bigger crop than they had in the preceding year.[15]

Futility has remained a hallmark of cropland-reduction schemes. In 1985, the government began rewarding farmers to remove croplands from production through the Conservation Reserve Program (CRP). This program's primary goal was to reduce the farming of land that was prone to erosion. By 1996, payments to farmers, at $50 an acre, reached $1.8 billion. The outlays leveled off, but by then the area idled by CRP was equivalent to the state of Michigan.

Despite the vast reduction in land under cultivation, food production remained approximately constant. For one thing, farmers largely offset the acreage removed from production by planting previously uncropped land. Like the land idled because of environmental concerns, the newly cultivated acreage was erosion prone. Second, farmers intensified their use of chemicals and pesticides on the land that remained in production. That represented another environmental setback in addition to thwarting any attempt to reduce agricultural surpluses.[16]

Even more absurd outcomes followed when the government resorted to production cutbacks to fix the mess created by dairy price supports. In 1983, Congress began paying dairy farmers to reduce production. The program did not prohibit other farmers, who did not join the program, from increasing their production. Consequently, when the first dairy support reduction program ended in 1985, the net reduction in dairy cows stood at a mere 10,000. The Agriculture Department's cost per cow eliminated was $100,000, more than one hundred times the value of a used dairy cow.[17]

Undaunted, Congress took another whack at the oversupply that it had created through price supports in the mid-1980s. The Dairy Termination Program shelled out more than $1.3 billion to farmers who agreed to slaughter their cows and take the next five years off. One California producer received a $20 million paid vacation, courtesy of the taxpayers. Once again, nothing prevented nonparticipating farmers from stepping up their production. The predictable result was that total milk production held steady. When the Agriculture Department announced in March 1986 that it planned to send 1.6 million dairy cows to slaughter, far more than anyone had predicted, the unexpected jump in supply threw the beef market into convulsion. Cattle ranchers lost millions and some went bankrupt.[18]

SOLUTION 3: DUMP THE SURPLUS ABROAD

There is nothing inherently wrong with American farmers producing more food than it takes to feed the American population. The rest of the world needs to eat, too. If farmers sell the surplus to foreign consumers, then the problems of overproduction disappear.

At least, things work out fine if the politicians keep out of it. But a brand-new set of problems arises when the U.S. government subsidizes the production or export of agricultural commodities. Now the American food merchants are underselling the foreign farmers, in many instances driving them out of business.

This is not an economically commendable example of production migrating to where costs are lowest. Rather, it keeps more than an economically justifiable number of U.S. farmers in business by increasing the number of foreign farmers who can't make a living. Credit the politicians with a clever scheme for exporting not only food, but also unemployment, and getting taxpayers to foot the bill. (To be fair, other countries pull the same stunt whenever possible, confirming that politicians are alike everywhere.)

One form of subsidization that creates this mischief is food-based foreign aid. In this scheme, the U.S. government purchases American farmers' output and ships it to foreign countries for distribution to the hungry. If the farmers in those countries have difficulty competing with cheap imports, imagine how well they do against food that is given away.

It is hard to argue against emergency food relief when a natural disaster threatens a country's population with starvation. But if the U.S. government expends massive sums to retain developing countries as a permanent outlet for American farmers' excess production, those countries are unlikely to become self-sufficient in food. As a consequence, they may remain perpetually on the brink of a food crisis.

The further the government has gone down this path, the more bizarre the outcomes have become. In 1991, the Agriculture Department hit on a foreign solution to the previously described stockpile of excess dairy products. The program consisted of buying butter from farmers for almost $1.00 a pound and selling it to foreigners for about $0.60 a pound. At a time when some Americans were struggling to pay for milk, the Agriculture Department was spending $50 million to dump 140,000 tons of dry milk abroad at distressed prices. A House Agriculture Committee report on the 1990 farm bill found that the amount of dry milk shipped to El Salvador exceeded the total amount consumed in that country. Naturally, El Salvador's milk prices fell and its milk production plunged.[19]

Agricultural export subsidies are especially troubling where U.S. production costs are higher than in countries with climates more suitable to the crop, such as tropical climates are for raising cotton. As cotton production in West Africa and other low-cost regions has grown, American cotton farmers have held their place in the world market by obtaining bigger subsidies and trade barriers. In fact, the $4 billion of subsidies shelled out in 2003 enabled U.S. growers to expand their exports even as lower-cost producers increased their production. Columbia University Professor Jeffrey D. Sachs estimated the resulting cost to African producers at $300 million a year, "a literally life-and-death difference for large numbers of impoverished households teetering on the brink of survival."[20]

The misery created by cotton subsidization represents only a small piece of a much larger problem. Congress has also shoveled taxpayers' dollars to American farmers to help them unload wheat, rice, and corn at prices well below their production costs. The strongest defense that the United States can offer for practicing protectionism while preaching free trade to the developing world is that other developed countries engage in similar hypocrisy. All told, the World Bank estimates that if farm subsidies and tariffs were eliminated, global wealth would increase by as much as half a trillion dollars and 150 million people could climb out of poverty by 2015.[21] Not surprisingly, America's do-as-we-say-not-as-we-do policy generates massive international bad will.

Dumping surplus production overseas can be criticized on fiscal, humanitarian, and foreign policy grounds. One might therefore expect enterprising office seekers to make political hay out of the many drawbacks to exporting the glut. One would be disappointed in that expectation, however. The Democratic candidates for the 2004 presidential nomination did not make these points to challenge the incumbent Republican administration. Instead, they staked out protectionist policies of their own. In so doing, they made no courageous stand on principle, but they showed that they understood how the system works. Farmers astutely vote according to who will deliver for them, rather than along party lines. Punishment for bucking their interests is swift and merciless.

SOLUTION 4: FEED THE CORN TO AUTOMOBILES

Up to a point, people can solve the problem of overproduction, without any need for government intervention, simply by eating more. As prices tumble in response to a glut, consumers can afford to consume greater quantities of food. Or drink.

In the early nineteenth century, farmers unloaded their excess corn production by distilling it into whiskey. As liquor production escalated, liquor prices plummeted. By the 1820s, per capita consumption of booze exceeded five gallons a year, compared with less than one gallon today.[22] Public drunkenness and alcohol-related diseases proliferated.

The contemporary analogue to selling corn as whiskey is to sell it as cheap ingredients of processed food. High-fructose corn syrup sweetens soft drinks. Corn-based bulking and binding agents, combined with a corn-fed chicken, produce the chicken nugget. Snack foods of various kinds proceed from extensive processing of low-priced commodities.

Food companies and restaurants could capitalize on the reduced cost of ingredients by lowering prices, but that would lower their revenues. Their preferred strategy, therefore, is to increase the size of the portions. Americans have taken the bait by stepping up their daily per capita intake of calories by more than 10 percent over roughly the past quarter-century.[23] The incidence of obesity has consequently increased.

Not only does inducing Americans to eat more have public health drawbacks, but there is ultimately a limit to how much they can eat. Fortunately, corn has the potential to satisfy another appetite: It is the automobile-loving nation's appetite for fuel. Corn can be distilled not only into whiskey, but also into grain alcohol, or ethanol. A gasohol martini, one part ethanol to nine parts gasoline, can run a car.

According to its advocates, ethanol is an elixir for a wide variety of economic ills. Aside from supporting corn prices by sopping up excess production, they say, using ethanol as fuel reduces the United States' dependence on foreign oil. Moreover, as an octane booster for gasoline, ethanol is environmentally sounder than the lead formerly used for that purpose. Ethanol, an oxygenate, reduces harmful emissions by helping fuel burn better. Finally, valuable by-products of ethanol production include feed grain for animals, carbon dioxide for soft drinks, and high-fructose corn syrup.

No matter what the problem is, ethanol is purportedly the solution. After the United States and its allies invaded Iraq to depose Saddam Hussein in 2003, some South Dakota members of the Veterans of Foreign Wars began putting up billboards promoting ethanol use. The billboards depicted Mount Rushmore, along with a red, white, and blue gasoline pump and the slogan, "Way to Go America." Organizers of the effort explained that the goals were to reduce U.S. dependence on foreign oil and keep American soldiers out of wars arising from the need for that oil. Filling up with ethanol, said the vets, was a way for people to "step up and get involved" in supporting the troops.[24]

Developing additional demand is hard to object to, in principle. It is simply good business practice to seek new applications for an existing product. Ordinarily, though, it is left to consumers to judge whether the new application justifies buying more of the product.

To cite a classic example from the annals of consumer marketing, baking soda was originally used in baking, as its name suggests. Church & Dwight Company, the manufacturer of the Arm & Hammer brand, later expanded the market by alerting consumers that baking soda "absorbs odors from stinky foods in your refrigerator and freezer to keep other foods (like ice cubes) from tasting funky."[25] Many homemakers began keeping an open box of baking soda in their refrigerators, without any further prodding in the form of federal income tax rebates.

Within the agricultural field, various organizations have sought to stimulate demand by uncovering previously unrecognized health benefits of their products. The U.S. Highbush Blueberry Council has trumpeted that U.S. Department of Agriculture Human Nutrition Center researchers have ranked blueberries number one compared with 40 other fresh fruits and vegetables in antioxidant activity. Antioxidants, says the Council, "help neutralize harmful by-products of metabolism called 'free radicals' that can lead to cancer and other age related diseases."[26] Consumers can evaluate such claims and decide whether to start eating more blueberries, all within the context of ordinary market forces. (One could argue that the blueberry growers have already received a subsidy in the form of government-funded research, but for now let's concentrate on the big stuff.)

On the face of it, the same logic ought to extend to ethanol. If it truly fills a need more effectively or more cheaply than other products previously available, then ethanol is bound to succeed in the marketplace on its merits. After competing with gasoline for the first half-century following the advent of automobiles, however, ethanol was the clear loser.

Samuel Morey developed an engine that ran on ethanol and turpentine way back in 1826. Henry Ford's first automobile, the 1896 quadricycle, was built to run on pure ethanol. During the 1930s, there was a vogue for ethanol blends in the Midwest. World Wars I and II temporarily stimulated demand for ethanol as a fuel and gasoline. From the late 1940s to the late 1970s, however, commercial fuel ethanol essentially disappeared from the United States.

Did the long decades of honest failure under the free enterprise system discourage the ethanol advocates? Not in the least. They sucked up their guts and followed a principle as American as apple pie: If at first you don't succeed, ask the government for a handout.

This effort to salvage defeat from victory proved wildly successful. The Energy Tax Act of 1978 exempted blends containing at least 10 percent alcohol from the $0.04-a-gallon federal gasoline excise tax. This effectively amounted to a $0.40-a-gallon subsidy for ethanol. In 1980, Congress provided insured loans for small ethanol producers, placed a tariff on foreign-produced ethanol, banned retaliation against ethanol resellers, and extended the gasohol tax credit. Subsequent legislation in 1983 and 1984 boosted the subsidy to $0.50, then $0.60 a gallon.

The demand for bigger and bigger tax breaks was understandable, as the unsubsidized economics of ethanol were horrendous. A gallon of ethanol contained only about two-thirds as much energy as a gallon of gasoline, according to the Agriculture Department. With ethanol representing one-tenth of the gasohol blend, substitution of gasohol for gasoline would be expected to reduce gas mileage by 3.3 percent, an estimate that Department of Energy analysis found to be optimistic in practice. (With drivers getting fewer miles to the gallon, by the by, the ethanol advocates' claims of reduced dependence on imported oil were weakened.) The Agriculture Department also calculated that it cost $1.60 to produce a gallon of ethanol, at a time when gasoline was wholesaling for $0.60 a gallon. Tax subsidies lowered ethanol's price to about $0.30 less than the prevailing gasoline wholesale price, but even this great big helping hand from Uncle Sam was not enough.[27] Ethanol production was profitable only when the price of corn was low. Like other farm commodities, corn experienced price highs as well as lows. By 1985, the majority of ethanol producers were out of business.

"Quitters never win," the ethanol promoters told themselves. Their defiant response to failure was to launch a new phase of government cooperation with the private sector. If ethanol couldn't succeed in the market, even with a generous tax incentive, then mandating its use might just do the trick. The Energy Policy Act of 1992 required specified automobile fleets to begin purchasing vehicles capable of operating on alternative fuels. Conveniently, E-85, a blend of 85 percent ethanol and 15 percent gasoline qualified as one such alternative fuel.

Meanwhile, the gasohol tax credit continued, although the rate dropped off to $0.54 a gallon in 1990. In the mid-1990s, with the cost of oil at $18 a barrel, the government was footing the bill for ethanol at a rate of $23 a barrel.[28] By 2004, the tax break was costing taxpayers an estimated $1.4 billion a year.[29]

Ethanol subsidization reached the height of absurdity in 1995 and 1996. As the result of a poor crop, corn prices doubled to $5 a bushel. Ethanol producers, or at least the ones that hadn't gone bankrupt a decade earlier, faced a devastating cost squeeze. In stepped state governments with subsidies designed to keep the ethanol plants solvent. After subsidizing an industry into existence to deal with a chronic corn glut, the people's representatives diverted additional tax revenues to address the consequences of a corn shortage.

By digging themselves in ever deeper with market intervention, politicians demonstrated that ethanol was the wrong solution to the problem of excess corn production. The simpler and less expensive remedy was to let the market continue the centuries-old progression toward fewer, more efficient workers employed in growing corn. Where was the market failure that necessitated a subsidy for a fuel consistently rejected by the market?

The ostensible market breakdown involved an externality. The argument went that drivers would surely reject gasohol produced under free-market conditions, but society at large would be the loser. The individual consumer decisions wouldn't take into account the collective benefits of cleaner air and reduced dependence on oil-producing sheikdoms. Unless government gave drivers a price inducement to tank up with ethanol, the product's less direct benefits wouldn't be realized.

This argument contains a fatal flaw. Although using ethanol as a fuel has hidden benefits, it also has hidden costs. In response to incessant calls for increased ethanol subsidies, the Department of Energy estimated in 1986 that each dollar of resulting extra farm income would cost consumers and taxpayers roughly four dollars.[30] The income gained by corn farmers through higher prices is largely offset by the increased cost of feed grain for livestock producers. Consumers in turn get hit by higher meat prices.

As for the supposed displacement of fossil fuels, a complete assessment must take into account the energy consumed by ethanol production plants, as well as energy used in growing, harvesting, and shipping the corn to the plants. In 1991, the Department of Energy estimated that all told, it required 85,000 to 91,000 British thermal units (BTUs) to produce one gallon of ethanol containing the energy equivalent of 76,000 BTUs.[31] It appeared, in short, that ethanol production represented a net detriment to the effort to reduce dependence on imported oil.

To be sure, the energy equation improved if the feedstock for producing ethanol was changed from corn to switch grass, a plant customarily used for hay. Switch grass, however, couldn't boast the political backers that corn could attract. In the arithmetic of ethanol incentives, BTUs counted less than votes and campaign contributions.

Technological advances may be improving the corn-based ethanol energy-use story. Still, the controversy continues. David Pimentel, a Cornell entomologist with a long-running involvement in the subject, maintains that it takes 29 percent more energy to produce a gallon of ethanol than the gallon yields. The Agriculture Department claims, on the contrary, that ethanol yields 35 percent more energy than its production requires. Average figures aside, producing ethanol appears to be energy-inefficient in drier corn-growing areas, where the crops must be irrigated with the help of natural-gas-powered pumps.[32]

Turning finally to the supposed environmental benefits of ethanol, it is striking that environmentalists are among the product's severest critics. According to the director of the Sierra Club's energy program in Washington, DC, ethanol decreases carbon monoxide, but increases smog by stepping up evaporation of the gasoline with which it is mixed. Furthermore, the Green Party's 2002 Minnesota gubernatorial candidate maintained that expanding the existing ethanol program as it was then structured would encourage cultivation of huge fields of corn under conditions that would require massive doses of chemicals and promote soil erosion.[33] Other research has concluded that mixing ethanol with gasoline can increase emissions of the toxic pollutant acetaldehyde and boost the likelihood of seepage of toxins such as benzene into groundwater.[34] A Department of Energy study found no significant environmental benefit to gasohol.[35]

The policy that makes the most economic sense isn't always the one that makes the most political sense. As Jerry Taylor of the Cato Institute observes, "If you want to be president of the United States, you have to go through the Iowa caucuses, which means if you don't bow down and worship ethanol, you're a dead man politically."[36]

Beyond that fact of political life, ethanol enjoys the enthusiastic support of food processor Archer Daniels Midland Corporation (ADM). Long-time chairman Dwayne Andreas is credited with persuading President Jimmy Carter of the benefits of ethanol in 1978.[37] At least, in Andreas's view, ethanol would help the country if ADM's 70 percent share of production, circa 1981, was not impaired by government-subsidized loans to small, competing producers or by Brazilian imports.[38]

Archer Daniels Midland Corporation's success in winning high-level backing for the ethanol subsidy and its other pet causes is not the product of charm alone. Generous contributions to a long string of politicians of both major parties have also played a role. Andreas was a member of President George H. Bush's Team 100, consisting of donors of $100,000 in soft money.[39] In the 1992 presidential campaign, Andreas, his family, and ADM ranked third among the Democrats' largest contributors and first among the Republicans, according to the Center for Responsive Politics.

Beyond supporting their electoral efforts, Andreas helped out politicians in such ways as underwriting the military school education of one of Vice President Hubert Humphrey's children. When Iowa's Tom Harkin was sued for libel in 1986 in connection with a statement made during a campaign, there was Andreas with a $10,000 contribution to the senator's legal defense fund. When Senate Majority Leader Bob Dole's wife became head of the Red Cross, Andreas's foundation came through with a $1 million donation. Dole's Better America Foundation received a $100,000 contribution from the same source.

President Richard Nixon's secretary, Rose Mary Woods, recalled that in 1972, Andreas made a personal visit to deliver an unmarked envelope containing $100,000 in $100 bills. The cash resided in a White House safe for about a year. Then, under the heat of the Watergate investigation, Nixon decided to give it back.

The zeal for supporting the work of public servants, which Andreas likened to tithing, occasionally landed him in hot water. In 1993, he and his wife had to pay a fine for exceeding the legal limit in contributions to political candidates. Casting his bread on the waters, however, certainly brought rewards to Andreas and ADM. The Cato Institute has described ADM as "the most prominent recipient of corporate welfare in recent U.S. history."[40]

To be fair, a handful of politicians, including Senator John McCain of Arizona, have defied ADM by criticizing the ethanol tax break or even seeking its repeal. Former representative and 1996 Republican vice presidential nominee Jack Kemp of New York told Congress that it ranked at the top "of all the stupid ideas in America."[41] House Ways and Means Committee Chairman Bill Archer called the tax exemption "highway robbery"[42] and tried, but failed, to abolish it.

In 2006, President George W. Bush devoted a portion of his State of the Union message to promotion of additional government support for ethanol derived from both corn and switch grass.[43] Despite the valiant efforts of a few, feeding corn to cars appears likely to survive for at least several more years as a dubious solution to the problem represented by the United States' ability to produce more corn with fewer farmers than in an earlier age.

THE BOTTOM LINE

To anyone with a rudimentary understanding of arithmetic, the increased efficiency of farming over a long period has a straightforward implication: As the number of people that each agricultural worker can feed increases, the fraction of the labor force employed in agriculture goes down. At least, that is what happens if the government stays out of it. In time, the displaced workers get redeployed into more productive areas, where they will make a bigger contribution to the nation's economic well-being.

Leaving well enough alone, however, is not the credo that politicians live by. Instead, they see things as they are and ask why not. Why not, in this case, keep folks down on the farm by supporting prices at some arbitrary level? When overproduction predictably results, the politicians refuse to connect the dots. "I am absolutely convinced," declared Senate Agriculture Committee Chairman Patrick Leahy of Vermont in 1990, "that simply bringing down the dairy price supports is not a way to cut production."[44]

The next step is to pay some farmers not to produce. When the other farmers step up their production, negating the impact of the crop reduction plan, politicians' minds start working overtime. They hatch schemes to dump the surplus abroad in the guise of providing foreign aid. They even contrive to turn it into motor fuel at a gigantic cost to taxpayers.

The politicians' ingenuity knows no bounds. In March 1991, Senator Leahy introduced an amendment to the Gulf War emergency appropriations bill. It consisted of a plan to eliminate the surplus in milk powder by requiring milk processors to add milk powder to fluid milk. Leahy enthusiastically declared that milk would taste better and richer as a result of the new standard. Never mind that milk processors were already producing a small quantity of extra-thick milk for the few consumers who preferred it. Despite the absence of any evidence of unfilled demand, Leahy persuaded

59 of his 99 colleagues to support the measure. In a rare outbreak of common sense, the plan was later dropped by the House–Senate conference committee.[45]

It is tempting to dismiss the entire U.S. agricultural policy as a joke, except that certain of its consequences are decidedly unfunny. They include massively increased food costs for consumers, nutritional problems, devastation of other countries' agricultural sectors, deterioration in foreign relations, and assorted environmental hazards. Without demonstrating a bona fide market failure that requires correction, the government has unleashed a host of troubles by intervening in the economy.

6

Location and Misallocation

Like every other successful occupier of real estate, corporations pay close attention to location. But when they decide where to locate a plant or headquarters building, they don't think only about pleasant vistas and convenient transportation. Companies also consider which location comes with the biggest tax break.

When a city attracts a corporate facility through financial inducements, the local residents cheer about the new jobs that will accompany it. Few voters see the bigger picture: They are sacrificing tax revenue to lure a company away from another city, which in turn is taking a hit to its pocketbook to lure a company from a third city. By pitting cities against one another, the corporations are gaining at the expense of taxpayers in all cities.

To understand how the game works, consider the following telephone conversation involving two fictitious chief executive officers, Clyde Clark of Superior Fasteners and Ward Wayne of Olympic Ball Bearings:

CLARK: Hey, good buddy, how were you hitting 'em this weekend?
WAYNE: A little on the comme ci, comme ça side, to tell you the truth. My drives were all going right down the middle of the fairway, but I couldn't sink anything longer than a three-foot putt.
CLARK: Well, let me get to the main reason I called. I understand you're planning to replace your Gotham City factory with a larger facility.
WAYNE: That's right. It's going to be our biggest plant. We'll upsize our Gotham City workforce by 25 percent.

CLARK: I bet it's going to be something to see. By the way, did I mention that we've decided to tear down our Metropolis factory and put up a bigger one?

WAYNE: You don't say. I'll bet your mayor is happy about the city getting those new jobs. Not to mention the extra tax revenues.

CLARK: Yeah, well that's what I was thinking about. You know, it isn't absolutely essential for us to build the new plant in Metropolis. Why, I bet a lot of other cities would give their eyeteeth to get us to relocate. And in terms of dollars and cents, eyeteeth translate into some pretty fancy tax breaks.

WAYNE: You got that right! I can tell you without even checking that our city council would offer you a humongous tax holiday if you were to pick that operation up and move it to Gotham City.

CLARK: I'm not surprised to hear that. It would be the same here, if you decided to pull up stakes and build that new ball bearing plant in Metropolis. (Pause.) Hey, good buddy, are you thinking what I'm thinking?

WAYNE: I'm way ahead of you, brother. If we both relocate, you can get lower taxes here in Gotham City and I can get lower taxes over there in Metropolis. And what's the big deal about moving one of our plants? We're only talking an hour by corporate jet.

CLARK: It's even sweeter than that, Ward. Once our own cities find out that we're thinking of relocating our plants, they'll probably offer us some fairly hefty tax incentives not to leave. If we play our cards right, we could wind up with impressive improvements to our bottom lines, without going to the trouble of moving our management people or replacing the ones who can't relocate.

WAYNE: I am truly psyched about this idea, Clyde. How soon can we flesh it out at my club and get in a quick 18 holes while we're at it?

IT HAS TO COME OUT OF SOMEBODY'S HIDE

This fictitious account incorporates a touch of hyperbole. Real companies don't consciously collude to squeeze cities for location-based tax incentives. But the economic result is the same as if they did: When Corporations X and Y obtain tax concessions to relocate, Cities A and B suffer a collective loss of tax revenue.

Somebody has to make up that shortfall. That somebody is likely to include local businesses that lack the negotiating power to extract tax breaks. Small service providers such as hair salons and shoe repair stores can't generate much fear at City Hall by threatening to pull up stakes. It is a safe bet that if they vacate their premises, their customers will continue getting haircuts and replacing their soles. The business will go to other establishments or to new ones that emerge to fill the demand. Employment among stylists and cobblers will show no net change, nor will the tax revenues generated by their activities.

Small businesses that cater to the local population have little leverage to negotiate for tax relief, but large companies that sell their products to a national or global market are in a strong position. They can choose to locate in any number of cities that meet certain requirements, such as adequate transportation and good schools for employees' children. Therefore, if cities offer tax incentives to attract factories and corporate headquarters, the big national and global companies will inevitably unload part of their tax burden onto small, local companies.[1]

PRETTY DETAIL OF AN UGLY PICTURE

The unfairness of this arrangement might be expected to generate howls of protest. But politicians don't get blasted for offering location-based tax incentives. They escape criticism because the electorate typically sees only part of the picture.

There is credible evidence that tax incentives for corporate relocation pay for themselves.[2] Municipalities stand a good chance of earning back the sacrificed revenues through taxes generated by increased growth in the local economy. Even hair salons and shoe repair stores benefit. When a major new plant or corporate headquarters opens, highly paid managers who migrate to the city become customers of the local businesses.

But that happy outcome shows only the winner's side of the story. Increased prosperity in the city that gains a new corporate employer is matched by reduced prosperity in the city that the corporation forsakes. The victorious city may ultimately make up the tax receipts that it sacrifices to attract a company, but the losing city's tax receipts will only go down.

The costs of location-based economic incentives will be even less apparent if City X loses out to City Y in one corporate location competition, but beats out City Z in another. In that case, residents of City X and City Y will both see location-based tax incentives in a favorable light. In no city involved in the great game of pass-the-beanbag will taxpayers recognize that the benefits are illusory. Collectively, the cities are only transferring a chunk of the tax burden from large, national and global corporations to small, local businesses. The only ways to get out of this box are for the cities to shift the tax burden directly to individuals, reduce services, or increase their debt to offset lost revenues.[3]

Voters' failure to see the whole picture is not entirely a matter of chance. The politically astute corporations that benefit from the cities' generosity make sure they loudly commend the government officials for their enlightened, business-friendly policies. On close examination, those policies are friendly only to *certain* businesses. But that is not a distinction that the office holders have time to acknowledge. They are too busy taking credit for creating jobs.

Note that *creating* is appropriate to the situation only to the same extent that shipping potatoes from Boise to Scottsdale qualifies as creating potatoes in Arizona. When a company relocates, city officials merely help transfer existing jobs from one locale to another. Jobs get created in response to growth in demand for goods and services. Granting location-based tax breaks merely influences *where* jobs will be created.

While on the subject of fallacies, let's clear up one more. The reasoning goes as follows: Tax reductions are inherently good. Therefore, it is a good thing if corporations can shake down cities for tax concessions.

The flaw in the logic is obvious when it involves only a shift of the tax burden, rather than an overall lowering of taxes. But we have implicitly assumed that the city has no unproductive expenditures that it can eliminate to offset the corporate tax concessions. Staunch advocates of tax cutting will insist that *every* government entity has fat to be trimmed. If so, the concession granted to the relocating company can genuinely represent a net reduction in taxes.

But suppose that a particular city has wasteful expenditures that can be cut from its budget. The city should wield the axe and reduce taxes in a way that distributes the burden optimally among all businesses and individuals. There is no good reason to earmark the budget savings exclusively for relocation incentives.

ALTERNATIVE STRATEGIES

The paradox of location incentives is that each city attracting a corporate facility reaps a benefit, yet collectively, all cities wind up in a worse position. No net new jobs are created in the process. Instead, the corporations auction off a fixed pool of jobs to the highest bidders. The cities make their bids in the form of tax breaks, which result in higher taxes for local businesses that can't participate in the legal blackmail scheme.

Make no mistake about it: There is nothing inherently wrong with cities competing for corporate facilities. If they do, there will necessarily be winners and losers, but the victors needn't feel sorry for the vanquished. Houstonians don't have to concern themselves about the standard of living in Miami, or vice versa. On the other hand, neither city ought to object if its rival benefits from a new strategy that makes every city better off. That is what could happen if cities agreed to compete on a basis other than location-based tax incentives.

The rational course, if the cities would only agree, is to swear off tax giveaways as a tool for attracting employers. Instead, they can vie for factories and headquarters by investing in themselves. For starters, they can develop good schools, which are a prime attraction for corporations contemplating relocation of employees. Excellent education also produces a high-quality labor force, which helps corporations in their local recruitment. Spending that leads to a low crime rate is another effective way to lure companies and their employees.

Moderate tax rates on the general population, rather than in incentives for relocation, represent another quality-of-life benefit. What's more, if local businesses (the ones that can't obtain tax breaks by threatening to leave), pay moderate taxes, the tax expenses that they pass on to their customers are moderate as well. That keeps the cost of living down, yet another aid to corporations' efforts to attract top-notch employees.

When cities collectively invest in schools, crime prevention, and tax reduction, it benefits society at large, rather than a handful of corporations with disproportionate bargaining power. Assar Lindbeck, former chairman of the committee for the Nobel Prize in Economics,[4] captured the essence of this enlightened approach with the following image:

> It is not by planting trees or subsidizing tree planting in a desert created by politicians that the government can promote . . . industry, but by refraining from measures that create a desert environment.[5]

WHAT THE RESEARCH SHOWS

Logic indicates that location-based tax incentives are counterproductive. Still, it might not work out that way in practice. Perhaps the tax giveaways are more cost-effective for American cities than common sense would suggest.

In point of fact, that is what the research initially seemed to indicate. Tax incentives first became a major factor in city-to-city competition for new businesses in the 1970s.[6] Economists began to study the phenomenon and formed a favorable impression.

These early studies suffered from fatal flaws in methodology.[7] Some measured the success of incentives by counting how many incentive programs were in operation. In effect, the authors of those studies said that it didn't matter whether a program produced any worthwhile result. Incredibly, other early studies tried to determine how effective the incentives were by asking the companies that were benefiting from the tax breaks. Naturally, those respondents assured the interviewers that the programs were highly effective and unquestionably worth renewing. In other words, "We like the giveaways, so keep them coming."

Research methods have improved since the early days of location-based tax incentives. Certain obstacles to measuring the benefits remain, but it is clear that the programs don't invariably work out as intended. The biggest hoped-for effect is generally to bring jobs to the city that grants the tax break. In some cases, the tax reductions instead encourage companies to replace workers with labor-saving machines.[8]

Certain tax benefits merely influence corporations' decisions about where to locate within a metropolitan area. Workers don't benefit materially from such programs. If a new factory is constructed a suburb or two away, they can either commute or move closer to their new place of employment.

Yet another practical problem with location-based incentives arises when companies renege on their promises after collecting their benefits. To be sure, cities have learned from such experiences. They now try to protect themselves with clauses that reclaim the tax preferences if the corporation doesn't live up to its end of the bargain. But a company may nevertheless get away with reneging. On the one hand, if the project works out badly and the corporation loses money, it may become judgment-proof by virtue of financial weakness. On the other hand, a large, financially strong company might simply refuse to honor its promise to maintain employment at a stated level. If the city presses its case, the company can threaten to eliminate even more jobs, potentially forcing the city to back down.

A RAY OF HOPE

The politicians who hand out tax incentives are fully aware that corporations are playing them off against one another. In the early 1990s, the country's governors met in Washington, DC, to discuss the problem. They pledged to forgo individual company subsidies in favor of general improvements in the economic climate, a pact that quickly broke down. Like other agreements to refrain from competition, each participant had a substantial incentive to break ranks. Once one city offered a tax incentive, others had to respond in kind.[9]

Then, almost miraculously, a possible way out of the box appeared. Actually, human rather than divine intervention was pivotal, in the person of Professor Peter Enrich of the Northeastern University School of Law. He argued in a 1996 article[10] that the states' competition to grant location-based tax incentives was creating a race to the bottom that injured their citizens' interests. Enrich contended that the incentives conflicted with the U.S. Constitution's Commerce Clause,[11] which authorizes Congress to regulate commerce among the states.

The framers of the Constitution, Enrich noted, aimed to eliminate the state-against-state conflicts that prevailed under the Articles of Confederation. Customs barriers and economic retaliation were the order of the day. The framers believed that the road to prosperity for the young nation lay in union, rather than division. Citing this historical background, Enrich concluded that the Commerce Clause constrained location-based tax incentives, just as it constrained other efforts by states to advance their own economies at the expense of the national economy.

In 2004, after hearing oral arguments from Professor Enrich, the United States Court of Appeals for the Sixth Circuit ruled that Ohio's investment tax credit violated the Commerce Clause. The suit began when DaimlerChrysler decided to replace its Toledo Jeep assembly plant and extracted $300 million in city and state tax incentives to build the new plant in Toledo. At the urging of consumer advocate Ralph Nader, Enrich took up the case. He didn't prevail on all points, but he was able to characterize the court's decision as "an important turning point in the fight against the endless proliferation of tax breaks for large, mobile businesses."[12] Enrich hoped the ruling would prompt wider public discussion of states' sacrificing their tax bases in futile efforts to outbid competing jurisdictions.

Legal challenges may go on for years. There is hope, however, that the courts will succeed where the politicians have failed. Quite possibly, the states and cities will be able to end their equivalent of the nuclear arms race. Chief executive officers (CEOs) could be major losers, however. With location-based tax incentives rejected by the Commerce Clause, they might have to devote their golf outings to inventing new ways to collect corporate welfare.

AN OFF-TARGET INVESTMENT THEORY

Location-based tax incentives might seem uniquely ill-conceived, but no one should underestimate the creative scope of booster-minded politicians. They have managed to devise another scheme for local business development that is just as loopy. It goes by the name of *economically targeted investments* (ETIs).

In the 1970s, sentiment for restraining government spending was running strong. As elected officials couldn't help but notice, city and state employee pension plans were accumulating huge pools of money. Like bears to honey, the office holders were instinctively attracted to the loot. They duly put their minds to figuring out how to get their paws on it.

Luck was with them. Not all the money was tagged for immediate disbursement to retired teachers and firefighters. A substantial portion was being invested to provide future retirement benefits for current state employees. These conditions provided a convenient cover story: The government would move some of the pension fund's dollars out of run-of-the-mill stocks and bonds and put them to work for the benefit of the citizenry. They would instruct the pension system's managers to invest in in-state business opportunities that provided an ostensible social benefit such as facilitating homeownership or generating jobs.

In the politicians' minds, everyone came out ahead when public pension plans made economically targeted investments. The targeted companies got a financial shot in the arm. That enabled them to keep state residents well-housed and off the unemployment roles. The politicians, in turn, could claim credit for fostering homeownership or creating jobs.

Best of all, according to the politicians' arithmetic, these wonderful benefits were obtainable at no cost. Diverting dollars into ETIs from other investments didn't require taxpayers to put any extra money into funding the public employees' pension plan. As a matter of fact, a smart consultant could probably produce financial projections ostensibly proving that ETIs would boost the pension plan's investment returns. If one could believe the numbers, this meant that ETIs made it *less* costly for taxpayers to provide retirement benefits for state and city workers.

SERVING TWO MASTERS

There is a fatal flaw in this seemingly idyllic arrangement. An economically targeted investment program creates a conflict in managing the pension fund. Predictably bad consequences arise from attempting to serve two masters.

The managers of a public pension fund are responsible for ensuring the future availability of cash for the public employees' promised benefits. Accordingly, job number one is to avoid major investment losses. Achieving this objective spares legislators the embarrassment of having to go back to the taxpayers for additional money.

Avoiding big losses is a key objective for a public employees pension fund, but it is not the whole story. Subject to controlling the risk, the managers are also supposed to maximize long-run investment performance. The more money the fund earns, the fewer dollars taxpayers have to kick into the plan.

Balancing the objectives of keeping losses low and returns high is challenging in itself. Each time a potential investment comes up for consideration, the managers must carefully weigh its upside against its downside. Whether looking at a stock, a bond, or an office building, they have to ask, "Among all the investment opportunities currently available to us, does this one offer us the highest return for the risk we're able to incur?" This already difficult analysis becomes far more complicated when politicians introduce criteria that have nothing directly to do with investment performance, such as the state's unemployment level or homeownership rate.

It is not inconceivable that if the planets align properly, a circumstance will arise in which a single action can fulfill two unrelated but worthy purposes. One happy day, a state pension plan's managers might honestly conclude that their investment objectives could best be advanced, at that juncture, by writing a check to an in-state company that must lay off workers unless it receives a massive cash infusion. But if this ever happens, it will go down in the annals of financial history as one of the most astonishing coincidences of all time.

In this example, the unlikelihood of the ETI being the pension plan's best available investment doesn't automatically follow from the supplicant company being financially troubled. At the right price, the stocks and bonds of distressed companies sometimes represent excellent investments. *Vulture capitalists,* professional money managers who specialize in such securities, stand to realize huge gains if the companies regain their footing. These investments entail considerable risk. But a public pension fund might be able to spread the risks over many different distressed companies. In the context of a widely diversified portfolio, a modest stake in a temporarily depressed business could be a suitable investment.

The problem, then, is not that the ETI company is financially challenged. Rather, the concern is the process by which the company gets selected for the pension fund's portfolio. If the decision is based solely on the company's investment merits, there is no cause for alarm. But if the company can raise the capital it needs only with a helping hand from the state legislature, it means the market has determined that it does *not* offer a satisfactory reward for the risk. In that case, the pension plan managers can invest in the ETI only if they deviate from their duty to maximize the plan's return, subject to controlling risk.

The same logic applies to an ETI that does not involve distressed companies. Suppose that a company is just starting up or expanding an already successful operation. Investment professionals have plenty of experience evaluating companies in those circumstances. Using benchmarks derived from similar companies, they can determine the appropriate price for the shares, based on the company's prospective or existing sales and earnings.

If the public pension plan decides to invest at that price, it is acting in accordance with its fiduciary duty. And it needs no prodding from the state legislature to make the investment. But what if the pension plan buys the shares, driving up the price in the process, solely to obey the legislature's directive to make economically targeted investments? In that case, the fund is paying a price that other investors don't find satisfactory for the risk. Put another way, the fund is subsidizing the company with lower-cost capital than the company can obtain in the free market. It is extremely difficult to reconcile this activity with the pension plan's mission of ensuring a comfortable retirement for police officers and sanitation workers.

All these problems arise before even considering what could be the ETIs' biggest drawback. So far, we have merely pointed out that mandating economically targeted investments will divert the public pension plans' investment assets from best to second-best or fourth-best opportunities. But what if politicians go beyond requiring ETIs in the abstract and recommend specific investments to the pension fund's managers? Chances are, the companies receiving those powerful endorsements will have strong ties to the politicians making the recommendations. As investment merit gives way to cronyism, the likelihood of major losses increases.

REAL-WORLD EVIDENCE

As with location-based tax incentives, common sense predicts that economically targeted investments will do more harm than good.[13] In both cases, though, examining the record is a good check on intuitions about the matter. It turns out that the results are no less dismal for investing pension assets in companies than for luring them with tax breaks. In fact, some of the outcomes have been monumentally bad.

In 1980, Alaska's public employee and teacher retirement funds lent 35 percent of their total assets ($165 million) for mortgages within Alaska. Well-established investment principles oppose such extreme concentration in a single type of investment or within a single geographic region. The wisdom behind that practice became apparent in 1987, when the price of oil fell. As a result of Alaska's economic dependence on that commodity, home prices plummeted. An extraordinary 40 percent of the retirement funds' loans either became delinquent or resulted in foreclosures.[14]

Connecticut tried to preserve jobs in 1989 by investing $25 million of the State of Connecticut Trust Funds in Colt's Manufacturing Company. The Hartford-based company had suffered major setbacks in the preceding five years, losing its government contracts to produce the Colt .45 revolver and the M-16 rifle.[15] Aside from the company's financial precariousness, some citizens might have questioned whether propping up a firearms manufacturer accorded with the high-minded social purpose behind economically targeted investments. But they didn't get to debate the issue for very long. Three years after the state got involved, Colt's filed for bankruptcy. The pension plan ultimately lost approximately 80 percent of its investment.[16]

The Kansas Public Employees Retirement System's $65 million investment in Home Savings Association became worthless when federal regulators seized the thrift in 1991. That was only one of the more dramatic losses that the Kansas public pension plan incurred. Write-offs exceeded $200 million[17] in a program that had been hailed in the late 1980s as a model for ETIs.

Even if public pension plans don't endanger their solvency through badly conceived economically targeted investments, they drag down their investment performance. A 1983 study by Alicia Munnell, who later served on President Bill Clinton's Council of Economic Advisers, found a 2 percent reduction in returns as a result of ETIs.[18] Economists M. Wayne Marr, John L. Trimble, and John R. Nofsinger reported that the 1990 annual return for state and local government employee pension plans with ETI programs was lower than for those without them. The difference, 5.82 percent versus 8.07 percent, was statistically significant.[19] This reduction of investment performance represents a real cost to taxpayers. The less money the fund earns on its investments, the more they must contribute.

WHY NOT GO WHOLE HOG?

Incredibly, the Clinton administration tried to carry the bad idea of economically targeted investments even further. In September 1994, Secretary of Labor Robert Reich proposed extending the concept beyond public employee pension plans by encouraging corporate pension funds to seek out ETIs.

Reich's proposal had an air of inevitability. Public pension plans' aggregate $1.4 trillion of investment assets was a bagatelle compared with the dollars residing in private-sector pension plans. The Labor Secretary's scheme promised to let the politicians into a $3.4 trillion sandbox.[20]

Fortunately, substantial obstacles stood in the way of Reich's plan. Most important, the private pension funds, unlike their public cousins, were subject to the Employee Retirement Income Security Act of 1974.

This law expressly requires fiduciaries of pension assets to discharge their duties solely in the interests of the active and retired employees and for the exclusive purpose of providing benefits to them.

Reich contended that it was nevertheless permissible for private pension plans to seek out investments with ancillary benefits to society as a whole. He gave examples such as affordable housing, infrastructure investments, and start-up companies. It was only necessary, he said, that such investments match the risk and return characteristics of other available opportunities. Skeptics were not reassured. They recognized that investment judgment could easily be skewed by corporate managers with their own agenda, including the desire to curry favor in Washington.

Opposition to Reich's proposal resulted in the introduction of a bill to restrict promotion of economically targeted investments by the Labor Department and other federal agencies. The proposed legislation, sponsored by Representative Jim Saxton (R–NJ), passed in the House of Representatives. It didn't advance beyond the Senate's Committee on Labor and Human Resources, but the impetus for pushing private pension funds into ETIs eventually faded.

THE BOTTOM LINE

Every financial scheme hatched by politicians is unsound in its own way. Location-based incentives and ETIs are two harebrained ideas that illustrate especially well the range of mischief achievable through unwarranted intervention in the market.

Location-based tax incentives transfer money from state and local governments to mobile corporations that can exploit the system. Other taxpayers, including businesses more firmly rooted in the community, must make up the difference.

Economically targeted investments by public employee pension plans present a serious conflict of interest. Fiduciaries can't safeguard the government workers' nest eggs at the lowest possible cost to taxpayers and simultaneously promote the politicians' economic development goals. What's more, the targeted investments are likely to involve political, rather than bona fide economic targets.

The mere fact that location-based tax incentives and ETIs are economically foolish doesn't entirely disqualify them from consideration. In a democratic system, citizens have the right to embrace a bad idea. The premise of self-government is that the people's judgment can be trusted, *provided the ideas are presented to them honestly.* Politicians rarely satisfy that requirement.[21]

In the hoopla surrounding tax incentives designed to lure businesses to town, the shift of the tax burden isn't made explicit. Neither do the public officials highlight that in aggregate, local governments lose money by striving to outdo one another in handing out tax breaks. Voters see the benefits of the incentives, but not the costs.

Similarly out of sight is the drag on the investment returns of public employee pension plans that results from economically targeted investments. Neither will many taxpayers see the connection between that drag and the cost of providing for future retirement benefits. The extra funding requirement simply disappears in the thicket of budget numbers.

There is an honest way to invest tax dollars in a business that can't attract capital on its merits in the free market. It consists of making the expenditure directly from the state's operating budget. As part and parcel of the honest approach, the public officials must justify the outlay with a credible story of market failure.

Politicians are allergic to such straightforward methods. Their predilection for subterfuge requires them to disguise their handouts to unsound enterprises as legitimate investments by public employee pension funds. It may not be textbook democracy, but it ensures that influence-buyers get something for their money.

7

Getting the City to Play Ball

Politicians aren't satisfied with interfering in markets for basic needs such as food and shelter. Their uncontrollable urge to intervene extends to recreation. On the face of it, professional sports attract enough interest from Americans to thrive without the added support of government handouts. Team owners have nevertheless convinced much of the public that subsidies for athletic stadiums represent legitimate uses of taxpayers' money. How this wasteful activity came about is a familiarly depressing, yet fascinating story of governmental intrusion.

America's first enclosed ballpark opened in 1862 at the Union Grounds in Brooklyn. Over the next 90 years, increasingly elaborate sports facilities sprang up around the country. The economic motivation was straightforward. By excluding nonpaying spectators from the games, the organizers of professional teams could recover their costs, such as the players' salaries, and earn a return on their investment. Driven by a healthy desire for profit, the entrepreneurs either built stadiums or arenas at their own expense or paid rent to other capitalists who built and operated them.

In 1953, the rules of the game started to change with the opening of Milwaukee's publicly funded County Stadium. The taxpayer dollars used to construct a ballpark helped lure the Boston Braves baseball team to the city—the first major league franchise relocation in half a century. Milwaukee's innovation put municipalities into the new business of providing playgrounds for team owners, instead of for children. By the late 1990s, public subsidies to professional sports facilities were running an estimated half billion dollars a year.[1]

The price tag for a new baseball stadium typically comes to $500 million, while National Football League (NFL) stadiums go for $350 million to $400 million. On average, the official public subsidy on these facilities amounts to 35 percent to 40 percent of the total cost. But outlays for required new infrastructure, such as roads and bridges, can push that number higher, depending on how the accounting is done. That still leaves something for the team owners to contribute, but in many instances they can avoid coming up with anything out of their own pockets. Instead, they generate the necessary cash by selling stadium naming rights to corporations or by licensing seats.[2]

As with any other case of governmental intrusion in the economy, it is appropriate to ask what market failure is corrected by public financing of sports stadiums and arenas. Somehow, the owners of professional sports teams flourished in the era when they procured sites for their games without government handouts. No federal tax-supported municipal bonds were issued to finance the fabled ballparks of yesteryear. Now, in contrast, the taxpayer routinely picks up a big part of the tab. To figure out whether this change makes economic sense, we must first consider what the taxpayers are getting for their money.

BUT DOES IT MAKE MONEY?

The initial level of economic analysis is to ask whether local governments break even on sports facilities: Do they earn back in tax revenues what they contribute in tax subsidies? Study after study, over 30 years, has answered that question with a resounding "no."

In 1974, Benjamin Okner of the Brookings Institution examined publicly funded stadiums around the United States. He found that most of them generated insufficient revenues to cover the costs incurred by government. In 1990, Pepperdine University's Dean Baim analyzed government subsidies on 14 stadiums. He calculated that in aggregate, they had a total net accumulated value of negative $139.3 million. In 13 out of 14 cases, the governments kicked in more tax dollars than they reaped from the projects. James Quirk and Rodney Fort came to a similar conclusion in 1992. A significant portion of the stadiums that they studied—10 out of 39—failed even to cover their operating expenses, excluding depreciation, much less debt service.[3]

At least in the period covered by these early studies, the majority of publicly financed stadiums collected enough in rent, plus a share of parking and concessions revenues, to cover operating costs. For the most part, it was only the capital costs that the municipalities failed to recoup. Since then, however, competition for professional sports franchises has escalated. Nowadays, teams negotiate low or even zero rent payments and routinely keep all the revenue from parking and concessions. As a result, taxpayers not only pick up the tab for financing the stadium, but also eat the cost of operating it.

Congress inadvertently accelerated this unfortunate trend through a provision of the 1986 Tax Reform Act. The rule denied tax-exempt bond financing for a stadium if revenues from the facility covered more than 10 percent of debt service. Perversely, that gave municipalities an incentive to collect less rent and ancillary revenue and burden taxpayers with operating costs formerly borne by the teams.

Advocates of pouring public funds into sports facilities aren't deterred by overwhelming evidence that cities lose money on the deals. In fact, the prosubsidy crowd argues that the unprofitability of stadiums is exactly why government should get into the game. They contend that some of the stadium's economic benefits accrue to the community at large. And because those benefits aren't captured by the facility's owner, the stadium is a losing proposition when considered on a stand-alone basis. Unless government steps in to absorb the loss, the reasoning goes, the stadium will never get built and the community will never realize the potential benefits. This is the market failure that public funding of stadium supposedly corrects.

The alleged generation of benefits to the community at large expands the economic analysis. Stadiums don't pay for themselves in tax revenues. But can public financing be justified if we also take into account economic benefits beyond those directly realized by the stadium owner?

This broader analysis hasn't produced a unanimous verdict. On the one hand, University of Pennsylvania researcher Edward Shils found in 1985 that Philadelphia's economy reaped over $500 million from the presence of its professional sports teams in 1983. Similarly, in 1993 Kenneth Clark concluded that the New York Yankees baseball club contributed $200 million a year to the Big Apple's economy. In sharp contrast, Baltimore researcher Hal Lancaster calculated in 1986 that the city had realized a trifling $200,000 a year from its football team. Interestingly, Lancaster drew his somewhat negative conclusion after the Colts moved to Indianapolis in the middle of the night in 1984. As for Shils's more upbeat finding, it is probably worth noting that his study was funded by a consortium of Philadelphia's pro sports franchises.[4]

Results vary widely in these economic impact studies because the researchers make widely varying assumptions about the *multiplier effect*. The basic idea is that the employees of the sports team and the stadium are bound to spend some percentage of their income in the local economy. This incremental demand for goods and services creates new employment and spending. The tough part is estimating the total effect of such recycling of new money in the local economy. Economists tackle the problem by multiplying the team employees' aggregate salary figure by a multiplier somewhere between 1.2 and 3 times. There is no objective, universally accepted basis for deciding where the correct multiplier lies within that range. It is safe to assume, though, that if the team owners are the ones paying for the impact study, the researchers will pick a number near the high end. Because of the highly arbitrary choice of multiplier, economic impact studies have limited credibility.

A more defensible way to evaluate the impact of sports franchises is to compare the economic performance of cities that have or don't have a franchise. Robert Baade of Lake Forest College has used this approach to study the broad impact of public funding of stadiums, beginning in the 1980s. In a 1987 analysis of nine cities that either launched new stadiums or attracted new professional teams, Baade found no significant economic impact on economic growth. Five of the nine cities, he reported, suffered significant *declines* in the percentage of regional income captured by their metropolitan areas.

Subsequent studies by Baade and his Lake Forest College colleague Richard Dye corroborated the initial findings.[5] Then, in 1994, Baade examined 32 metropolitan areas that either gained or lost a professional sports team between 1958 and 1987. Only two showed a significant relationship between the presence of a team and per capita growth in personal income. Of those two, the presence of a team had a positive effect in one city (Indianapolis) and a negative effect in the other (Baltimore). Baade obtained similar results when he looked at metropolitan areas, instead of cities. The presence of a sports stadium had no effect on per capita income in 27 out of 30 metro areas that either gained or lost a stadium. In the remaining three (St. Louis, San Francisco/Oakland, and Washington, DC), having a stadium had a significantly *negative* impact.[6]

How is it possible for a metropolitan area to experience a *reduction* in per capita income as a result of having a professional sports team or a stadium? The answer lies in the jobs that stadium activity generates. They are generally low-paying and seasonal positions—ticket takers, ushers, parking lot attendants, and the like. When a city devotes its economic development subsidies to creating this sort of employment, it develops a comparative advantage in unskilled, seasonal labor. As a result, long-run future growth becomes concentrated in low-paid jobs.

Defenders of public sports subsidies counter that the local population's income must rise as a result of the money spent at stadiums and surrounding restaurants. The flaw in that argument is that expenditures on tickets on sporting events might simply represent money *not* spent on other leisure or entertainment activities within the same metropolitan area. In that case, building a stadium and bringing in a professional sports franchise does not produce new income for the locals. It merely reduces the revenues of the metro area's movie theaters and nightclubs as well as restaurants that are not near the stadium.

An equally plausible guess about the facts is that large numbers of fans come from outside the metropolitan area and spend money at the stadium. That money could represent dollars they decided not to spend on entertainment in their hometowns. While we are tossing scenarios around, we should include the athletes and executives who arrive along with a new team. Conceivably, they choose to live in the area and spend the bulk of their large salaries within the local community.

There is no end to the hypothetical outcomes that prosubsidy and antisubsidy partisans can dream up. But the real test is what actually happens, as measured by rigorous quantitative analysis. Overwhelmingly, the verdict of hard-core research is that having a sports team or a new stadium doesn't help the local economy.

If anything, the chances of a citywide economic benefit from a sports stadium have declined over time. The newer stadiums are expressly designed to let the owners capture as much of the revenue generated by the games as possible. Modern sports facilities provide restaurants, museums, and nightclubs. That makes it tough for other businesses to set up shop nearby in hopes of profiting from the fans' pregame or postgame spending.

(Reportedly, the model emulated by today's owners is Walt Disney World, a project conceived on the principle of making sure that visitors spend as many of their vacation dollars as possible at Disney-owned enterprises. According to lore, Walt Disney resented the way the success of his first theme park, Disneyland, enriched many surrounding small businesses.)[7]

The prosubsidization claim best supported by economic data is that if a stadium attracts a professional football team (or prevents one from leaving), housing prices go up. According to an analysis by Edward Coulson of Pennsylvania State University and Gerald A. Carlino of the Federal Reserve Bank of Philadelphia,[8] people are willing to pay for the lifestyle advantage of living in a city where they can attend NFL games. As a result, apartment rents in central-city areas are 8 percent higher in NFL cities than in non-NFL cities. That makes residential property more valuable, resulting in higher property tax receipts. Carlino and Coulson conclude that in most cases, the resulting revenue gain more than offsets the annual cost to the city of subsidizing the stadium. (They are eminently fair in their calculation of the subsidy, including such items as police and fire services.)

Carlino and Coulson's research represents a useful contribution, but not everyone would view high rents as evidence that a sports team is providing an economic benefit. A general rent increase doesn't boost income within the city. It just transfers income from renters to landlords, with some of the transferred funds getting siphoned off by the tax collector.

Using Carlino and Coulson's average figures, the city pays $27 million a year for a stadium and generates $50 million a year in additional property taxes. The taxes come out of the hides of renters and property owners, whose aggregate income does not rise. From a fiscal viewpoint, the city could achieve the same effect, with less rigmarole, by forgoing the stadium subsidy and raising taxes by $23 million a year.

If the local economy doesn't benefit in the conventional sense of generating jobs or income, who does profit when a city shells out tax dollars to build a stadium and lure a sports franchise to the city? The clear winners are the team owners.

It is not even the case that a portion of the subsidy trickles down to the fans. That might happen if the subsidies came in a form that reduced the marginal cost of admitting one more fan to the stadium. The team owners would then have a possible incentive to pass along part of the subsidy, that is, to reduce ticket prices to attract more fans. In reality, though, the municipality subsidizes a team's fixed costs: construction costs and rent. Those costs are the same, no matter how many fans show up. As a consequence, the team owners pocket the whole subsidy.[9]

ROBIN HOOD IN REVERSE

Stripped to its essentials, public financing of stadiums amounts to taxing ordinary citizens to increase the wealth of team owners. To state the obvious, an individual has to be exceptionally wealthy to become a team owner in the first place. Soaking the poor and the middle class to make the wealthy wealthier hardly fits the definition of a public purpose warranting government intrusion.

Bestowing public benefits on well-heeled owners doesn't necessarily make them just a little wealthier than they already were. In 1989, investor Eli Jacobs bought the Baltimore Orioles baseball team for $70 million. Maryland tax dollars then went to build the team a $200 million stadium, which greatly increased the value of the franchise. After just four years, Jacobs unloaded the Orioles for $173 million. Even to the megarich, a $103 million profit is not trivial.

In a similar vein, when the Texas Rangers baseball team decided it needed an up-to-date stadium in 1990, the cost was estimated at $190 million. One of the team's principal owners, billionaire Richard Rainwater, probably could have scraped up or borrowed the cash at a decent market rate of interest. Instead, the Rangers broadly hinted that unless the government of Arlington provided land and loans on attractive terms, they would pull up stakes and relocate to Dallas or Fort Worth.

Arlington capitulated, agreeing to guarantee $135 million of the construction costs, in exchange for a whopping $5 million (3.7 percent) annual rent. The city's voters consented to pay for the interest on the stadium bonds through a hike in sales taxes. That increase was on top of a rate that was already among the nation's highest.[10]

The Rangers put up no cash, instead financing their share of the construction costs through a ticket surcharge. True, the Rangers franchise kicked in some land that it owned. But that land was part of the original inducement to the team to relocate from Washington, DC, paid for with taxpayers' dollars.[11]

In exchange for its negligible out-of-pocket contribution and (perhaps more important) for agreeing not to skip town, the Rangers received much more than a field and seats. To begin with, the package included office space for the team's management, plus additional space that the team could rent to tenants. The Rangers retained all profits from leases it negotiated on that taxpayer-provided space.[12] In addition, the Rangers obtained an option to buy the stadium once the accumulated rental payments reached a total of $60 million, along with an additional 270 acres of surrounding real estate. Profits from developing that land belonged entirely to the team.

Yet another sweetener was a swiftly enacted state law authorizing the newly created Arlington Sports Facilities Development Authority to exercise eminent domain. This was the first time in the history of Texas that a municipal authority was empowered to seize an unwilling private citizen's property for use by other private citizens. The Authority exercised that power by condemning and turning over to the Rangers a 13-acre parcel that the family owners had refused to sell for half its appraised value. In the ensuing lawsuit, the jury awarded the family $4 million.

The value of the deal that Arlington accepted to prevent the Rangers from bolting was quickly reflected in the team's franchise value. In 1991, *Financial World* estimated that the franchise was worth $101 million, ranking it a low sixteenth in the major leagues. Just three years later, the Ballpark in Arlington opened, replete with the luxury suites and club seats that represented important new revenue streams. The Rangers further capitalized on their new facility by selling permanent seat licenses, an innovative contractual arrangement that permitted holders to transfer their rights to buy season tickets. Now, the Rangers franchise was valued at $157 million, boosting it to third place among major league teams. Improved performance could not account for the rise in value, as the Rangers had still never made it to the postseason.[13]

The City of Arlington's gift kept on giving. When Rainwater and his partners sold out in 1998, they pocketed a nifty $250 million. That was three times the price that they had paid in 1989.

It was an especially good payday for one small participant in the deal. George W. Bush, who served as the team's public face, collected a $15 million share of the proceeds. Bush had initially invested just $606,000, most of it borrowed, and increased his ownership stake along the way through stock options. In the interim, as journalist Joe Conason has wryly observed, Bush successfully ran for governor of Texas on a platform of emphasizing self-reliance over dependence on government.[14]

With individuals as well-known as George W. Bush participating in "give-us-a-stadium-or-we-leave" maneuvers, the objections to subsidized sports facilities haven't remained entirely beneath the public's radar. People appear to recognize that boosting taxes to support sports stadiums represents little more than a transfer of wealth from the poor and middle class to the rich. Several surveys have found that more than 60 percent of respondents oppose the use of tax dollars to build or improve professional sports facilities. In one case, 56 percent favored selling existing publicly owned arenas to the highest bidder. That position was supported even by 39 percent of those who said they regularly attended professional sports events.[15]

Another source of the disgruntlement may be government's failure to recover the cost of the subsidies from the direct beneficiaries, the sports fans. Taxing the broadcasting rights to the games is an example of how that equitable outcome could be achieved. But in many cases, the general population pays through such mechanisms as an increased tax on liquor or diversion of lottery proceeds.[16] More problematic still is the financing of a subsidy through a sales tax, as in the case of the Texas Rangers' stadium. As a percentage of income, a sales tax falls most heavily on low earners. Disproportionately burdening low-income folks to enrich well-heeled team owners could account in part for the resentment that arises when a team compiles a lousy won-lost record.

The Cincinnati Bengals NFL franchise was slapped with a lawsuit after persuading Hamilton County, Ohio, in 1996 to foot the bill for a new $458 million stadium, then deteriorating to its worst-ever record, two wins and 14 losses, in 2002. County Commissioner Todd Portune, who filed the ultimately unsuccessful lawsuit as an individual taxpayer, huffed, "We're the butt of every NFL joke. How would that make you feel?"[17] Portune really became incensed in 2001, when it came to light that the Bengals had been among the NFL's most profitable franchises in 1996, even as owner Mike Brown was claiming that the team couldn't remain competitive without taxpayer support.

Finally, all this taxpayer support covers only local subsidies and doesn't include the massive federal subsidy provided through municipalities' issuance of tax-exempt bonds to finance the stadiums. Interest on those bonds is exempt from federal income tax so municipalities pay lower interest rates than private borrowers. Over the life of the stadium, by one estimate, the interest rate subsidy could total about one-third of the facility's construction cost.[18]

DEALING CRAFTILY WITH THE FACTS

Confronted with hard data showing that the financial benefits of publicly financed stadiums flow exclusively to the team owners, the prostadium forces typically respond with obfuscation.

First, they ignore the evidence. The boosters brush aside the economic studies and just go right on talking about new jobs that will be created for souvenir sellers and the like. They fail to mention, in the case of a replacement facility, the jobs that will be eliminated at the old stadium. The advocates of subsidization stubbornly insist that consumers will increase their entertainment budgets to attend sports events, rather than spend less on other kinds of entertainment.

Acting as if no one had ever refuted the notion, supporters of taxpayer-funded sports facilities cite examples of local economies that were supposedly turned around by publicly financed stadiums. They contend that one section of Cleveland ("the Flats") became rejuvenated because of Jacobs Field, even though the Flats isn't part of the Jacobs neighborhood and was already on the upswing before the stadium was built. One stadium developer claimed that there were 36 new retail establishments within two blocks of second base at Jacobs Field. Researchers who checked the accuracy of that claim were told by an aide to Cleveland's figure that the actual figure was 20. They found that even that number was too high, unless the count included parking lots and garages.[19] Stadium promoters credit Camden Yards for turning around Baltimore's Inner Harbor, yet that area was bustling for a decade before the ballpark opened. The revival was largely attributable to the National Aquarium, which is open for 280 more days annually than Camden Yards.

The second strategy adopted by the prostadium forces is to discredit the conclusions of the economic studies as the ravings of academics who have probably never even visited a modern sports facility. A leading backer of Phoenix's Banc One Ballpark simply brushed aside painstaking research on the substitution effect, by which consumers shift spending to sports events from other entertainment. It was all bull excrement, he declared.[20]

Again and again, researchers hear that, despite what previous studies have shown, "our city is different."

Third among the strategies for confusing the opponents of publicly financed stadiums is the technique of countering legitimate analysis with pseudoanalysis. The studies that promoters order from obliging consulting firms differ in an essential way from bona fide research. Instead of focusing on objective economic data, such as growth in employment or tax revenues, the hired-gun studies rely on surveys in which the respondents speculate on future economic behavior. The squishy numbers that emerge from this process preclude any rigorous analysis.

Wishful thinking runs rampant in reports ordered by the team owners. Consultants asserted in 1992 that Denver's proposed new stadium would bring about a pedestrian overpass from Union Station to the ballpark plaza, new housing in the immediate vicinity, an international shopping district, and a new 23rd Street viaduct. An artist's rendition of improvements to 21st Street envisioned wide sidewalks and shops. Seven years later, the street looked about the same as in 1992. Little new housing had materialized and the "international shopping area" remained mostly a warehouse district. Neither had the pedestrian overpass been built. The viaduct was the only piece of the vision that had been fulfilled.[21]

DIVERTING THE FOCUS

Sometimes, ignoring, discrediting, and countering with disinformation all fail to undercut the evidence that the stadium's alleged economic benefits are bogus. At that point, the stadium boosters switch their story. It turns out that the real reason for diverting millions of dollars from other public purposes is to improve the quality of life for residents.

A good example of this switch occurred when Cleveland's Gateway downtown sports facility project came under fire for generating only 2,000 permanent jobs, instead of the 16,800 predicted by its boosters. Thomas Chema, the project's former spokesperson, first denied ever making such a prediction. Then, he complained that the critics were overlooking Gateway's true benefit—image enhancement.[22]

In proclaiming the qualitative benefits of taxpayer-financed stadiums, the promoters start to sound like the bunco artist Professor Harold Hill in *The Music Man*. They promise that life will be more interesting, hometown pride will flourish, even that racial harmony will blossom.[23] Cleveland supporters of public financing actually told researchers that since the new ballpark opened, the city's bicycle messengers were smiling more.[24]

Straying ever further from verifiable results, the promoters argue that professional sports preserve diversity of opinion in the media. Sporting events, they contend, sell newspapers. Conceivably, therefore, in some cities, the presence of a team has kept a second daily newspaper afloat that otherwise would have folded. Just possibly, that newspaper uncovered some instance of government corruption and thereby improved the quality of life for the city's residents. The argument seems strained, to say the least, but the connection between sports and newspaper sales probably helps explain why daily newspapers tend to editorialize in favor of stadium proposals.

Supporters of publicly financed sports facilities also try to transform the quality-of-life argument into a dollars-and-cents proposition by drawing a connection with corporate location. To attract large employers, they contend, a city must project a major-league image. A professional sports franchise, say the prosubsidy forces, is an essential ingredient.

This reasoning is not entirely unfounded. In deciding where to locate, a corporation's management certainly considers the ability to recruit a high-caliber workforce. Quality of life, in turn, is a factor in attracting good employees to the city where the company operates.

Quality of life, however, is not the sole determinant of corporate location. Corporations also take into account costs of transportation, energy, taxes, and labor. Nor is a professional sports franchise the only consideration in gauging the quality of life. Others include climate, population density, crime levels, quality of education, and the arts. Understandably, public relations campaigns for stadium subsidies do not devote much effort to evaluating the relative importance of sports franchises within this context.

To be fair, quality-of-life considerations have begun to attract attention from legitimate researchers, as opposed to the owners' hired producers of "facts on demand." As one academic authority points out, bona fide economic analysis of the psychic income generated by sports franchises can restore the honor of public officials:

> This redefinition enables decision makers to retain their integrity while supporting public subsidy of a facility. It is an alternative to the contorted and embarrassing shenanigans to which many of them have

resorted to this point. Instead of relying on the wistful "spin" that external sources will invest in the community as a justification for public subsidy of facilities, emphasis is shifting to measuring the benefits that accrue to existing residents living within it.[25]

Aspects of the psychic income created by construction of a stadium include pride in living in a "major league" city capable of completing a major civic project, opportunities for social bonding through following the team's ups and downs, and an overall sense of vitality.

There is nothing inherently wrong with taking these qualitative benefits into account in evaluating a stadium proposal. But they cannot be divorced from the fiscal considerations. Like any other benefit, a boost to community spirit must be measured against the costs.

Putting a price tag on qualitative benefits is no simple task. The ideal way to account for psychic income, from the team owners' standpoint, is to assign it an infinite value. That way, the prostadium forces can sweep away all dollars-and-cents objections to the proposed subsidy. A fairer approach, however, is to survey the city's residents to find out how much the team is worth to them.

The basic technique consists of asking a representative sample of residents a question such as the following: "What's the largest amount you'd be willing to pay in taxes every year to prevent the [TEAM NAME] from leaving the city?" Multiplying the average figure by the number of taxpayers in the city provides an estimate of the total psychic income associated with the proposed stadium. That figure can be compared with the annual cost of the required subsidy to determine whether the expected benefit justifies the cost.

This isn't just some mad professor's pipe dream, but rather a method that has been applied in real life. Residents of Lexington, Kentucky, were asked how much they would pay to support a new basketball arena for the University of Kentucky team and a baseball stadium intended to attract a minor league franchise. The result was that residents valued the basketball facility at $311,000 to $610,000 a year, which would suffice to cover debt service on a stadium costing $3.71 million to $7.28 million. That was just a tiny fraction of the arena's projected $100 million cost. Similarly, Lexington residents indicated that they would pay for a baseball stadium costing no more than $7.06 million, substantially below the projected $10 million to $12 million price tag.[26]

The key point is that voters mustn't get dazzled by glitzy public relations campaigns emphasizing quality-of-life benefits. A city has finite financial resources. The appropriate fiscal decision is whether subsidization of a sports facility offers a bigger payoff in lifestyle than alternative investments. In making their choices, voters might want to bear in mind that the idea of raising taxes to build a stadium wouldn't come up at all if team owners couldn't play one city off against another.

The ability to pit cities against each other pretty well guarantees that once a team has gotten full mileage out of a multimillion-dollar subsidy, it will turn around and demand a new tax-supported stadium. The owners' sense of entitlement will not be diminished an iota if they have failed to deliver a championship to the intensely loyal fans, even after receiving a great, big helping hand from the public sector. Owners see themselves as a class of the deserving rich. They expect as their due government handouts to cover a basic cost of business. The owners aren't dissuaded from that view by the fact that sports franchises covered their occupancy costs out of their own pockets for many decades before they figured out how to work the system.

HOW DO THEY GET AWAY WITH IT?

Why, in the face of solid arguments against the idea, are team owners so often successful in persuading municipalities to build stadiums for them? It is because the owners are more strongly motivated and therefore better organized than the opponents of public subsidies. They are determined to prevail as a function of how the professional sports leagues operate.

In campaigning for a publicly financed stadium, the team owners typically form a powerful coalition with other potential beneficiaries. These include contractors with the political connections to obtain construction contracts from the city, unions representing the construction workers, and investment banks that stand to earn fees by underwriting the bonds that will finance the project. Daily newspapers tend to jump on the bandwagon, recognizing that local sports news sells papers. Many local politicians likewise side with the prostadium forces, seeing advantages to being identified with popular athletes.

On the other side are small businesses that would be displaced by the new stadium, sentimental defenders of the old stadium, antitax activists, and people living near the proposed construction area, who don't want stadium-related activities to disrupt their neighborhood. This ragtag assemblage is sometimes joined by advocates of higher spending on other social services. Usually, though, those allies get bought off during the negotiations by promises of increased outlays for their favored programs. The common thread among the disparate elements of the antistadium forces is that they have less money and less media clout than the prostadium forces.

Team owners can throw more dollars than their opponents have available into "economic impact studies" with assumed income multipliers that favor their case. The reason is that they have a huge financial stake in the outcome. By contrast, no single member of the antistadium forces faces a big enough financial loss to justify kicking in big bucks to a public relations war chest.

On referendum day, construction union members and others with direct interests in the outcome turn out in force. To a large extent, those with less at stake don't bother to vote. If the subsidy proposal nevertheless fails, the strongly motivated team owners and their allies immediately begin organizing a new campaign. Meanwhile, with no new referendum on the immediate horizon, the ad hoc antistadium coalition loses steam. Its members simply have to turn their attention to other things going on in their lives.

The team owners maintain their focus because they have so much to gain. This is true even if they don't contemplate a quick sale in the manner of Eli Jacobs. Owners who are in the game for the long haul stand to profit immensely from receiving a modern stadium with revenue-producing features that their existing facility lacks.

Generating incremental revenues from luxury suites and club boxes is critically important because of professional sports leagues' revenue-sharing requirements. The leagues need to preserve competitive balance, which is essential to maintaining spectator interest, in the face of financial advantages enjoyed by teams in bigger metropolitan areas. For example, the NFL divides broadcasting revenues equally among the teams. The pro football league also requires the home team at each game to hand over 40 percent of the gate receipts to the visiting team. All professional sports major leagues, however, allow teams to keep 100 percent of the nonticket revenues generated by their arenas or stadiums. Therefore, the main way that a team can increase its profits is to shift operations from an existing stadium to a new one with more amenities that produce nonticket revenue.

If the owners of just about any other kind of business asked the city to shell out several hundred million dollars to build them an improved facility, the response would be swift and succinct: "Build it yourself!" Professional sports team owners, however, routinely succeed in their petitions. Their pitch is simple: "If you don't give us a stadium, we'll move the team to another city that will." Fearful of being blamed for losing the beloved local team, the politicians cave in to the owners' extortion.

Threats to pull up stakes would fail if the team owners couldn't count on receiving competing offers of a stadium from cities without a professional franchise in their sport. But if the sports fans in another city are that eager to see football or basketball, why doesn't the city already have a team? After all, suppose a city had unfilled demand for another form of entertainment, such as movies or bowling. Entrepreneurs could be counted on to plug the gap without any need for the local government to lure them from elsewhere.

The answer is that a group of investors cannot simply decide to launch a National Football League or National Basketball Association franchise. They have to obtain a franchise from the league and there are fewer of those than there are metropolitan areas large enough to support teams. If the would-be owners can't obtain a franchise from the league, they are out of luck, because there is no other league in that sport. The leagues exhibit classic monopoly behavior, artificially keeping the supply (of teams) below the level of demand.

As a result of this legal restraint of trade, the team's owners can easily play one city off against another to get a fancier stadium. Not only do they not have to pay for the construction, they don't even have to pay rent.

The politicians who submit to the owners' shakedown get hailed for saving professional baseball or hockey in their city. It is a cozy deal for everyone. Everyone except the taxpayers, that is.

THE BOTTOM LINE

Financing sports stadiums is a money-losing proposition for municipal governments. The numbers don't work even if we take into account income generated in the local economy by a professional sports franchise. Neither do arguments about intangible benefits stand up to scrutiny.

The net effect of tax subsidies, as former Houston Mayor Bob Lanier stated, is that "the average working person is asked to put a tax on their home, or pay sales or some other consumer tax, to build luxury boxes in which they cannot afford to sit."[27] When polled, the majority of people say that they oppose the use of public funds to build professional sports facilities. Given a chance to put a value on the potential of a stadium to enhance their quality of life, city residents don't necessarily come up with a figure as large as the proposed subsidy.

Subsidization of sports facilities is a comparatively transparent case of government providing a solution to a nonexistent problem. For many decades, sports teams built or rented their ballparks or arenas on their own. Politicians got into the act only when team owners realized that they could shift their occupancy costs onto the taxpayers by threatening to pull up stakes. The leagues abetted this hustle by ensuring that there would always be fewer franchises than cities capable of supporting franchises.

Owners counter that the world has changed. Players, they lament, have gotten greedier than in the days when they played for the sheer love of the game. To pay for the higher salaries, teams must either get financial help from their cities or give up trying to obtain the outstanding players who can bring championships. If they don't sign those stars, competitive balance will disappear. The big-market teams will dominate the small-market teams through sheer financial power.

There is no reason to suppose that players ever wanted to earn less than their talents merited. Salaries are higher now than in the past because teams' revenue opportunities have expanded. A star player helps a team not only to fill more seats in the stadium, but also to garner more broadcasting revenue, sell more luxury suites, and generate more merchandise sales.

Teams seek stadium subsidies specifically to increase revenue in the categories that league rules don't force them to share with other teams. If the leagues were serious about maintaining competitive balance, they could extend the revenue-sharing requirements to additional categories. If they really got cranked up to ensure competitive balance, the leagues could even allow multiple teams in the biggest metropolitan areas, which are large enough to support several.

Granted, no individual city's voters have the power to alter the leagues' revenue-sharing arrangements. If a city's residents want to attract or retain a professional sports franchise, they may have no choice but to fork over the money that the owners demand. It would be nice, though, if the voters were at least presented with an honest description of their choice.

Instead, they are bombarded with bogus economic studies, paid for by team owners and their allies. Faced with the need to pick numbers out of the air, the authors pick numbers that just happen to say, "Go for it!" The pseudoanalyses disingenuously portray shifts of spending from one form of entertainment to another as evidence that professional sports teams promote economic expansion.

When those arguments collapse of their own weight, the stadium boosters fall back on squishier claims of quality-of-life enhancements. One thing is pretty clear. When the taxpayers subsidize a sports facility, the quality of life improves for the team owners. But it is not clear at all that the rest of the populace gains anything in exchange for the money extracted by the visible hand of government.

8

Art of the State

In June 1998, the Supreme Court of the United States took a stance on a matter of dire importance to the national well-being. For the moment, controversies surrounding the death penalty, abortion, firearms, and church–state relations would have to remain on hold. But at long last, the American people knew whether it was consistent with the Constitution to deny Karen Finley's bid for public funding to smear her naked body with chocolate.

Performance artist Finley has also blazed creative frontiers by painting with her own breast milk, staging a bondage scene involving Winnie-the-Pooh and friends, and writing love poetry with lines such as the following:

> I shot myself because I loved you.
> If I loved myself, I'd shoot you.[1]

These examples by no means define Finley's artistic limits. In a 1999 piece, she disrobed on stage, then offered to let audience members lick chocolate off her body in exchange for $20 donations. A 1992 installation allowed the patrons to participate in the creation of the art. On arrival, visitors were given cups of red wine, shown a wall decorated with tiny flags of every country in the world, and asked to spit on the flag of their choice. Finley also spoofed domestic arts queen Martha Stewart with a book that advised readers, among other things, to celebrate the month of June by growing marigolds in their armpits.[2] In July 1999, she posed for *Playboy,* both naked and wearing chocolate. By the way, Finley doesn't have a one-track mind when it comes to selecting food to slather over her body. An early performance employing canned yams generated a passionate critical response.[3]

But it was Finley's original chocolate smearing, as part of a 1989 performance entitled, "We Keep Our Victims Ready," that gained her judicial immortality. The following year, the National Endowment of the Arts (NEA) rejected Finley's grant application on the grounds that the content was inappropriate. Along with three other artists—including one whose art consisted in part of urinating on stage and turning a toilet bowl into an altar—Finley sued in 1991 for reinstatement of her grant. The suit also challenged the constitutionality of a 1990 law requiring the NEA, in awarding grants, to consider general standards of decency and to respect the American public's diverse beliefs and values.

The "NEA Four" won the suit, seemingly ensuring for all time people's right to view publicly funded, naked chocolate smearing. The U.S. Court of Appeals for the Ninth Circuit ruled that the phrase "decency and respect for the diverse beliefs and values" was unconstitutionally vague and restricted artists' viewpoints. To the dismay of devotees of food art au naturel, however, the Supreme Court reversed the Ninth Circuit, ruling that it was constitutional for the government to consider whether a project satisfied general standards of decency. "Within politics there is a boundary," Finley later commented. "I found that boundary."[4]

Although the Supreme Court decided the case by a vote of eight to one, the decision divided the justices, just as Karen Finley's art divided her conservative critics from her liberal supporters. Writing for the majority, Justice Sandra Day O'Connor stated that requiring the NEA to consider public notions of decency posed no threat of censorship of ideas. Lone dissenter Justice David Souter, on the other hand, contended that such a standard would naturally harm artists whose work disrespected traditional American values or who simply held nonmainstream ideas of art.

Justice Antonin Scalia, despite siding with the majority, sharply criticized O'Connor's rationale. Joined by Justice Clarence Thomas, he disputed O'Connor's interpretation that the law merely admonished the NEA to give some consideration to decency and that if Congress had gone beyond such "advisory" language, it indeed would have violated the First Amendment. Moreover, Scalia contended, it would have been perfectly consistent with the Constitution for Congress to prohibit funding for certain viewpoints. "It is the very business of government to favor and disfavor points of view on innumerable subjects, which is the main reason we have decided to elect those who run the government, rather than save money on making their posts hereditary."[5] To Scalia, the key issue was the

First Amendment's requirement that Congress make no law abridging freedom of speech. In requiring the NEA to consider decency, he said, Congress neither abridged the speech of those who disdained the American public's beliefs and values nor abridged indecent speech.

AN END TO RANCOR

On the face of it, the squabble over the decency requirement appears intractable. Conservatives are adamant in their opposition to the NEA funding decisions that gave rise to the 1990 law that the aggrieved artists sought to rescind. Specifically, the conservatives remain enraged over an exhibit that included homoerotic photographs by Robert Mapplethorpe and the provocatively titled photograph "Piss Christ" by Andres Serrano. Liberals, for their part, declare that they won't have the Religious Right's views imposed on them and regard Karen Finley and her fellow plaintiffs as champions of free speech. Finding a middle ground between these positions appears beyond the capability of even the most skillful mediator.

In reality, the conflict could be resolved by a simple, if radical solution: Terminate government funding of the arts.

Imagine a situation in which all art exhibitions and plays are funded privately, either by for-profit or by nonprofit organizations. In this context, artists are free to offend a portion—even a majority—of the public, provided someone appreciates their work sufficiently to bear the production costs. Those who find the art repugnant are free to stay away and to refrain from providing financial support.

Rejecting this peaceful resolution, politicians have put government into the business of funding art through the NEA. As a result, taxpayers are compelled to contribute to the production of art that offends many of them. Furthermore, artists such as Karen Finley have succeeded in passing themselves off as victims of censorship. This claim distorts the meaning of *censorship*. As commentator George F. Will has noted, regarding the NEA decency requirement:

> People so inclined are unconstrained after the statute as they were before it to exercise their right to express themselves by urinating on stages and smearing themselves with chocolate. They just cannot expect the public to pay for such affronts to its sensibilities.[6]

Putting an end to public bankrolling of the arts would clarify the situation. There would be no federal funds to cut off. No artist could then complain of being silenced by the government.

By rights, removing government from the scene is a position that ought to unite the two warring camps. The gap is not really unbridgeable between individuals who find public urination irredeemably offensive, no matter how artistically it is done, and those who perceive a serious, important social message in Karen Finley's confrontational work. Both groups should recognize a danger in mixing the arts with politics.

Once government gets into the business of paying for art, it must inevitably decide what art is. Philosophers have been addressing the question for centuries without ever laying it to rest. In that light, conservatives and liberals alike should be apprehensive about the answers that emerge from the logrolling and pork barreling of the political process.

What's more, government procurement carries with it a duty (not always well executed, to be sure) of obtaining good value for the taxpayers' dollars. This means that the bureaucracy must not only figure out what art is, but also which art is good art. When government functionaries take up a question that mired in subjectivity, people should *really* start to worry.

Politicians may not all know fine art, but they understand the art of the possible. Predictably, they will quickly set aside irresolvable aesthetic questions. They will concentrate instead on what they know, which is trading goodies for votes and influence. One option is for the politicians to decide which art to fund on the basis of which choices will pay off best in the next election. That implies pandering to the lowest common denominator in taste. Another possible strategy is to cadge campaign contributions from wealthy elites who yearn for Treasury subsidies to promote their own artistic preferences.

WHO WILL GUARD THE CUSTODIANS?

Defenders of public funding of the arts will likely reply that these concerns are merely hypothetical. They will claim to have foreseen the problems of improper political influence and government control of (as opposed to support for) the arts. What's more, the advocates of public funding will assure us, they have set up firewalls around funding decisions.

The safeguard that ostensibly prevents federal dictation of cultural standards is a rule requiring that individuals outside the government be brought into the grant process. Since the establishment of the National Endowment for the Arts in 1965, the outsiders' participation has taken several forms. Congress has established a National Council on the Arts, consisting of 26 private citizens, appointed by the president, with expertise and records of achievement in the field. Congress has also instituted peer review panels to evaluate grant proposals, specifying that the panelists be diverse in their ethnic background and artistic viewpoints. Since 1990, the panelists have been instructed to view applications exclusively on the basis of artistic merit and excellence.[7]

These protections are akin to the rules for ensuring the impartiality of juries. Skilled trial lawyers know how to work the system to empanel jurors sympathetic to their case. The sole constraint is the opposing side's attempt to do likewise. In politics, it is more difficult to achieve balance. The party that currently holds a majority has more than a 50 percent voice in the selection process. Stacking blue-ribbon panels to predetermine the outcome of a so-called objective investigation is a long-standing Washington tradition. In this culture, there is little chance that pure artistic merit will determine who gets fed at the NEA trough.

Connections may play a sizable role. In 1990, journalist Mark Lasswell reported that Karen Finley received her controversial NEA grant from a panel that included her frequent collaborator, musician Jerry Hunt. That panel also recommended an award to Hunt. The writer Geoffrey Wolff served on a panel that gave his brother, writer Tobias Wolff, a $20,000 NEA grant. The panel that awarded $5,000 to artist Amanda Farber included her stepmother.[8]

It is customary for individuals highlighted by such exposés to protest that they are victims of innuendo. No matter how unfounded any specific insinuation of favoritism may be, the appearance is certainly not good. Subsequent to the period discussed by Lasswell, Congress curtailed the NEA's power to make grants to individuals, putting the emphasis instead on arts organizations. Still, influence by nonaesthetic considerations is an unavoidable problem of direct government support of the arts.

APPLYING THE APPROPRIATE TEST

In view of the government's unsuitability for rendering aesthetic judgments, it is wise to return to first principles when considering how to provide art to the populace. The question is not whether art is necessary. That much we can take for granted. Along with recreation and spiritual expression, art is one of the things people desire, beyond the standard necessities—food, shelter, and clothing.

The only controversy is whether the government's intrusion into decisions about how arts dollars should be spent serves any useful purpose. Politicians would undoubtedly create a furor if they began promoting basketball over football or the Miami Dolphins over the Green Bay Packers. Why, then, should a government agency rule that certain art forms or certain arts organizations will get larger allocations of resources than others?

An appealing alternative to giving elected officials control over aesthetic judgments is to let people decide how much art they want, what art forms to enjoy, and which artists' work to appreciate. For convenience, we could label this approach *democracy*. Politicians would get into the act only if they could demonstrate a market failure.[9]

In reality, it would be surprising to discover that the market has failed to produce enough art and therefore requires prodding from the government. Civic-minded citizens regularly demonstrate their willingness to pay for far more art than they can personally consume. It is routine for museum patrons to bear the cost of exhibitions that run for several weeks, even though they plan to attend for only a few hours on a few days. By contrast, we seldom observe people—even exceptionally wealthy people—purchasing larger quantities of mundane household items than they or their families plan to use. The willingness to subsidize other people's enjoyment of art reflects a passion that transcends ordinary, self-interested economic behavior.

This passion can translate into massive amounts of money. In 2005, the *New York Times* reported that San Francisco real estate heiress Carole Shorenstein Hays infused $1 million into a struggling effort to bring playwright August Wilson's *Gem of the Ocean* to Broadway. It closed after a run of only two months. (Critic John Simon labeled the play "a big, bustling mess,"[10] calling it the occasional clinker to which a talented dramatist such as Wilson was entitled.) According to the *Times,* Hays "seemed not to care in the least that she had lost $1 million on the play."[11] She explained that she had grown up loving the theater and derived faith, hope, and verve from it. Hays spoke also of her commitment to important American playwrights such as August Wilson: "*Gem of the Ocean* is an important work," she said. "It would be a shame if people didn't get a chance to see it."[12]

If certain consumers are willing to pay for the satisfaction of seeing a work of art produced, more art must be available than consumers are willing to pay for to gratify their aesthetic appetites. Accordingly, the proposition that subsidies are required to ameliorate an undersupply of art is doubtful on its face. But all the same, let's consider economists' findings on the subject.

INTERVENTION: PRO AND CON

In a 1987 article,[13] Noël Carroll of the Cornell Sage School of Philosophy and the Center for the Performing Arts discusses several rationales that have been advanced for government funding of the arts. (He excludes such activities as commissioning artists to design stamps and government buildings.) Carroll finds problems with each rationale:

■ *Government has an obligation to reverse deterioration in the aesthetic environment.* The notion is that the market economy has produced landscapes marred by fast-food restaurants and used-car lots and a lifestyle dominated by tawdry, mass-produced consumer products. By vigorously funding the arts, it is argued that government may be able to reverse the resulting destruction of psychic health. This rationale requires the government to fund only art that satisfies aesthetic needs, which implies works that are beautiful or sublime. Not all contemporary art meets that standard. Carroll cites Luis Buñuel's motion picture *The Andalusian Dog* as an example of highly regarded[14] art that does not produce an aesthetic experience. The film is probably best known for its opening sequence, which depicts a woman's eye being slit by a razor. Subsequent scenes show a woman poking a severed hand with her cane, ants emerging from a hole in a man's palm, and a woman's armpit hair attaching itself to a man's face. Carroll contends that art lovers should be disturbed by denial of funding to "darkly expressive artworks"[15] of this sort while the government picks up the tab for friendly, joyful works. The government will undoubtedly affect the evolution of art, he maintains, if it underwrites only one type of art. From the contemporary art world's viewpoint, says Carroll, such a policy would be considered regressive.

- *Funding the arts can stimulate the economy by, for example, attracting tourists.* It may be difficult to discern how economic stimulus arises from funding a new work by an individual artist, as opposed to funding a city arts center. Even so, Carroll considers this rationale acceptable, but only if the project satisfies two rarely met conditions. First, the government must be convinced that no alternative, comparably expensive form of intervention would produce greater prosperity in the targeted area. Second, in the case of national funding, the government must justify stimulating tourism in one geographic region rather than another.

- *Failure to fund the arts may lead to unemployment among artists.* It is potentially defensible for the government to strive to reduce unemployment caused by discrimination, argues Carroll, but that is unlikely to apply to out-of-work artists. Furthermore, unemployed artists may be unemployable as artists, rather than simply unemployable. For example, unemployed poets may be able to support themselves by working as journalists or copywriters. It is unclear, he says, that the government's duty extends to guaranteeing them the jobs they most desire.

- *Fairness demands that if the government subsidizes sports stadiums, it must subsidize the arts as well.* Carroll questions whether *either* (or for that matter, any) leisure activity should be state-subsidized. Chapter 7 exposes fatal flaws in the arguments supporting publicly financed stadiums. Using those decidedly wasteful projects to justify government funding of the arts would compound the offense.

- *Government funding is justified by the arts' moralizing function.* As with Rationale 1 (reversing aesthetic deterioration), this one justifies funding of only one type of art. It doesn't justify funding art that either provides no moral uplift or achieves the opposite. Favoring the morally uplifting variety may skew the development of art in damaging ways.

A 2003 working paper by economists Cécile Aubert, Pranab K. Bardhan, and Jeff Dayton-Johnson[16] makes a case for subsidization by considering the competition between mass-produced goods and nonstandardized goods. For example, Hollywood movies and *auteur* cinema[17] aren't perfect substitutes for each other. The authors argue that the unaided market fails to produce enough of the nonstandardized goods for several reasons:

- *Consumers don't necessarily know which kind of nonstandardized goods they like best.* The likelihood that they'll discover their preferred varieties increases as the volume of production rises. But without subsidies, profit-maximizing companies won't undertake enough production to make this happen.

- *Consumers don't necessarily know what kind of nonstandardized goods they'll like in the future.* Some works of art that are now widely appreciated were regarded as excessively avant-garde and, consequently, were not wanted by consumers at the time that they were produced. Producers dependent on near-term recovery of their costs might never have produced those goods, making today's art lovers worse off than they are as a result of past subsidization.

- *Consumers like to consume the same art that their neighbors consume, partly because sharing the experience is part of the value of cultural consumption.* Big producers may be able to steer people's preferences toward mass-produced goods through aggressive marketing, which enjoys the advantage of economies of scale.

- *Future production of certain kinds of art depends on preserving a process.* The authors cite the example of music performed on the *bayan,* a small accordion from Russia and Ukraine. Future performances depend on the continued training of instrument makers and players. If current training isn't subsidized, future audiences may not be able to hear *bayan* performances.

The authors support their arguments with formidable quantitative analysis. On the other side, several authorities have opposed government funding of the arts for reasons rooted in both political science and aesthetics. The following paragraphs provide a sampling.

Edward C. Banfield, late professor emeritus of government at Harvard University, notes that museum visitors and concert attendees tend to be more prosperous than the average taxpayer.[18] Government support of the arts therefore constitutes a wrong-way income transfer from the less well-off to the more well-off. Banfield also contends that the introduction of direct funding of the arts through the NEA in 1965 gave rise to an arts establishment consisting of private associations, state art agencies, and the congressional art caucus. This coalition, he says, is intent on expanding the scope of public support by attracting new supporters, which will in turn justify larger government outlays. Citing Ronald Berman, former chairman of the NEA's sister agency, the National Endowment for the Humanities, Banfield argues that the arts constituency has pursued its objectives by determinedly exempting artistic activity from critical standards.

The late Ernest van den Haag, psychoanalyst, academic, and 1972 Senior Fellow for the National Endowment for the Humanities, also weighs in on the subject.[19] He points out that the distinction is rarely made between arguments for the arts, on the one hand, and arguments for government support of the arts, on the other. It is true, says van den Haag, that the arts give pleasure to some and employment to others. But so does whiskey, a commodity for which few advocate government support.

A valid argument for federal funding, van den Haag maintains, must demonstrate that the arts benefit the community at large. This includes individuals who wouldn't voluntarily pay for art or else couldn't afford to. The purported benefit obtained through arts subsidization, says van den Haag, is a contribution to national cohesion or shared values. He denies that the arts play such a role in the United States. Sports and television, which *do* contribute to national cohesion, thrive without subsidization, he points out.

Van den Haag further argues that an art subsidy attracts to the field people who would not become artists without it. Those individuals differ from artists who are interested in its intrinsic rewards and are willing to incur the large risk of earning a low income. The pseudoartists, van den Haag maintains, will inevitably compete for subsidies more successfully than real artists. They will exploit the knowledge that it is easier for the holders of the purse strings to justify grants for art that is already fashionable than for truly original art. In short, taxpayer-supported subsidies are likely to stimulate production of mediocre art.

MUST GOVERNMENT BE THE SELECTOR?

Our recap of the pros and cons doesn't yield a slam-dunk case for subsidies. But suppose for sake of argument, we concede the existence of a market failure in the production of art. Let us further grant (notwith-standing the demonstrated willingness of patrons to outspend their own consumption capability) that the government alone can make up the shortfall. It doesn't automatically follow that the government must influ-ence the menu of available art by funneling money through an agency such as the NEA.

If the NEA did not exist, the government would still be steering vast amounts of money to the arts. Donations to arts organizations are de-ductible from federal income taxes. It is consequently less costly, on an after-tax basis, to write a check to the local museum or symphony than would be the case if the deduction didn't exist. By lowering the price of the psychic gratification derived from supporting the arts, the government induces people to buy more of that psychic gratification than they other-wise would.

A tax preference offers the advantage of not compelling people to fi-nance art that they find objectionable or simply uninteresting. It also by-passes the administrative costs of a grant-making apparatus. To be sure, writing the arts into the tax code represents an intervention in the market. But it preserves the market element of leaving the choice in consumers' hands, instead of making it the object of political horse trading.

Leaving the choices to people who care deeply about art is appropriate in light of the highly subjective nature of artistic tastes. Some music lovers would rather have more chamber music concerts, even at the cost of hav-ing fewer organ recitals. Others feel exactly the opposite. The nature of the marketplace is that no individual is likely to be completely satisfied with the programming mix that emerges from audience ticket purchases and tax-benefited private donations. But neither is the government likely to raise the overall level of satisfaction by favoring certain types of musical performances over others.

THE POLITICS OF ARTS SUBSIDIZATION

History teaches us that art subsidies are not really about advancing the arts. The NEA came into being in 1965, when President Lyndon B. Johnson signed the National Foundation on the Arts and the Humanities Act (NFAHA). Forty years later, it is difficult to make a persuasive economic case for subsidizing art through such an entity. A reasonable inference is that supporters couldn't make a viable case in 1965, either. As it turns out, the legislation's origins had nothing to do with market failures or rates of return on public investment in the arts.

"Johnson had never felt at ease with the arts, but he had good reasons for supporting [the NFAHA],"[20] writes critic and curator Michael Brenson. For one thing, says Brenson, LBJ was aware that his predecessor John F. Kennedy had received a great deal of favorable press for supporting the arts. Johnson also hoped that creating a federal art agency would win him backing from the East Coast liberal establishment that opposed his policy on Vietnam. Finally, Johnson viewed culture as a weapon in the Cold War and as a way to gain recognition of the United States as a great civilization.

Edward C. Banfield relates that New York City's "culture industry" was the single most powerful proponent of establishing the National Endowment of the Arts. The bill's supporters noted that subsidies to the New York cultural institutions would generate benefits for hotels, restaurants, and shops through tourist trade. Naturally, says Banfield, they didn't argue their case on the basis of such overtly commercial considerations. Instead, the NEA's advocates talked about improving America's image and boosting its prestige by officially recognizing the arts. "No politician was fooled by this rhetoric, of course,"[21] Banfield comments.

The rationale for creating the NEA wasn't that without it, a market failure would deny people the art they craved. The legislation emerged from a happy confluence of Lyndon Johnson's short-run political objectives and New York City's conviction that its retail businesses deserved a gift from the rest of the nation's taxpayers. The NEA's supposed public benefits included combating the Communist bloc, improving the nation's image, and—as recounted by Banfield—benefiting the poor and relieving tension in urban ghettos. It was questionable, at best, that supporting the arts was the most effective means of achieving these lofty goals.

COMPOUNDING THE ERROR: GOVERNMENT-FUNDED BROADCASTING

Not content with its dubious intrusion into the arts through creation of the NEA in 1965, Congress established the Corporation for Public Broadcasting (CPB) through the Public Broadcasting Act of 1967. Nobody, least of all parents, suggested that a market failure was causing Americans to spend too few hours watching television. Rather, the ostensible problem involved the quality of programming available on commercial television.

The CPB strives to improve the quality of telecasting by providing roughly 15 percent of public television stations' funding. With the federal dollars, the stations purchase broadcast rights and services from the Public Broadcasting Service (PBS), a private, nonprofit media enterprise. Additionally, the CPB provides some funding to PBS and to member stations of National Public Radio.

Inevitably, government funding of the CPB has generated controversies similar to those that have surrounded the NEA. In lieu of nudity and sacrilege, however, the major bone of contention has been alleged political bias. With news and public affairs programs figuring prominently in PBS lineup, and with CPB's funding controlled by politicians whose antics are scrutinized by those programs, periodic clashes over the CPB budget are inevitable.

In 2005, the flare-up featured Democratic accusations that under Republican control, the CPB was promoting a conservative agenda. The CPB board replied that it was merely trying to correct a prevailing liberal bias in PBS programming. President George W. Bush's administration cited in particular an episode from the *Postcards from Buster* series in which an animated rabbit visited two families headed by lesbians.

Continuing the tit for tat, liberals scored CPB Chairman Kenneth Tomlinson for surreptitiously paying a consultant to monitor the PBS program *Now* for political bias in its selection of guests. The consultant rated each of the show's guests "L" for liberal or "C" for conservative. Liberals complained that the methodology was itself biased. Senator Chuck Hagel (R–NE) was classified "L" solely, according to *New York Times* columnist Frank Rich, because he voiced doubts about the administration's policy on the Iraq war in a discussion devoted primarily to praising Ronald Reagan.[22]

It was, in fact, a bit of a stretch to call Hagel a liberal. Prior to the congressman's most recent reelection, his voting record had garnered low ratings from classically liberal interest groups. He received a rating of just 8 percent from the AFL–CIO labor organization and 0 percent from the League of Conservation Voters (LCV). Organizations usually classified as conservative awarded Hagel high ratings, including 100 percent from the

Christian Coalition and an A from the National Rifle Association. Proto-typical liberal Ted Kennedy (D-MA) was Hagel's reverse image, with rat-ings of 100 percent from the AFL-CIO and 0 percent from the Christian Coalition.[23]

Senator Charles Schumer (D-NY) contributed to the spectacle. Fol-lowing a time-honored tradition, he suggested that critics of government support for public television were trying to murder Big Bird. To drama-tize the danger posed by Republican efforts to cut CPB's budget by 25 percent, Schumer displayed a picture of the beloved avian from PBS's *Sesame Street* and a herd of rampaging elephants. Big Bird, along with his friends Bert and Ernie, was shown fleeing for his life.

A LOAD OF RED HERRINGS

Sadly, the serious arguments on behalf of the Corporation for Public Broadcasting aren't much better, intellectually speaking, than the politi-cians' grandstanding. They boil down to praise for the high quality of PBS programs and cheers for the educational benefits provided by public television stations. Neither represents a valid rationale for broad govern-ment funding.

Bill Reed, the president of public television station KCPT in Kansas City, made both arguments during an appearance on the June 21, 2005, edition of *Jim Lehrer News Hour* on PBS. Public broadcasting, he main-tained, offered the airwaves' best nonviolent children's programming, as well as superior public affairs programs. Reed also pointed to his station's educational role in the community. This included service to 200,000 K-12 students and collaborations with nine area colleges and universities that brought distance learning to 50,000 people each year.[24]

Many citizens agree with Reed that public television provides better content than commercial television. They act on that conviction by sup-porting their local stations through financial contributions. Viewers' con-tributions are the lifeblood of public television stations, since they receive only about 15 percent of their funding from the CPB.

If the federal government ceased kicking in cash, the stations might have to schedule even lengthier fund-raising telethons than they already do. That would represent a hardship for some, but quality of life would improve in an important way: Politicians would no longer have an incentive to vituperate about alleged political bias on PBS. The key point is that it is possible to agree wholeheartedly that PBS's public affairs programming is a national treasure, without believing that the government should exercise the power of the purse strings over it.

As for public television stations' educational programming, there is certainly an argument for public support *of that specific activity*. Education is a classic public good, producing benefits to society at large, rather than exclusively to its consumers (the students). Subsidization prevents demand for education from falling below the optimal level.

By this reasoning, government funding is appropriate for televised education, provided it is at least as cost-effective as alternative means of providing comparable services. (In the case of distance learning, substitutes might be much costlier.) But public television stations cannot legitimately use their educational role to justify subsidization of their public affairs programming. Any funds provided by the government ought to be earmarked for educational programs.[25]

THE BOTTOM LINE

Proponents of government funding of the arts delight in comparisons that demonstrate just how miserly the American government is about promoting culture. One advocate has stated that the United States spends 38 cents per capita on the National Endowment for the Arts, while in Canada and France, per capita support of the arts totals $32 per annum.[26] Comparisons with military expenditures are especially popular, such as noting that the NEA's annual budget is equivalent to about five inches of a B-1 bomber.[27] In Great Britain, the Arts Council's chairman observed in 1985 that his agency's funding amounted to the interest on one year's interest on the capital cost of the Trident nuclear missile program.[28]

But an outlay of taxpayers' dollars can't be presumed valid merely because it is small. Neither can ideologues of the right or the left legitimately attack government funding of arts organizations or public television on the grounds that they dislike the output. Subsidizing anticorporate screeds is an unwarranted use of government funds, but so is underwriting exhibitions of wholesome paintings approved by the Moral Majority.

Government funding of the arts is unjustified because it doesn't redress a demonstrable shortcoming of the marketplace. The case was weak in 1850, when the economic essayist Frédéric Bastiat argued against art subsidies,[29] and it hasn't strengthened with the passage of time.

On the whole, it would be better to leave funding of the arts and the airwaves to the audiences. In their collective wisdom, art lovers could then decide how much naked-body chocolate smearing is the right amount. By voting with their dollars, viewers could steer public television stations toward their desired mix of right-wing-biased and left-wing-biased commentary. The Supreme Court would be freed to concentrate on weightier matters. Congress could focus on initiatives that have a genuine chance of redressing the nation's real problems. Best of all, the public would get welcome relief from a particularly contentious variety of political bombast.

II

RESTRAINT
OF TRADE

9

Stock Arguments

It is a common human failing to assume that if something goes wrong, it has to be somebody's fault. This presumption qualifies as a systematic error, because certain calamities are objectively nobody's fault. Similarly mistaken is the automatic conclusion that one's troubles are somebody *else's* fault. In certain cases, the victims are undeniably the authors of their own misfortunes.

What, if anything, should be done about these chronic misperceptions is debatable. Some public-spirited citizens might favor intensive psychological counseling. Others would balk at the huge cost. No reasonable person, however, would advocate using wrongheaded notions of blame to justify government intervention in the marketplace. That would constitute economic folly. From a political viewpoint, however, the very same policy could represent a masterstroke.

A case in point involves people losing money in the stock market. Most of the time, nobody is at fault. Losses occur for countless reasons other than Wall Street sharpies manipulating prices or otherwise defrauding investors. A company may develop a marvelously innovative product yet see its stock price fall, simply because a competitor introduces an even better product. Sometimes, too, the shares of unquestionably solid companies drop with no hint of dishonest dealing. Instead, they trade down because a normal, cyclical slowdown in economic activity causes the stock market as a whole to decline.

These are risks that people who invest in stocks must resign themselves to bearing. The principle involved is the financial analogue of the sports world's "no pain, no gain" dictum. People are free to choose the no-pain alternative—an investment that poses no material risk of principal loss. The catch is that they must accept a very modest reward. Interest rates on three-month United States Treasury bills ranged from 6.36 percent to as little as 0.90 percent in the 10 years ending in 2004.[1] Over the same period, by contrast, common stocks (measured by the Standard & Poor's 500 Index) produced an annualized total return of 11.93 percent.[2] To achieve the higher return on their savings, however, investors had to tolerate some pain. In 2000, the value of the S&P Index fell by 10.14 percent.[3]

If they so desired, politicians could take the high road on this matter. They could treat investors as grown-ups who must take responsibility for their own choices. But that would represent a failure to appeal to the darker side of human nature, where the vote-capturing potential tends to be greater. The more astute response is to pander to people's belief that if they lose money, it must be the consequence of some inherent unfairness in the market. Politicians capitalize on that delusion by vowing to outlaw the nefarious trading practices that caused their misfortunes.

A FUTILE WAR ON VOLATILITY

To be sure, there are instances in which investors who take a bath are justified in pointing the finger. Suppose a corporation falsifies its financial statements. By overstating its profits, the company inflates the perceived value of its stock. Investors have a legitimate gripe if they buy at a high point and then see the stock price plummet once the deception comes to light.

Like any other kind of commercial fraud, phony accounting is a suitable focus for law enforcement agencies. Going after the perpetrators may deter other companies from committing similar crimes.

Punishing securities dealers when the market goes down produces no comparable benefit. It doesn't prevent the market from falling the next time a change in economic conditions calls for that response. A sensible person would not expect a government agency ever to undertake such a doomed mission. Sensible people, however, underestimate politicians' capacity for folly.

The Securities and Exchange Commission (SEC) labels itself "The Investor's Advocate" and details how it "protects investors and maintains market integrity." The agency recounts that it came into being after countless investors lost their fortunes in the October 1929 stock market crash. Referring to the boom years that preceded the debacle, the SEC writes, "It is estimated that of the $50 billion in new securities offered during this period, half became worthless." Congress addressed the problem, the narrative continues, by establishing the SEC "to protect investors" and "to promote stability in the markets."[4]

For an indication of how well the SEC has succeeded in stabilizing the markets, consider the bloodbath that followed the dot-com mania of the 1990s. According to the Joint Economic Committee of Congress, "nearly $3 trillion of market value [was] erased between March 2000 and January 2001, as the technology-rich NASDAQ plunged by 45 percent."[5] As for the goal of protecting investors, many initial public offerings of Internet companies became every bit as worthless as the new securities offered in the 1920s. Dot-com holders could console themselves with the thought that *their* valueless stocks had come to market only after meeting the elaborate filing requirements instituted by the SEC. (The agency is careful to point out that it doesn't endorse the securities offerings that it oversees, but merely informs investors whether they have met the legal requirements for sale to the public.)

To his credit, the Joint Economic Committee's chairman, Representative Jim Saxton (R–NJ), linked the NASDAQ index's collapse to "data indicating that a sharp economic slowdown was underway by the middle of 2000."[6] Here was a hint, at least, that fluctuations in the stock market reflect forces beyond the government's power to regulate. It might not be too large a leap to suppose that if stock prices are inherently uncontrollable, attempting to control them could have undesirable consequences.

The damage can multiply when the government pursues the dubious goal of stability with policy tools that may actually have the opposite effect. That is a potential flaw of two important components of SEC regulation: *short sale restrictions* and *circuit breakers*. The following sections describe the impact of these policy measures, as well the effect of initial margin requirements, an antivolatility device administered by the Federal Reserve. Finally, we investigate another mission that the SEC pursues in the name of protecting investors. The prohibition on insider trading illustrates the complications that arise when the government sets out with the simple-seeming goal of making markets fair.

SELLING THE SHORT SELLERS SHORT

There are two ways in which a company's stock can be priced incorrectly. It can be too low or it can be too high. Either way, financial decision makers receive a false signal. They rely on stock prices to identify the most attractive investment opportunities available in the economy. When a stock deviates from its intrinsic value, it steers capital away from the most productive opportunities for constructing new factories, retail establishments, utilities, and transportation facilities. Whether a stock is overpriced or underpriced, it contributes to a misallocation of society's scarce resources.

It follows that if politicians must inject themselves into the stock market's operations, they ought to be just as concerned about a stock trading too high as they are about it trading too low. But that is not what their actions indicate. Market regulations make it considerably harder for investors to correct an overpricing than to correct an underpricing.

The way to help *raise an underpriced stock* to its proper level is to buy it. Politicians encourage this action. They even portray it as patriotic. "Own a piece of America!" the office holders exhort their constituents.

Out of the same eagerness to steer the nation's capital into its highest and best use, politicians should encourage investors to restore *overpriced* stocks to their proper levels. A simple, well-known technique can achieve that purpose. It is called *selling short* and this is how it works:

> An investor believes XYZ Corporation's current stock price of $35 exceeds fair value. She therefore agrees to sell at $35, even though she doesn't own any shares. To make good on her obligation to deliver the stock that she has sold, the investor pays a fee to borrow shares from another investor, who does own the stock.

> Suppose the short seller's judgment proves correct and XYZ falls to $30. She realizes her profit by buying shares at the new price to replace the shares she borrowed. Her profit is $35 − $30 = $5 a share, less commissions and the fee she paid for borrowing the stock.

> Because the investor is betting on a decline in XYZ's price, she risks a loss if the stock rises. If XYZ's price increases to $40, the investor is in the hole by that amount less the price she paid, or $5. In addition, she is out of pocket for the borrowing fee and commissions.

Bias toward the Long Side

Short sellers' pursuit of trading profits helps to keep share prices in line with their intrinsic value. In that respect, their actions are every bit as socially useful as the purchases of stock that politicians routinely applaud.

The fact that short sellers rectify overvaluations, instead of undervaluations, doesn't detract from their contribution to efficient allocation of economic resources.

The dot-com frenzy of the late 1990s dramatically underscores this point. At the time, a minority of market participants questioned the basis of the sky-high valuations of many Internet-based stocks. To the extent that the skeptics restrained the rise in prices by selling short, they mitigated the multitrillion-dollar losses that investors later suffered. It is hard to see how the public was served by hampering the short sellers' attempts to act on their conviction.

If anything, short sellers deserve special commendation, because they take greater risks than stock buyers. Consider again the investor who buys XYZ Corporation in the belief that it is cheap at $35. The most that this optimistic investor can lose is $35 a share (plus commissions), because the stock can't trade below $0. On the other hand, there is no upper limit on the stock price. The short seller's potential loss is therefore unlimited.

Even though short sellers incur large risks while helping to direct capital to its most productive use, they get far less respect than investors who "go long" (buy stocks). In fact, politicians treat them as pariahs. Owning a piece of America is deemed patriotic, but selling short is regarded as vaguely traitorous.

During 1989 hearings on short selling, Representative Dennis Hastert (R-IL, and later Speaker of the House) described the practice as "blatant thuggery."[7] Some overseas critics have taken an even harsher stance. In 1995, the Finance Ministry of Malaysia proposed caning as a penalty for short selling.

Constraining Good Practices to Prevent Bad Ones

Government regulations in the United States reflect the politicians' bias by making it harder to sell short than to go long. For one thing, the "uptick rule" stipulates that an exchange-listed stock can be sold short only at a price above the previous reported price.[8] In addition, the Securities and Exchange Commission requires brokerage firms to maintain more capital in support of their short positions than is the case for long positions (inventories of stocks).

How does the government justify hamstringing transactions that might restore overvalued stocks to their proper prices? Here is the official rationale provided to the public:

The SEC has traditionally held the belief that protections against abusive short selling are important for issuer and investor confidence, and has enacted prophylactic rules designed to curb manipulative behavior.[9]

It is hard to argue in principle with a curb on short selling that is demonstrably abusive. But if selling short at a price below the last previous sale is self-evidently abusive and manipulative, we might reasonably infer that it is also inherently abusive and manipulative to *buy* a stock at a price *above* the last previous sale. No government regulation, however, prevents traders from creating a stampede by paying a higher price on each successive trade. Regulators presume that manipulation is occurring only when traders "pile on" a stock that is going down.

The official justification for singling out short sales for special regulations is unpersuasive. Other available tools are as effective in curbing manipulation on the short as on the long side. For example, it is illegal to *paint the tape*. This abuse consists of a series of sham transactions in which two colluding market operators buy and sell a stock to each other at successively higher prices. The rising price creates the illusion that the stock is going up for some valid reason. Painting the tape also works in reverse, with the confederates trading at successively lower prices to create the illusion of a bona fide price decline. Enforcing rules against practices such as painting the tape ought to be a sufficient deterrent to *abusive* short selling. There is no obvious justification for promulgating additional, one-sided rules to control *nonabusive* short selling.

True Origins of the Short Sale Restrictions

In reality, the government's policy of tilting the market against short sellers is the product of the cries for reform that followed the 1929 crash. On Black Tuesday, October 29, massive selling produced record trading volume. The ticker tape fell behind by two-and-a-half hours and stocks lost 12 percent of their value. During the months of October and November, $100 billion of paper wealth evaporated.[10] Contrary to legend, there were no documented incidents of ruined speculators leaping from office building windows. Nevertheless, images of catastrophe and despair became fixed in the public mind.

Investors who had previously bought on margin[11] at historically high valuations suffered horrendous losses. Politicians saw little gain in suggesting that stock buyers were in some small way responsible for their own misfortunes. Neither was it very satisfying to fix the blame on excessive creation of credit during the 1920s, followed by a sudden tightening of the money spigot. That was how many insightful observers interpreted the events, but politicians couldn't expect to get much traction by pillorying the governors of the Federal Reserve. They correctly perceived that they could better satisfy the public thirst for recrimination and revenge by attacking Wall Street fat cats.

The potentially salable story was that wealthy short sellers not only profited from the crash, but caused it. Inconveniently enough, there was little evidence to support such a claim. In November 1929, the New York Stock Exchange found that only about 0.01 percent of outstanding shares had been sold short.[12]

Dry statistics, however, made less of an impression on the public than colorful stories. On November 29, 1929, the prominent stock market operator Ben Smith turned bearish and reportedly rushed into a brokerage shouting, "Sell 'em all! They're not worth anything!"[13] As the stock market's downturn continued, the press demonized Smith, along with renowned speculator Jesse Livermore, who had astutely gone short before Black Tuesday. Both received death threats.

Unsubstantiated rumors arose of organized bear raids, funded by Europeans intent on undermining the U.S. market. Yet in May 1931, the New York Stock Exchange found that the total proportion of shares sold short had risen only to 0.035 percent. Shares held on margin—representing speculative purchases—were more than 10 times as numerous. The exchange uncovered no bear raids. Its analysis found instead that the continuing decline resulted mainly from liquidations of long positions, along with forced sales by margin traders.[14]

In 1933 and 1934, a Senate investigation of Wall Street's affairs likewise discovered no evidence of bear raids. It did, however, succeed in eliciting denunciations of short selling. Otto Kahn, head of the brokerage house Kuhn Loeb, told the senators that profiting from the misfortunes of others was "inherently repellent to the right-thinking man."[15]

The political hoopla reinforced the popular misimpression that short selling was a central cause of the 1929 crash. In the end, though, Congress introduced no legislation to outlaw the practice. The main way in which the government clipped the short sellers' wings was the Securities and Exchange Commission's 1938 adoption of the uptick rule. The New York Stock Exchange had voluntarily imposed the rule on its members in 1931.

A Long Record of Futility

By failing to prohibit short selling outright, Congress actually displayed uncustomary intelligence on an economic matter. In all likelihood, an outright ban would have failed in the end. The futility of similar actions over the preceding three centuries strongly suggests that markets need some traders to take the short side, regardless of what politicians think.

The Amsterdam stock exchange prohibited short selling in 1610, but the rule was disregarded and subsequently repealed. Similarly, in 1734 Great Britain voided sales in which the seller did not possess the shares. The law was considered unenforceable and ignored until its repeal in 1860.

When the French stock exchange reopened after the Revolution of 1789, short selling was prohibited. Napoleon contended that short sellers were treasonous, because they hoped for a drop in the prices of government securities. The French ban was eliminated in 1882.

An 1864 American attempt to restrict short sales of gold lasted for just 15 days. Britain outlawed short sales of bank stocks in 1867, but both investors and the courts disregarded the prohibition. On the whole, government efforts to hamstring short selling were judged to aggravate the problems they were intended to remedy.[16]

The Real Beneficiaries

It is difficult to discern a public benefit in constraining short selling that doesn't entail fraud or stock manipulation. The harder it is for the critics to express their opinion in the market, the further above its intrinsic value a stock such as Enron[17] can go. That means greater losses for shareholders later on, when an accounting fraud comes to light. From a broader economic perspective, obstructing short sellers interferes with efficient allocation of resources. Overvaluation of selected stocks steers investment capital toward comparatively unproductive uses.

If the uptick rule and other impediments to short selling help neither investors nor society-at-large, who does stand to benefit? The answer is the insiders and managers of the companies most in need of healthy discipline by short sellers. They love to see their net worth and stock-price-based bonuses shielded from efforts to price their overvalued shares properly.

THE LOUDER THEY SCREAM, THE HARDER THEY FALL

In 2004, the SEC agreed to an experimental suspension of the uptick rule for the 1,000 largest stocks. The depth of the market in such shares minimized concerns about possible manipulation by short sellers. Although the SEC's pilot project did not make it as feasible in all instances to correct overvaluations as undervaluations, it was a step in the right direction.

Conceivably, there are even some politicians open-minded enough to entertain the idea of making short selling easier, rather than harder. They might not be convinced by the theoretical arguments alone, however. Indeed, a bit of caution would be justifiable. After all, it might turn out that the companies most determined to fight the short sellers really are targets of unfounded attacks, as they frequently claim. In that case, the public interest might better be served by keeping short sellers on a short leash.

University of Chicago Economist Owen Lamont shed light on this question by studying the acrimonious battles between short sellers and the companies on which they focused their efforts.[18] He found that the companies' managers employed hardball tactics to thwart the shorts. These included:

- Expressly designing stock splits and distributions to disrupt short selling.
- Coordinating with owners of company stock to withdraw shares from the security lending market, thereby "squeezing" the shorts, who must borrow shares to implement their trades.
- Making accusations of illegality.
- Bringing lawsuits.
- Requesting probes by government authorities.
- Hiring private investigators to scrutinize the short sellers.

Inflated rhetoric was another feature of the struggles. One company told speculators who were shorting its stock, "Your activities are mean, shameful, and loathsome. They are motivated by appalling avarice and greed, and they will not be permitted to go unanswered."[19]

Lamont's analysis focused on cases in which companies mounted defenses against short sellers or accused them of wrongdoing. He excluded companies that resorted to other forms of harassment. These included:

- Preventing a short seller from asking questions at the annual meeting by drowning him out with a loud, extended coughing fit.
- Illegally driving up the share price through an illegal "corner," that is, a purchase of all available shares.

- Issuing death threats. (One person reportedly threatened in connection with shorting the stock of Tel-Com Wireless Cable TV
  was later found slain, execution-style in Colts Neck, New Jersey.)[20]

For the 270 companies that employed more conventional methods between 1977 and 2002, average stock performance was poor following the
anti-short-seller actions. Over the subsequent year, the companies' shares
performed 2.34 percent a month worse than the market averages. Over
the three years subsequent to taking up the cudgels, the short-battlers'
stocks retreated 42 percent vis-à-vis the market.

Judging by Lamont's results, the short sellers were generally correct in
perceiving overvaluation in the stocks of the companies that responded
with legal threats or financial countermeasures. In fact, Lamont reported
that short sellers became more convinced that they were right when their
activities prompted a company to lash out. "The louder they scream, the
better the short," said one.[21]

Yet Another Dubious Intrusion

Critics of short selling might counter that perhaps the short sellers manip-
ulatively drove down the prices of "innocent companies,"[22] as Congressman Hastert suggested in the 1989 hearings on the topic. That suggestion
is undercut, however, by economist Lamont's finding that fraud was a frequent cause of price declines in the companies he studied. In fact, he found
that of the four companies that testified in the hearings in which Hastert
decried alleged victimization by short sellers, two were subsequently
charged with fraud. (The other two went bankrupt within two years of
the hearings.)

Lamont comments, "A striking feature of the sample [of companies in
the study] is that ex post, many of the firms taking action are indeed fraud-
ulent or have a product that simply does not work (or both)."[23] With such
attractive targets available, it hardly makes sense for short sellers to attempt
to beat down stocks of indisputably sound and fairly valued companies.

This is especially so in view of the high cost of being wrong on the
short side, where the potential loss is unlimited. Short sellers also face the
risk that a bull market in stocks will boost all shares, including those that
already look overvalued. In 2003, the prominent short-selling fund
Rocker Partners LP lost 35.6 percent as the value of the Standard & Poor's
500 Index soared by 26.4 percent.[24]

The stock market goes up in more years than it goes down. This means the deck is stacked against short sellers before the government gets into the act. It smacks of overkill to make it even harder for short sellers to return overvalued stocks to their proper levels.

But that is the conclusion reached by applying elementary principles of economics. The political logic follows an entirely different path: Stock prices affect the wealth of corporate managers and insiders. Those individuals have a vested interest in seeing the government hinder the short sellers. Failing to kowtow to that interest could entail a huge sacrifice of campaign contributions.

THE FOLLY OF CIRCUIT BREAKERS

To examine the second variety of ill-advised rule making, let's consider the market from the viewpoint of a professional stock trader whom we will call Brittany.

She earns her livelihood by capitalizing on minor price fluctuations that occur in the course of the trading day. Amid the market's often hectic activity, buy and sell orders don't always arrive in a nice, steady fashion. Sometimes, for no reason related to a stock's intrinsic value, sellers temporarily outnumber buyers. For a brief moment, the stock dips below its fair price.

When Brittany spots a fleeting bargain of this sort, she snaps up some shares. Before the trading day ends, conditions may reverse. That is, buyers of the stock may momentarily outnumber sellers, causing the stock to trade above its appropriate level. At that point, Brittany will sell her shares, netting a small profit on the round trip.

She doesn't make long-run bets on stocks—even if "long" is defined as overnight. Between one day's close and the following day's opening, any number of events could radically alter conditions. A government agency could release a sharply disappointing economic report, the president could deliver alarming news in a televised address, or a panic could sweep the Asian stock markets. Rather than expose herself to such risks, Brittany leaves her trading positions "flat" at the end of every session. She either sells all the shares she owns or neutralizes their risk by making offsetting short sales.

Brittany has no grandiose purpose in mind; she is just trying to make a living. But by buying or selling whenever a stock's prices get slightly out of line, Brittany and her fellow professional traders provide an immense service to the economy at large. They help smooth the rise and fall of stocks in response to news that affects their value.

What would happen if traders ceased trying to profit from every short-lived misvaluation? Prices would begin to lurch more violently in response to each bit of news. Owning stocks would become a much riskier proposition. That higher risk would be reflected in lower valuations for stocks. By extension, capital would be more expensive for corporations, meaning that they would invest less capital in their businesses. Economic growth and job creation would suffer.

A Tough Day on the Trading Floor

Keeping in mind the social value of professional traders, let's visit Brittany during an exceptionally tough day in the market. Right after the opening bell, stocks began bumping lower. Brittany bought a lot of cheap-looking shares. Unfortunately, they kept getting cheaper as the market continued to slide.

By the afternoon, the decline ranked among the worst Brittany had witnessed in her dozen years in the business. She was resigned to finishing the day with a loss, but the picture wasn't entirely bleak. Experience had brought her a keen understanding of *market technicals*. She believed that a drop of another percentage point or two would precipitate buying by inveterate bargain hunters seeking to purchase shares at the lows. That would spark a rally, giving Brittany a chance to trim her losses rather than sell at the bottom.

On this occasion, Brittany can't rely on her feel for the market. A price drop of just one more percentage point will trigger the exchange's circuit breaker. This government-mandated rule temporarily shuts down trading if prices fall by a stated amount. If the circuit breaker is activated close enough to the end of the day, trading will shut down before the session's scheduled conclusion and will not reopen until the following morning.

Even though Brittany believes the market will rebound if left alone, she can't wait to find out whether she's right. Getting trapped overnight in her positions by a trading halt is not an option. Her only choice is to sell all her stocks quickly, before prices fall further and the circuit breaker goes into effect.

The artificially induced selling by Brittany and others in her predicament helps to drive stock prices lower. This might seem odd, since the circuit breaker's ostensible purpose is to stabilize a falling market. But achieving a useful result isn't the criterion by which politicians decide to introduce or perpetuate stock market regulations.

Consider the Evidence

To be fair about it, short-run traders like our fictitious Brittany represent just one variety of stock market participants. Other shares are held by long-run investors who rarely trade. They would hardly notice if trading automatically shut down as a result of prices falling by a specified amount.

Whether circuit breakers contribute helpfully to the market's operation depends on the complex interaction of all the players. But the mere presence of complexity doesn't mean that it is impossible to make an informed judgment about the advisability of prearranged trading halts. Experience sheds some light.

Congress instituted circuit breakers in 1988, in response to the record stock market decline of October 19, 1987.[25] The first time the New York Stock Exchange's circuit breaker was triggered, on October 27, 1997, the regulators concluded that the mechanism might have accelerated price declines in the final minutes of trading. According to the Securities and Exchange Commission's study of the incident, concerns over the likelihood of an early stock market close may have transferred selling pressure to the futures market. There, traders could obtain swifter execution in the limited remaining time. It could be that the futures led stocks down to the circuit breaker's trigger point, which was then a 550-point decline.[26]

Given that it took a decade for the circuit breaker to be activated, academic researchers have only a small sample of observations to study. Consequently, they have been obliged to approach the question indirectly. But even a data-constrained analysis, when conducted by serious researchers, sheds more light than a study compromised by political objectives. Congress instituted circuit breakers at the recommendation of the Presidential Task Force on Market Mechanisms (also known as the Brady Commission). The impetus was largely Congress's desire to demonstrate that it was doing something to respond to the 1987 crash. Bona fide analysis leaves it unclear whether circuit breakers are effective or counterproductive.

Researchers from the University of Michigan and the University of Wisconsin considered the evidence of trading halts on individual stocks.[27] These shutdowns represent a miniature version of circuit breakers, which apply to all stocks. The notion behind a trading halt is that extreme stress can temporarily impede the flow of information to investors. A temporary suspension of trading gives investors time to catch up on information. When trading resumes, the market should swiftly and smoothly establish a new consensus price for the stock. The researchers found that reality failed to match the theory. On the first full trading day after a stock got halted, it was 50 percent to 115 percent *more* volatile than under similar market conditions, when no halt was imposed.

A study funded and published by the Federal Reserve Bank of Atlanta[28] paid students at Georgia Institute of Technology to trade in simulated stock market sessions. The researchers varied the conditions among the sessions, testing for effects of instituting or not instituting a circuit breaker. Their results indicated unequivocally that circuit breakers had no beneficial effect in reining in unwarranted price swings. In fact, one type of circuit breaker (a temporary trading halt, as opposed to an automatic shutdown for the balance of the day) appeared to have a detrimental effect.

Sticking with the Plan

All in all, the evidence offers little reason to believe that government-instituted circuit breakers have improved the operation of the stock market. But that is hardly surprising, considering the underlying idea. The dubious premise is that investors will incorporate information more effectively into stock prices if the government prevents them from acting on that information.

Politicians fail to grasp that artificially blocking a stock market slide for a few hours doesn't alter the underlying economic reality. If corporate earnings are deteriorating, they will continue to deteriorate whether or not Congress permits the Dow Jones Industrial Average to reflect the change. All that a circuit breaker achieves is to put politicians on record against a stock market decline.

In a perfect world, the lack of solid evidence supporting circuit breakers would have consequences. Politicians would admit their error and abolish a useless and potentially harmful restraint on the market. In the real world, however, elected officials are no more likely to speak out against circuit breakers than they are to stand up for short sellers. Taking the position that sounds good is more expedient than championing a policy that actually does some good.

THE IMPOTENCE OF MARGIN REQUIREMENTS

Yet another way that Congress has tried to keep the stock market on an even keel is by controlling investors' efforts to boost their profits through borrowing. The Securities and Exchange Act of 1934 authorizes the Federal Reserve to impose limits on *buying on margin*. Reducing market volatility is one of the rationales for this power, along with the equally dubious objectives of preventing investors from taking on too much debt and steering capital to more productive uses.

The connection between margin loans and stock market instability is firmly established in the popular imagination. Economist John Kenneth Galbraith's account of the 1929 crash[29] assigned a central role to the previous lending to stock buyers by brokerage houses. Regulatory reports on the 1987 meltdown[30] reinforced the idea, although computerized program trading became the villain of choice in that affair. Even so, rigorous research disputes the notion that the Federal Reserve can narrow the market's fluctuations by manipulating the rules for margin buying.

Explaining the Alleged Link with Volatility

The mechanics of margin buying are simple. Suppose investor Bob expects the share price of Idiotronic Corporation to rise from $25 to $30. He can buy 100 shares at a total cost of $2,500. If his bet pays off as he expects, his profit is $5 a share, or $500. That represents a return of $500 on his $2,500 investment, or a 20 percent gain before commissions. Alternatively, Bob can augment his capital of $2,500 by borrowing $2,500 from his broker. He can then afford to buy 200, rather than just 100, shares. In that case, a $5 rise in Idiotronic's share price generates gross proceeds of $6,000 when Bob sells. He repays the $2,500 that he borrowed, leaving the $2,500 he invested plus a $1,000 profit. His gain is $1,000 /$2,500 = 40 percent, before commissions and interest on the borrowed money.

Making a 40 percent return on investment is better than making a 20 percent return, so the appeal of buying on margin is easy to understand. Equally easy for investors to understand—at least after the fact—is the disadvantage of buying on margin when the market goes the wrong way. Using the facts of the preceding example, suppose that Idiotronic shares fall by $5, instead of rising by that amount. If Bob has bought on margin, he sells at $20, generating gross proceeds of $4,000. After repaying his borrowings of $2,500, he's left with $1,500, or $1,000 less than his initial capital of $2,500. That represents a loss of 40 percent on the money he put up, before commissions and interest. Had Bob not bought on margin, his loss before commissions would have been only $500, or 20 percent.

This potential for amplifying gains and losses, which financial analysts call *leverage,* fosters the belief that margin buying increases stock market volatility. In a rising market, investors supposedly get intoxicated by the prospect of gains. Instead of merely purchasing as many shares as they can afford, they borrow from their brokers and purchase about twice that number. This hyperactive buying allegedly drives up prices more dramatically than fundamental conditions warrant.

According to this story, it is even worse when the market starts heading down. Investors who have borrowed become subject to *margin calls*. That is, their brokers demand repayment of the investors' loans when losses reduce the equity (nonborrowed capital) in their accounts below a stated level.[31] At that point, the investors are obliged to deposit additional equity in their accounts.

If the investors are unwilling or unable to put up additional equity, they must sell some of their shares and use the proceeds to reduce their margin debt. These sales are not prompted by investors' perceptions of the value of their stocks. In fact, if investors had the financial wherewithal, they would probably buy more shares to take advantage of the dip in prices. According to those who associate margin buying with market volatility, this forced selling produces a larger price drop than fundamental conditions alone would create.

The Plea: "Not Guilty"

The Tech Wreck of 2000 inevitably put the spotlight on margin requirements.[32] With investors experiencing massive losses in Internet-related stocks, numerous observers identified leverage as the culprit. Economist Paul Krugman declared that margin lending would eventually be seen as a factor no less important to the 2000 sell-off than program trading was to the stock market crash of October 1987.

If the problem was runaway speculation, fueled by margin buying, there appeared to be a simple way to stop pouring gasoline on the fire. All the Federal Reserve had to do, in the view of some politicians, was to increase the initial margin rate.[33] Senator Charles Schumer (D-NY) proposed a boost to 60 percent from 50 percent, where the rate had stood since 1974.

Chairman Alan Greenspan, however, rejected calls for the Federal Reserve to rein in speculation with tighter margin restrictions. True, total margin stood at $265 billion, the highest level since the government began regulating it in 1934.[34] But as big as the number was in absolute terms, it represented only 1.5 percent of the market's total value.[35] That made it unlikely, in Greenspan's view, that clamping down on margin buying would materially affect stability.

Greenspan wasn't trying to duck responsibility. He was just being realistic about the Federal Reserve's power over the market. Voluminous research has failed to demonstrate a definitive link between margin requirements and volatility.

In 2001, Peter Fortune, a senior economist at the Federal Reserve Bank of Boston, summarized nearly 30 years of research. He found no solid statistical evidence that stock returns responded to changes in Federal Reserve margin requirements. Fortune further concluded that the research made no clear case for active management of margin requirements by the Fed.[36] The Federal Reserve Board conceded in 1984 that no one had demonstrated that regulating margins dampened fluctuations in stock prices.[37]

Considering the plausible link between margin buying and market volatility, previously outlined here, some readers may be puzzled by the absence of a statistical connection. This is a case in which plausible explanations can be devised on both sides of the question. It could be that the investors who rely on margin tend to buy at low points and sell at high points in prices. This would mean that margin buyers cushion, rather than accentuate, the market's ups and downs. If so, clipping margin buyers' wings with tighter margin restrictions wouldn't have the desired effect of reducing volatility.[38]

In the end, what counts is not the ability to offer a clever explanation for what might be, but the wisdom to be guided by what is. Over the past few decades, the Federal Reserve has shown that wisdom by declining to exercise its power over margin requirements. Raising and lowering the rate might make politicians feel better, but would provide no other material benefit.

The country would be better off if other government officials followed the Federal Reserve's example by concluding that a lack of demonstrated effectiveness is sufficient reason to refrain from using a policy tool. In fact, there are many instances in which regulators would do everyone a big favor by sitting on their hands. As the following section demonstrates, it is difficult to achieve unambiguously good results even with the best of intentions.

INSIDE THE INSIDER TRADING LAWS

On October 6, 2005, stockbroker Edward Leadbetter of Fort Wayne, Indiana, purchased 500 shares of Appoline Pharmaceuticals at a price of

$47.19 for his client, Margaret Delaney. Leadbetter considered the stock a prudent investment for Mrs. Delaney, a widow hoping to earn money on her investments to help pay for her daughter's college education. Appoline had reported steadily increasing earnings over the past five years. What's more, two of the company's highly promising drugs were well on the way toward final approval by the Food and Drug Administration. Leadbetter was no get-rich-quick artist, but he saw potential for a substantial price rise in Appoline shares over the next 12 to 18 months.

One day after a sizable chunk of Jessica Delaney's college savings went into Appoline Pharmaceuticals stock, a bombshell struck. On October 7, Appoline's management announced that it was voluntarily withdrawing its largest-selling and most profitable drug, Impaxadril, from the market. New tests revealed that patients using the pain reliever had experienced an alarmingly high rate of heart attacks. In reaction to this devastating news, the price of Appoline shares plummeted to $34.86, representing a one-day decline of more than 25 percent. In one brutal trading session, Jessica's college fund was reduced by over $6,000.

It was hardly a glorious day for the management of Appoline Pharmaceuticals. News reports indicated that the company's senior executives had become aware of Impaxadril's fatal side effects on September 16, 2005. Instead of acting immediately to protect the public, management waited three weeks before halting shipments of the drug.

Appoline's spokesperson, however, pointed with pride to one aspect of the unfolding public relations disaster. Between September 16 and October 6, there had been no pattern of suspicious trading in the company's shares. The stock had not begun to slide in advance of the withdrawal of Impaxadril. In fact, the price had moved slightly higher over the period.

This was in sharp contrast to several recent cases where shortly before a company disclosed unfavorable news to the public, its shares fell precipitously. In those incidents, the stock price movements strongly suggested that inside information had illegally influenced the market. Someone within the company had either sold with the benefit of advance knowledge of the announcement or leaked the news to others.

The absence of insider trading at Appoline gave bragging rights not only to the company's management, but also to securities regulators. Here was tangible evidence that their recent, high-profile prosecutions of corporate insiders were achieving the goal of deterrence. White-collar criminals now knew that they couldn't get away with prematurely profiting from material information about their companies.

Regulators would have been hard-pressed, however, to identify the victims of the insider trading violations. Suppose that bad news caused a given stock to fall from $30 to $20. Whether insiders exploited nonpublic information to bail out at $30 or whether they didn't, the result for noninsiders who owned the stock was the same. They suffered a $10-a-share loss.

On the other hand, it was easy to find a poster child for the harm that arose because the executives of Appoline Pharmaceuticals did *not* violate the insider trading laws. Consider Jessica Delaney, whose college fund lost over $6,000 when the news about Impaxadril became public. Her financial setback could have been averted by illegal insider trading.

Suppose the insiders had sold shares between the time they became aware of Impaxadril's fatal side effects (September 16) and the date that the company disclosed the information (October 6). Their sales would have pushed down the price, so that the stock wouldn't have been trading as high as $47.19 when stockbroker Leadbetter bought it. That would have prevented Jessica Delaney from suffering the full $12.33-a-share loss from $47.19 to $34.86.

With luck, other investors might have gotten wind of the insider trading in Appoline Pharmaceuticals. If enough of them had dumped their shares, the entire price decline would have occurred before any unsuspecting investor could suffer a one-day, 25 percent shellacking. In that case, Jessica Delaney would have been $6,000 closer to affording a college education than she actually was on October 5, 2005.

The Cost of Excluding Pertinent Information

The story of Jessica and her college fund is fictitious, but similar outcomes are repeated every trading day. The information that changes the value of a company's shares is not always as dramatic as a decision to suspend sales of a major product. But every time the insider trading prohibition prevents material information from being digested and evaluated by the market, a gap opens between the stock's price and its true value.

From a social welfare standpoint, stock market regulation should strive for parity, rather than disparity, between price and value. The stock market serves society by steering investors toward the most productive uses for their capital. If stock prices misstate the value of companies in a given industry, that industry will attract less investment or more investment than it should. The economy will consequently achieve less than its full potential, making people generally less well off than they could be.

In this light, a law that causes shares to diverge from their true value can't be judged an unqualified success. Even so, few if any politicians would dare to question the insider trading ban. The self-described public servants justify their marketplace interventions on grounds of alleged market failures. Yet, what could demonstrate market failure more plainly than a stock trading at a price other than what it is worth, thanks to a law that guarantees that result?

Not beyond Challenge

Even though politicians treat the insider trading prohibition as a sacred cow, questioning its validity isn't an undertaking of the lunatic fringe. In 2004, the *Financial Analysts Journal* featured a debate on the subject by two distinguished leaders of the investment profession.[39] By way of background, the *Financial Analysts Journal* is published by the CFA Institute. This organization awards the Chartered Financial Analyst designation and describes its purpose as "lead[ing] the investment industry by setting the highest standards of ethics and professional excellence and vigorously advocating fair and transparent capital markets."[40]

Dean LeBaron, founder of Batterymarch Financial Management, argued that preventing insiders from trading makes no sense if one of the stock market's primary functions is (in technical language) accurate price discovery. LeBaron advocated encouraging insider trading at all times, provided insiders were required to identify their buy and sell orders. That, he explained, would alert other investors that the buying or selling might be based on information not generally available.

Jack L. Treynor, president of Treynor Capital Management, took the anti-insider-trading side of the argument. He reasoned in part that securities dealers (otherwise known as "Wall Street") can lose money if inside information enters the market between the time they buy a stock from one customer and sell it to another. There is a social benefit in protecting dealers from such losses, Treynor contended, because dealers provide valuable liquidity to the market. By enabling investors to buy and sell stocks comparatively easily, dealers increase the attractiveness of investing in the market. Treynor concluded that insider trading laws probably contribute to the health of capitalist societies. "But those laws don't protect the little guy," he added. "Instead, they protect some rich, powerful big guys—dealers."[41]

In short, two eminent investment experts debated the wisdom of prohibiting insider trading. One concluded that the ban was a bad idea. The other endorsed it, but rejected a key justification that's typically advanced for the law. If insider trading were legal, say the politicians, the little guy couldn't compete on even terms with the "big shots." Yet Treynor, who supported the insider trading prohibition, concluded that it is primarily the big shots who benefit from it.

THE BOTTOM LINE

The misdirection arising from insider trading rules echoes the verdict on short selling restrictions. Restrictions on short sales assist corporate executives' attempts to prop up their appropriately faltering stock prices. The insider trading prohibition protects Wall Street dealers, rather than the broad investing public that politicians claim to serve.

Even so, it is not self-evident that abolishing the insider trading restrictions is the correct solution. Research suggests that countries that enact insider trading rules enjoy certain benefits. These include comparatively low-cost capital, accurate stock prices, and market liquidity.[42] (Oddly, the finding of increased price accuracy conflicts with the intuitive notion that withholding inside information from the market makes pricing *less* accurate.)

In light of the complexities involved, the government should step gingerly when contemplating an intrusion in the stock market. Politicians act on a different set of premises: What is best for the country isn't their primary consideration. Allowing buyers and sellers to set prices for investment capital, barring irrefutable evidence of market failure, is sound economics, but it isn't the best way to win votes. Candidates gain more by reinforcing investors' conviction that if they lost money by betting on the direction of stock prices, it must be somebody else's fault.

The policy tools that legislators have created to control volatility range from ineffective to counterproductive. Commanding the market to be stable is an act of economic hubris. But that doesn't prevent it from also being a politically astute strategy.

10

What Is Wrong with Payola?

On July 25, 2005, New York Attorney General Eliot Spitzer announced a $10 million settlement with Sony BMG Music Entertainment in a payola investigation. Spitzer continued his probe of other record companies as well as the nation's largest owners of radio stations. He vowed to expose and exact punishment for illegal payments by the record companies to induce radio stations to devote airtime to their artists.

Details of the illicit practices painted a sordid picture. Internal documents revealed station programmers being plied with expensive vacations, plasma television sets, and plain old cash. Record company officials threatened to yank promotional support, such as concert tickets, if stations failed to place certain records on their playlists.

One e-mail recounted problems that arose when Sony attempted to rig record selections by paying its own representatives to call in requests. "My guys on the inside say it's the same couple of girls calling in every week and that they are not inspired enough to put on the air," an executive complained. He urged his colleague to locate some new callers: "They've got to be excited. They need to be going out, or getting drunk, or going in the hot tube [sic]"[1]

To individuals a bit older than the teenagers who constitute the prime record-buying audience, it all sounded like a broken record. Way back in 1959, congressional hearings on payola captivated the nation. The scandal caused the downfall of Alan Freed, the disc jockey credited with coining the term *rock and roll*. Freed pleaded guilty to two counts of commercial bribery, began drinking heavily, and died in 1965.

Things worked out much better for Dick Clark, another nationally famous disc jockey at the center of the hearings. Clark was obliged to divest interests in music publishers and record companies that were seen as creating conflicts of interest, but he enjoyed a long and successful postscandal career. The difference, in the view of music writer Kerry Segrave, was that "slick and hyper"[2] Freed enraged the establishment. In particular, he tolerated unruly behavior by teenagers attending rock-and-roll concerts that he organized. On Clark's *American Bandstand* television program, by contrast, the youngsters adhered to a dress code and the performers executed many fewer pelvic thrusts than on other telecasts.

The 1959 congressional hearings spawned amendments to the Communications Act that made undisclosed payola a crime and led to the adoption of new antipayola regulations by the Federal Communications Commission (FCC). In addition, the larger radio stations removed the opportunity for disc jockeys to receive payments by transferring their control of the playlist to program directors.

Neither the government's reforms nor the industry's actions ended payola. In 1964, the FCC reported allegations that the practice continued. The going rate for payments to program directors in the mid-1960s was reportedly $25,000.[3] At some smaller stations, disc jockeys continued to pick records. A lengthy FCC investigation resulted in the conviction of deejays Freddy Baez and Hipolito Vega of WHOM in Los Angeles for payola and perjury.

Columnist Jack Anderson thrust payola into the spotlight yet again in 1972. He charged that program directors and disc jockeys were receiving vacations, prostitutes, cash, and cars for plugging songs. Anderson also added a new wrinkle by claiming that some payola was in the form of drugs.

A major scandal broke out in 1973, when an executive of CBS's Columbia Records unit told investigators that the company's promotion budget concealed $250,000 of annual payola outlays. Columbia Records chief Clive Davis was subsequently fired, ostensibly for improperly spending company funds on his apartment and a bar mitzvah. Senator James Buckley (R-NY) demanded a federal payola investigation. The Justice Department, assisted by the FCC and Internal Revenue Service, along with four grand juries, spent two years investigating the practice.

Several indictments followed, and in 1976, four Brunswick Record Company executives received fines and prison terms.[4] In addition, an executive of Gamble-Huff Records pleaded no contest to payola charges. All told, 25 individuals pleaded guilty to various charges arising from this round of federal investigations.[5] Almost as soon as the probe wound down, the FCC announced that it would hold new hearings, based on additional information that it had received.

The House Oversight and Investigations Subcommittee looked into payola again in 1984. This time, the allegations involved payments by record companies, funneled through independent record promoters, to get songs onto the playlists of certain key radio stations. Those lists were used by trade publications to assess the popularity of current releases and also by lesser stations to formulate their own playlists.

NBC Nightly News rekindled concerns in 1986 by charging that the independent promoters had links to organized crime. Senator Al Gore (D-TN) announced that the Senate Permanent Subcommittee on Investigations would investigate the new form of payola. In 1989, a Los Angeles grand jury indicted independent record promoter Joe Isgro on 57 counts of, among other things, payola, mail fraud, and conspiracy to distribute cocaine. The ensuing trial ended abruptly when the judge ruled that federal prosecutors had violated rules of evidence by withholding a key document.

In short, payola investigations were a very old story by the time New York Attorney Spitzer entered the fray. The purchase of airtime didn't end with the celebrated 1959 congressional hearings, although it continually evolved into new forms. Almost a half-century later, Spitzer declared that payola was pervasive in the music business.[6]

What's more, the post-1959 scandals represented less than half the story of the remarkable persistence of pay-to-play schemes. An earlier version, involving performers instead of disc jockeys, was mentioned in Richard Rodgers and Oscar Hammerstein's 1945 movie musical, *State Fair*. In fact, the buying of exposure for music substantially antedated *Variety*'s 1938 introduction of the term *payola*.[7] Pay-to-play was common even in the nineteenth century, long before commercial recordings and radio arrived on the scene. Originally, the allegedly improper payments involved live performances and sheet music sales.

Early attempts to stamp out pay-to-play arrangements proved no more effective than subsequent efforts by Congress and the FCC. After more than a century of futility, it might be time for politicians to take a different view of the matter. Perhaps criminalizing payola is a wrongheaded attempt to abolish a market that should exist, in the interest of fairness and economic efficiency. If government officials were to consider this possibility, they would merely be catching up with an analysis produced almost 50 years before the Spitzer payola investigation.

WHAT FRAUD?

Payola was perceived by many as a new phenomenon in 1958, when the subject came up in a congressional inquiry into broadcasting industry corruption.[8] In the music business, however, it had become a major topic of discussion by the early part of the decade. Since the end of World War II, the focus of radio programming had shifted from live performances of big bands to the broadcasting of records. Disc jockeys picked the records for their programs and commented on the music they aired. The deejays' increased prominence paralleled the record companies' growing recognition of the impact of airtime on record sales. As a result, the record spinners displaced bandleaders as the main recipients of payments.

By 1956, press coverage of payola prompted a response by economist Murray Rothbard.[9] That was also the year Elvis Presley first topped the charts, with "Heartbreak Hotel." It wasn't entirely coincidental that rock and roll was rapidly gaining popularity as payola was attracting increased scrutiny. The payola controversy reflected much more than a debate over what constituted proper commercial practices.

Rothbard began by distinguishing between a legal fraud and a mere deception. Selling a box labeled "cereal," but actually containing hay, would constitute a legal fraud, he said. By contrast, if a self-proclaimed expert on metaphysics charges for a lecture and disappoints the audience with his poor mastery of the subject, he has at worst deceived them. The attendees obtained no express warrant describing exactly what metaphysics is and what sort of lecture they could expect. Although the deception might be objectionable, said Rothbard, the purpose of the law is not to enforce all forms of morality. (Indeed, legislating morality has a deservedly bad reputation among Americans.)

Against this backdrop, Rothbard asked who was legally defrauded if a disc jockey accepted money from a record company to play its records. Certainly not the record company, which duly received the airtime for which it paid. Neither could competing record companies claim that they were defrauded. The disc jockey had authority over the playlist and had entered into no agreements with the competitors to play their records.

That left the disc jockey's employer as the only party that might have been legally defrauded. The station was paying the disc jockey to use his best judgment in choosing records on the basis of their quality and popularity. If he allowed his judgment to be swayed by the payments, he was not giving his employer what he promised.

But what if the station knew about the payments? As long as the disc jockey's ratings remained high, advertisers would continue to pay high rates for the station's commercial time. In that case, no one could legitimately contend that the station had been defrauded.

Furthermore, Rothbard pointed out, accepting payola wouldn't necessarily compromise the disc jockey's choice of records. After all, he would have an interest in continuing to pick the records that would ensure high ratings. High ratings would in turn support his continued employment. If payola became widespread, argued Rothbard, the payment rate would be roughly the same for every record company. The disc jockey would then be able to exercise his best judgment, uninfluenced by any single company's special favors.[10]

Under these conditions, the station would benefit from having the disc jockey receive compensation directly from record companies. Suppose that the annual compensation required to attract a disc jockey of the desired caliber is $200,000.[11] If the disc jockey can collect $25,000 a year in payola from various record companies, the station will have to offer only $175,000 per annum to fill the slot. The total compensation package of salary and payola will make the position more attractive to the disc jockey than alternative employment that pays $190,000 a year.

Rothbard acknowledged that the radio station's listeners might have had a valid complaint about deception. They trusted the disc jockey to play the records he considered the best. If he instead allowed monetary considerations to influence his choices,[12] his fans were entitled to feel cheated. But they were not legally defrauded. They had no express warrant from the disc jockey stating that he would rely entirely on his judgment about the records' merits. What's more, the audience hadn't paid to listen to the disc jockey's broadcasts. That left them with even less of a claim than the individuals who, in Rothbard's illustration, paid to hear a lecture by a professed master of metaphysics and were disappointed.[13]

AN OLD THING UNDER THE SUN

The distributors and recipients of payola are indebted to the late Professor Rothbard for rehabilitating their reputation.[14] But merely demonstrating that they aren't engaged in fraud smacks of damning them with faint praise. The fact is that payola serves a useful economic function. If the public properly understood this function, payola traffickers would be able to hold their heads high.

Ever since the era before recordings, when sheet music sales represented the main action, industry executives have operated on a simple principle: The best way to persuade people to buy music is to arrange for them to hear it. Only the specific methods of getting music into consumers' ears have changed.

Paying for public exposure began about 100 years before payola became a fixture in radio broadcasting. The London music publisher Novello promoted its sheet music through performances by members of the Novello family.[15] It was a less costly form of marketing than advertising. British composer Arthur Sullivan was another practitioner of pay-for-play. Before famously teaming up with William Gilbert, Sullivan secured public performances for his song "Thou'rt Passing Hence" by ceding a share of the royalties to Charles Santley, a leading baritone of the day.

American music publishers further developed pay-to-play by employing *song pluggers*. These colorful characters contrived to get the publishers' songs heard in a wide range of venues, including beer halls, department stores, the Coney Island amusement park, vaudeville, Broadway theaters, the St. Patrick's Day parade, and in one instance, a nudist colony. Deals were struck with organ grinders. Some pluggers performed on the sidewalk, while others—including the young George Gershwin—promoted new songs to motion picture audiences during intermission. Irving Berlin and Jerome Kern were among the other musical luminaries who got their start as pluggers.

The quest to get music heard continued after records supplanted sheet music as the industry's key product. In the 1930s and 1940s, publishers vied to get their songs included in the repertoire of dance bands. Many prominent bandleaders accepted compensation for selecting material proffered to them. Some were careful to pick only songs that suited the style of their orchestras, but others damaged their popularity through lack of discrimination.

In lieu of participating in pay-to-play arrangements by accepting cash, some bandleaders formed their own publishing companies. They could then agree to perform songs by not-yet-prominent songwriters, giving the tunes valuable exposure. As publishers, they could capture some of the value that their performances created by collecting a portion of the songs' royalties.

Radio became a competitive ground for music companies through broadcasts of the bands' live performances. After World War II, the "big band" era ended and the focus of radio programming shifted to recorded music. The disc jockeys who hosted the programs attracted personal followings and consequently became major influences on musical taste.

Throughout this history, music industry executives recognized that some forms of exposure were more valuable than others. During the period in which the key objective was to get songs performed onstage, it was generally acknowledged that a big-name singer could do more for a song's sales than a lesser-known vocalist. Al Jolson, who was billed as "The World's Greatest Entertainer," could almost automatically turn a song into a hit by singing it. Publishers were willing to pay for that marketing muscle. They routinely gave Jolson a cut of the royalties, listed him as a collaborating composer or lyricist or, in one case, presented him with a racehorse. Quid pro quos to other stars included free sheet music, arrangements, rehearsal rooms, accompanists, comedic introductory material, clothing, jewelry, and cash.

These arrangements, like the later payments to disc jockeys, were commonly described as *bribery*. That term has an undeniably unsavory connotation. But let's consider the transactions in economic terms.

The vaudeville headliners, through sales of sheet music that wouldn't otherwise occur, created value for the publishers whose songs they performed. But the performers couldn't capture any part of that value through the salaries they received for performing. That money came from theater ticket sales. In the absence of payments from the publishers to the performers, the publishers would get a free ride on the performers' talent and popularity. Critics of pay-to-play arrangements must explain why such an arrangement would have been more equitable than allowing performers to benefit from the value they created.

There is nothing unusual, in the business world, about spillover benefits of the sort that Al Jolson created by featuring a song in his act. Consider a prestigious retailing chain that agrees to locate an anchor store in a shopping mall. The high-profile department store will act as a magnet for shoppers who will also patronize the mall's specialty stores and restaurants. On the strength of that spillover business, the developer will be able to charge higher rents to the other tenants than the mall locations would command without the anchor store's presence.

In negotiating the anchor store's lease, the managers of the prestigious retailing chain will surely demand a price concession to reflect the value they create for the developer. Indeed, they would be poor businesspeople if they neglected to capture some of that value.

Nobody coins derogatory terms to describe the big-name retailer's intelligent business practice. The company doesn't get accused of seeking a bribe. The department store operator is simply participating in the profits it creates for others, just as Al Jolson did by accepting remuneration for transforming songs into hits.[16]

Today, just as in vaudeville days, consumers buy the music they hear. Radio stations create value for record companies by playing their records. The value arises not only from acquainting listeners with the tunes, but by indicating that the records are popular. When it comes to entertainment, consumers want not only what they like, but also what everybody likes.

Radio stations face a predicament much like that of the vaudevillians of old. They create value for record companies, but they can't capture that value through their main source of revenue, which is advertising for products other than records. If the record companies don't pay for airtime, they are free riding on the radio stations. Again, the question for critics of pay-for-play is, "What's fair about that?"

The retailing industry again provides a helpful analogy. In the intensely competitive business of branded consumer products, supermarket shelf space is extremely valuable. Shoppers can't buy a product if it isn't on the shelf. The more prominent the location is on the shelf, the more valuable the space is to the manufacturer. Recognizing the value that their shelf space creates for consumer goods manufacturers, supermarkets charge manufacturers for it, openly and legally. What, then, is reprehensible about radio stations capturing a portion of the value that their airtime creates for record manufacturers?

The difference, critics of payola might say, is that records ought to be selected on their merits, rather than for financial reasons. But this objection could also apply to the supermarket. Shoppers want to be able to buy the products that offer the best quality or best value for the money. Auctioning off the shelf space might not invariably result in those items being the ones available for sale.

With radio airtime, as with supermarket shelf space, the force of competition allays concerns about consumers' well-being. If shoppers find that a supermarket carries only poor-quality and overpriced products, they will take their business elsewhere. Whatever the store gains by selling shelf space to manufacturers, it will sacrifice through reduced sales to customers. Similarly, listeners will abandon a radio station if it plays unappealing and unpopular songs. That will be costly, because the rate that the station charges for its commercial time is proportional to the size of its audience.

Fears that either inferior potato chips or unpopular pop songs will be forced on unwilling consumers are unwarranted. Some readers may regard both mass-marketed branded goods and today's top-selling records as junk. But if those judgments are valid, the fault lies with the taste of consumers. Neither the sale of shelf space nor payola can induce them to buy products they don't want.

Rothbard doesn't do the distributors and recipients of payola justice by merely absolving them of fraud. Pay-to-play transactions constitute a legitimate market for a resource. Payola or something closely resembling it is essential if airtime is to be allocated for the maximum benefit to society.

PAY-TO-PLAY IS HERE TO STAY

Market practices invariably override attempts to outlaw the economically necessary function of pricing airtime. In the wake of Sony BMG's settlement of payola charges with New York Attorney General Spitzer, rock musician Jacob Slichter described the elaborate mechanisms that record companies have devised to circumvent payola restrictions. For example, bands perform at festivals organized and broadcast by the radio stations, without getting paid as much as they ordinarily receive for live concerts. This practice, referred to by one executive as "Show-ola," ensures the bands' records at least a modest amount of airtime.

A more important subterfuge involves operators who call themselves "independent record promoters." These gatekeepers shell out substantial amounts to radio stations. Although the payments, according to Slichter, are ostensibly for the privilege of looking at the stations' playlists, they are really, "as those in the business know, to get their clients' songs on the air."[17] The independent promoters then charge their record company clients for the supposed service.

This arrangement differs in form, but not in substance, from conventional payola. In lieu of cash flowing directly from the record company to the radio station, an intermediary takes a cut. Also, the payment of cash by the record company follows the receipt of cash by the radio station, instead of the two actions occurring simultaneously. These cosmetic changes make it difficult to establish a quid pro quo, that is, an exchange of cash for airtime. The transaction therefore escapes the prohibition on undisclosed payola, enabling the necessary market in airtime to function.

FORECLOSING DISCLOSURE

Slichter's account shows that when the government suppresses payola, virtual payola inexorably emerges to perform its essential economic function. Whether diluted or taken straight, payola puts most radio stations in no jeopardy of being victimized by commercial bribery. The larger stations headed off that problem, following the 1959 congressional payola hearings, by eliminating the disc jockeys' authority over the playlist.

Just one possible objection remains.[18] Because the radio spectrum is finite, radio stations must obtain government approval to operate. Regulators attach certain duties to the right to operate. This leads in turn to the notion that by assigning airtime on the basis of financial consideration, rather than according to the records' merits, the radio station betrays a public trust.[19]

Ronald Coase, who was awarded the Nobel Prize in Economic Sciences, points out that this objection has little practical significance.[20] Eliminating payola wouldn't make artistic merit the primary consideration for a record's inclusion in a radio station's playlist. It would instead eliminate a revenue source, making the station even more dependent on advertising revenues related to products other than records. That would shift the station's emphasis further in the direction of attracting the largest possible audience, to maximize the rates it can charge advertisers for its commercial time. Mass appeal, rather than aesthetic considerations, would become even more predominant in selecting records.[21]

Congress didn't focus on this point when it amended the Communications Act in 1960. The lawmakers did, however, provide a seemingly simple solution to the problems they perceived in radio stations' fulfillment of their obligations to the public. Instead of outlawing payola per se, the legislators prohibited *undisclosed* payola. The notion was that radio listeners wouldn't be harmed by pay-to-play arrangements as long as they knew that records were being selected for financial reasons, rather than on merit alone.

The FCC had a strict view of what constituted adequate disclosure. In early 1960, before Congress enacted the amendments, the commission unveiled its own response to the 1959 payola scandal. The FCC spelled out what was required, in its view, for radio stations to comply with certain existing provisions of the Communications Act. Under the tightened rules, stations would have to make announcements when they played records supplied at no charge by record companies. The announcements would have to state that consideration had been received for playing the records and specify who had provided the consideration. Additional announcements would be required whenever stations played records that were to be featured at record hops[22] and other outside activities, where airtime was to be exchanged for payment of a performer's fee, donation of records, or the use of a hall.

The broadcasting industry objected to these onerous requirements. In the course of amending the Communications Act, Congress was sympathetic to the broadcasters' complaints. According to Coase, however,

> no attempt was made to discover whether it might be possible to devise a form of announcement which would alert listeners to the fact that payments were made by record companies whose records were played (so that the "deception" could be prevented) without the clutter of announcements to which broadcasters objected.[23]

As a practical matter, radio stations were left with two ways to conduct the economically necessary market in airtime. One method was to engage in subterfuges such as the use of "independent record promoters" as middlemen. The other was to accept payola surreptitiously and face prosecution from time to time. Consequently, an activity that is deemed legitimate in most other industries remains a shady or criminal practice in broadcasting.

FOLLOW THE MONEY

Some system for allocating radio airtime is bound to exist, no matter whether payola is deemed lawful. A market mechanism is more economically efficient than other approaches to allocation. Furthermore, a pricing system for airtime could operate openly, given reasonable disclosure requirements.

In light of these facts, it is strange that Congress hasn't devised an approach to allocating airtime that avoids recurring payola scandals. Periodic prosecutions divert law enforcement resources from crimes that, unlike payola, have clearly identifiable victims.

The answer to this riddle is straightforward. Outlawing payola is a means of suppressing competition. It is axiomatic that the louder Big Business brays about competition as the United States' lifeblood, the more vigorously it presses Congress for insulation from competition. Big record companies are no exception to the rule, as demonstrated by the historical context of the 1959 payola scandal.

During the years 1948 through 1955, an average of 78 percent of the records on *Billboard*'s top 10 Hit Parade were produced by four companies—Capitol, Columbia, Decca, and RCA-Victor. Their share never dipped below 71 percent in those years, but in 1956 it fell to 66 percent. The major producers' market share declined steadily over the next three years until in 1959, the four companies accounted for only 34 percent of the top 10 hits. Their weakening grip on the music business was paralleled by a loss of dominance of number-one hits by the royalty collecting agency ASCAP to its main rival, BMI.

The cause of these changes was clear. Rock and roll arrived on the scene, thanks mainly to smaller, independent record companies such as Chess and Sun. The old-guard companies continued to concentrate on the more traditional popular music that had dominated the charts until the mid-1950s. Unfortunately, for them, record sales moved increasingly to a rock-and-roll beat. A list of artists achieving number-one hits in the early and late 1950s tells the story:[24]

1952	**1959**
Leroy Anderson	Paul Anka
Jimmy Boyd	Frankie Avalon
Percy Faith and His Orchestra	The Browns
Joni James	Dave "Baby" Cortez
Vera Lynn	Bobby Darin
Al Martino	The Fleetwoods
Patti Page	Wilbur Harrison

Jo Stafford	Guy Mitchell
Johnny Standley	The Platters
Kay Starr	Elvis Presley
Lloyd Price	Santo & Johnny

As 1952 chart-toppers, "I Saw Mommy Kissing Santa Claus" and "Auf Wiederseh'n Sweetheart" were displaced by 1959's "A Big Hunk O' Love" and the raucous "Kansas City," the companies with a big stake in the older-style music launched a counterattack. They capitalized on the view, widely held by parents of the teenagers who avidly bought the rock-and-roll records, that the new music was unwholesome.

Since at least 1951, trade sources had noted that payola was employed most aggressively by producers of a rock and roll's predecessor, rhythm and blues. For the independent record companies producing R&B and rock and roll, payola was a matter of necessity. They lacked the vast marketing organizations and established stars of the major record companies. Their only option was to work assiduously at the local level, angling for airtime by courting disc jockeys.

It was essential for small companies to get their records exposed quickly in this manner. Under the compulsory licensing feature of U.S. copyright law, a publisher doesn't obtain exclusive production rights when it buys a song from a songwriter. Any other publisher can produce the song, without the songwriter's permission, as long as it pays the songwriter a standard royalty. The result is that if a small company release becomes a hit, a big company can quickly produce its own "cover" of the song, performed by a bigger-name artist. Faced with a severe loss of sales to the major company's version, the independent must garner as much airtime as possible in its brief window of opportunity.

With payola in their arsenal, the independents managed to compete successfully against companies with much bigger bankrolls. Their success, however, made them vulnerable to allegations that immoral business methods were foisting immoral music on the public. Rock and roll was so manifestly bad, its detractors said, that only bribery could account for its presence on the airwaves. Politicians leapt at the chance to portray themselves as defenders of public morality and before long, the congressional payola hearings were front-page news.

In a remarkable exercise in spin control, the crusade to ban pay-to-play arrangements was portrayed as upholding David against Goliath. Congressman Oren Harris (D-AR) kicked off the payola inquiry by asserting that small record companies were being driven out of business because they lacked the means to survive the unfair competition of payola. In reality, all record companies appear to have given payola to disc jockeys. But it was the small companies that depended on it to stay in the game with better-capitalized competitors.

The effort to squelch the upstarts, disguised as moral rearmament, succeeded. Congress cracked down on payola through the 1960 amendments to the Communication Act. The companies that were financially able thereupon stepped up their other promotional activities, including advertising in the trade press, sales calls, and personal appearances by performers. Small record companies, which relied on wholesale intermediaries, couldn't compete with the big companies' powerful distribution systems.

As the independents were forced to cut deals with the major companies or sell out to them, the majors reasserted their control. By 1979, more than 85 percent of the U.S. market was in the hands of six companies—CBS, Capitol, MCA, Polygram, RCA, and Warner Communications.[25] To be fair, the majors owed much of their success to adapting to the changing tastes in music. They also benefited from the consolidation that normally occurs as an industry matures. But it didn't hurt that Congress had stomped on the independents' most affordable means of challenging them.

A LONG-PLAYING RECORD

Viewed in isolation, the events of 1959 through 1960 might not persuade every reader that the antipayola crusaders' true objective was to limit competition. Motives are hard to prove and lobbyists are skilled at covering their tracks. Over the long history of popular music, however, the major companies have consistently demonstrated their aversion to capitalism, "red in tooth and claw."

In the 1890s, sheet music publishers banded together agreed to stop paying singers to perform their songs. It was a standard attempt by an industry to beef up its profits by eliminating a cost of competing. Like most such efforts, it broke down through cheating. Publishers covertly made deals with the stars and when their perfidy was uncovered, the pact collapsed.

An ambitious attempt to root out pay-to-play agreements—then known as the "payment system"—occurred in 1916. John J. O'Connor, business manager of *Variety,* organized the Music Publishers Protective Association (MPPA). Its avowed goal was eradicating the "evil custom"[26] of paying singers and musicians to perform songs, which was alleged to be anticompetitive.

The result was mainly to drive pay-to-play agreements underground. Publishers agreed to abide by the MPPA's rules, but in lieu of paying performers directly, instead cut them in on song royalties. The MPPA reportedly plugged this loophole in 1917, but the rules against cut-ins were never stringently enforced. Before long, publishers were offering cuts of the royalties in exchange for having their songs used as flip sides for piano rolls and recordings of hit songs.

Cut-ins survived despite repeated efforts to root them out. In 1956, Elvis Presley topped the charts with "Heartbreak Hotel," written by steel guitarist Tommy Durden and songwriter Mae Boren Axton. Thanks to his shrewd manager, Colonel Tom Parker, Elvis received a co-songwriting credit for consenting to sing the tune.[27]

Parenthetically, it is interesting to speculate why *Variety*'s business manager took on the task of organizing the Music Publishers Protective Association. Economist Coase, following an earlier writer on the subject, suggests that payola may have been soaking up dollars that otherwise would have bought advertising in *Variety.* In its coverage of the MPPA, however, *Variety* referred to O'Connor as a music publishing industry "outsider," without bothering to mention his name.[28]

Unsuccessful in restricting competition through voluntary compliance, the MPPA eventually—perhaps inevitably—turned to the federal government. The industry association's opportunity arose with passage of the National Industrial Recovery Act of 1933. That Depression-era legislation empowered the members of an industry to formulate codes of conduct that became binding when signed by the president. In essence, the government's idea was to set aside, for the time being, its previous emphasis on fighting monopolies. By instead allowing companies within an industry to cooperate, the New Dealers hoped to revive business through a boost to corporate profits.

In formulating a code for the music publishing industry, the popular music wing pushed hardest for prohibition of pay-to-play schemes. The companies sought to ban not only direct cash payments to performers, but also indirect inducements such as the provision of free arrangements to bandleaders. MPPA Chairman John G. Paine made it clear, in the 1934 hearing on the proposed code, that the reason he sought federal help in suppressing the payment system was its heavy cost to the industry. He didn't point out that most industries, at most times, could improve their profits by agreeing to restrict competition, but that doesn't constitute a sound economic argument for encouraging anticompetitive pacts.

After the usual bureaucratic delays, the music publishing industry's proposed code won National Recovery Administration approval and became effective on March 18, 1935. On May 27, however, the United States Supreme Court declared the National Industrial Recovery Act unconstitutional. Along with other industries' codes, the MPPA's brainchild became inoperative.

Undaunted, Chairman Paine promptly submitted essentially the same code to the Federal Trade Commission (FTC), which was authorized to approve rules of fair trade practices for an industry. The FTC noted, however, that an antitrust suit was pending against ASCAP, to which the music publishers belonged. In addition, an independent music publisher had complained that some publishers were subsidiaries of motion picture producers. Those companies, which also owned movie theaters, had captive outlets for exposing their music to potential sheet music buyers. They didn't need the additional plugs of live performances in hotels and restaurants, which were the only ones available to the independents. The FTC's chief examiner concluded that the MPPA's proposed rules would spell the doom of the independent publisher. In 1938, the FTC rejected fair trade practice rules for the music publishing industry.

The last major campaign to eliminate payola, prior to the congressional hearings of the 1950s, was waged by the Music Publishers' Contact Employees Union. The song pluggers who constituted the membership feared that their services would no longer be needed if music companies could obtain satisfactory exposure for songs simply by writing checks to performers.

As economist Coase notes, this particular complaint highlighted an economic inefficiency associated with suppressing pay-to-play agreements. By blocking the replacement of one form of promotion with another, less resource-intensive one, a ban on pay-to-play tends to reduce the gross national product.[29] In any event, the song pluggers' effort foundered, partly because another affiliate of the American Federation of Labor, the American Federation of Musicians, had payola recipients among its members.

THE BOTTOM LINE

It is hardly surprising that record companies would want to beef up their profits by limiting competition. Neither is it out of character for an industry to seek the government's collusion in its schemes. But there is no legitimate reason for the government to take up the cause.

Pay-to-play arrangements have proven durable for well over a century in the music business, despite repeated efforts to eradicate them. Two lessons can be drawn from the experience. First, one way or another, music producers will spend money on the only form of promotion that sells their product effectively—getting it heard by consumers. Second, payola performs a necessary function of pricing airtime, a valuable resource.

Economists figured this out 50 years ago. Politicians can be forgiven for taking a while to catch up, but it should be clear by now that payola isn't going away. Payola should be recognized as a legitimate activity, much like the consumer goods manufacturers' payment for shelf space at supermarkets. If accompanied by disclosure that doesn't clutter up the airwaves, payola could come out of hiding and the government could cease tying up vast resources in pointless investigations and prosecutions.

11

What Is Big Brother Watching?

Congress could choose to concern itself with poverty, failing schools, environmental dangers, terrorism, or the moral quandaries presented by advances in medical science. All these issues seem likely to affect the national well-being more profoundly than the accuracy of television audience ratings. Politicians' long-standing interest in the subject illustrates why voters should question the rationales advanced for government intervention into ordinary commercial activities. Behind most lofty purposes are self-serving interests with lots of cash to spread around.

A CALL TO ARMS

When people gripe about the quality of television programs, they typically blame the networks' habit of aiming for the lowest common denominator of viewer intelligence. In 2004, Senator Conrad Burns (R-MT) offered an alternative hypothesis. "It's impossible to achieve a high quality of broadcasting," he declared, "if shoddy audience measurement practices are permitted to proliferate."[1]

Stephen Miller, a legislative fellow in Senator Burns's office, later revealed that Congress considered the quality of television ratings a public interest issue. The crux of the matter, he said, was whether the ratings were fair and accurate.[2] Burns vowed that if existing laws didn't give the Federal Trade Commission (FTC) the necessary authority to ensure that ratings were run in the public's best interest, he would seek to create federal oversight through new legislation.[3]

Despite politicians' instinct to expand their control over economic activity at every opportunity, two of Burns's congressional colleagues spoke up against his crusade. Representatives Dan Burton (R-IN) and Jesse Jackson Jr. (D-IL) decried federal ratings of television audience ratings as an unnecessary intrusion. "Should it be the Federal government's responsibility to inform Americans that *American Idol* was last week's number-one show in its timeslot?" they asked.[4] In Burton and Jackson's view, the boardroom, rather than the halls of Congress, was the proper place to debate the reliability of technology employed by the main television audience rater, ACNielsen.

The push for increased intervention in television ratings involved a great deal of dissimulation. Much of the criticism of existing ratings methods emanated from companies that represented major obstacles to improving the system. Proponents of an expanded role for government even depicted the arcane details of audience measurement as a civil rights issue. To explain how this tangled web was woven, it is necessary first to give a flavor of the nonpolitical challenges facing ratings providers.

THE CHALLENGES OF MEASURING AUDIENCES

There is no cost-effective way to determine what every single television viewer in the United States is watching at a given moment. Therefore, audience measurement is invariably based on a sample of the population.[5] The sample consists of a small portion—as little as 0.004 percent—of the total population being analyzed.

Even so, the data collected on the sample can accurately reflect the viewing habits of the entire audience if the sample is representative of the total population. In pursuit of that ideal, rating companies strive to construct samples with the same demographic breakdown as the full television audience. Weighting factors include family size, sex, income, education, age of the head of household, and access to cable television.

The practical challenges of creating and maintaining a valid sample are formidable. About half of the households randomly selected for the sample decline to participate. Those who do agree grow tired, after a time, of following the required procedures.

As a consequence, the rating company must continuously refresh its sample with new participants. That is an expensive proposition. To the extent that the surveyor tries to control its costs, the sample may lose some of its precision in representing the full audience.

Three basic surveying methods are available to ratings providers:

1. Diaries.
2. Meters.
3. Telephone surveys.

Each method has its own operational challenges.

Diaries

The diary method requires families to write down what they watch and mail in their records. Only about 50 percent of the diaries are typically usable.[6] The rest are either filled out incorrectly or else never get mailed back. Many viewers don't log in their selections while watching television, but instead wait until the deadline for mailing in their diaries. At that point, they attempt to reconstruct what they watched, possibly with the help of a copy of *TV Guide*. Some individuals, perhaps embarrassed to admit that they watch certain programs, fill out their diaries dishonestly.

Meters

The best-known form of direct monitoring of viewers' program choices is Nielsen's *Peoplemeter*. This is a box with buttons that people use to log in every time they tune in their televisions. The Peoplemeter's major drawback is button-pushing fatigue. As a result, Nielsen may undercount subcategories of the television audience that are disproportionately prone to neglect their duty.

When Peoplemeters replaced diaries in some of Nielsen's surveys, ratings on children's programs plummeted. According to one explanation, the youngsters were less conscientious about pushing the button than their mothers had been about filling out the diaries. As another consequence of the introduction of Peoplemeters, ratings on sports programs skyrocketed. Once again, the proposed explanation assumed that the woman of the household had been filling out the diary. According to this view, wives hadn't realized how much time their husbands were devoting to watching sports. According to this story, the husbands punched the buttons religiously because they feared that the television would shut off if they didn't.

A major disadvantage of metering is its high cost. The expense isn't a big issue for the national networks, but is significant at the local level. Only the largest regional TV markets (about a quarter of the total) can afford to pay for electronic measurement. Others have to rely on the less accurate diary system. (Where the Peoplemeter is not yet in use, some local stations employ devices known as *set meters,* which automatically go into action when viewers turn on their sets.)[7]

Telephone Surveys

Calling people to ask what they are watching is prone to several kinds of distortion. For one thing, many viewers are reluctant to give information over the phone because they fear that the caller is actually a salesperson. Also, the interviewees' responses may be influenced by the interviewer's attitude or tone. Finally, some respondents misrepresent what they watch, hoping to present themselves in a more favorable light.

Potential technological solutions to the inaccuracy of ratings are already available, but some of them conjure up images of George Orwell's Big Brother.[8] One such technology is already used in cable-based pay-per-view service. In this system, a button on the viewer's remote control device enables a customer to order a program. Pushing the button signals the cable system operator to unscramble the desired channel. The same technology could record what is showing on the television set at all times, but consumers would probably consider the practice an invasion of privacy. Similar objections doomed a method briefly employed in the 1970s. The technology consisted of trucks driving through neighborhoods and recording the program being viewed on every TV set.

THE BACK STORY

When Senator Burns launched his campaign to regulate television audience ratings in 2004, he wasn't entering virgin territory.[9] In 1963, the House of Representatives conducted hearings in the wake of a cease and desist order by the FTC. That agency ordered several audience measurement companies to stop misrepresenting the accuracy and reliability of their reports.

In response to the government's concerns, the broadcasting industry established an accrediting bureau, the Broadcast Rating Council, by special permission of the Justice Department. The organization, which is now known as the Media Rating Council (MRC), sets minimum standards for ratings companies involved in television, radio, multimedia, print, and the Internet. An independent accounting firm audits the companies' compliance with the standards. A key point is that ratings companies aren't compelled to obtain MRC accreditation.[10]

Nobody, including the ratings companies, suggests that the present system produces perfect audience measurement. But gains in accuracy have a price. It comes down to how much advertisers and media companies are willing to be charged by the ratings providers for incremental improvements in the system.

Media companies' reluctance to foot the bill isn't the only obstacle to better audience measurement. Broadcast and cable television networks actually go out of their way to distort the ratings by revising their offerings during *Sweeps* weeks, the quarterly ratings periods for local stations. Ratings in those weeks determine advertising rates for the succeeding three months.

To maximize their Sweeps week ratings, local television stations air their most sensational material. Broadcast networks lend their local affiliates a helping hand by replacing regular series with star-studded specials. Cable networks, for their part, schedule new programs instead of reruns. As a result, advertising rates reflect the local stations' skill in artificially pumping up viewership for short bursts, rather than their ability to deliver large audiences week in and week out.[11] The bottom line is that whatever they may tell Congress and the public, media companies are more interested in high ratings than in accurate ratings.

NOT EVERYONE IS FLATTERED BY A TRUE REFLECTION

Sweeps create a dilemma. The high stakes, combined with the media companies' efforts to rig the results, put a premium on accurate ratings.

Diaries, which historically have predominated in local markets, aren't up to the task. But better measurement costs more than local stations have been willing or able to pay.

In May 2002, Nielsen forced the issue. Choosing Boston as a test market, the company replaced diaries with Peoplemeters for local ratings. The impact on ratings was immediate and profound. Ratings plummeted by almost a third at some local stations, while cable ratings skyrocketed.

This result didn't surprise knowledgeable analysts. A family that regularly watches *Law & Order* is likely to list the program in its diary even if it misses the show one week. The same family will forget having seen part of an obscure cable show that it had never previously watched. Peoplemeters corrected such errors, but the local Boston stations didn't regard that as an improvement. Many of them stopped using Nielsen altogether.

Additional opposition to Peoplemeters arose as ratings declined for certain prime time shows geared to African Americans. Examples included *The Parkers, Girlfriends, Eve,* and *Half & Half.* Nielsen attributed the change to an improvement in accuracy over the diary method.

That answer didn't satisfy Congressman Gregory Meeks (D-NY). He thundered that minority shows would get canceled because of the ratings drops. In his opinion, axing the programs would "harm minority empowerment" and "set back the cause of equal representation." To some, this harm didn't warrant the same outrage as segregated schools or discriminatory hiring. The liberal *New Republic* gibed that Meeks didn't appear concerned about "[s]etting back the moral gravity of the civil rights movement by wasting it on TV ratings."[12]

The Congressional Hispanic Caucus Institute likewise portrayed the ratings controversy as a matter of minority group empowerment. If Latinos were being accurately counted by Nielsen, the research unit argued, advertisers and broadcasters would be vigorously tapping into their substantial purchasing power. The absence of day-to-day programming catering to Latinos, the Institute maintained, proved that they were not.

This logic, presented in a policy brief, seemed a trifle strained. In fact, the authors noted that the data limitations were more severe than they had foreseen. As a result, they could claim only to be "inferring that Nielsen (television) ratings may not be correct in reflecting the television rating habits of Latinos in the United States."[13] Nevertheless, the Institute's researchers were resolute in their conclusion that the government needed to step in. For starters, they said, "Congress should engage Latino advocacy groups in a public-private partnership to alert the business community of the purchasing power of Latinos."[14]

Although that jargon-laden recommendation was slightly vague, the Institute's second proposed action step was a veritable blueprint for action. The Institute advocated fostering competition in the ratings business through small-business incentives. In short, like any other group of politicians, the Hispanic Caucus hoped to get some federal dollars laid on its constituents.

FOLLOWING THE MONEY

Surprise of surprises, business interests in ethnic communities were not the only ones with a financial stake in the controversy over diaries versus Peoplemeters. News Corporation, headed by media mogul Rupert Murdoch, generously supported the minority groups' anti-Peoplemeter campaign, which labeled itself, "Don't Count Us Out/Queremos Ser Contados." According to the *New York Times,* News Corporation spent nearly $2 million organizing news conferences and demonstrations, operating phone banks, and advertising in newspapers and on television stations around the country.[15]

Little imagination was needed to guess why News Corporation took such a strong interest in the issue. Its two New York stations depended heavily on minority audiences. Reduced ratings on minority-oriented programs hit Murdoch right on the bottom line.

The likelihood that the new results represented an improvement in accuracy didn't sway the billionaire publisher's view of the matter. Inconveniently for the Don't Count Us Out line of reasoning, ratings for certain minority-oriented cable network programming *increased* following the introduction of Peoplemeters. In the March 2004 New York ratings, the reported black viewership of the Black Entertainment Network soared by 180 percent and Telefutura's reported Hispanic audience jumped by 83 percent.[16]

This effect was part of a general finding that the diary method had been overstating the viewership of broadcast networks, compared with that of cable networks. Black households, the new technology indicated, were devoting 54.2 percent of their viewing time to cable, not the 39.2 percent suggested by diaries.[17] Rupert Murdoch had a particularly strong financial stake in keeping advertisers in the dark about this particular trend. News Corporation was more concentrated in traditional broadcasting, with less of a stake in cable, than the corporate parents of the ABC, CBS, and NBC broadcast networks.

DOLLARS AND SENSITIVITY

Notwithstanding the spin doctoring by the opponents of Peoplemeter deployment in local ratings, the device was neither new nor unproven when Nielsen started installing it in Boston in 2002. Nielsen introduced the Peoplemeter for national ratings in 1987. Broadcasters initially complained, as ratings points shifted from high-rated to low-rated shows and from broadcast to cable networks. Eventually, however, Peoplemeters came to "set the standard for TV measurement in the United States," according to *BusinessWeek*.[18]

Media expert Randall Rothenberg put the case bluntly, saying that the potential undercounting of minority views was not Rupert Murdoch's real concern about the "new" technology:

> His actual worry is that Peoplemeters will be better than the diary system currently in place to measure audiences. He's not alone: All mainstream media companies are scared to death of improved measurement.[19]

According to Rothenberg, broadcasters and advertising agencies benefit from inaccurate measurement. Uncertainty, he explained, fosters an inflated notion of the effectiveness of mass media. For that reason, said Rothenberg, broadcasters opposed the Peoplemeter from the time it was introduced for national ratings, a decade-and-a-half earlier.

Rothenberg wasn't unique in identifying the users of the ratings as the primary obstacles to the improved accuracy they claimed to desire. The *Wall Street Journal* wrote:

> For 2 decades, networks correctly worried that better data would show declining ratings, and they didn't want to pay for an upgrade. For their

part, ad agencies accepted the rickety system because starting a competitor would be exorbitantly expensive for them.[20]

The hypocrisy became flagrant when Nielsen started to roll Peoplemeters into local markets. In October 2003, News Corporation Fox Television Station Group agreed to buy Nielsen's Peoplemeter data in all nine of the top-10 markets in which it owned stations. That decision was supported by 16 years of industry experience with Peoplemeters in the national market. Presumably, that gave broadcasters a sufficient opportunity to identify any irremediable technical problems. It was only in February 2004, after the Peoplemeter test-run data showed a sharp drop in Fox stations' ratings, that News Corporation tried to talk Nielsen into postponing the launch of commercial service.[21]

All of a sudden, News Corporation and its allies were blitzing the media with accusations of racially biased ratings. Black activist Al Sharpton burst into the office of Susan Whiting, president of Nielsen, to deliver a tongue-lashing while reporters huddled outside.[22] News Corporation's tactics were so aggressive that several other media companies dissociated themselves from the Don't Count Us Out campaign. They concluded that they were better off working with Nielsen to fix the shortcomings in its methods.

Proving the adage about politics making strange bedfellows, Senator Hillary Clinton (D-NY) volunteered for duty in the war against Peoplemeters. Clinton was ideologically remote from the conservative Murdoch. In fact, Murdoch's *New York Post* had long delighted in blasting the former First Lady, at one point running the headline "Shame on Hillary" after she embraced Palestinian leader Yassir Arafat's wife.[23] But according to the *New York Amsterdam News,* which serves the African American community, Senator Clinton's loyalists were "definitely opposed to any rating system that would affect their political base among minorities."[24]

Understandably, the anti-Peoplemeter public relations campaign dwelt on race more than on News Corporation's profit margins. One not-too-subtle newspaper advertisement depicted a black family watching television while a white man wearing a white suit stood in their living room, watching them. The ad was headlined, "Nielsen has control over what you watch. So shouldn't somebody be watching Nielsen?"[25] That dubious reasoning omitted both the networks' control over what viewers watch and the Media Rating Council's long-standing mandate to watch Nielsen.

RACE MATTERS (UP TO A POINT)

To be fair, there was a plausible case that race had at least a small influence on Peoplemeter readings. Unlike diaries, the new technology required all viewers in the household to push buttons every time they sat down to watch TV. The Don't Count Us Out campaigners argued that black and Hispanic households had a higher fault rate (failure to push the button) than white households. The minority groups' program choices, argued the coalition, were consequently undercounted.[26]

Also, in testimony before the Senate Committee on Commerce, Science and Transportation, Univision President Tom Arnost buttressed his case for government intervention with statistical evidence. He claimed that in Nielsen's Peoplemeter sample, 18- to 34-year-old Hispanic males, Spanish-speaking households, and large Hispanic households were underrepresented. Arnost even showed that Nielsen's May 2004 national ratings for the total Los Angeles audience indicated lower viewing of Spanish-language programs than the company's Hispanic-only local ratings for the same period—a statistical impossibility. He concluded, based on such technical glitches, that federal oversight was necessary.[27]

The experts were not unanimous, however, in criticizing local Peoplemeters on racial grounds. One veteran of media research who testified in favor of expanded government regulation was Gale Metzger. Metzger formerly chaired the Board of the Advertising Research Foundation and was a key force behind SMART, a 1990s Nielsen competitor. He stated that it was unfortunate that the local Peoplemeter discussion had focused mainly on issues of minority measurement. "While I believe audience measurements should be inspected for all important population subgroups," he said, "I do not believe race or ethnicity is the primary issue with the LPM."[28]

Neither did every advocate of minority interests perceive a benefit in tightening the reins on Nielsen. One opponent of new regulation was the National Urban League, which describes itself as "the nation's oldest and largest community-based movement devoted to empowering African Americans to enter the economic and social mainstream."[29] National Urban League President Marc Morial stated that a bill proposed by Senator Burns in 2005 "would make it nearly impossible to make improvements in TV ratings technology [and] would make it harder to more accurately measure people of color and television audiences." Opposing the legislation as well were civil rights activist Jesse Jackson and Asian-language broadcaster KTSF (San Francisco).[30]

Finally, fairness to Nielsen requires acknowledging the steps that the company took to ensure adequate representation of minority groups. Nielsen stated that in New York it *overrepresented* black and Hispanic households, relative to 2000 Census Bureau figures. Management's rationale was the possibility that the census had undercounted the two groups.[31] Also, the company cooperated with a task force charged with reviewing minority-related measurement problems. Nielsen reported in March 2005 that it was committed to implementing many of the task force's recommendations.[32]

THE RATINGS STRUGGLE ESCALATES

In May 2004, the Media Rating Council (MRC) declined to accredit Peoplemeters for local markets, citing unspecified performance issues that its audit had identified. But the Council's action scarcely constituted a stinging rebuke of Nielsen. For one thing, the MRC praised the Peoplemeter technology as an improvement over the diary system. What's more, the Council strongly urged the News Corporation to suspend its anti-Peoplemeter campaign immediately.[33] MRC Executive Director George Ivie later said that the Council was happy with Nielsen's responsiveness. He described the company as "very engaged in the MRC process for the LPM [local Peoplemeter] markets and responding to our concerns with focused improvement plans and initiatives."[34]

Even though it hadn't yet achieved accreditation for Peoplemeters in the New York local market, Nielsen decided to go forward. The company pointed out that when it introduced the new technology in Boston in 2002, the MRC accredited the new system subsequent to the commencement of operations.[35] Later, after somebody leaked the details of the MRC's audit to the press, Nielsen stated that it was working on the identified flaws, which involved just four out of 85 audited areas.

Nielsen had indicated that it planned to convert the 10 largest local television markets to Peoplemeters by the end of 2005. In response to the company's decision to proceed in New York, Spanish-language media company Univision Communications sued to block the company's Los Angeles launch.[36] Nielsen responded by charging that Univision was trying to maintain inflated and inaccurate ratings on its own programs as its competitors' ratings rose.[37]

When the court ruled against Univision, the anti-Peoplemeter forces carried the battle to Washington. News Corporation pushed the idea of increased government oversight of the ratings. Tom Herwitz, president of station operations, asserted that this intervention was necessary to protect consumers from Nielsen's monopoly practices.[38] Never mind that Nielsen doesn't sell its services to the public, making it difficult to establish what harm consumers were incurring at the ratings company's hands. News Corporation and the Don't Count Us Out coalition received another setback when the Federal Trade Commission decided that television ratings were best left to private business. Murdoch's crusade continued nevertheless.[39]

News Corporation's lobbying bore fruit in July 2005, when Senator Burns introduced a bill grandly entitled the Fairness, Accuracy, Inclusivity, and Responsiveness in Ratings (FAIR Ratings) Act. Burns enlisted three Republican Senators as cosponsors. In the House, Representative Vito Fossella (R–NY) introduced the bill and attracted 13 cosponsors; two Democrats agreed to attach their name to the bill.[40]

The proposed legislation would make MRC accreditation mandatory for companies offering their ratings as a basis for determining advertising rates. By the by, the bill's supporters received more than $90,000 in campaign contributions from News Corporation's political action committee (PAC) in 2005.[41] To put that figure in perspective, the PAC's 2004 disbursements to individuals totaled $130,500.[42] Despite the Fox network's conservative editorial line, 55 percent of the 2004 disbursements went to Democrats. For corporations, participating in the political process is not about advancing a philosophy; it is about making friends in high places.

It wasn't clear how big a threat the proposed FAIR Ratings Act posed to Nielsen. By the time Burns introduced the bill, the Peoplemeter had achieved full accreditation in Boston and San Francisco, although it was still awaiting the MRC's blessing in New York, Chicago, and Los Angeles.[43] On the other hand, Nielsen reported that if the bill passed, its local Hispanic service in 19 local markets would have to close down for lack of MRC accreditation.[44] This was hardly a desirable outcome, if the News Corporation/Don't Count Us Out campaign's true intent was to empower minority groups.

Also worth considering is the freedom that media companies enjoy under the nonmandatory system. Suppose they suspect that political pressure on the MRC is the main factor blocking accreditation of a service they consider superior to the alternatives. The media companies can buy the service, based on the ratings provider's past record of ironing out the remaining technical problems.

COMPETITION—ACTUAL AND POTENTIAL

Government intervention isn't usually the first resort of consumers or businesses who are dissatisfied with a service. Ordinarily, the swifter and more effective solution is for a competitor to provide a better or less expensive service. In the case of television ratings, though, media companies complain that ACNielsen has no serious competitor.

It doesn't automatically follow, however, that it is the government's duty to step into the breach. The shortcomings of present audience ratings partly reflect the unwillingness of networks, local stations, and advertisers to pay for something better. To some extent, tight purse strings also explain the absence of a major alternative supplier of TV ratings.

In 1994, the three major broadcast television networks created a competitor to Nielsen. The Systems for Measuring and Reporting Television (SMART) received $40 million in funding from 30 telecasters, advertisers, and agency sponsors. But after failing to achieve full industry support, SMART closed down in 1999.[45]

Perhaps, as media consultant Erwin Ephron suggests, the market's need for a single set of accepted ratings represents a stiff barrier to entry for companies wishing to compete head-on with Nielsen.[46] On the other hand, Nielsen doesn't have the field all to itself. Other companies collect and disseminate specialized ratings. One tracks the viewership of news programs. Another focuses on Latino audiences.[47]

Capitalizing on a gap in local ratings in small markets, former Meridian, Mississippi, station manager Marc Grossman launched Real Ratings, using a computerized phone calling system. Notwithstanding claims about barriers to entry, Grossman managed to raise the necessary capital from private investors. And as a Nielsen spokesperson noted, starting a ratings company requires no special license. "All you have to do is collect, process, and report the data."[48]

Even small-scale competition, or for that matter, the possibility of future competition, can keep a market giant on its toes. Astute managers recognize that complacency in the face of rapidly evolving technology can be fatal. The penalty may be getting knocked out of a market position that once appeared unassailable. This hazard is described in a classic 1960 *Harvard Business Review* article, "Marketing Myopia."[49] The author details how an entire industry (rail transportation) stagnated because it failed to focus properly on its customers' needs.

By all appearances, ACNielsen circa 2004 wasn't waiting around to be knocked off its perch by an upstart. Expanding the use of Peoplemeters to local markets was an example of a technological improvement adopted under no immediate competitive threat. And aware that some local markets might be too small ever to afford Peoplemeters, Nielsen invested heavily to upgrade its diary-based surveys. The company poured more than $34 million into research, development, and implementation of the improved (and twice-as-expensive) diary. Among other things, Nielsen made the diary easier to read, enabled viewers to indicate when the television was on but not being watched, and stepped up the volume of mailing to demographic groups with low response rates.[50]

Finally, overseas experience suggests that competing ratings providers can survive, despite a supposed structural tendency toward monopoly. European telecasters purchase audience measurement through Joint Industry Committees (JICs) or Media Owner Committees (MOCs). These entities periodically take bids from several different providers and award contracts to provide ratings, based on such factors as cost, reliability, and technology.[51] If American networks are sincere about desiring competition, they may be able to foster it by creating their own JIC or MOC, provided the arrangement can past muster under the applicable antitrust rules.[52] As a matter of fact, refining the antitrust rules to facilitate such an arrangement might be a constructive, nonintrusive way for Congress to help the users of television ratings.

THE BOTTOM LINE

As time goes on, audience measurement is only getting harder. People are increasingly skipping commercials, which weakens the link between the ratings and their value to advertisers. Additional challenges arise from the proliferation of channels and new ways of using television, such as TiVo, games, and DVD.[53] Audience ratings fail to capture TV-watching outside homes, on college campuses and in bars, gyms, hotels, and offices.[54]

Challenges are nothing new in the ratings business, however. When ACNielsen began using Peoplemeters for national ratings in 1987, things didn't go smoothly right away. But the company responded to its customers' criticisms and won them over to the new system. Nielsen achieved this without immediate competitive pressure or a government-legislated system of mandatory accreditation by the Media Rating Council.

Judging by the marketplace's record of working out the kinks, it is hard to justify expanded involvement by Congress. It is certainly indefensible to act at the behest of media companies that simply don't like the message delivered by the improved data. If the reality is that cable television is capturing a larger audience share than a more primitive surveying method suggested, then hurray for media companies that shrewdly placed large bets on cable. For the losers, the proper message to send is that it isn't government's role to indemnify capitalists against bad guesses.

The case for intrusion isn't strengthened by the happenstance that a technological advance caused ratings to drop on some (although not all) minority-oriented programs. Down that path of false fairness lies a law requiring ratings to be *inaccurate*. In any case, it is hard to argue that the sociological ramifications of a canceled television program should be anywhere near the top of lawmakers' agenda.

Television ratings represent an especially ludicrous example of politicians asserting that they can make the economy function better by intervening. The true impetus for this bogus reform is not a breakdown of the market, but rather the desire of certain market participants to rig the system in their own favor. Political support for the charade comes from both Republicans and Democrats. It is a sad commentary that bipartisanship is often difficult to summon on matters as vital as national security, but is easy to obtain when the mission caters to vested interests.

12

Getting Cash and Making the Rent

Politicians of the left and of the right differ in their code words. Liberals depict themselves as caring people who refuse to consign those in need to the mercy of impersonal market forces. Conservatives preach self-reliance and extol the virtues of competition. But in their heart of hearts, office seekers across a broad ideological spectrum share a fundamental conviction: Government intrusion is the solution to all economic problems, real or perceived. The only difference between Republicans and Democrats involves the interest groups they prefer to subsidize.

Not even the simple act of withdrawing cash from an automatic teller machine (ATM) is a matter that politicians can leave alone. In a competitive market, banks and consumers ought to be capable of working out the best way to pay for the convenience of instant access to cash. But leave it to politicians to turn the question into a rich opportunity for demagoguery.

Governments of only a few cities in the United States engage in the folly of regulating rents. Pricing leases on residential property is another straightforward matter for the users and providers of the service. The reason for discussing rent control along with other unwarranted intrusions is that it persists in the face of manifestly disastrous economic consequences. Citizens who hope to free the marketplace of ill-advised government intervention need to recognize what they are up against in terms of politicians' determination to stick with counterproductive policies.

NEED READY CASH?

Following the War for Independence, the American people were determined to secure the rights for which they had fought with such determination and valor. It took about as long from the end of the war as the war had lasted,[1] but in the end the nation enshrined a list of sacrosanct rights in the Constitution. The enumerated rights included, among others, the right to speak freely, to assemble peacefully, to worship according to one's conscience, to bear arms, and to avoid self-incrimination.

Not included in the United States Bill of Rights was the right to free use of an ATM. Nevertheless, in 1997 Massachusetts State Senator W. Paul White became incensed when he was obliged to shell out $3.00 to obtain cash in California. "Nobody should have to pay for the right to use an ATM machine," the indignant legislator declared.[2]

Did the patriots of Lexington and Concord die in vain? Not so. The ability to get folding money at any hour of the day or night is not an inalienable right. It is a service, like online movie tickets or satellite radio, that exists because somebody risked capital on a new idea. Politicians' attempts to dictate the pricing of ATM service represent just one more case of unwarranted intrusion in ordinary commerce.

Remembering Why Companies Innovate

The memory may be fading, but in bygone years it was hard for people to lay hold of their own cash. To convert part of the balances in their checking accounts into 10- and 20-dollar bills, they had to trek to branches of their banks. Inconveniently enough, the banks were open mainly during hours when many of those people worked. Running short of cash on a weekend meant raiding the children's piggy banks, finding a merchant willing to cash a personal check, or refraining from any sort of cash transaction until Monday.

Somehow, people managed. They would still be managing somehow if a combination of technology and profit motive hadn't brought about one of the greatest quality-of-life improvements of the past generation. Thanks to the introduction of the automatic teller machine, cash is available whenever depositors want it.

No intelligent adult imagines that banks have incurred the formidable expense of installing ATMs out of sheer altruism. As with any other investment in their business, bankers expect their outlays on cash machines to contribute to profits. The basic strategy is to attract and retain depositors by providing the service enhancement of 24-hour access to cash. By earning interest on the freshly opened accounts and by doing other types of business with the new customers, the bank hopes to realize a profit on its investment in ATMs. Banks may also profit through cost reductions achieved by handling routine customer transactions through ATMs instead of tellers.

Keeping Shirkers off the Network

In theory, there's another way to profit from installing ATMs. A bank could charge its customers a dollar or two for each use of an ATM. But the industry hasn't followed that path. The proliferation of cash machines indicates that banks can justify the investment without collecting usage fees from their own customers.

Use of a bank's ATM by the customers of *other* banks raises different issues. "Foreign usage" is possible because enterprising financial services companies have undertaken to organize ATM networks. Customers of any bank in a network can obtain cash from an ATM of any other participating bank. This arrangement multiplies the convenience factor for ATM users, but poses a potential difficulty.

Once a bank joins a network, its customers enjoy access to all the ATMs on the network. Unless the network somehow blocks it, the bank can then become a free rider. That is, it can cease building ATMs or even save money by eliminating some of its existing ATMs. By this stratagem, the bank shifts the considerable cost of building and maintaining ATMs onto its competitors, while still being able to match any other bank in convenience offered to customers.

Failure to prevent free riding would produce a bad outcome for consumers. Every bank would have an incentive to sponge off its competitors. They would all hold back on building ATMs. The result would be fewer ATM locations than the true economics would justify and less convenience for bank customers.

Fortunately, the networks prevent free riding through "interchange fees." Each time a customer of Alpha Bank uses an ATM owned by Beta Bank, Beta Bank receives a payment from Alpha Bank. This charge reduces Alpha Bank's incentive to make ATM service available to its customers only through competitors' machines. Interchange fees save consumers from a world in which banks vie to provide as few ATMs as possible.

Competing Strategies

Barring political interference in the matter, the networks' participating banks face a range of strategic options in dealing with the costs they incur through interchange fees:

- A bank could recoup the interchange fees by charging its customers for their use of other banks' ATMs. These amounts wouldn't be collected at the ATM, but through service charges on customers' monthly account statements.

- A bank could collect a fee, as part of the ATM transaction, each time another bank's customer uses one of its ATMs. In addition to generating additional revenue, a bank with an especially large number of ATMs could employ this strategy to lure depositors away from competitors. The opportunity to avoid foreign use fees would make it worthwhile for consumers who regularly use its conveniently located ATMs to switch their accounts. Some consumers might avoid the fees by traveling an extra distance to use a different bank's ATM. That would reduce the foreign-fee-imposing bank's revenue from interchange fees.

- A bank could do neither of these, concluding that its optimal strategy is to maximize its opportunity to earn interchange fees while also attracting and retaining customers with a low-fee policy that doesn't charge them for using other banks' ATMs.

All three approaches have been observed in the marketplace. Competing banks have adopted different strategies and modified them based on the results. As the competitive landscape has changed, banks have revised their strategies.

To economists, this constant jockeying for advantage is a good thing. It leads to cost-effective use of the resources employed in providing banking services. That, in turn, contributes to overall economic growth.

Nothing is required of politicians to make it all work smoothly, except to refrain from actions that hamper vigorous competition. Those actions might include paying off campaign contributors by enacting rules that tilt the playing field in favor of selected factions within the banking industry. Another example would be waiting until after business innovators have incurred the substantial technological and financial risks of introducing ATMs, then proclaiming that consumers have a right to use them for free.

Politicians have proven themselves psychologically incapable of meeting the simple requirement of standing aside and letting competition work. True to character, legislators haven't been content to let the market sort out the best ways to provide and price ATMs. Instead of letting consumers take their business to the firms that offer the most attractive trade-off of convenience and cost, office holders have striven to limit the banks' choice of strategies.

Politicians Respond to the Outcry

Prior to April 1996, charges for noncustomer use of ATMs were not allowed in 35 states. The nationwide Plus and Cirrus ATM networks also prohibited them. In April 1996, the two networks lifted their restriction. By April 2001, the practice was permitted in all states except Iowa, which maintained an administrative ban. At that time, the fees averaged $1.39.[3]

Not surprisingly, consumers objected to paying for a service they had previously received with no explicit charge.[4] Advocacy groups took up the cry. "Imagine stopping at the ATM at your local gas station late at night to get $20 to pick up diapers or milk and being hit by an extra charge of $3.90 because you're not at your local bank," wrote the Public Campaign.[5] That was the allegedly outrageous fee that a gas station in Rock Springs, Arizona, was charging its customers for ATM use.

Never mind that the convenience of being able to use an ATM late at night is the very reason anyone would pay $3.90 to use an ATM. For similar reasons, people willingly pay premium prices for items such as milk and diapers at all-night convenience stores when the need is urgent and other retail establishments are closed. Advocacy groups weren't agitating for price limits on convenience store merchandise, but the new ATM fees hit a hot button. By 1998, the Public Campaign maintained, 80 percent of the public favored outlawing noncustomer charges.[6]

Naturally, consumers were *not* opposed to being able to get cash in places they had never dreamed of getting it before the advent of ATMs. These included sports stadiums and national parks. Foreign usage fees helped banks justify the cost of installing and maintaining ATMs in low-volume locations of that sort, but people nevertheless rankled at paying for the service.

Sensing dissatisfaction that they could capitalize on, politicians sprang into action. In California, the cities of Santa Monica and San Francisco prohibited banks from charging noncustomers for ATM use, acting by city council vote and by referendum, respectively. In New Jersey, Woodbridge and Newark outlawed the practice. The cities' bans, however, were enjoined by federal district courts, which ruled that the National Bank Act preempted state and local action.

At the national level, elected officials demonstrated that interfering in ordinary commercial transactions is not the province of any single party or ideology. In the House of Representatives, a ban on noncustomer ATM usage charges was proposed by Maurice Hinchey (D-NY) and the sole independent member, Bernie Sanders of Vermont, a self-described democratic socialist. In the Senate, a similar measure was advanced by conservative Republican Alfonse D'Amato (R-NY).

Cash machine fees furnished D'Amato with an attention-grabbing issue in a difficult—and ultimately unsuccessful—reelection battle. He attacked what he called "the abusive practice of double ATM charges."[7] Consumers, he complained, were being "walloped"[8] by the fees.

"Senator Pothole," as D'Amato was known for his dedication to constituent service, garnered plenty of publicity by decrying ATM fees, but ultimately achieved nothing on the legislative front. He first proposed a fee restriction in 1997, but failed to recruit any support from fellow Republicans on the Banking Committee, which he chaired. To get his measure before the full Senate, D'Amato tried tacking it onto a 1998 banking bill. The Senate voted down his amendment by a vote of 72 to 26.[9]

The Great Cause Lives On

In the end, discontent over foreign fees on cash machines failed to launch a second American Revolution. To this day, the U.S. Constitution does not guarantee the right to use ATMs. But politicians both liberal and conservative remain dedicated to the proposition that ordinary commercial activity must never proceed unimpeded. They continue to regard every technological and business innovation as an opportunity to override the market's wisdom.

RENT CONTROL: FACT-RESISTANT POLICYMAKING

Rent control is such a commonly invoked illustration of foolish intervention in the marketplace that it is fair to ask whether one more discussion is merited. Other subjects in this book, such as taxpayer-financed sports stadiums, savings subsidies, and payola, represent less worked-over territory. But rent control is worth spending a few pages on for the very reason that its folly is so solidly established. Few topics offer a starker contrast between sound economics and political blather.

Economists' almost unanimous disdain for rent control is well documented. A survey of the early 1990s found 93 percent of the profession agreeing with the statement that placing a ceiling on rents reduces the quantity and quality of available housing. That represented a tie for highest level of economists' concurrence on an issue (93 percent also agreed that the usual effect of import tariffs and quotas is to reduce general economic welfare).[10] The nearly universal agreement strongly suggests that economists consider rent control faulty on the basis of bedrock theory and empirical evidence and not on the basis of ideology.

The Case against Controls

The case against rent control is easy to understand. For decades, textbook writers have felt comfortable in presenting the argument to beginning students of economics. A quarter-century ago, one such author wrote of "rather overwhelming evidence"[11] that laws limiting rents failed to protect tenants from the consequences of housing supply rising less swiftly than demand. He offered the following explanation:

- Rent controls directly cause landlords to receive less-than-normal returns on their investments in housing.
- The landlords respond by shifting their activities to other types of investment or into other geographic regions where rents aren't controlled.
- Construction of new rental housing consequently declines.
- The low rate of return on rental housing makes it unprofitable for landlords to maintain existing buildings. Consequently, the available housing deteriorates in quality.

- Rent controls aggravate the problem of scarce housing. With the price of housing held below the equilibrium level by rent controls, the quantity supplied falls below the quantity demanded. A genuine shortage results.

The author of this particular recital of the case against rent control, Campbell R. McConnell of the University of Nebraska-Lincoln, encouraged his readers to verify his points by constructing a simple supply-and-demand diagram. Since his intended audience was students in introductory economics courses, it is reasonable to infer that the arguments against rent control don't lie beyond the intellectual grasp of the average politician.

If office seekers nevertheless continue to defend rent control, they can't claim that they have been too busy to keep up with current economic research. McConnell detailed the flaws in rent control in 1981. And it wasn't news at the time. The undesirable consequences of New York City's rent controls, instituted in 1943, had already been apparent for decades.

Subsequent studies have confirmed the wrongheadedness of artificially restricting rents. Consider some of the empirical findings reported in a survey of research published in the years from 1986 to 2003. Various studies examined the effects of rent control in New York City; Brookline and Cambridge, Massachusetts; and Berkeley and Santa Monica, California. Researchers found that instead of increasing the supply of available rental housing, as intended, rent controls reduced the supply. Also contrary to the government's intentions, the restrictions promoted gentrification, a process in which affluent residents displace a diverse, mixed-income population. Rent stabilization, a modified form of rent control, provided a substantial subsidy to comparatively affluent sections of Manhattan but little benefit to middle-income neighborhoods in Manhattan and the city's other boroughs. Far from helping the poor, rent control magnified the usual disparity whereby rent consumes a higher percentage of income in low-income households than in high-income households.[12]

Particularly troubling is a 1991 article that reported materially worse maintenance in New York City apartments than in the United States as a whole. Even compared with Chicago, another city with an old stock of housing and a large poor population, New York renters were more likely to have leaking roofs (14.0 percent versus 9.6 percent), broken heating (26.1 percent versus 8.6 percent), or broken toilets (5.6 percent versus 2.2

percent). Was it a matter of New York landlords being greedier than Chicago landlords? Cutting back on maintenance is a self-defeating sort of greed if vacancy rates are high enough that an unhappy tenant has a genuine option of finding a different apartment. But when rent controls hold down the supply, while also squeezing the landlord's cash flow, cutting corners on maintenance is a predictable response.[13] When the government tries to reduce this effect through law enforcement, it incurs additional costs that would be avoided if rent control weren't in effect.

In the absence of rent control, landlords would also be less tempted to convert buildings to condominiums or cooperatives. That is one way of escaping the vise of rising costs and static rents. Rent-controlled tenants who don't want to buy their apartments represent obstacles to a conversion. Offering those tenants a financial incentive is the legal and ethically proper way to induce them to relocate. Some landlords, however, resort to pressuring tenants to leave by cutting back on maintenance. Right-thinking people naturally deplore such tactics. The government, let us hope, will enforce the housing code vigorously. But while well-intentioned individuals work toward a solution through their deploring and their enforcing, tenants suffer with leaking roofs and broken toilets. The pain and discomfort caused by some substandard maintenance would be avoided if landlords weren't trying to extricate themselves from buildings doomed by rent control to perpetually inadequate profits.

Farce Does Not Come Cheap

Inequity is a recurrent theme in the sad chronicle of rent control. In New York City, a combination of rent controls, high property taxes on apartment buildings, and regulations on development have discouraged construction of new housing and accelerated the deterioration of existing units. Builders of new housing, to be offered at market rates, can't hope to attract middle-class tenants who currently inhabit rent-controlled apartments or who benefit from direct government housing subsidies. Consequently, it is only profitable for developers to build luxury apartments. In the resulting two-tier market, the worst of the regulated housing eventually becomes inhabited by the poor. The rents they pay are at least as high as those paid by middle-class tenants for the better-quality segment of the price-controlled apartments.[14]

The government's misguided attempts to promote social objectives through rent control have also burdened the economy with massive dead-weight costs. These include substantial administrative costs, as well as the cost of litigation. In addition, scarce supply imposes extra costs on renters in finding apartments, as well as forcing them to make side payments for the privilege of moving into their dwellings. In one case several years ago, a sublet was available at the legal limit of 10 percent above the regulated rate, but only to a renter who was willing to buy a $2,500 painting from the artist with the primary lease.[15]

Further costs to the system arise when landlords try to induce tenants to surrender rent-controlled or rent-stabilized apartments. The landlords may plan to take the apartments off the rent control rolls, occupy the apartments themselves, or realize greater value from their holdings by demolishing and replacing the buildings.

To encourage tenants to relocate, landlords offer cash incentives. The inducements typically range from $30,000 and $100,000, but can sky-rocket to $1 million when one tenant is in a position to hold up a major redevelopment project. Renters may also receive windfalls such as bigger apartments at no increase in rent, moving expenses, or a week in a hotel. These benefits are not the result of hard work or risk taking, but rather of having the luck to be in the right place at the right time. Lawyers, brokers, and managing agents who facilitate the deals earn fees ranging from $1,000 to $100,000.[16]

The necessity of buying out lawful tenants raises costs to landlords and ultimately to other city residents. And it is paralleled by the cost of evicting tenants who don't actually occupy their apartments. Under the law, absentee tenants aren't entitled to benefit from rent restrictions, so they try to conceal their true status. When they are caught living out of state or surreptitiously subletting to tourists, the rent control abusers commonly stop paying rent and tie the landlords up in court. This cat-and-mouse game took a ludicrous turn in 2005 when a landlord in a high-rent Manhattan neighborhood hired a private investigator to get the dirt on Bozo the Clown.

Larry Harmon, the character's 80-year-old alter ego and owner of the Bozo trademark, rented a two-bedroom apartment for $1,719.27 a month. Under the rent stabilization rules, his rent increases were capped, provided he used the apartment as his primary residence. As it happened,

Harmon and his wife spent much of their time in a California condominium. The private detective interviewed Harmon's Los Angeles doorman, tracked down his cable television bills, and caught his wife saying that California had become the couple's primary residence. Claiming a violation of the rent-stabilization laws, the landlord sued.

The clown protested that his reason for spending so little time in New York was that he was frequently on the road. "I just wanted to bring laughter and love to the world," he explained. "But New York was my home and my pivot point."[17] In the end, though, Harmon conceded that New York wasn't his primary residence and agreed to a doubling of his rent to $3,600.

Bozo was not the only celebrity benefiting (at least for a time) from the rent subsidy ostensibly meant to assist New York's downtrodden. Cyndi Lauper is another featured player in the annals of New York City rent laws. With hits such as "Girls Just Want to Have Fun" and "Time after Time," the pop star racked up millions of record sales during the 1980s.[18]

Lauper and her husband, actor David Thornton, originally rented their apartment on upscale West End Avenue in 1992 for $3,250 a month. They evidently considered that a fair rent, given market conditions. In 1996, however, the show biz couple sued Shlomo Baron, from whom they had sublet the apartment. The apartment was rent-stabilized at $508, but the building was able to lease it for $2,400 to Baron, who said it wouldn't be his primary residence. When Lauper and Thornton got wind of the arrangement, they claimed violation of the rent stabilization laws and sued for the amounts they had paid above the stabilized rate, plus damages.

Later, the building terminated its lease with Baron. The singer and her husband demanded a reduction in their rent to the rent-stabilized rate of $508. Although the court agreed in principle, it calculated a higher rent, based on a different formula. Lauper and Thornton fought on, but in 2005, the state court of appeals ruled that the couple must pay $989.

Economists would say that the pop diva was still getting a pretty good deal, paying only 30 percent of the market rate of 13 years earlier. All the same, the hearts of Lauper's fans went out to her. "Cyndi doesn't even own a Beverly Hills Mansions [sic] or a multimillion dollar apartment," wrote one defender. "When Cyndi was a new artist she got screwed [because] Columbia Records paid new artists practically nothing, [because] they paid BABS[19] and Mick Jagger all the big money. Cyndi only got paid like 3 cents for albums sold overseas."[20] Evidently, certain hardship cases require special insight to recognize.

Politicians' Stances

Despite the ludicrous situations to which it gives rise—not to mention black markets and bribery—attempts to rein in rent control have been rare. Reluctance to attack the sacred cow isn't strictly a matter of party. Republicans may surpass Democrats in uttering paeans to free enterprise, but the fault lines are less clear when it comes to measuring results.

New York State took a tentative step toward reining in rent restrictions in 1971 by instituting vacancy decontrol. Under this modification of the rules, price controls were lifted when a tenant moved out of an apartment. In 1974, however, vacancy decontrol was repealed. At that time, Republican Malcolm Wilson was governor and Republicans controlled both houses of the state legislature.[21]

In 1997, the GOP controlled one house of the legislature and Governor George Pataki, a Republican, was inclined toward a free market approach. The resulting attempt to overhaul the rent laws, however, succeeded in lifting price controls on a mere 23,000 renters out of nearly one million in the pool. This change hardly left controlled rents as a benefit exclusively for the poor. The criteria for kicking the 23,000 renters out of the system were annual income of more than $175,000[22] and monthly rent above $2,000.[23]

One might think that some enterprising New York City politician would try to capitalize on the unfairness and economic distortions that rent control fosters. Identifying a problem and championing reform is a proven formula for electoral success. It wouldn't be a matter of siding with the rich against the poor, given the extent to which the subsidies flow to comparatively affluent New Yorkers. But that's not a story office seekers are eager to tell, regardless of party.

When asked where he stood on rent control and rent stabilization laws, Republican Mayor Michael Bloomberg came down squarely in favor of extending the 60-year-old authorization. "The bill comes up for renewal in 2003, and I'm in favor of renewing it," he declared.[24] In the 2005 mayoral race, Bloomberg's most controversial position involving rent control was his opposition to repealing the Urstadt Law, which placed administration of the controls in the hands of New York State. Bloomberg had initially supported repeal, but subsequently concluded that the city couldn't afford rent control's administrative costs. Eliminating the cost to taxpayers altogether, by abolishing rent control, was not even hinted at by the candidate of the party traditionally most vocal in espousing free market principles.

Among the Democrats, the main contenders for the 2005 mayoral nomination likewise balked at offering voters a choice on a profoundly important economic issue. Like Bloomberg, Fernando Ferrer, Virginia Fields, Gifford Miller, and Anthony Weiner all treated the Urstadt Law as the main controversy associated with rent control. (Unlike the Republican incumbent, however, they favored repeal.)[25] In lieu of competing on the basis of offering fresh ideas, the Democrats vied to demonstrate the vehemence of their opposition to any relaxation of rent control. City Council Speaker Miller exceeded his rivals in that contest, according to a tenant advocacy group that endorsed him.[26]

Why They Remain Silent

Rent control is a chestnut for chroniclers of economic folly, but it provides a valuable insight into the political system. Here is a public policy question with important social and economic ramifications. A group that is well informed on the matter has come down on the side of reversing the present policy, by an overwhelming margin of 93 to 7. It wouldn't necessarily constitute a failure of democracy if, after thoughtful debate, the government rejected the economists' position. But it can't be counted as a success that no major candidate is willing even to present to the electorate a viewpoint supported by both elementary economic theory and the stark evidence of six decades.

The reason for the disparity between serious analysis and politicians' rhetoric is no mystery. Although rent control harms society as a whole, it provides immensely valuable subsidies to a segment of the population. That segment doesn't consist of the poor, in whose name office seekers defend rent ceilings. But the merits of a subsidy make little difference to politicians. The critical consideration is that the beneficiaries of rent control are organized and they vote. By responding to pressure from this special-interest group, elected officials eliminate the option of implementing the policy that is fairest to all.

If the disastrous consequences of rent control were more widely understood, more enlightened policies might stand a chance. But educating the public requires patient effort and willingness to take an unpopular stance. In that sort of situation, so-called political leaders are reluctant to lead. They prefer to wait until the parade is underway, then scramble to the front.

THE BOTTOM LINE

The phrase *bipartisan consensus* has a positive ring. But the chief point on which the views of the Republicans and the Democrats converge is that their meddling is essential to every economic interaction. Depending on their purported political philosophies, office seekers speak of empowering the people or promise to unleash the power of entrepreneurship. But the power that all politicians understand at the gut level is the power of the government to misallocate resources for political gain. From that perspective, even the simplest commercial transaction, if it occurs outside the watchful eye of Uncle Sam or his local affiliates, represents a missed opportunity.

III

TELLING IT
LIKE IT ISN'T

13

Honesty Is the Worst Policy

What if Washington, DC, experienced a sudden outbreak of honesty?

One consequence would be a startling change in the economic rhetoric of the party in power at the time. The new commentary might sound something like this:

> We invite the public to judge the administration by the economy's performance during our watch. Consider what has happened to the key statistical measures.
>
> Interest rates are down by a full percentage point. This has made it easier for businesses to borrow for expansion, which includes hiring additional workers. The lower interest rates have also made it easier for businesses to eliminate certain jobs by acquiring the latest labor-saving equipment. In time, the resulting improvement in productivity will create new jobs to replace the ones that were lost. But for now, the displaced workers will be spending some time on the unemployment rolls. We should also point out that as a result of the drop in interest rates, retirees who depend on the income from Treasury bills and certificates of deposit have had to tighten their belts a notch.
>
> The price of an average home has risen by 10 percent. That is great news for the millions of families whose home equity value represents a vital component of their savings. Of course, it is not such great news for those who are still struggling to become first-time homeowners. The spike in housing prices has jerked the brass ring a few more inches out of their reach.

Inflation has eased. That means reduced strain on the budgets of our seniors living on fixed incomes. It also means sleepless nights ahead for a lot of folks who maxed out on their consumer credit lines. They figured their salaries would continue to rise in line with a high rate of inflation, making it easier for them to repay their debts in the future. Looks like they guessed wrong.

The administration's economic achievements don't stop there. Unemployment is down, making it tougher for many small businesses to hire qualified workers at wages they can afford to pay. Finally, the world has given the administration's economic policies a resounding vote of confidence by boosting the dollar's value relative to other major currencies. As a result, U.S. manufacturers are finding it harder to export their goods.

So when you go to the polls this November, the question you ought to ask yourself is, "Are you better off than you were four years ago?" We're confident that the answer will be a resounding, "Maybe yes, maybe no."

Nobody should count on ever hearing anything remotely resembling these remarks. Brutal honesty is an accusation that is unlikely ever to be leveled at White House economic spokespersons. Nor is excessive candor a trait of the opposition's congressional leaders and presidential aspirants. Their task is to make sure that voters get the benefit of a one-sided account of everything that's going wrong with the economy.

Both parties generally agree that good times are good for everybody, the presumption being that if unemployment is low and inflation isn't out of hand, voters will tilt toward the incumbent party. Conversely, politicians reckon that a high level of job loss will create widespread insecurity. The tide will then shift toward throwing the bums out.

Certainly, it is possible for a segment of the population to be disadvantaged by a trend that benefits the majority, or vice versa. But politically speaking, there is little danger in overlooking this subtle point. The small group that is out of synch is simply not worth worrying about, unless it is especially well organized or known for having high voter turnout. The main deviation from the presumption that good times are good for everyone consists of obligatory grousing by liberals that the least well-off in society are reaping too few of the benefits.

Viewing the state of the economy in black-and-white terms makes it easy for politicians to match their rhetoric to prevailing conditions. There are just three simple rules to remember:

1. *If the economy is hovering between strength and weakness:* Paint as bright or as bleak a picture as possible, depending on whether your party is in or out of power.

2. *If the economy is booming:* Claim credit, no matter whether your party is currently in power.

3. *If the economy is in recession:* Blame the other party, no matter whether it is currently in power.

Starting with the premise that the purpose of political discourse is to win votes rather than to guide the electorate toward objective reality, let's consider some strategies for implementing the three basic rules.

PAINTING A FUZZY PICTURE

Politicians tell the story of the economy largely in statistics, such as the unemployment rate, the size of the federal deficit, and the inflation rate. This is a succinct way of describing how things are going. A number presented with no frame of reference has little meaning to voters, however.

It is one thing for Franklin Roosevelt to say, in his second inaugural address in 1937, "I see one-third of a nation ill-housed, ill-clad, ill-nourished." A 33.33 percent destitution rate is a bad number by anybody's standard. But what about a 6 percent unemployment rate or a 2 percent inflation rate? Most people hearing these figures without some historical basis of comparison could do little more than nod sagely and say, "Could be better, could be worse." As for federal deficits, the numbers are so gigantic, relative to the dollar figures that people ordinarily deal with (annual salary, cost of a college education, and so forth), that they find it difficult to attach any meaning whatsoever to them. It is like trying to imagine how much more uncomfortable one would feel at 300° than at 200° Fahrenheit.

The only way to transform economic statistics into meaningful gauges is to put them into context. Fortunately for politicians, no federal statute dictates *which* context must be used for a particular statistic. That leaves plenty of room to frame the latest number in the most helpful way for the politician delivering the speech.

If unemployment stands at 6 percent, the president can point out that it is down from the previous month. It might even be the lowest number in the past year. These comparisons give the impression that the country is headed in the right direction, leaving voters to attribute it all to the administration's wise policies. Members of the opposition party, however, might just as correctly be able to point out that the unemployment rate was only 5 percent when *their* last president left the White House.

Another effective way to frame a statistic is to cite the average rate of the previous four years. Or the previous 20 or the previous 50 years. There is no inherently correct time frame in this exercise. The point is to determine which comparison period makes the present number look especially good or especially bad.

It isn't necessary to select a comparison period that is in any way relevant. Many statistical series are inherently jerky over very short periods. The jumpiness reflects such things as measurement problems and imperfect formulas for seasonal adjustment. On top of that, the numbers are subject to later revision. As a result, a seemingly large one-month move may disappear in a subsequent restatement.

To get a true picture of the underlying reality, it is best to smooth out the random fluctuations. This can be achieved by standard techniques such as calculating an average of the latest three months. Politicians, however, don't denigrate a spurious month-over-month change as a statistical quirk. To them, it is an opportunity to proclaim that their plan is working or to decry the opposing party's miserably failed policies.

If no other means of distorting the statistics presents itself, there's always the option of citing absolute numbers in lieu of percentages. For example, politicians can blame their opponents for producing the largest federal budget deficit ever. The fact is, however, that the numbers get bigger over time as the population and the federal budget grow. As a consequence, a deficit that is far from the largest ever, as a percentage of the budget or of gross domestic product, may happen to set a new high in dollars.

Historical comparisons are even more specious when the dollars are conveniently unadjusted for inflation. A popular variation on this theme consists of blasting the other side for a record-high price for gasoline or heating oil. The trick consists of avoiding any mention that in terms of purchasing power, the current price is actually lower than in certain past periods.

TAKING CREDIT WHERE NOT DUE

The natural alternation of prosperity and hard times provides another vast opportunity for misrepresentation.

Cyclicality is a built-in feature of any economy. As an economy expands, companies step up production to increase their inventories. They also spend on new plant and equipment, which generates business for producers of capital goods.

To pay for all this, companies borrow money, which puts upward pressure on interest rates. Higher interest rates discourage further investment by business. Eventually, companies reach a point at which they have added enough inventory and new productive capacity to satisfy anticipated demand. That reverses the economy's momentum. Sometimes, the slowdown-inducing effects are compounded by a shock to the economy, such as a surge in energy prices. The resulting business downturn likewise puts self-correcting forces into motion.

Thanks to the economy's built-in stabilizers, an expansion goes on for only so long before being followed by a recession. After a while, the recession ends and a normal cyclical rebound begins. At that point, the administration congratulates itself for putting the country back to work. In reality, the president's main accomplishment consists of sounding credible while claiming credit for the inevitable. With equal plausibility, the administration might list the return of spring among its achievements.

Suppose you're running for president against the incumbent party and by a stroke of good luck, the country is in recession on Election Day. No matter how many reasons voters may have to dislike you, the dissatisfaction with the state of the economy is probably going to help your cause. If you win, you will probably wind up in a position to portray yourself as an economic miracle worker.

It will be almost three months before you are sworn into office. Since the Depression, the median duration of recessions has been just 10 months. No economic contraction has lasted more than 16 months.[1] There is a good chance then, that the most you will have to do is get the electorate to cut you some slack for up to a year. You don't have to be a public relations genius to hold the critics at bay for that long. Just keep deploring the mess your predecessor handed over to you.

The customary honeymoon period enables you to claim that your economic plan is working, even though the numbers continue to look sickly.

People will be tolerant, as long as you repeatedly remind them that it will take a while for your remedy to achieve the desired effect. Don't agonize over the correctness of your specific policies. Most cold sufferers recover after taking the proverbial two aspirin and drinking lots of fluids. The recession is pretty sure to end of its own accord, well before it lasts long enough to become *your* recession.

How about the other case, in which your party loses power just before a recovery begins? Concede nothing. Claim that the economy is finally responding to actions that your party took when it held the White House. There is no dishonor in asserting that your policies worked, but only with a lag. After all, the current administration almost certainly spent its first few months reminding voters that it would take a while for its plan to produce results.

Even if you have the bad luck of witnessing a long and vigorous expansion while the other party is in power, you can still talk about lags with a straight face. Simply argue that the current, sustained prosperity has nothing to do with the present administration's economic policies. Assert that it is all because of structural reforms that your party instituted 8, 12, or even 20 years earlier. The more outlandish your claim the better. After all, the most far-fetched economic thesis is the hardest one to disprove.

PLAYING THE BLAME GAME

Offloading blame for bad times is just as important as hogging credit for good times. A politician who handles both tasks well can emerge with an invaluable, albeit totally undeserved, reputation for infallibility in economic policy. As with claiming credit, talking about lags is an essential tactic in the battle to assign responsibility.

If your party is in power when a recession begins, you can blame it on the previous administration's failure to rein in corporate greed and speculative excesses. Never mind trying to find an empirical connection between business ethics and the business cycle. Anyone concerned about logic will note that it is an elementary error to assume that if A preceded B, A caused B. But that doesn't deter the press from publishing the morality tale that corporate scandals produced a loss of confidence, which in turn produced a business downturn.

What if a recession begins right after your party hands over power to your opponents? In light of your past emphasis on lags, logical consistency would demand that you take responsibility. We are dealing with politics, however, not philosophy. Use your imagination.

You might ridicule anyone who suggests that the slump represents a delayed response to your previous actions. Rather, you can say, the economy has screeched to a halt because consumers and corporations have suddenly pulled in their horns. They are frightened, you can explain, that the new administration will (*choose one or more*):

- Raise taxes.
- Reduce taxes for the rich.
- Increase spending.
- Cut back essential programs.
- Handicap businesses with costly new regulations.
- Remove all restraints on corporate avarice.

In short, economic policies always work with a lag, except when it's inconvenient for your party if they do.

A COLOSSUS FLAILING IN THE WIND

The reality that government policies have a weak connection with short-run economic performance is not the view that politicians prefer to espouse. It portrays them as ineffectual, potentially even irrelevant. A true account limits their role to confusing the public about what is actually going on and who is responsible.

Having spent their entire lives in pursuit of power, politicians would rather believe that when they finally get the reins, they will have some control over events. Furthermore, the speeches they have made during their quest have omitted self-aggrandizement as a motivation for seeking office. Instead, the politicos have emphasized their desire to "give something back" to ordinary Americans.

To work ceaselessly to persuade voters of their altruistic motives without believing it themselves would make politicians superhuman cynics or outright sociopaths. Based on observation, most politicians don't fit into either of those categories. Therefore, it has to be hard for them to assimilate the notion that if they get elected, they will be powerless to head off a recession or cut it short once it begins.

Aside from their own psychological needs, the notion of the president as a colossus flailing in the wind is anathema to politicians for more practical reasons. Election campaigns are about three things:

1. Registering sympathetic voters.
2. Making sure they show up.
3. Persuading undecided voters to vote the right way.

(Well, four things, if we also consider managing the polls. This includes such activities as disqualifying voters who are likely to go the wrong way, siphoning off an opponent's votes by placing on the ballot a nonserious candidate with a similar name, and plain fraud.)

The point of the persuasion component of electioneering is to lead the voter to a straightforward, unambiguous action—a vote for a particular candidate. There is no space on the ballot for the voter to evaluate the candidate on a scale of one to five. When the ballots are tallied, a holding-the-nose choice of the lesser of two evils counts no less than a vote cast in the belief that it will help to make the country a better place to live.

This is not a realm in which it pays to deal in nuances. The job is to frame the voter's choice in black-and-white terms:

- *We* stand for jobs, national security, and education.
- *They*—by implication, if rather improbably—are against those things.

No points are awarded for subtlety.

Imagine, under these conditions, attempting to conduct an intelligent discussion of economic policies and their consequences. It is a nonstarter. The way to get X's on the ballots is to reduce it all to a simple message, such as:

Your neighbor is out of work and you could be next. Throw out the rascals who got the country into this mess.

or

You've never had it so good. Don't mess it up by changing leaders.

There is no room in this stripped-down debate for questioning underlying premises. No one can afford to raise the possibility that neither the incumbent nor the challenger can influence short-run economic conditions by tinkering with fiscal policy. Yet that is the lesson of the past several decades.

FORGET ABOUT FINE-TUNING

Up until the Depression, the federal government made little effort to counteract the business cycle. Even Franklin Roosevelt, in the early stages of his presidency, refrained from heroic measures to stimulate aggregate demand for goods and services. He initially adhered to the established wisdom of striving to balance the federal budget, a policy more likely to accentuate than attenuate a business slump.

In the first phase of the New Deal, Roosevelt focused on allowing companies to suppress competition and raise prices. This was supposed to boost companies' profits, inducing them to step up production, which would get the economy moving. In response, businesses enthusiastically began seeking ways to beat the system, giving rise to voluminous litigation. The Supreme Court cut the scheme short in 1935 by ruling that the National Industrial Recovery Act of 1933 was unconstitutional.

Only as the Depression dragged on to the point of seeming intractability did FDR attempt to stimulate aggregate demand through deficit spending. Instead of raising taxes or cutting back expenditures to keep the federal budget in balance, he sought to prop up aggregate demand by temporarily allowing expenditures to exceed revenues. The 1936 publication of John Maynard Keynes's *The General Theory of Employment, Interest and Money*[2] provided intellectual cover for Roosevelt's new approach. In addition, Federal Reserve Chairman Marriner Eccles had come up with the same idea independently.

The extent to which Franklin Roosevelt's fiscal activism contributed to ending the Depression remains a hotly debated topic. In any case, subsequent administrations embraced the idea of stabilizing the business cycle by adjusting the levels of taxes and government spending. The notion of being able to bend the economy to their will appealed to politicians of both major parties. Confronted with the contrast between his stated aversion to big government and his fondness for active fiscal policy, Republican Richard Nixon famously declared, "We are all Keynesians now."[3]

Politicians' ambitions for economic management grew beyond dealing with the extreme conditions observed during the Depression. At the height of confidence in stabilization policies, in the 1960s, economists even spoke of *fine-tuning*. Armed with computer models, they contended that they could prescribe policies capable of preventing the economy from ever again teetering into recession. Their claims gained credibility from a long, unbroken expansion that lasted from early 1961 through late 1969.[4]

Things did not go as well in the 1970s, however. Severe recessions, high unemployment, and sharply escalating inflation undercut the belief that stabilization policies could keep the economy on a nice, even keel. In fact, economists have come around to the view that governmental attempts to smooth out the cycle are counterproductive.

It turns out that the lags politicians commonly talk about, usually to manipulate public perceptions of the effectiveness of their policies, are real. The problem is that econometric methods aren't precise enough to predict the length of the lags. By the time a tax cut aimed at stimulating the economy kicks in, the economy may already be turning around of its own accord. The effect will be like proverbial gasoline on a flame, sending the economy into an overheated state inevitably with bad consequences. Restraining a booming economy isn't exactly a policy objective that politicians emphasize, but pursuing it runs a similar timing risk. Instead of heading off an inflationary overexpansion, the government may wind up aggravating a recession.

Even if they could accurately estimate the length of the lag with which a fiscal measures would take effect, economic policymakers would still face a major obstacle. They would have to forecast the state of the economy at the point at which their policies would begin to have an impact. Unfortunately, economists find it difficult to glimpse into the future. In fact, sometimes even the present is murky. On October 2, 1990, Federal Reserve Chairman Alan Greenspan told his fellow Federal Open Market Committee members, "The economy has not yet slipped into a recession."[5] But according to the subsequent deliberations of the economists charged with dating business cycles, the economy had begun to contract three months earlier, in July.

Getting the timing right isn't the only problem in implementing fiscal policy. For one thing, people tend to save a lot of the incremental income they receive from temporary tax cuts. By failing to spend the extra cash, they undercut the intended stimulus. In addition, tax cuts and increases in government spending generate fears of future deficits. That drives up long-term interest rates, which actually depresses economic activity, contrary to the politicians' desires.[6]

None of this, by the way, represents a radical assessment of the effectiveness of fiscal policy. As University of California, Berkeley economist Alan J. Auerbach wrote in 2003:

> The difficulty of practicing countercyclical fiscal policy has been a staple of macroeconomics textbooks for decades. With the typical postwar recession lasting less than a year and discretionary fiscal changes subject to information, political, and economic lags, knowledgeable policymakers have understood the daunting task they faced. But the strong support for this most recent "stimulus package" reminds us that policymakers may go where economists fear to tread.[7]

The "recent stimulus package" to which Auerbach alluded was the Job Creation and Worker Assistance Act that President George W. Bush signed on March 9, 2002. In response to the first recession in a decade, Congress had approved tax incentives for business spending on equipment and software, as well as a temporary extension of unemployment benefits. At the time, it wasn't yet known whether the economy was still in recession. Three weeks before Bush signed the legislation, however, the National Bureau of Economic Research (NBER) had preliminarily estimated that real gross domestic product increased by 1.4 percent in the fourth quarter of 2001. The NBER subsequently designated November 2001 as the conclusion of the recession against which the President and Congress took up arms in March 2002.

Even former Clinton chief economic advisor Laura D'Andrea Tyson, who confesses to harboring "Keynesian sensibilities,"[8] acknowledges that attempts to fine-tune the economy rarely work:

> When governments try to fight recessions by cutting taxes or increasing spending, they almost always get the timing wrong. By the time the tortuous budgetary process yields a new policy, the recession is over and the fiscal stimulus is no longer warranted. Nor, unfortunately, is it easily reversed, especially if it takes the form of a tax cut.[9]

THE OTHER PLAYER

In addition to the imprecision of fiscal policy, there is another highly inconvenient fact for politicians seeking to claim credit for prosperity: The second major lever for influencing the economy, monetary policy, is out-side their control. Adjusting the availability of credit in response to chang-ing conditions is entirely the purview of the Federal Reserve.

The Federal Reserve Board is designed to be insulated from political pressure. Its governors are appointed for 14-year terms. Once confirmed, they can't be removed by the president or Congress except for criminal acts.

Surely, it would be unrealistic to claim that the central bank's deci-sions to raise or lower interest rates are subject to no political influence whatsoever. But the Fed's monetary policy can be out of phase with the administration's fiscal policy. What's more, monetary policy affects eco-nomic activity with a lag, just as fiscal policy does. The Fed faces the same danger that the administration and lawmakers do of reinforcing a trend when they are actually trying to reverse the trend that preceded it.

If it sounds like *nobody* is in charge, that would be correct. A useful image of the U.S. economy is a boulder rolling down a hill, flattening everything that stands in its path. The president, Congress, and the Fed-eral Reserve run alongside the boulder, vainly trying to nudge it this way or that—often pushing in opposing directions. For the most part, the boulder will probably determine its own course.

A BETTER WAY

None of this implies that politicians' economic policies have no impact, positive or negative. A well-designed tax system can have a hugely favor-able effect on long-term economic performance. That is a good reason for politicians to modify the tax code to encourage investment and simplify the rules to reduce the resources devoted to exploiting loopholes.

Politicians have little incentive, however, to pursue long-term eco-nomic benefits. On Election Day it is hard to cash in on benefits that lie far off in the future. In addition, a permanent improvement in the nation's average economic performance has a highly undesirable effect: It makes the opposing party look good when it's in office.

Politicians, then, find themselves in a quandary. They can't control the economy in the short run. At the same time, they can't gain a clear electoral advantage from bringing about long-term improvements. The solution is clear: If the reality of economic policy and conditions isn't helping the political agenda, alter the public's perception of reality.

OUT OF THEIR MISERY

As an illustration of the games that politicians play with people's minds, consider some sleight-of-hand applied in 2004. It involved the *misery index*, a straightforward and highly intuitive indicator of economic conditions. The index simply adds the unemployment rate to the inflation rate. Being without a paycheck while the prices of life's necessities are going up is a good working definition of misery.

The misery index was the brainchild of Arthur Okun, who headed the Council of Economic Advisers at the end of President Lyndon Johnson's administration. His innovation caught on in a big way during the 1970s. At the time, the United States was reeling from the one-two punch of sluggish economic growth and high inflation.

Voters were puzzled by this turn of events. Economists had previously led them to believe that high unemployment automatically went along with low inflation. Conversely, people assumed that if policymakers tried to rein in inflation, they would slow the economy down and push unemployment higher. *Stagflation,* which combined high unemployment and high inflation, was a new and frightening phenomenon.

The worst of all worlds is exactly how a challenger to an incumbent president would like to portray prevailing economic conditions. So it is not surprising that Democratic Senator John Kerry dusted off the phrase "misery index" when he opposed Republican George W. Bush's bid for a second term in 2004. Kerry's aides meant to impress on the voters just how bad off they really were. The inference they hoped voters would draw was that the nation needed new leadership to pull it out of its misery.

There was one small hitch. When the Kerry campaign hatched its plan, in April 2004, the latest available reports showed unemployment at 5.6 percent and the Consumer Price Index 1.7 percent above its year-earlier level.[10] Adding the two numbers produced a misery index of 7.3 percent. Inconveniently enough, that was exactly where it stood in 2000, the last year of the administration of Bush's predecessor, Democrat Bill Clinton.[11] Denigrating Bush's performance on the basis of the traditional misery index hardly would have been an adept maneuver for his Democratic challenger.

It was time to shake the kaleidoscope through which politicians encourage people to view reality. The Kerry campaign issued a press release proclaiming that under President Bush, something called the "Middle-

Class Misery Index" had registered its worst deterioration ever. This sounded pretty serious. It made little difference to Kerry's advisers that according to their own numbers, the absolute level of middle-class misery was around the middle of its historical range.

Credit for creating a picture of the economy going to hell in a hand basket went to Gene Sperling and Jason Furman, former economic advisers to Bill Clinton and Al Gore, respectively. They cobbled together a new index consisting of median family income, college tuition, health costs, gasoline costs, bankruptcies, the homeownership rate, and private-sector job growth. Under Bush, the Kerry campaign reported, the index had posted its biggest three-year decline on record. (Note that the newfangled misery index differed from the familiar version in that a high number indicated good, rather than bad, economic conditions.)

Anyone with experience observing politicians' shenanigans would have suspected Sperling and Furman of cherry-picking statistics to make Bush's record look bad. After all, the president would have gotten better marks if the newly hatched index had included other plausible series such as mortgage interest rates, life expectancy at birth, and median home size.[12] But Kerry's advisers could indignantly wave off accusations of bias in constructing their new gauge. They had taken care to include one series—the homeownership rate—that had *improved* under Bush.

As it turned out, the bias in design of the new index wasn't a matter only of which statistics its creators selected. Kerry's aides were also careful about which *versions* of the statistics they chose. For example, they counted median family income on a pretax basis. That eliminated the increase in the amount of money people actually had available due to Bush's tax cuts. As for escalation in college costs, the Kerry team focused solely on increases at public colleges. Tuition increases at private colleges hadn't been as great. Similarly, the formula for calculating the Middle-Class Misery Index took into account the number of private-sector jobs, which was down, but excluded public-sector jobs, which happened to be up.

Kerry's new index rested on no economic theory more elaborate than plucking the worst numbers out of a large array of possibilities. It was rather like observing that a department store has recorded a respectable increase in profits, but arguing that it had a bad year because sales declined in a handful of product categories. Kerry's ploy was not only clever, but also difficult for Bush's staff to refute on news telecasts that allotted only a few seconds to each interviewee within a segment.

Even so, the challenger couldn't produce a picture of bad times that stood up under scrutiny. If Kerry's advisers were representing conditions fairly, then the United States must have been very well off under President Jimmy Carter. The Middle-Class Misery Index reached its highest level, prior to the Clinton years, during Carter's administration. At the end of 1978, however, unemployment stood at 6.0 percent and inflation was running 9.0 percent. That put Okun's misery index at 15.0, twice its level in early 2004 under George W. Bush. As Gregg Easterbrook of *New Republic* aptly asked, "Can you find one single person in the United States who would want a time-machine ride to the economic conditions of 1978?"[13]

None of this deterred the Kerry camp from declaring that in terms of economic performance, Bush had produced "the worst record of any president ever."[14] The claim was rendered even more ludicrous by the fact that "ever" went back only to 1976 because some of the statistics in Kerry's custom-tailored index weren't collected before that date. It is hard to imagine that Americans felt more miserable in 2004 than they did under President Herbert Hoover in 1932 when unemployment reached a staggering 23.6 percent.[15] As an exercise in reenvisioning reality, the Middle-Class Misery Index was remarkable for its audacity.

MAKING RECESSIONS RECEDE

No party has a monopoly on optical illusions. Republicans have also been energetic in their attempts to massage the numbers. They have focused on disassociating themselves from recessions. Understanding the GOP's gambits requires a bit of background on the dating of economic downturns.

The financial press sometimes defines a recession as two or more consecutive quarters of declining gross domestic product (GDP). For analytical purposes, however, economists rely on a less cut-and-dried approach. In their research on recessions, they use the starting and ending dates determined by the Business Cycle Dating Committee of the NBER. This private, nonpartisan research group gives considerable weight to GDP, as reported by the Commerce Department, but also emphasizes personal income, sales in the manufacturing and wholesale-retail sectors, industrial production, and employment. No fixed formula determines which other measures enter into the analysis in a given cycle.[16]

Politicians could choose to take a statesmanlike stance by going along with this convention. They could frankly acknowledge that recessions are naturally recurring features of economic life. Candidates for office could refrain from blaming a downturn on the other party and acknowledge that economic fine-tuning is futile.

So much for the honest approach. Getting into territory they are more familiar with, politicians insist that if the upleg of the cycle has been followed by a downleg, it must be somebody's fault and that somebody must be somebody else.

One strategy for winning the blame game is to name the current recession after a president who belongs to the other party. That is simple enough when the other party is in power. The bigger challenge is to shed responsibility for a recession that begins during one's own watch. Pulling off this feat may require playing politics with the NBER's recession-dating process.

The Republicans were strongly motivated to interfere during Ronald Reagan's presidency.[17] According to the NBER, the country had undergone two recessions within an unusually short span. The first occurred under Jimmy Carter in 1980 and the second under Reagan in 1981 and 1982. If only the Business Cycle Dating Committee could be persuaded to combine the two episodes into one long recession, the GOP could label the whole period the "Carter Recession."

That exercise in gentle persuasion failed, but the Republicans were not discouraged. Two decades later, the NBER determined that a recession had begun in March 2001. It was a bad break for George W. Bush, who took over from Bill Clinton in January 2001. If only the NBER had read the statistics a little differently, the GOP could have ostentatiously disavowed responsibility for a recession that began under the Democrats. But the Republicans were not about to take the recognized authority's verdict lying down. Instead, they decided to bypass the process. The Economic Report of the President, released in February 2004, unilaterally declared that the most recent recession had commenced under Clinton in the fourth quarter of 2000.

In fairness, the NBER's eschewing of a cut-and-dried rule for dating business cycles leaves room for bona fide debate. Two of the indicators that the NBER considers in the dating decision, industrial production and sales in the manufacturing and wholesale-retail sectors, peaked in mid-2000. That lent at least some support to the redating by the Council of

Economic Advisers (CEA), which issued the president's February 2004 report. Gregory Mankiw, chairman of the CEA, said that he made the call based on the available data.

Furthermore, there is no guarantee that the NBER's deliberations are entirely free of political considerations. Its Business Cycle Dating Committee members could have biases, even if not conscious. But it could hardly represent an improvement in objectivity for the CEA, a panel appointed by the president, to become the recognized authority for dating recessions.

The electorate would have been better served if the Bush administration hadn't bothered to try to override the NBER. No reasonable, informed observer would have held George W. Bush accountable for a recession that began within two months of his inauguration. From that perspective, attempting to shift the starting date by some trifling number of weeks was pointless. The Republicans might even have said it was pointless to squabble over responsibility for economic perturbations outside the government's control. But by politicians' standards, that would have been overdoing the honesty bit.

SLASHER IN SEARCH OF A RATIONALE

For politicians who aspire to be known for their honesty, an essential technique is to stick to one story. Naturally, if circumstances change, there's nothing dishonest about switching to a different policy recommendation. But it is slippery to stick with the same policy recommendation and replace the original rationale with a different one that better fits the new conditions. Attentive observers are likely to infer that neither the old nor the new rationale is the true one.

In 2000, George W. Bush ran for president on a platform of slashing taxes by $1.3 trillion. He had put together his proposal in the preceding year, with the help of economist Lawrence Lindsey. The candidate's adviser crafted the proposed tax cut package to promote long-run investment and growth, as well as to return the then-prevailing federal budget surplus to taxpayers. Lindsey also contended that the economy under President Bill Clinton was weaker than it appeared. He therefore regarded Bush's plan to reduce taxes as an insurance policy against an economic downturn.[18]

Notwithstanding Lindsey's concerns, however, the United States economy continued to expand in 2000. Real gross domestic product increased by a healthy 3.7 percent. Under the circumstances, it wouldn't have made sense for Bush to promote his tax cut proposal as an economic stimulus measure. As Wall Street economist Steven Roach declared, "The last thing we need right now is a big tax cut" that would overheat the economy.[19] To allay such concerns, Bush's campaign staff contended that his plan would not increase aggregate demand for goods and services.[20]

Bush instead presented his proposed tax reduction as a long-run benefit to the economy and as a means of returning the federal surplus to its rightful owners. Washington, he said, couldn't be trusted with the taxpayers' money. The Republicans positioned tax cutting, in *Business Week*'s words, as a structural reform "meant to generate more income for those bypassed by boom-time prosperity."[21] The strategy worked well enough. At least, it didn't derail Bush's quest for the White House.

By early 2001, the economy looked less robust. President-elect Bush kept talking up his plan to slash taxes. But now he resurrected from 1999 Lindsey's rationale that a tax cut would provide insurance against a recession.[22] That is to say, Bush now maintained, contrary to what his campaign had argued a few months earlier, that his plan *would* increase aggregate demand.

Inevitably, the economy lapsed into recession and, in November 2001, just as inevitably emerged from it. Following orthodox political practice, which no reputable school of economics upholds, President Bush blamed his Democratic predecessor for the former development and claimed credit for the latter. In his State of the Union address in January 2004, he crowed:

> The tax relief you [Congress] passed is working. And because you acted to stimulate our economy with tax relief, this economy is strong and growing stronger. . . . The pace of economic growth in the third quarter of 2003 was the fastest in nearly 20 years: new home construction, the highest in almost 20 years; homeownership rates, the highest ever.[23]

Bush's tax cut plan had morphed from a nonstimulative structural reform to insurance against a possible recession to, finally, the stimulus that overcame an actual recession. The spectacle of a solution in search of a problem was reminiscent of the highly variable rationale for the ethanol subsidy. *Barron's* took Bush to task for failing to stick up for the long-run benefits of cutting taxes, the justification on which he campaigned in 2000:

The president does defend his tax cuts, but all too often he claims now what he never believed then—that they were well-timed bits of counter-cyclical macroeconomic stimulus.[24]

Sticking to one story isn't a practice that comes naturally to politicians. They are more comfortable with variations on a theme. Without multiple versions of reality to draw on, there is no way to tell all of one's constituents what they want to hear.

But there is a risk in jumping from one policy rationale to another as economic circumstances change. Troublemakers who hold a brief for honesty in politics may keep track of a candidate's speeches, looking for inconsistencies. Even more annoyingly, the do-gooders may alert voters when a program, ostensibly designed to address a certain problem, is suddenly being defended on altogether different grounds. The voters might just conclude that the politician's true motivation is some third rationale that hasn't yet been mentioned.

THE BOTTOM LINE

Politicians have little impact on short-run economic performance. At best, they can (and do!) play the blame and credit game. They gyrate ingeniously and energetically to tattoo their opponents with responsibility for downturns in the business cycle. Never mind that downturns are the unavoidable complement to upturns, or else by definition there would be no cycles.

Politicians deserve criticism for overstating their role in creating prosperity, but they can legitimately assign some of the blame to another set of players. For economists who want to be inside the halls of power, the price of admission is agreeing to go along with the ruse. Party loyalty demands that they dumb down their theories to the level of potshots at the opposition.

Economists and politicians alike could elect to take the high road out of their mire of disingenuousness and distortion. They could stop pretending that the economy responds on cue when a wise administration decides to pick up or slow down the pace. Using their formidable communication skills, politicians could raise the level of the discussion from bickering over dubious short-term fixes. They could shift the focus to tax and regulatory reforms that would enable the American economy to achieve a greater portion of its long-run potential.

All of this *could* happen, but it won't actually happen without a profound change in politicians' beliefs. They will alter their present approach in economic debates only when they no longer perceive that honesty is the worst policy.

The onus is on the voters. Their task is to become knowledgeable enough to recognize dishonesty. If they then confront candidates by exposing their deceit, a change in politicians' behavior is possible.

14

Campaign Finance Reform: The Permanent Campaign

Campaign finance reform is one of Washington's longest-running farces. Every few years, exceptionally shocking irregularities come to light, generating enough public revulsion to initiate new legislation. But the enterprise is doomed from the outset because the mission of reform is in the hands of the chief beneficiaries of the irregularities.

The officeholders' perennial tactics include delay, dilution (sometimes occurring after the legislation has passed, when the furor has died down), and invention of new ways to evade the spirit of the law. Generation after generation of voters concludes that Washington has finally cleaned up the electoral process, only to discover later that it's as much of a cesspool as ever.

It's not obvious that putting a ceiling on campaign expenditures is appropriate public policy. Some politicians openly oppose spending limits on principle, arguing that they violate the First Amendment's guarantee of free speech. They may regard the reformers as wrongheaded, but there's no automatic presumption that advocates of spending caps operate on base motives. A sincere desire to do what's good for the country could lead to either a hands-off policy or an effort to prevent politicians from becoming beholden to major contributors.

Most office seekers, however, instinctively head for the low road. They sanctimoniously denounce the role of big money, especially in their opponents' campaigns. Hoping to score points with voters, they back purported reform that on closer examination constitutes pseudoreform. It is one more case of politicians telling it like it isn't and thereby making a mockery of the democratic process.

FUTILITY IN THE REFORM ERA

The charade of campaign spending limits began in the reform era after the Civil War. It was a time of high hopes for positive social change. Leaders of the progressive movement sought to broaden participation in the political process and curtail the power of party bosses and their machines. Campaign finance was a natural focus of their efforts.

A 1867 law banned the solicitation of campaign funds from Navy Yard workers. In 1883, the Pendleton Act outlawed solicitation of funds from all federal office holders. Thanks to that reform, civil servants could keep their jobs even if they declined to hand over a portion of their earnings to the campaigns of their political patrons.

The Pendleton Act set another powerful precedent by leaving a gaping loophole. Its restriction didn't apply to state and city government employees. That left the local party machines free to continue shaking down workers who were beholden to them for their positions. Anyone doing business with the municipality was expected to pony up as well.

Campaign finance gained prominence following the 1896 and 1900 presidential contests between Democrat William Jennings Bryan and Republican William McKinley. On the Republican side, campaign manager Mark Hanna created a highly effective quota system for corporate contributions, playing on fears of Bryan's opposition to the gold standard and protective tariffs. Banks and insurance companies' assessments were calculated as a percentage of their assets, while major corporations paid a specified percentage of their revenues.[1] The levy worked so well that in 1900 McKinley returned $50,000 of a reputed $250,000 contributed by Standard Oil, saying that the company had paid more than its fair share.[2]

Hanna didn't promise the corporate bankrollers any specific favors in exchange for their cash. Instead, he offered the prospect of "access" and a corporate-friendly administration. As in more recent times, that was enough to raise concerns about the influence of major contributors.

Meanwhile, reform-minded journalists began to uncover nefarious activity in the insurance industry. During 1904, the popular press published electrifying exposés of unscrupulous business practices, nepotism, and political lobbying that verged on bribery.[3] Responding to the resulting public outrage, in 1905 the New York state legislature formed a special committee to investigate the insurance industry. As general counsel, the legislature chose a prominent progressive lawyer, Charles Evans Hughes.

Among the items turned up by Hughes was a check for $50,000 written by one of the targets of the investigation, New York Life Insurance Company. The check was made out to the 1904 presidential campaign of Theodore Roosevelt. Republican Roosevelt was a champion of reform who had criticized his own party's tactics in the 1896 election, complaining that Hanna "advertised McKinley as if he were a patent medicine."[4]

During the same campaign, Roosevelt made a great show of returning $100,000 given by Standard Oil—after the contribution provoked a public outrage.[5] The Rough Rider ostentatiously declared that his campaign's policy was never to promise anything in return for funds except the square deal due everybody, contributor or otherwise. Nevertheless, said Roosevelt, accepting funds from Standard Oil would likely be construed as putting him under an improper obligation to the company.[6]

As Roosevelt was dictating the letter ordering his campaign staff to return Standard Oil's $100,000 contribution, Attorney General Philander Knox wandered into his office. "Why Mr. President, the money has been spent," Knox said. "They cannot pay it back—they haven't got it." Replied the president of the United States, "Well, the letter will look well on the record, anyhow."[7]

The revelations arising from the 1904 election were sufficiently embarrassing to induce Roosevelt to ask Congress to overhaul the campaign finance system. He called for a ban on all contributions to political parties and the institution of government funding of federal, state, and local campaigns.

Congress acted to quell the public outrage, albeit slowly. By the time the lawmakers passed the Tillman Act in 1907, they had substantially watered down Roosevelt's sweeping proposal. Instead of outlawing all contributions, the law prohibited only contributions by corporations and national banks. Neither did the 1907 reform cap contributions by individuals. That left the door wide open to many who had amassed huge fortunes through control of the corporations that were barred from giving. Furthermore, the Tillman Act applied solely to federal elections.

REFORMERS AND CIRCUMVENTORS—A DISTINCTION WITHOUT A DIFFERENCE?

Reformer Charles Evans Hughes's encounters with campaign finance didn't end with his work on behalf of the New York legislature. In 1916, he was the Republicans' presidential nominee, losing to the incumbent, Democrat Woodrow Wilson. Although Wilson, like Hughes, campaigned under the banner of reform, he relied on the large individual gifts that remained lawful despite the Tillman Act's ban on corporate funding. Wilson turned a blind eye as huge contributions poured in from transit moguls Thomas Fortune Ryan and August Belmont Jr., two individuals from whom he had self-righteously refused to accept money four years earlier.

Five years later, Hughes reentered the election financing picture when former Secretary of the Navy Truman H. Newberry was convicted of exceeding Michigan's campaign funding limit of $1,875. The charge arose out of Newberry's successful 1918 primary race for the Republican senatorial nomination, in which he defeated auto magnate Henry Ford. Hughes won a Supreme Court reversal of Newberry's conviction on the grounds that Congress had no jurisdiction over spending on primary elections. Besides exploiting that loophole, Hughes argued that Newberry had not personally overspent on the race for the Senate nomination. The campaign committee, not the candidate, had raised and disbursed the $180,000.[8]

The spirits of the reformer and the circumventor of campaign finance laws were united in the body of Charles Evans Hughes. This impartiality no doubt served him well in his subsequent job of Chief Justice of the United States Supreme Court.

PRESERVING THE ALL-IMPORTANT ESCAPE CLAUSE

In 1910, Congress mandated disclosure of the sources of campaign funds in House races and in the following year extended the requirement to Senate races. Disclosure wasn't required in electoral off-years, however. During the Harding administration, certain contributors took full advantage of that opening. They donated heavily to the Republicans, receiving access to government-owned oil deposits as their quid pro quo.

The resulting Teapot Dome scandal, in which the Secretary of the Interior was convicted of accepting bribes, triggered a fresh wave of outrage.

Congress dutifully tightened the disclosure requirements through the Federal Corrupt Practices Act of 1925. But the requirements were still not tough enough to have any real impact. Indeed, one journalist declared that campaign managers could drive a four-horse team through the 1925 Act.[9] Among other things, the Federal Corrupt Practices Act relieved candidates of liability under its provisions if they simply claimed to have no knowledge of money being spent on their behalf.

It became apparent just how huge that particular loophole was when Congress finally got serious about disclosure by passing the 1971 Federal Election Campaign Act. In 1968, under the looser, older law, candidates for the House and Senate reported just $8.5 million of expenditures. After the new law went into effect, Congressional candidates owned up to spending $88.9 million.[10]

Following the 1925 Federal Corrupt Practices Act, the next major opportunity for getting around the campaign finance laws arose from the Clean Politics Act of 1939. Also known as the Hatch Act, it expanded the Pendleton Act's prohibition of contributions by (as opposed to solicitation of) federal employees. Previously, about 70 percent of government workers had been excluded from the ban.

One year after the Hatch Act's passage, the Republicans sought to extend the ban to state government employees whose salaries were federally funded. Democrats revolted, on the principle that their big city political machines depended heavily on contributions from those state workers. In an effort to defeat the bill, they attached a rider calculated to scare off the large-donor-oriented Republicans. It limited individual contributions to $5,000 and expenditures by a party committee to $3 million in each presidential election cycle. To everyone's amazement, Congress passed the bill, rider and all.

That's not to say that the limitations accomplished the intended results. The Republican National Committee's general counsel declared that an individual could lawfully make $5,000 contributions to each of several state and local party committees. In addition, he contended, a party could legally form several national committees, each of which could spend $3 million. Through the latter dodge, the Republicans managed to spend $15 million on the 1940 election—five times the supposed limit. The Democrats managed only to double the alleged cap with a $6 million outlay.

Party chieftains continued to whittle the spending limits into irrelevance. To voters circa 1940, the $3 million ceiling on national committee spending seemed to limit total outlays in a two-party system to $6 million. By 1968, however, the joint tab reached $100 million. The Democrats formed almost 50 different committees to get around the single-committee limitation. Meanwhile, insurance kingpin W. Clement Stone made a mockery of the $5,000 individual limit by contributing $2.2 million to a smorgasbord of Republican committees and pro-Richard Nixon organizations. Once again, the reform that the politicians presented to the voters barely resembled the reform that voters actually got.

UNTIL THE NEXT OUTRAGE

The 1940s were followed by two decades of inactivity on the reform front. It wasn't that spending leveled off; on the contrary, the introduction of television advertising sharply increased the cost of campaigns. But without a scandal on the scale of Teapot Dome, the perennial public disgust over campaign finance never reached the boiling point.

Neither did the presidents of the 1950s and 1960s use their bully pulpit to demand congressional action. In fact, Lyndon Johnson went one better than the traditional tactic of watering down reform through delay. He named a bipartisan panel to look into the matter, then declined even to acknowledge its report.[11]

Finally, the dam started to crack. The 1968 presidential contest between Richard Nixon and Hubert Humphrey dramatized the ineffectiveness of existing campaign finance laws. Winner Nixon managed to block one proposed reform that might have actually achieved its purpose—public funding of campaigns.

The Federal Election Campaign Act of 1971 (FECA) raised hopes of palpable change by limiting candidates' media expenditures and restricting wealthy presidential candidates' spending on their own campaigns to $50,000. Once again, however, hopes of reining in the influence of big money on campaigns proved in vain. In 1972, Republican incumbent Richard Nixon managed to double his 1968 campaign spending. Challenger George McGovern spent four times as much as Hubert Humphrey had spent four years earlier.[12]

The 1971 Federal Election Campaign Act also left a major stone unturned by failing to create a single, independent agency to monitor and enforce the campaign finance laws. Instead, Congress left the fox with responsibility for the henhouse. The 1971 law assigned the Clerk of the

House and Secretary of the Senate to monitor compliance, along with the General Accounting Office.

AN APPARENT TURNING POINT

In addition to driving the cost of running for president to new heights, the 1972 election made history by spawning the Watergate affair. The scandal not only brought down Richard Nixon but also created a new groundswell for reforming campaign finance. Tales of illegal corporate contributions, money laundering in Mexico, and cash contributions in paper bags spurred the citizenry to action. Before long, letters demanding revision of the campaign finance laws accounted for one out of every four constituent letters to members of Congress.[13]

This time, Congress went beyond just making a show of reform. The 1974 amendment of the Federal Election Campaign Act finally adopted Theodore Roosevelt's proposal of 70 years earlier for public funding of presidential elections. Additionally, Congress limited expenditures on primaries and general elections. National committees could spend no more than $2.9 million on presidential races. Individuals were permitted to contribute no more than $25,000 in aggregate to all candidates in a federal election. Political action committees (PACs) had to limit their outlays to $5,000 per candidate. And to make sure everybody followed the rules, the 1974 law established a body to focus on enforcing the campaign laws, the Federal Election Commission (FEC).

DEFANGING THE ENFORCER

On its face, the FEC promised to be an effective cop. The law established it as an independent agency with sole discretion to determine whether a civil violation of the Federal Election Campaign Act has occurred. The commission also received primary responsibility for enforcing FECA, including exclusive jurisdiction for civil enforcement. That meant the FEC could conduct investigations, receive evidence, authorize subpoenas, and put witnesses under oath.

Passing the Federal Election Campaign Act allowed Congress to boast that it had finally put some teeth into the enforcement of the campaign finance laws. But members of Congress had no desire to put the cops on their own trail. Accordingly, they made sure to hamstring the commission in three insidious ways: The FEC has an impossibly cumbersome enforcement process, it lacks statutory enforcement powers, and its commissioners are chosen in a manner exquisitely designed to produce deadlocks.

Mandatory multistage procedures hamper the FEC in carrying out its seemingly far-reaching enforcement powers. Staff and resource limitations cause lengthy delays in dealing with the eligible cases. Targets of the subpoenas file motions to quash the subpoenas and if denied, simply refuse to comply. Going to court sets off a whole new round of research, briefs, and legal arguments. This can add years to an already painfully drawn-out enforcement process.

To throw one more monkey wrench into the works, Congress specified that the FEC would have six commissioners, with no more than three to come from any one political party. The natural consequence has been a split and deadlocked commission, with three Republicans offsetting three Democrats. It doesn't matter how serious an alleged campaign law violation may be. All further action can come to a halt if a 3 to 3 vote occurs at any stage in the process—opening a case, finding reason to believe that a violation has occurred, finding probable cause, filing a case in court, or appealing a court ruling.

It is small wonder that FEC Commissioner Scott Thomas and his executive assistant Jeffrey Bowman wrote in 2000 that the law's procedural requirements and the related time allowances make it difficult or even impossible to resolve a complaint in the same election cycle in which it is brought. They reported that the epithets flung at the hamstrung agency included "toothless watchdog," "dithering nanny," "lapdog," and even "self-licking ice cream cone."[14]

IT IS ALL IN THE EXECUTION

Having an even number of commissioners is not a unique feature of the FEC among federal administrative agencies. The International Trade Commission (ITC) also has six members, with three chosen from each party. But Congress provided that if the ITC commissioners deadlock on whether to proceed with an investigation, the investigation goes forward. The FEC's contrasting rule, by which a tie vote produces a stalemate, can lead to absurd results.

In 1996, the Dole for President campaign ran short of funds prior to the Republican Convention. The Republican National Committee (RNC) helped out by taking 12 members of presumptive nominee Robert Dole's staff onto its own payroll. When the Dole campaign received its grant of public funding for the general election, it returned 11 of the 12 staffers to the campaign's payroll.

On investigation of the incident, the FEC found that the Dole campaign had received an illegal contribution and the campaign entered into a settlement. But when the FEC's general counsel recommended investigating whether the RNC's shouldering of the staffers' compensation constituted an illegal in-kind campaign contribution, the commissioners split 3 to 3 on strict party lines and the matter ended. The bizarre conclusion: Dole's campaign *received* an unlawful contribution from the Republican National Committee, but that wasn't a good enough reason to explore whether the Republican National Committee *made* an unlawful contribution.

Not content with rigging the system to ensure deadlocks, Congress has impeded the FEC through its power to veto regulations issued by the commission. Two slapdowns occurred within the first year of the FEC's existence. First, a bipartisan coalition in the Senate rejected a rule that would have applied FECA contribution limits and disclosure requirements to congressional office accounts. These accounts, also known as *slush funds,* were intended to support constituent-related services, such as travel and newsletters. Second, the House blocked an FEC attempt to expedite the processing of disclosure reports by having candidates file them directly with the commission rather than with the House Clerk and Senate Secretary for forwarding to the FEC. Reportedly, the rejection was less of a substantive policy statement than a chance for Congress to demonstrate its power over the commission.[15]

In another 1975 skirmish, Congress put the FEC on a short leash by forcing it to come back for funding every year. The following year, the commission instituted random audits of congressional campaign committee disclosure reports, mimicking an enforcement approach employed to great effect by the Internal Revenue Service. Congress's reaction was swift and furious. Bipartisan coalitions emerged in both the House and the Senate to strip the FEC of its power or, at a minimum, enact amendments that would restrict the commission's use of authorized funds for random audits. In 1980, Congress managed to repeal the FEC's ability to conduct random audits. As a result, the commission could initiate audits only when a candidate's report betrayed glaring discrepancies. Another tactic for hamstringing the commission was requiring it to devote a substantial part of its appropriation to computer upgrades instead of enforcement.

UNDERMINING THE INTENT

Despite the many stumbling blocks placed in the Federal Election Commission's path, the post-Watergate reforms materially altered the practice of campaign finance. Beginning with the 1976 election, the presidential campaigns operated under a public financing system. Candidates could elect to receive public funds, provided they agreed to abide by ceilings on their expenditures and to refrain from raising any private money for their campaigns in the general election. Public financing's impact was highlighted in the 1985 report of a bipartisan commission headed by former Republican Congressman and Secretary of Defense Melvin Laird and former Democratic party chairman and U.S. trade representative Robert Strauss. The report found that the new system had opened up the electoral process, reduced undue influence of individuals and groups, and all but ended corruption in the financing of presidential elections.

Heartening though this news was for voters, it was gall to the politicians. The time had come to find some new way to shield campaign financing from scrutiny and restore influence and corruption. It would have been too audacious to attempt a frontal assault on well-established restrictions. Corporations and labor unions had long been prohibited from making contributions or expenditures to influence federal elections. As for individuals, the Federal Election Campaign Act had limited their contributions in an election cycle to $1,000 to a federal candidate, $20,000 to a national political party, and $25,000 to all recipients. With these rules firmly entrenched, the circumstances called for a sneak attack. Luckily for the politicos, an opening emerged in the form of *soft money*—campaign contributions that aren't subject to the customary ceilings.

Soon after the passage of FECA in 1974, the Federal Election Commission began to deal with a riddle posed by the legislation: What if a state party spent money on voter registration efforts and get-out-the-vote drives for an election that included both federal and state races? If the fund-raising limits for federal elections applied, the effect would be to limit state expenditures not controlled by FECA.

In 1976, the FEC decided that there was no reasonable basis for separating the state impact from the federal impact of voter registration and get-out-the-vote efforts. Therefore, the commission concluded, the state parties would have to pay for such activities exclusively with funds raised in accordance with the federal limits, otherwise known as *hard money*.

Just two years later, the FEC reversed itself. Now, an activity that affected both a federal and a state election could be financed with a combination of hard and soft money. The state party undertaking the activity could determine what portion of the outlay was affecting the state election and how much was affecting the federal election. In 1979, the FEC helped the national parties a bit more by permitting them to open nonfederal accounts and allocate expenditures between state and federal impact.

The allocation required no scientific formula. To the extent that the parties' allocation assumptions exaggerated the significance of state races, seekers of influence could now do what the campaign finance laws expressly forbade. They could effectively contribute to, and influence the outcome of, federal elections without regard to lawful spending limits.

A NEW SURGE OF SOFT MONEY

In 1987, a federal court found that the FEC's failure to provide guidelines for allocating expenditures on mixed (state and federal activities) was contrary to the law. According to the court, the potential for abuse was obvious and any improper allocation of nonfederal funds by a state party represented a violation. The court ordered the FEC to issue new regulations to ensure that allocation methods used by state and local party committees were in compliance with the FECA.

While the FEC pondered the matter, the 1988 presidential election took place, launching a fabulous new era of soft money. Fund-raisers for Democratic nominee Michael Dukakis began soliciting contributions of $100,000 or more from individuals, far exceeding the $1,000 single-candidate and even the $25,000 all-purposes limit for hard money. The soft money effort was handled by the Democratic National Committee's Victory Fund '88 committee, which had the same Boston address as Dukakis's national campaign headquarters. Bush's campaign denounced the Democrats' novel tactic as illegal then copied it. In fact, the Republicans' "Team 100" soft money campaign eventually recruited twice as many $100,000-plus individual and corporate contributors as the DNC's effort. To head the soft money drives, both parties tapped the individuals who had previously served as their candidates' chief fund-raisers.

After further prodding by the court, the FEC finally established new soft money guidelines in 1991. The regulations merely codified existing practices, and use of soft money to influence federal elections continued to grow.

Another growth surge followed the FEC's 1995 ruling that a mix of hard and soft money could fund not only voter registration and get-out-the-vote drives, but also certain television advertisements. The rationale was that some ads were run by the parties, rather than the candidates' campaigns, and discussed election issues instead of urging viewers to vote for a particular candidate. Once again, a guideline was needed; in this case, to determine what constituted an issue ad.

It so happened that the U.S. Supreme Court had previously established a "magic words" test for determining whether individuals other than candidates or organizations other than political parties could pay for ads with hard money. As long as an ad didn't contain certain words such as "vote for" or "vote against," said the high court, it could be funded with soft money. President Bill Clinton's 1996 campaign adopted the same magic words standard for the Democratic party even though the Supreme Court had specifically excluded candidates and parties from the standard on the grounds that their efforts were inherently campaign related.

The Democratic party began running ads that promoted its candidate by name and attacked Clinton's opponent, Robert Dole, by name. To qualify for soft money, even under the Clinton campaign's aggressive interpretation of the rules, the party's effort had to be separate from the Clinton campaign. Nevertheless, campaign officials wrote, edited, produced, and directed the ads. Bill Clinton himself was personally involved in the project.[16]

Inevitably, the Dole campaign soon began using soft money to finance a similar series of television ads. The FEC issued no advisory opinion to prevent the campaigns from misappropriating the Supreme Court's definition. Neither did it try to block the practice through its enforcement powers.

In the aftermath of the 1996 campaign, the public was treated to accounts of peddling benefits such as coffee at the White House and sleepovers in the Lincoln bedroom for contributions at specific dollar levels. Vice President Al Gore got into hot water for appearing at an event at a Los Angeles Buddhist temple that brought in $116,500 of allegedly illegal contributions. Gore denied knowing that the event was a fund-raiser, initially characterizing it as a "community outreach" event.[17] On a more ludicrous note, businessman Johnny Chung arranged to have President of the United States Bill Clinton photographed with the president of China's second-largest beer producer. The photo was later used in Chinese beer advertisements.[18] Chung eventually admitted circumventing individual limits on donations and pleaded guilty to bank fraud, tax evasion, and conspiracy.

In 1985, Melvin Laird and Robert Strauss had hailed the near elimination of corruption from the financing of presidential elections. Just over a decade later, corruption was rampant, with questions even of national security being raised. The problem that Congress had ostensibly fixed with public financing got unfixed by the introduction and expansion of soft money.

ANOTHER NARROW ESCAPE FROM REFORM

Considering the magnitude of the scandals surrounding the 1996 election, one might have expected a swift and sweeping reform. One would have been mistaken, however.

True, the Federal Election Commission's general counsel concluded that the Democratic National Committee's so-called issue ads were actually designed to promote Bill Clinton's nomination and election. Accordingly, the general counsel recommended that the Commission should find reason to believe that $47 million of media disbursements were illegally made by the DNC and illegally accepted by the Clinton campaign. The general counsel further recommended a finding of violations of spending limits and disclosure requirements by the DNC and the Clinton campaign. Finally, the general counsel had similar findings about the Republican National committee's soft money expenditures for issue ads on behalf of Robert Dole's campaign.[19]

When the FEC voted on the general counsel's enforcement recommendations in February 2000, however, the commissioners deadlocked at 3 to 3. Thanks to a system designed to produce such stalemates, the government's watchdog agency took no action against the soft money abuses that shocked the nation. Naturally, politicians took the message—actions have no consequences—as a green light to stretch the limits of soft money even further.

CONGRESS SHAMED INTO ACTION

Now Congress took up the cudgels for reform and clamped down on soft money as part of the Bipartisan Campaign Reform Act. The first version of the legislation, also called the McCain-Feingold bill after chief sponsors Senator John McCain (R-AZ) and Russ Feingold (D-WI), had been introduced in 1997. As a presidential candidate in 2000, George W. Bush indicated that he would support the bill as long as it regulated both traditionally pro-Democratic (labor unions) and pro-Republican (business) soft money contributors. He signed the law, with reservations, in 2002.[20]

On the face of it, McCain-Feingold restored meaning to the limits on individual contributions. Previously, corporations and labor unions had gotten around prohibitions on contributions to federal election campaigns by giving soft money. The new legislation barred corporations and labor unions from dipping into their own treasuries for soft money donations. From now on, they would have to raise the money through voluntary, individual contributions to their PACs.[21] McCain-Feingold also outlawed issue ads in the 60 days preceding an election.

But despite the severe constraints seemingly imposed by McCain-Feingold, seasoned observers doubted that they had heard the last of soft money. Long-time FEC-watchers wondered, based on its record, whether the commission would enforce the new rules effectively.[22] Indeed, according to a September 2004 ruling by the U.S. District Court, the regulations created by the FEC to implement McCain-Feingold's provisions created "an immense loophole"[23] for coordination of soft money efforts. Judge Colleen Kollar-Kotelly found that the FEC defied logic, devised creative new definitions of common words, and interpreted McCain-Feingold so narrowly that certain of its regulations would "foster corruption" and "invite circumvention of the law."[24] Unfortunately, Kollar-Kotelly's ruling came too shortly before the November 2004 election to curb the extensive use of soft money.

THE NEW ANTIDOTE TO REFORM—527S

The biggest controversies of 2004 didn't arise from new restrictions imposed by McCain-Feingold. The race between George W. Bush and John Kerry was noteworthy for complaints that the FEC was failing to enforce old rules on tax-exempt entities known as 527 groups.

Nonprofit political organizations can exercise their rights of free speech by publishing their opinions and underwriting voter mobilization drives. Federal laws and Supreme Court decisions that antedate McCain-Feingold set a condition: If a group's "primary purpose" is to affect the outcome of federal elections, it must register as a federal political committee. It then becomes subject to contribution limits rather than being allowed to raise unlimited amounts of soft money.

With other sources of soft money shut off, political operatives associated with both major parties created new 527s to fund issue ads. The Media Fund and Swift Boat Veterans for Truth spiritedly attacked the records of candidates Bush and Kerry, respectively, ostensibly focusing all the while on issues. The Media Fund ran an ad depicting a child held by a ball and chain, representing the bill for the Iraq war, and another featuring a woman telling Bush, "you lied to us" about dumping of toxic nuclear waste.[25] Phrases applied to Kerry by the Swift Boat Veterans included, "contempt for the military," "devious, self-absorbing, manipulative," and "no regard for the truth."[26]

To preserve the requisite issue ad fig leaf, the televised messages didn't actually tell viewers not to vote for the incumbent or his challenger. Officials of the 527 groups avoided even uttering the names of the candidates that they clearly favored but were not explicitly supporting. America Coming Together's President Ellen Malcolm told reporters, "We're going to win the election for Democrats up and down the ticket." John Kerry topped that ticket but by not mentioning his name, Malcolm apparently remained within the letter of the law.[27]

If the FEC had required the 527 groups to register as federal political committees, they wouldn't have been able to raise more than $5,000 from any individual. Red tape came to their rescue, however. The FEC hearings in the spring of 2004 culminated in a decision to delay making a decision. The 527s were consequently free to go after bigger tickets from the likes of Democratic billionaires George Soros and Peter Lewis and well-heeled Republicans such as T. Boone Pickens and Bob Perry. Contributions of $250,000 or more accounted for an estimated 80 percent of the 527s' funding.[28] With an emphasis on big-ticket donors, pro-Kerry and anti-Bush 527s raised $266 million. The other side got off to a slower start, as the Republicans initially relied on their superior fund-raising capabilities among small contributors. Pro-Bush and anti-Kerry 527s nevertheless drummed up $14 million.[29]

Predictably, accusations flew that 527 groups were illegally coordinating their efforts with election campaign committees. The Republican National Committee charged MoveOn.org, The Media Fund, America Coming Together, and America Votes of coordinating with the Kerry campaign, which in turn alleged that Swift Boat Veterans for Truth was coordinated with the Bush campaign. At the Democratic convention in Boston, The Media Fund and America Coming Together operated down the hall from the Democratic National Committee's finance committee.[30] In some instances, lawyers represented campaigns or political committees while simultaneously representing 527 groups.[31]

THE SACRED RULE—QUID PRO QUO

Along with carefully constructed loopholes, another perennial theme of campaign finance reform has been the debate over the contributors' motives: Does it follow, just because wealthy donors foot a large portion of the bill for a candidate's election, that they expect favors in return? During the height of a campaign finance scandal in 1997, President Bill Clinton protested:

> I do not agree with the inherent premise that some have advanced that there is somehow something intrinsically wrong with a person that wants to give money to a person running for office and that if you accept it, that something bad has happened.[32]

The long history of campaign finance provides voters ample reason for taking a dim view of such transactions. During the 1905 insurance industry investigation, Charles Evans Hughes asked New York Republican boss Thomas Platt whether candidates felt morally obligated to their large donors. "That is naturally what would be involved," Platt candidly replied.[33]

The contrast between the Clinton and Platt comments does not imply a philosophical division along party lines. Johnny Chung, the frequent visitor to the Clinton White House who confessed to violating individual donation limits, contributed $350,000 to the Democratic National Committee in the 1996 election cycle. His take on the process: "[T]he White House is like a subway: you have to put in coins to open the gates."[34]

PRINCIPLED OPPOSITION TO REFORM (REALLY!)

There are several possible responses to the seeming futility of attempts to reform campaign finance. One is to continue plugging loopholes in full knowledge that before long, new loopholes will require new plugs. Another disheartening response is to conclude that the system is irredeemably corrupt and resign oneself to it.

The third path, which is less obvious, is to reject the presumption that contributions ought to be restricted. A few politicians have openly opposed campaign contribution limits on principle, paradoxical though it may sound. Even more remarkably, the principle is loftier than preserving the right to sell out to the highest bidder.

After President Gerald Ford signed the 1974 FECA amendment that imposed spending ceilings for presidential campaigns and related outlays by national party committees, opposition emerged on First Amendment grounds. The objection didn't arise from a Republican versus Democrat or a left versus right conflict. Its three spokespeople were conservative Republican Senator James Buckley of New York, the liberal ex-Senator from Minnesota Eugene McCarthy, and the executive director of the New York Civil Liberties Union, Ira Glasser. The trio contended that contribution limits were unconstitutional and that disclosure requirements smacked of a police state.

To pursue their challenge to the 1974 campaign finance legislation, Buckley, McCarthy, and Glasser sued the Secretary of the Senate, Francis R. Valeo. The case went to the Supreme Court. On January 30, 1976, the justices handed down their decision.

In *Buckley v. Valeo,* the court ruled that limiting campaign expenditures by individuals, groups, or candidates indeed violated freedom of speech, because a primary effect would be to restrict the quantity of campaign speech. By the same reasoning, the court prohibited any limitation on what candidates could spend on their own behalf. Justice Potter Stewart commented:

> [M]oney is speech and speech is money, whether it is buying television or radio time or newspaper advertising, or even buying pencils and papers and microphones.[35]

Buckley v. Valeo was a complex decision. The justices decided that campaign expenditures by candidates could not be limited, but that direct contributions to candidates could be. They reasoned that when the money passed out of the givers' hands, it ceased to belong to them as speech. Contribution limits, said the judges, served the legitimate interest of protecting the integrity of elections. The justices also implied (and in 1980 affirmed in *Republican National Committee v. FEC*) that expenditure limits on *publicly funded* candidates were constitutional. Their rationale was that presidential candidates had the option of rejecting public financing and ignoring the limits. An additional component of the court's ruling required a change in the method of appointing FEC commissioners. Finally, the court upheld the 1974 legislation's disclosure and record-keeping requirements, rejecting the plaintiffs' objections.

Neither the advocates nor the opponents of campaign spending restrictions could claim an unqualified victory and the Supreme Court's 1976 decision didn't settle the constitutional issues once and for all. A 1978 ruling by the high court determined that corporations had nearly the same First Amendment rights as individuals. Many lawyers took this as an opinion that the 1907 Tillman Act ban on corporate contributions was unconstitutional.[36]

Combined with the FEC's loosening of distinctions between state and federal expenditures on voter registration and get-out-the-vote drives, the judicial modification of the 1974 legislation produced a gusher of soft money. In the 1974 elections, 608 political action committees representing business, labor, and other special interests donated a total of $12.5 million. By 1996, the figures had mushroomed to 4,079 PACs and $200.9 million.[37]

To compound matters, the PACs gave 90 percent of their money to the politicians in the best position to help them—the incumbents. That bias accentuated the overwhelming tendency of members of Congress to get reelected. Political action committee money reinforced the power of incumbency maintained by the creation of safe districts through gerrymandering. Between 1992 and 2004, according to Amy Walter and Jennifer Duffy of the *Cook Political Report,* the number of competitive races in the House of Representatives declined from 151 to 57.[38] Seven out of eight contests of 2004, in short, were decided before they began. Instead of facing serious opposition and being forced to respond to the demands of the general electorate, most of the "permanent representatives" were free to cater to the narrow interests of PAC sponsors.

Historian Thomas Fleming pointed out a supreme irony in the explosive growth of soft money in the wake of *Buckley v. Valeo* and certain pivotal FEC decisions. Campaign finance reform began in the post-Civil War era in reaction to a system of mandatory levies on government employees. During the 1990s, labor unions reasserted their influence on the Democratic party by contributing millions through their PACs. Among the largest donors were the American Association of State, County and Municipal Workers and the National Education Association. "We are back to extracting a percentage of government employees' income to finance political campaigns," wrote Fleming, "but now we call it union dues."[39]

THE BOTTOM LINE

In the years since James Buckley, Eugene McCarthy, and Ira Glasser went to court, others have argued or editorialized against campaign finance restrictions on principled grounds. People of good faith can disagree. Surely, however, openly opposing spending and contribution limits is more commendable than behind-the-scenes political maneuvering to derail, dilute, or evade reform measures.

The democratic way is to put the choice to the people. In a perfect world, campaign finance reform's supporters would emulate its principled opponents by stating their positions plainly. The unprincipled opponents would meanwhile refrain from covertly building loopholes into proposed legislation. Voters could then choose between unrestricted spending and restrictions that might achieve the objectives represented by their sponsors.

In the real world, voters rarely encounter such straight-up-and-down choices. Legislators' approach to anything that involves reforming their own behavior follows a predictable pattern:

- Publicly debate a potpourri of bona fide reforms.
- Behind closed doors, craft a package of watered-down measures full of hidden loopholes.
- Pass the pseudoreform bill with bipartisan support, hoping that the public debate will leave voters falsely believing that the talked-about reforms actually made it into the legislation.
- Proudly declare that the problem has been solved for good.
- Resume business as usual, using the new gimmicks necessitated by the pseudoreforms.

Despite such gambits, vigilant voters can move the system closer to the ideal by insisting on truth in labeling of candidates and their proposals. To achieve that goal, it is also essential for journalists to perform their watchdog function. The media must ruthlessly expose dissembling, whether by Democrats, Republicans, or independents. Truly objective journalism does not consist of accepting politicians' disingenuous statements at face value and reporting them uncritically.

Most important of all, voters must remember that the job will never end. Even if zealous scrutiny resulted in every single elected official being ousted for campaign finance violations, others would quickly arise in their place. Politicians are engaged in a permanent campaign to create a safe environment for trading favors for cash. Their opponents in this effort—the people they are ostensibly elected to serve—can't afford to rest.

15

Here's That Rainy Day

Here's that rainy day they told me about
And I laughed at the thought that
It could end this way.[1]

The basic idea of a retirement insurance fund is hard for anybody of any political persuasion to oppose. Certainly, conservatives and liberals could disagree over whether the plan should be managed in the private sector or by the government. Libertarians might object to making participation compulsory. But who could object to people accumulating the necessary financial resources to live their twilight years in dignity instead of dependency?

Happily, this noble vision is a realizable objective, thanks to the miracle of compound interest. The simple formula involves setting aside a portion of people's income throughout their working lives. Prudently invested, the savings grow into big enough nest eggs to generate respectable postretirement incomes. Here is how it works:

A worker contributes $250 to a retirement fund every quarter for 40 years. By the end of the period, she has paid in a total $40,000. But she has also earned interest at a rate of 5 percent. Compounded quarterly, the accumulated interest comes to $85,535. Her account consequently has a total value of $127,535, of which only about one-third represents the cash she paid into the fund.

Naturally, honest and efficient administration is essential to the plan's success. There is nothing mysterious or untested, however, about creating a sound insurance program—particularly when the power of compound interest is harnessed. The main requirement to make the plan work well is a solid set of actuarial assumptions. The administrators need an estimate of the average number of years that participants will survive to collect benefits after retiring. There is a tremendous built-in advantage, when it comes to generating actuarial assumptions, in working with a pool of insured individuals that includes most of the employed people in the United States: The law of large numbers kicks in with a vengeance.

It is well within the power of insurance professionals to design a retirement program capable of remaining solvent under almost any conceivable circumstances. Therefore, the nation's retirement system should just hum along from one year to the next. The plan's ability to meet its future obligations should not hinge on highly debatable assumptions about future economic growth or productivity rates. Providing old-age income ought to generate no more excitement than any number of other inherently dry statistical processes.

Instead, the U.S. Social Security system is perennially mired in crisis and controversy. Conservatives tend to be more outspoken on the issue, but many liberals also express concern. The critics differ mainly on the severity of the problem they perceive and the question of whether it can be fixed by mere tinkering or necessitates a complete overhaul:

> [T]he program faces a long-term deficit and policymakers should make changes to it sooner rather than later.—*Peter A. Diamond and Peter R. Orszag, The Brookings Institution*[2]

> By 2018, Social Security's tax income is projected to be insufficient to pay currently scheduled benefits. This shift from positive to negative cash flow will place increased pressure on the federal budget to raise the resources necessary to meet the program's ongoing costs.—*David M. Walker, Comptroller General of the United States*[3]

> Fact: The current system will require a total of $25 trillion (in today's dollars without inflation) more in revenue than it will receive in taxes over the next 75 years, according to the Social Security Administration.—*David C. John, The Heritage Foundation*[4]

> For years, outside experts, various presidential commissions, and the Social Security system's own trustees have warned that the national re-

tirement program is headed toward bankruptcy.—*Michael Tanner, Fox News*[5]

Social Security has been financed as a Ponzi scheme and the Ponzi scheme is about over.—*John Cogan, Hoover Institution*[6]

It has taken a special talent for the federal government to create a financial nightmare from an idea so eminently executable. The key to achieving this feat has been misrepresenting Social Security to the electorate. If voters were to receive an honest explanation of the scheme, they might very well demand a genuinely fresh approach to financing retirement. Political careers built on the status quo would be jeopardized.

Even now, as the inexorable necessity of reform forces its way onto the political agenda, politicians continue to dissemble. They promise to preserve the dream embodied by Social Security, but soft-pedal the unavoidable costs of repairing the system. To understand how they are sidestepping the tough issues, it is necessary first to examine how the predicament arose.

SURVEYING THE MESS

The fundamental flaw in Social Security is that it is not a self-funding insurance program. If it were that sort of well-designed system, each generation's savings would be invested for several decades. As one generation reached the end of its working life, the huge pot of money into which its savings had grown would be tapped for that generation's retirement income. It would make no difference how many members of the succeeding generation were entering the workforce. Those younger people's payroll deductions would fund *their* retirement. What could be simpler, fairer, or more reliable? Members of every generation would receive what was coming to them. No one would be burdened with supporting a previous generation.

Unfortunately, the qualities of simplicity, fairness, and reliability have made self-funding insurance a political nonstarter for the politicians. (Politicians don't object to fairness, per se. But they are willing to sacrifice it for the greater good of hustling votes.)

The level of Social Security benefits that current retirees receive is not determined by the investment performance of their savings, as it would be in a self-funding insurance program. Rather, Congress decrees what the size of the payout shall be. The Social Security Administration (SSA) disburses the prescribed amounts without respect to how much the retirees' savings earned (or could have earned) over the preceding decades.

Where does the Social Security Administration get the cash to pay those benefits if not from investment accounts set up for the retirees with the funds they have paid into the system? The SSA taps the huge inflow of money from younger people who are still in the workforce. It is assumed that when the time comes for today's workers to retire, the succeeding generation's contributions will be handed up in a similar way.

In theory, this "pay-as-you-go" approach can actually work, provided one all-important condition holds: The current workforce always must be large enough, relative to the size of the retired population, to pay enough into the system to cover current retirees' benefits. Consider another simple illustration:

> Suppose that based on levels determined by Congress, the average retiree's annual benefit is $16,000. There are currently four active workers for each member of the retired population. Their average wage and salary income is $30,000. Therefore, to pay for the retirees' income, the workers and their employers must contribute an average of $16,000 ÷ 4 = $4,000, which amounts to 13.3 percent of the average worker's income. If the ratio of active workers to retirees falls to three-to-one, then the required contribution per worker comes to $16,000 ÷ 3 = $5,333, or 17.8 percent of the average worker's income. With only two workers per retiree, the required percentage is 26.7 percent. At some point along this continuum, the system becomes an unaffordable burden for the active workers.

The scenario in which Social Security becomes unaffordable isn't so wildly improbable that it can safely be ignored. The population doesn't grow at a nice, steady pace that ensures a consistent ratio between workers and retirees. Birth rates fluctuate, making some generations bigger than others.

At present, the large post–World War II baby boom generation is approaching retirement age. As the boomers exit the workforce, the ratio of active workers to retirees is expected to decline from 3.3:1 currently to about 2.2:1 by 2030.[7] Barring a steep increase in payroll deductions (as specified by the Federal Insurance Contributions Act, or FICA), the Social Security system will start taking in less than it is paying out by 2018.[8]

This is what the Hoover Institution's John Cogan meant by declaring that the *Ponzi* scheme is about over. The late Charles Ponzi gave his name to a scheme for creating the illusion that people are earning extraordinary profits by investing in a business venture. In reality, the swindler uses new participants' money to pay off earlier rounds of participants. No funds actually get invested in a bona fide enterprise. The deception is sustainable as long as the organizer continues to recruit victims at an increasing rate. Inevitably, though, it becomes impossible to attract enough new participants and the fraud collapses.

Ponzi's particular form of chicanery is a useful model for explaining Social Security although politicians don't usually choose it. They prefer a bookkeeping fiction that conveys a more positive impression, the so-called Social Security trust fund.

DON'T TRUST, BUT DO VERIFY

The politicians' rosy depiction of Social Security suggests that workers' contributions are carefully shepherded into a trust fund. The very phrase suggests a future financial state superior to mere security. After all, in the popular imagination, "trust fund babies" invariably live in ease or even debauchery.

According to the way the government keeps the books, the money deducted from workers' paychecks resides in a fund that the SSA invests in supersafe United States Treasury obligations. It would seem to follow that the workers' promised benefits are certain to be available when they retire. Likewise for the next generation and the one after that.

In reality, the phrase "trust fund," as applied to Social Security, is just words. Yes, the Social Security Administration receives interest-bearing IOUs from the Treasury when it hands over the cash it has collected. The Treasury then uses the cash, along with the revenues it receives from other sources, to cover a variety of government expenditures. Instead of sitting in a fund earmarked for future retirement benefits, workers' FICA payments generate an entry on the Treasury's balance sheet.

The problem with this arrangement is not any significant risk that the Treasury will fail to pay its obligations when they come due. Rather, the

flaw involves the total amount of money that the Treasury owes to the Social Security Administration. It has no particular connection to the aggregate size of the benefits that Congress has promised the workers.

As long the SSA, in Ponzi-like fashion, rakes in more from current
workers than it shells out to retirees, its Treasury IOUs sit undisturbed,
collecting interest. When (as must happen in light of the present demo-
graphics) the outflows begin to exceed the inflows, the interest can initially fill the gap. As the shortfall increases, however, the SSA must start
redeeming its IOUs, which are structured as bonds. The Social Security
Administration freely acknowledges that the federal balance sheet entry
labeled as the Social Security trust fund will not suffice to keep the system afloat:

> These bonds totaled $1.5 trillion at the beginning of 2004, and Social
> Security receives more than $80 billion annually in interest from them.
> However, Social Security is still basically a "pay-as-you-go" system as
> the $1.5 trillion is a small percentage of benefit obligations.[9]

Eventually, the IOUs will be entirely liquidated, but the system will
still be paying out more than it is taking in. The Treasury won't have re-
neged on any commitment to Social Security. Nevertheless, it will dawn
on tomorrow's retirees that they are on the wrong end of a rat hole into
which billions of dollars are disappearing.

FROM DAY ONE

Misleading though it is to depict Social Security as a trust fund, the deception might be partially excused if certain historical facts existed. Suppose that at the outset, elected officials had devised as sound a system as
they knew how, given the information available at the time. Imagine also
that certain demographic factors subsequently changed in ways that could
not possibly have been foreseen. In that case, the politicians could be
faulted only for lacking the gift of prophecy, not for acting in bad faith.

This is precisely the self-vindicating story that politicians have promoted. During the Great Depression, so the tale goes, progressive statesmen reinvented the federal government as a force for positive social
change. They resolved to abolish once and for all people's fear of spending

their twilight years in the poorhouse. These visionaries enacted a plan whereby, in the words of the Social Security Administration, "the workers themselves contribute to their own future retirement benefit by making regular payments into a joint fund."[10]

At least for the first few decades, the story continues, the enlightened leaders' decision to take bold action was vindicated. Social Security proved to be "the most successful government program ever."[11] Problems arose only when life expectancy unexpectedly increased. That meant large numbers of people began living for many years beyond the customary retirement age of 65. Suddenly, the actuarial assumptions that had worked splendidly for several decades no longer applied. Far from exposing a flaw in the original design of Social Security, the change reflected health benefits brought about by other reforms of the no-longer-passive federal government.

In 2004, the Democratic presidential nominee, Senator John Kerry summarized this version of history with a quip. When Social Security began, he noted, the ratio of current workers to retirees was 13 to one. "Your life expectancy was 62," said Kerry. "Sixty-five retire. Life expectancy 62. Thirteen people paying in. It works."[12]

The fact is, however, that Social Security was neither actuarially sound at the outset nor later thrown off balance by an otherwise welcome increase in life expectancy. One essential element of a sound retirement insurance fund is long-run reliance on the power of compound interest. In 1935, President Franklin Roosevelt was not solely concerned with providing future retirement benefits to that era's young workers who would have many years for their savings to grow through investment. Rather, he wanted to provide immediate relief to people already on the verge of retiring and facing bleak financial prospects.

FDR couldn't tap the federal budget for that purpose, given the strains arising from tax revenues lost through the period's severe contraction in business activity. His only alternative was to have SSA begin paying benefits right away, funding the outlays with deductions from the paychecks of current workers. Accordingly, in January 1937, one Ernest Ackerman received the first Social Security benefit—a one-time, lump-sum payment of 17 cents. In 1940, monthly benefits commenced.[13]

The workers of the 1930s became the next generation of retired workers. Because their contributions had already been spent on the preceding generation's retirement benefits, the system had to repeat the gambit of forcing then-current workers to cough up the cash. Therefore, the SSA was playing catch-up ball from the outset. Periodic benefit increases by Congress made certain it would never get caught up.

THE FUZZY MATH OF LIFE EXPECTANCY

Turning to part two of the politicians' Social Security fable, people are indeed living more years beyond retirement than in the past. But most discussions of the topic greatly overstate the magnitude of this rise in life expectancy and its impact on the system.

An increase in life expectancy from 59 (men) and 63 (women) in 1935 to 76 for children born in the new millennium[14] appears to constitute a revolutionary change. To a large extent, though, the increase represents a reduction in deaths of individuals before they reach working age. The fact that a greater percentage of children survive to adulthood should have no effect on a soundly structured retirement plan. It means that there will be more retirees to collect benefits one day, but it also means that more workers will be paying into the system. Consider the following hypothetical example:

> A family has three children. One survives to age 70 and one to 80, while the third dies of an incurable childhood disease at age 6. The average life span among the siblings is $(70 + 80 + 6) \div 3 = 52$. One of the siblings in turn has three children. By the time they are born, a cure has been found for the childhood disease that killed the third sibling in the previous generation. The three members of the new generation live to ages 70, 80, and 75, respectively. Their average lifespan is $(70 + 80 + 75) \div 3 = 75$. On the face of it, life expectancy has increased from 52 years to 75 years. But for those who survive past childhood, life expectancy is exactly the same in the second generation, at 75, as in the first: $(70 + 80) \div 2 = 75$. Despite the advances in medical science, people who live long enough to enter the workforce still survive for an average of 10 years after retirement, just as they did when life expectancy was 23 years shorter.

The real-life demographic figures produce similar arithmetic. Of males born in 1875, 53.9 percent survived to age 65 in 1940. The comparable ratio for males born 50 years later and scheduled to reach 65 in 1990, was 72.3 percent. The corresponding figures for females were 60.6 percent and 83.6 percent. Thanks to dramatically reduced death rates in infancy and childhood, life expectancy *from birth* increased by about 15 years. Life expectancy *from age 65,* however, grew only from 12.7 years for males born in 1875 to 15.3 years for males born in 1925. The increase for men who lived long enough to begin collecting benefits was less than three years. For females, the increase was just under five years, from 14.7 to 19.6.[15]

These demographic statistics debunk the notion of Social Security beginning as a well-conceived program and running into trouble only because people began living much longer—a change to be celebrated rather than lamented. Candidate Kerry presented a misleading picture in 2004 by suggesting that Social Security initially worked because few workers lived very long after starting to collect benefits. From the program's inception, the long-run balance between money going in and money going out was precarious, irrespective of longevity. In a pay-as-you-go system, periodic crises were bound to occur.

Congress's wide latitude to increase retirees' benefits compounds the scheme's vulnerability. The amounts previously paid into the system place no ceiling on future payouts, as they would be in a genuine retirement insurance program. In fact, legislators have a powerful incentive to heap favors on the over-65 crowd. Voter turnout is much higher among the old than among the young. According to the Census Bureau, 72.2 percent of citizens aged 65 to 74 voted in the 2000 presidential election. The ratio was only 36.1 percent for citizens aged 18 to 24 years.[16] Dispensing goodies to seniors can be politically wise even if it imposes a staggering burden on the young folk.

STAGES OF DENIAL

A program that has the status of a sacred cow, combined with certain fiscal doom, creates acute stress for an elected official. The psychological strain generates a predictable response—denial. This response in turn causes the sufferer to grasp at hopes for a painless solution. Apparent salvation variously appears in the form of convening blue-ribbon panels, juggling tax rates and retirement ages, and assuming that acceleration in economic growth will somehow bail out the system.

The politicians' denial represents an unwillingness to confront the unpredictability of the future level of gross domestic income. The higher the country's income, the easier it is to support its retired population. But because no one knows for certain what the future income will be, the percentage of U.S. income that will be required to support retirees is subject to risk. The only question is who will bear that risk.

If Congress promises a specified level of benefits to workers within a given age bracket, it eliminates risk for one segment of the population. But the action does not reduce the chances that slower-than-expected future economic growth will create a larger-than-hoped-for burden on the active workforce. Congress has not eliminated any risk from the system. Instead, it has entirely shielded older workers from the risk and fully exposed younger workers to it.

Politicians have a distinct aversion to dealing with this inconvenient intrusion of reality. Deciding how to distribute economic risk is a responsibility they are loath to accept. They prefer to pretend that a proposal to link retirement benefits to investment returns (which reflect economic performance) *introduces* risk into the system. In so doing, they retreat further and further into denial. Three stages of the syndrome can be identified.

Stage One of denial consists of refusing to acknowledge that a problem exists. Twelve-step programs, such as Alcoholics Anonymous, emphasize that the essential first step toward a cure is to admit that one has a problem. Politicians who cannot bring themselves to that initial action have no chance of escaping their dependence on the pay-as-you-go mentality.

Fortunately, Social Security's incontrovertibly bleak financial projections have shocked some politicians into reaching the second stage of denial. In Stage Two, the subject accepts the fact that the Ponzi scheme cannot continue but refuses to confront the consequences of ending it.

The difficulty in progressing beyond Stage Two is not that the range of options is dismayingly large. In reality, only a few choices are available, and all of them are politically unappealing.

If the choice is to continue paying current retirees' benefits through deductions from current workers' paychecks, the politician must acknowledge that outflows from the system are beginning to exceed inflows. The government must close the gap by some combination of reduced benefits and increased taxes. As a practical matter, however, balancing the system through a tax increase would burden young workers to a degree that would trigger a revolt.

Alternatively, the government could replace the present system with a genuine retirement insurance plan. For workers young enough to have compound interest work for them for several decades before they retire, implementation of this reform is simple. It is a matter of flipping the switch and letting the thing run. But for the retired and the almost retired, new funding will be needed after inflows from current workers cease and the SSA draws down all its Treasury IOUs. There are four possible ways to come up with the money required to pay the benefits already promised to older workers:

1. Raise taxes.
2. Increase the national debt.
3. Create money through Federal Reserve policy, a potentially inflationary solution.
4. Reduce spending on other government programs.

To a seasoned politician, the solution is obvious:

1. Propose a reform that will ensure retirees' financial security for all time.
2. Remain suitably vague about which unpalatable but unavoidable choices the reform will entail.
3. When a compromise plan eventually emerges from Congress, blame the opposition for all its unpopular features.
4. Explain that the choice was either to accept an imperfect bill or continue to subject people to uncertainty over financial security in their golden years.

Working its special magic, the political process has landed on both horns of the ultimate dilemma. Congress has accepted legislative imperfection while also perpetuating the uncertainty surrounding the funding of promised benefits. Compromises have spread the pain around, but left future retirees in the lurch as before.

This outcome constitutes Stage Three of denial. It consists of acknowledging that a problem exists, confronting the consequences of dealing with it, and then punting. The pathology of the third stage is exemplified by the work of the bipartisan National Commission on Social Security Reform created by President Ronald Reagan in December 1981.

A FOREORDAINED FAILURE

The commission's stated goals were to "propose realistic, long-term reforms to put Social Security back on a sound financial footing and forge a working bipartisan consensus"[17] to enable the proposed reforms to be enacted by Congress. The bipartisan structure precluded a financially responsible resolution.

Republican Alan Greenspan, the commission's chairman, favored replacing the pay-as-you-go system with a bona fide retirement insurance plan. A model was readily available in the plan adopted in the preceding year by Chile. Some commission members, including Senator Daniel Patrick Moynihan (D-NY) and Representative William Archer (R-TX), supported at least a partial switch to a private insurance plan. To AFL-CIO President Lane Kirkland and most of the Democratic appointees, however, any consideration of privatizing Social Security was heresy.

In the end, the Social Security commission proposed a patch job rather than an overhaul. The reform legislation that President Reagan signed into law in April 1983 called for new taxes to reduce the projected gap between workers' contributions and retirees' benefits. To trim the cost of benefits, the age for qualifying for full retirement benefits was bumped up in stages from 65 to 67 by 2022. In addition, the new setup extended coverage to employees of nonprofit organizations and new federal workers while ending state and local government workers' previous freedom to opt out of the system.

Contrary to Reagan's hopes, the commission proposed no break from the failed practice of taxing current workers to support current retirees. It missed the chance to begin exploiting the power of compound interest more effectively. The resulting legislation did not call for the long-term investment of workers' contributions to fund their own retirement. Washington, in short, remained in denial, refusing to come to grips with the inevitability of recurring crises under the existing arrangement.

Alan Greenspan put the best possible face on the work of Reagan's commission. The Social Security system, he proclaimed, was fixed for at least the next 75 years.[18] Only one-fifth of the way toward that horizon, however, President Bill Clinton was declaring that Social Security needed to be saved.

Clinton's warning led to a year-long national debate over the program's future.[19] It was a puzzlement to voters old enough to remember that the problem supposedly had been fixed in 1983. For a politician facing an election every two to six years, deferring a problem is just as good as solving it. In fact, when the solution necessitates paying the piper, deferring the problem is a downright superior choice.

MORE ARTFUL DODGING

So it was that three presidencies after the Greenspan-led panel allegedly ensured the solvency of the nation's retirement program, George W. Bush convened the President's Commission to Strengthen Social Security. Senator Moynihan returned to the scene as cochair along with Time Warner cochief operating officer Richard Parsons. The panel included such acknowledged experts as former Congressman Bill Frenzel (R-MN) and the aptly named Thomas R. Saving of Texas A&M University.

The commission proposed three possible models for reforming Social Security. All options included some form of personal savings accounts. Here, at last, was a path out of the darkness. Sadly, the commission's December 2001 report failed to spur Congress into immediate action.

In 2004, the presidential debates provided depressing evidence that deferral continued to be the politicians' preferred strategy. Bob Schieffer of CBS News pointed out to Democratic candidate John Kerry that Greenspan had said that that Social Security could not possibly meet its promises to retirees without recalibrating. That is, the numbers would not work unless Congress either cut benefits or raised the retirement age. Given that Kerry had said he would not change the benefits, Schieffer asked, did that mean he would leave the problem for the next generation to solve?

Kerry replied that, in so many words, the hullabaloo about a Social Security crisis was old hat. During the 1990s, he said, "[W]e heard the same thing. And we fixed it. In fact we put together a $5.6 trillion surplus in the 90's that was for the purpose of saving Social Security."[20] Kerry's message was seductively reassuring: As long as the federal government managed to run a surplus, it could always come up with the cash to pay retirees what they had been promised.

On the positive side, Kerry dispensed with the customary pretense that the funding for Social Security benefits was segregated in some sort of trust fund, safe from the financial follies of future Congresses and presidents. His remarks even hinted at an ability to think ahead—at least up to a point:

> Now if, later on after a period of time, we find that Social Security is in trouble, we'll pull together the top experts of the country, we'll do exactly what we did in the 1990s, and we'll make whatever adjustment is necessary.[21]

The adjustments that Kerry expected yet another blue-ribbon panel to recommend had nothing to do with creating a self-supporting system. The senator proposed neither raising the retirement age nor reducing payouts to retirees. He did talk about boosting taxes, at least on top-bracket earners. That would make a dent in the near-term funding shortfall. But rescinding some of President George W. Bush's tax cuts wouldn't address the fundamental problem. The baby boomer bulge generation's benefits imposed too big a burden for the succeeding generation's workers to bear through taxes.

Kerry refused to acknowledge any problem with keeping Social Security on its doomed pay-as-you-go basis. It was analogous to an alcoholic sleeping off the effects of a binge with every intention of going on another bender as soon as he sobered up. In fact, Kerry's recommended hangover cure smacked of "the hair of the dog that bit you."

During the same debate, George W. Bush at least touched on the underlying issues. He discussed his proposal to allow current workers to put a portion of their Social Security payments into private savings accounts. This would address the existing pay-as-you-go system's ineffective harnessing of the power of compound interest. Bush didn't go so far as proposing to replace Social Security with an actuarially sound insurance program, but he deserved credit for challenging his opponent's presumption that any reform smacking of privatization was self-evidently evil.

The soft spot in Bush's argument involved "transition costs." Creation of private savings accounts would provide for current workers' retirement benefits through their own contributions, but it wouldn't help those about to retire. The 60-somethings hadn't been benefiting from compound interest for 40-odd years. If current workers began putting a portion of their contributions into private savings accounts, instead of surrendering the full amount to pay for current benefits, the government would somehow have to make up the difference.

Debate moderator Schieffer estimated this transition cost at a trillion dollars over the succeeding 10 years. Kerry contended that Bush would have to fill an even larger "hole in Social Security" if he created private savings accounts. Citing the Congressional Budget Office, he estimated the gap at two trillion dollars.[22] Schieffer then put Bush on the spot by asking where he proposed to get the money.

There were only four possible answers that the president could give—higher taxes, increased borrowing, potentially inflationary monetary expansion, and reduced spending on other programs. Displaying keen political instincts, Bush avoided choosing any of these politically unpopular paths. "[O]f course we're going to have to consider the costs," he said and left it at that.[23] Bush's response, regrettably, continued the long tradition of denial. He acknowledged the problem and proposed a sensible solution, but ducked the question of how to finance his solution.

After his 2004 reelection victory, Bush placed Social Security reform at the top of his domestic agenda, but he neglected to line up adequate support within his own party for a fight that was certain to be tough. To make matters worse, he never presented a clear answer to the question of how to fund the transition costs. As a result of political miscalculations, the president lost an opportunity for material progress toward a financially sound retirement insurance program in the United States.

THE BOTTOM LINE

Generations of workers have viewed Social Security as their savings for a rainy day. Now, that rainy day has come. While the politicians remain in various stages of denial, the cost of repairing the system mounts. Michael Tanner of the Cato Institute estimates that the tab increases by $320 billion for each two-year election cycle by which a solution is delayed.[24]

Politicians are more concerned with appearing to do something about the problem than they are interested in actually solving it. But applying Band-Aids such as a higher retirement age merely enables Washington to remain addicted to blue-ribbon panels. Even the politically difficult step of instituting personal accounts represents a partway solution.

A genuine insurance retirement program is the mature, responsible way to head off recurring crises. Under such a plan, each cohort of workers would provide for its own future retirement income by investing a portion of its own paychecks. No longer would workers have to worry about the next generation's willingness to pay for their retirement. The system would fully harness the power of compound interest. That would certainly represent an improvement over the 2 percent return that present retirees earn on money paid into the system through payroll taxes.[25] Most refreshing of all, a bona fide retirement insurance program would not rely on a mythical trust fund.

Contrary to the charges sometimes hurled by the present system's defenders, a bona fide insurance plan need not gamble workers' retirement savings on the ups and downs of the stock market. Models for responsible, long-run investment strategies are readily available in the private pension fund world. Each cohort of workers' contributions could be invested in the same conservative, broadly diversified portfolio. Such an approach would eliminate the danger of any individual's retirement income being lost through speculation on singularly bad stocks recommended by an unscrupulous stockbroker.

It would even be possible under a genuine insurance retirement program to preserve a feature hailed by many for equity reasons.[26] The present payout arrangement provides low earners a higher percentage of their working wages than high earners. If a political consensus favored retaining that characteristic, it could be achieved within the context of a pooled investment fund for each cohort of workers. The lower earners' retirement accounts would simply be credited with something more than their per capita share of the portfolio's investment returns.

The electorate might just go for this sensible proposal if it were presented honestly. A candid discussion would include forthright dealing with the matter of funding near-term retirees' benefits, given that current workers' current payments into the system would no longer be used for that purpose. One suggestion, by Boston University economist Laurence J. Kotlikoff, involves a federal tax on business cash flow. He calculates that the levy would begin at around 8 percent and decline to a permanent level of approximately 2 percent within 40 years.[27]

Sadly, the emotionalism surrounding Social Security minimizes the chances of any politician putting a comprehensive solution on the table. Instead, voters will probably continue to hear accusations that any step more substantive than fine-tuning the existing mess constitutes an attempt to wreck the finest government program ever devised. A nagging question will remain unanswered, however: How can reform wreck a system that is already in ruins?

16

A Case of Insurance Fraud

A pit bull is not a bull any more than a guinea pig is a pig or a sea
lion is a lion. Even a child understands that calling an item by a
certain name doesn't make it that thing. Politicians nevertheless
maintain the pretense that the scheme that they label "deposit insurance"
is bona fide insurance.

The misnomer becomes obvious when we contrast federal deposit insurance with the operation of authentic insurance plans. Real insurance
companies don't shell out benefits for claims they haven't insured. They do
create incentives to reduce the frequency of events that give rise to claims.

Although bank failures produce economic losses and someone must
absorb the losses, there is a considerable downside to insulating depositors
from the losses and making taxpayers the ultimate fall guys. Worst of all,
deposit insurance may actually increase the incidence of bank failures.

Only through assiduous misrepresentation can such a problematic
program enjoy close to universal popularity. Contrary to what the public
has been led to believe for the past 70 years, the original impetus for
adopting deposit insurance wasn't a desire to protect savers. It is yet another case of politicians working overtime to prevent voters from understanding the issues.

BENEFITS WITHOUT PREMIUMS

The strongest indication that federal deposit insurance is insurance in
name only is its practice of paying for larger damages than its policies

cover. Genuine insurance companies are too determined to remain solvent to do anything like that. In the real-world insurance industry, complaints about insurance companies tend to come on the other side, alleging stinginess about honoring legitimate claims.

Consider a family that buys a home for $300,000 and insures it for the purchase price. Buoyed by a general rise in the real estate market, the house's value subsequently increases to $500,000. The insurance company urges the owners to increase their coverage to reflect the appreciation. The family, however, decides against paying the higher premium for the higher home value.

A natural disaster destroys the house, resulting in a loss of $500,000. But the insurance company's claims adjuster authorizes a check for only $300,000. Hearts go out to the family members for their loss, but they chose to bear $200,000 in risk above the amount of their coverage. Economizing on premiums, they gambled and lost.

Reasonable people must concede that the outcome can't be otherwise. The insurance company would fail if it habitually paid out claims above the amount for which it collects premiums. If insurance companies failed to conduct their business in an economically sound manner, they would have to cease operations, thereby depriving consumers of the benefit of insurance.

THE UNBUSINESSLIKE BUSINESS
OF INSURING DEPOSITS

Insurance companies, which sensibly pay only what policyholders have contracted for, stand in sharp contrast to the government's surrogate, the Federal Deposit Insurance Corporation (FDIC).[1] Beginning with its inception during the Great Depression of the 1930s, the FDIC operated under a legal limitation on the size of commercial bank deposits that it could insure. The Banking Act of 1935 capped coverage at $5,000 per account. For the next four decades, however, the FDIC almost invariably protected all depositors of failed banks, whether fully insured or not.

The FDIC's usual procedure was to merge the failed bank with a healthy bank. To induce the healthy bank to take over the insolvent institution, the FDIC either assumed the failed bank's loans or reimbursed the acquiring bank for any losses it incurred in the deal. Thanks to this unbusinesslike way of doing business, depositors with only partial coverage got all their money back when their banks failed. They fared much better than the family that suffered a $200,000 loss by declining to insure the full value of its home.

As early as 1950, Senator Paul Douglas (D-IL) warned that the FDIC's mode of operation was effectively obligating the government to protect uninsured as well as insured depositors. In the absence of a crisis, however, the practice continued. Deposit insurance kept digging itself into a deeper hole.

In 1980, the nation's twenty-third largest bank, First Pennsylvania, went bust by betting heavily—and wrongly—on the direction of interest rates. That, one would think, was an unfortunate turn of events for the bank's owners. But one would be wrong. Due to prohibitions then in place on interstate banking, the FDIC couldn't find a healthy bank to acquire First Pennsylvania. Deeming the bank essential to its community, by virtue of its size, the FDIC provided financial assistance to keep it afloat. The Federal Reserve and a consortium of large banks also lent a hand.

This time, not only the uninsured depositors but also the shareholders were made whole, even though their equity had been wiped out when the bank went belly up. Bailing out the providers of risk capital, who are entitled to all of the upside in the venture, runs directly counter to the spirit of free enterprise. As an old adage has it, "Capitalism without bankruptcy is like Christianity without hell."[2]

TOO BIG TO FAIL

Following the First Pennsylvania affair, the FDIC began to worry that uninsured depositors were becoming too blasé to exert much discipline over banks. During 1982 and 1983, it let some smaller banks fail without protecting uninsured depositors from losses. But as soon as a really big bank failed, the FDIC reverted to form. Politicians' rhetoric about standing up for the little folks was once again exposed as a sham.

In 1984, Continental Illinois was the nation's seventh largest bank and number one in commercial and industrial lending. When Contilly hit the skids, the FDIC provided $1.5 billion in aid and raised another $500 million from a group of banks. In conjunction with the Office of the Comptroller of the Currency and the Federal Reserve, the FDIC devised a rescue plan. It promised to protect all depositors without regard to the legislated $100,000 ceiling on deposit insurance.

Howls arose from congressmen whose constituents had lost portions of their uninsured deposits in other bank failures during the preceding two years. Why, they demanded to know, did the FDIC treat Continental Illinois differently? The House Banking Committee dragged out of Comptroller of the Currency Todd Conover a statement that regulators were unlikely to allow any of the 11 largest multinational banks to fail. Phrasemakers promptly declared that the government had adopted a "Too Big to Fail" policy. Stocks of the favored banks immediately climbed vis-à-vis the market averages.

In response to the public outcry over perceived favoritism toward the biggest and richest banks, the FDIC modified its stance. When the First National Bank of Oklahoma City became insolvent in 1986, the insurer allowed the bank's holding company to go bankrupt and its shareholders to be wiped out. But even though the FDIC stopped protecting some parties who had no contractual right to its protection, bigness remained a rationale for bailing out uninsured depositors.

What's more, bigness was gradually defined downward. In 1990, the FDIC stepped in to protect all depositors of National Bank Washington (DC), which was only the 250th largest or so. Even depositors at the bank's offshore office in the Bahamas benefited from the insurer's largess. Based on its location, critics charged that National Bank Washington was actually bailed out because it was too *political* to fail.

Eventually, public dissatisfaction over the abuse of the too-big-to-fail doctrine led to reform. Further impetus came from the mushrooming cost of bank failures and, especially, savings and loan failures. The FDIC Improvement Act (FDICIA) of 1991 expressly prohibited the FDIC from protecting a bank's uninsured depositors and other nondepositor stakeholders. Consistent with political traditions, though, the lawmakers provided a loophole: The FDIC could protect uninsured claimants in part or in whole if not doing so would have a severely negative impact on economic conditions or the country's financial stability.

The loophole didn't immediately or entirely undo the reform. For one thing, invoking the "systemic risk exemption" required the recommendation of the Federal Reserve Board of Governors and the approval of the Secretary of the Treasury in consultation with the president. Additionally, the new law tightened procedures by requiring that the FDIC sharply increase the banks' premiums if its reserve fell below 1.25 percent of insured deposits. This change gave the banks an incentive to prevent the FDIC from tossing money at uninsured depositors.

Still, the government's resolve to refrain from bailing out a very large bank hasn't been tested since the 1991 reform. Skeptics believe that when the test comes, the politicians will fail with flying colors. In 2002, Donald Kohn stated in his confirmation hearings as a nominee for the Federal Reserve Board of Governors, "No depository institution should be insulated from market forces by being considered too big to fail."[3] A newsletter focused on central banks commented, "Perhaps fortunately, nobody in the markets actually believes that doctrine."[4]

The good news is that the FDICIA forced the deposit insurers to become somewhat more businesslike. The lawmakers discovered an elementary technique employed by bona fide insurance companies: charging higher premiums to high-risk customers. By the same principle that requires poor drivers to pay more than good drivers for auto insurance, Congress concluded that unsound banks should get charged extra, giving them an incentive to become sound. It was a positive step. Still, the FDIC's historical practices don't look anything like the behavior of an honest-to-goodness insurance corporation.

ANOTHER DISTINGUISHING FEATURE

Bona fide underwriters of insurance pay out claims no greater than the amounts for which their policyholders have insured themselves. An authentic insurance company goes a step further. It seeks to reduce the number of claims that it is required to pay.

Some unscrupulous companies pursue that goal by trying to avoid honoring legitimate claims. Regulation and the threat of litigation keep such behavior under reasonable control. A further constraint is the resistance a company encounters in selling new policies when it has a reputation as a weasel. But legitimate methods of keeping claims low, such as requiring policyholders to avoid dangerous behavior, have the happy side-effect of benefiting society.

Corporate wellness programs illustrate how the provision of insurance leads to a reduction of underlying risk. A University of Michigan analysis of employee health insurance at Steelcase Corporation concluded that every smoker generated $285 a year of incremental health care expense. Ford Motor Company sought to avoid such costs by sponsoring a self-help smoking cessation program. According to a study by the American Institute of Preventive Medicine, 45 percent of the program's participants quit smoking. Ford's strategy was hardly an isolated example. A 1999 report found that 91 percent of companies were paying for some type of wellness program, up from 78 percent a decade earlier. Studies had shown that unhealthy lifestyles cost employers enough in incremental health insurance to justify the expenditure.[5]

Through legitimate strategies for minimizing claims, insurance companies collectively reduce the frequency of claims. Fewer people suffer injuries and the underwriters that contribute the most to this socially desirable outcome enjoy the greatest financial benefit. The result pleases everyone, except perhaps tort lawyers, who have fewer clients.

DEPOSIT INSURANCE LACKS THE FEATURE

Does deposit insurance have a comparable effect of reducing damage by promoting risk-reducing behavior? Let's test the proposition. We can observe whether the introduction of federal deposit insurance at a discrete point in time induced behavior likely to reduce the incidence of failures by depository institutions. These include not only commercial banks, but also savings banks, savings and loan institutions, and credit unions.

Federal deposit insurance came onto the scene through passage of the Banking Act of 1933. Coverage under a Temporary Deposit Insurance Fund began on January 1, 1934, and the Banking Act of 1935 created the FDIC. In the 1930 to 1933 wave of bank failures, depositors, shareholders, and other creditors suffered aggregate losses of $2.5 billion. Adjusting for inflation, the total hit was equivalent to about $25 billion at the time of the most dramatic failure of depositary institutions in recent memory, the savings and loan (S&L) crisis of the 1980s.[6]

The S&L debacle necessitated a government bailout of the relevant deposit insurance program, the Federal Savings and Loan Corporation (FSLIC). Estimates of the cost of the bailout range from $150 billion to $200 billion,[7] or six to eight times the losses suffered in the legendary Depression-era bank failures. In short, a half-century after federal deposit insurance was adopted in the wake of a financial calamity, a much larger calamity occurred. On the face of it, it would be absurd to argue that the so-called insurance program for deposits has reduced the risk of the events that give rise to claims.[8]

THE COST OF FAILURE

If all this sounds like cognitive dissonance, don't worry, it is. Nearly every pundit, scholar, and politician talks about federal deposit insurance in glowing terms. One authority, writing in 2000, called it "remarkably successful since it was signed into law some 66 years ago."[9]

The program's defenders, however, can't point to success in the sense of preventing claim-triggering events. Deposit insurance hasn't eliminated failures of depository institutions. It has succeeded only in altering the distribution of the associated losses.

In an economy with no deposit insurance, some banks fail and their depositors suffer substantial losses. With deposit insurance in place, some banks still become unable to meet their obligations, but the depositors suffer no losses. This doesn't mean that the losses have magically disappeared. Instead, the deposit insurer has transformed them into costs that include payments to depositors, assumptions of bad loans, financial assistance to the troubled institutions, and the insurer's operating and administrative expenses.

Economist Eugene White has toted up these costs and reached a provocative conclusion. His study covers the commercial banks' insurer, the FDIC, in the period from 1945 to 1994. White maintains that the tab has probably exceeded the cost of bank failures that would have occurred if deposit insurance had not been adopted.

White's conclusion rests in part on his estimate of the number of failures that would have occurred if the United States had not adopted deposit insurance. By enabling small, weak banks to continue attracting deposits despite their precarious financial state, the innovation halted a trend of merger and consolidation of the nation's highly localized banking industry. Had the consolidating tendency been allowed to continue, White says, "Both the destruction of weak banks and the formation of larger banks would have produced a stronger banking system with fewer losses."[10]

Economists can debate the assumptions underlying this contrafactual analysis of history as it didn't happen. What is beyond dispute is that the cost of bank failures has remained large. As White notes, however, the costs have become invisible to the individual depositor. Instead of manifesting themselves as wipeouts of a small number of people's savings, the costs of bank failures are spread across all depositors and hidden in the insurance premiums paid by the banks.

WHAT'S SO BAD ABOUT FEELING SECURE?

Spreading the cost of bank failures might not seem a bad solution to the problem. After all, what's wrong with making the phrase, "like money in the bank," mean what it implies? Surely, there is a social benefit in giving people certainty that their nest eggs are secure.

The catch is that the same benefit could be obtained at a price far below the cost of operating the FDIC and bailing out depositors whenever a failure occurs. (Eugene White's historical study put these costs at $770 million a year, in 1982 to 1984 dollars.) Regulators could simply require banks to offer deposit accounts consisting of Treasury bill mutual funds. By segregating these accounts from their other assets, the banks could truthfully represent them as having the ultimate safety of the U.S. government's backing. Aside from avoiding all the costs of bailouts and administration, notes White, this solution would eliminate the bad incentives that deposit insurance creates for institutions.[11]

To understand how a seemingly constructive program destroys wealth through bad incentives, let's first consider the position of savers in a world without deposit insurance. Instead of being restrained by a limit on insurance coverage, individuals can invest as much of their savings as they desire in the ultrasafe T-bill mutual funds that White proposes. Once savers satisfy their appetite for security, they can invest the balance of their assets in higher-return vehicles, understanding that they must accept, as a trade-off, greater risk on that portion of their assets. Examples of higher-risk, higher-return investments include annuities, corporate bonds, and stocks, as well as uninsured bank deposits.

In this environment, banks can't compete for people's savings just by advertising that their deposits are insured. Instead, they must demonstrate their soundness. Few consumers have the expertise to judge a bank's soundness on their own, but they constitute a big market for credit ratings provided by companies with skill in assessing banks' finances. The need to obtain the highest ratings gives banks a strong motivation to manage their affairs responsibly.

BAD INCENTIVES FROM GOOD INTENTIONS

Introducing deposit insurance does not give depository institutions an incentive to demonstrate that they are sound. Savers are concerned only with the soundness of the insurer. Freed of the need to appear conservative, the shareholders can pursue high-risk ventures with huge potential payoffs.

With an insurer standing behind it, a bank can use the depositors' money to make risky bets on the direction of interest rates. Alternatively, it can lend at high interest rates to extremely speculative oil producers, betting that rising energy prices will enable the precariously capitalized borrowers to pay off their loans. If the bets go wrong, the shareholders will lose their investment, but no more. On the other hand, if the bets with the depositors' money work out favorably, the bank's shareholders will realize far greater profit than they could have by speculating with only their own capital.

Without deposit insurance, savers would never consent to bankrolling the shareholders' leveraged speculation. They would be too worried about losing their savings, with no chance of participating in the bank's potential winnings. But knowing that their deposits are insured, the savers don't even bother to analyze whether their money is being invested prudently or recklessly. If depositors don't care, some banks' owners will inevitably choose the reckless path.

An even more insidious form of bad incentives can arise from the link between ownership and management. The bank's controlling shareholders can effectively name themselves to the key executive posts. In those roles, they collect generous compensation packages based on reported profits. The greater the risks they take with depositors' money, the more they stand to take home in incentive-based pay.

This arrangement became incredibly sweet in the prelude to the S&L crisis. As a result, of previous bungles, regulators wound up with title to more failed thrift institutions than they could unload on qualified buyers. According to the official rules, an acquirer of a failed S&L had to put up a meaningful amount of equity. The regulators adhered to the letter, if not the spirit, of the rules by accepting various forms of paper and promises in lieu of cash.

Without putting any real wealth at risk, a group of shrewd operators could gain control of a savings and loan and its valuable charter. They would then greatly expand its deposits by paying premium interest rates to savers. The rates might have been higher than the S&L's operations could actually support, but that didn't impair the institution's ability to attract deposits. Knowing that their deposits were insured, savers made no effort to determine whether the S&L was financially viable.

The operators invested the money in ultra-high-risk real estate ventures, hoping to realize spectacular gains. (Speculative-grade corporate bonds, popularly referred to as *junk bonds,* were a highly controversial but small component of most S&Ls' investment portfolios.) The so-called thrift institution's owners collected huge bonuses on the resulting profits—while they lasted. This compensation alone returned to them whatever negligible equity they had invested to gain control of the S&L.

When the dicey investments went bust and the thrift institution failed, the owners simply handed the keys back to the regulators. Providing for depositors was the deposit insurer's responsibility. For the canny S&L operators, it was a low-risk, yet extremely lucrative way to speculate with other people's money. And it was only possible in an industry that enjoyed the dubious blessings of deposit insurance.

SOME MORE BAD OUTCOMES

The S&L crisis illustrated the perverse incentives that deposit insurance creates for depository institutions. But that wasn't the only hard lesson that emerged from the S&L debacle. Divorcing an institution's deposit-gathering capability from its financial soundness had additional bad consequences.

For one thing, the losses arising from the bad incentives exceeded the available insurance. At that point, the politicians turned to the taxpayers. The cost of bailing out the savings and loan depositors was laid on all taxpayers, without respect to the balances (if any) in their savings accounts. Part of the tab for such largess to a few ended up falling on families too strapped to accumulate savings and therefore unable to benefit directly from the availability of deposit insurance. This is a fundamental flaw in a system that spreads the cost of bank failures around instead of allowing them to fall on a small number of depositors. Even those who can't afford to benefit end up paying.

Yet another problem with deposit insurance that the S&L crisis exposed was the danger of leaving a back door for the politicians. The $150-billion-plus bailout confirmed what many skeptics had long suspected: Even though deposit insurance was advertised as a self-supporting system for protecting deposits, the government was the ultimate guarantor.

Knowing that the federal government backstops the insurance—in practice, if not as a matter of law—legislators instinctively take the easy way out. If more bank examiners are needed, but budgets are tight, the lawmakers find a project with a bigger political payback and allocate the funds there. When powerful bank lobbies complain that the requirements of qualifying for deposit insurance are too onerous, the eager-to-please officeholders snap into action. They loosen the standards for maintaining financial soundness, thereby ensuring that more banks will fail in the future.

These lessons will probably be unlearned as the memory of the S&L crisis already seems to have faded. Small failures continue and sooner or later, a full-force disaster may strike again. Deposit insurance continues to be an enabler for the politicians whose character weaknesses create these catastrophes.

Taxpayers, who will foot the bill for any future calamities, might wish to reflect on this incontrovertible principle: If deposit insurance didn't exist, the need to bail it out would never arise.

SOME KIND OF BACKSTOP IS NEEDED

Horror is the reaction most likely to be encountered by anyone making the radical suggestion of doing away with government-sponsored deposit insurance. Some Americans have a living memory of the bank runs of the Depression. The episode is a terrifying image even to those who have only read about it or seen it depicted in movies. It keeps them ever mindful that a replay of that era's massive withdrawals could destabilize the entire financial system. Why, in this light, would any sane person want to undo one of President Franklin Roosevelt most unquestionably beneficial reforms?

Defending deposit insurance as part of FDR's legacy is a misreading of history. But people's concern about systemic risk is valid. Financial experts have long recognized that the unique character of the banking business makes some sort of safety mechanism necessary.

Whenever a bank fails in a world without deposit insurance, it is extremely painful for the institution's depositors, creditors, and shareholders. A few isolated failures don't bring down the nation's financial structure, however. That risk arises because the depositors are unable to distinguish between sound and unsound banks. They have neither the resources nor the expertise to monitor their respective banks' loan portfolios. Depositors can't tell how heavily exposed their particular banks are to losses in the economy's current trouble spot. Reports that some banks are unable to meet withdrawals will probably be accompanied by rumors about others.

Before long, the *contagion effect* can precipitate runs even at sound institutions. Drained of cash, the banks will no longer be able to renew maturing loans to businesses that want to finance their growth. Instead of lending for economic expansion, banks will soon be calling in loans as a means of raising cash to meet withdrawals. Not only will many depository institutions face potential ruin, but credit will stop flowing to business. A deep recession may result.

Two general approaches have evolved to prevent the economy's inevitable hiccups from devastating the financial system whenever one bank fails. One method has failed repeatedly and the other has consistently worked well. Using their peculiar logic, America's politicians have opted for the failed approach and have made it a sacred cow.

CHOICE 1: DEMONSTRATED FAILURE[12]

The first approach to containing shocks is to insure banks' liabilities. In the early nineteenth century, this mainly meant the notes that banks sold to investors. At the time, deposits were a less important source of funds than nowadays.

New York established a government-sponsored insurance plan for bank liabilities in 1829. The Safety Fund Banking System required participation of all banks that renewed their state charters. The banks paid annual assessments of 0.5 percent of their capital until their cumulative assessments equaled 3 percent of capital. If a participating bank failed and its assets didn't suffice to redeem its notes and deposits in full, the safety fund was tapped to make up the difference. Vermont adopted a similar plan in 1831 and Michigan copied New York's scheme in 1836.

Michigan's insurance fund collapsed in just six years. The others survived for about 30 years, but after 1842, New York's safety fund lost credibility. Its 0.5 percent annual assessment generated too little cash to redeem failed banks' liabilities promptly. When a New York bank failed, the claims of noteholders and depositors traded at steep discounts to face value. It was the market's way of saying that the state's insurance was worthless.

Despite this abysmal record, eight states adopted state-sponsored insurance programs following the Panic of 1907—Kansas, Mississippi, Nebraska, North Dakota, Oklahoma, South Dakota, Texas, and Washington. By then, deposits had become a major component of the banks' liabilities. One thing that didn't change, however, was the consistent failure of the insurance schemes.

Just six years after its launch, Oklahoma's fund found itself too short of cash to reimburse failed banks' depositors immediately. It took six more years for the fund to build its assets up to the level of its liabilities. Almost immediately, bank failures precipitated by the southwestern agricultural depression returned the fund to an illiquid state. The fund was dissolved in 1923, still $7.5 million in the hole on its obligations to depositors.[13]

Following a similar trajectory, Kansas abandoned deposit insurance in 1929 with $7.2 million of unpaid claims. Nebraska's fund went defunct in 1930 owing $20 million. In 1925, Texas allowed banks to switch from the insurance scheme to an alternative system of posting a bond with the state, leaving $15 million of claims unpaid.[14]

Even the demise of the second wave of state-sponsored deposit insurance failed to kill the idea entirely. Several states launched deposit insurance schemes for thrift institutions. They went under at a brisk clip in the 1980s.[15]

Apologists for deposit insurance can point to specific design flaws in each of the failed deposit insurance programs. They can make "for want of a nail" arguments in every case. But wherever politicians get involved in the economy, political influence quickly follows. The last thing that lobbyists for risky banks want is for bank examiners to be highly trained, well compensated, and sufficiently numerous to cover the territory effectively. Neither do the risky banks want any system of differential, risk-based deposit insurance premiums to classify them as candidates to pay premium rates. Instead, they want to be free riders, extracting their full share of the benefits of deposit insurance but contributing disproportionately to the system's risk.[16]

All too characteristically, in 1933 Congress launched a new round of assured disaster by enacting federally sponsored deposit insurance. Their decision ignored not only all previous experience, but also an alternative model with a demonstrated record of success.

CHOICE 2: PROVEN SUCCESS

The second approach to dealing with the systemic risk of bank failures is to create groups of banks that are financially responsible for one another. Under this arrangement, a failed bank's assets are liquidated to repay its noteholders and depositors. Whatever liability remains is covered by the group's members.

In a system of joint responsibility, no danger arises from undercharging for insurance coverage. The banks within the group waste no time debating the amount of premiums required to cover future losses, which are unknown. Instead, when a failure occurs, they determine how much cash is needed to satisfy all claims, then assess themselves for the full amount. Depositors don't have to worry about their claims exceeding some arbitrary limit such as $100,000. The members of the group are responsible for the full amount.

Knowing that they are on the hook for any losses within their group, the banks make certain no member free rides by taking excessive risks. Unlike politicians, the banks have a powerful incentive to monitor their peer institutions effectively. If a member of the group fails to toe the line, the group can boot it out. That sends a clear signal to investors and depositors that the renegade bank is too shaky to entrust with their money. Recognizing that the resulting stigma could bankrupt them, the bank's owners steer well clear of reckless lending.

Suppose that despite the incentive to manage its affairs prudently, a bank gets into financial difficulty through an extraordinary run of bad luck. By prior arrangement, the members of its group provide loans to preserve its liquidity. They also ensure the continuity of a market in its notes.

A mutual surveillance pact doesn't alter individual depositors' lack of the expertise needed to monitor their banks' loan portfolios. Experience teaches them, however, that the other banks are performing that task and enforcing discipline. A report of trouble at one or two banks doesn't raise a suspicion that every bank is in trouble. The result: No contagion, no systemwide bank run, no drying up of business credit. A system of mutual responsibility accomplishes what deposit insurance has invariably failed to achieve.

Two conditions are essential to success. First, the group must be small enough to make monitoring economically worthwhile. If the group consists of too many banks, the failure of a single bank will have little impact on the other members' pocketbooks. That reduces the member banks' motivation to remain vigilant. Second, the members must not be so geographically dispersed that keeping an eye on one another becomes impractical.

Skeptical readers are bound to question whether this approach actually works in practice. It does. Two versions worked extremely well in the years before Congress introduced federally sponsored deposit insurance. They consisted of clearinghouses at the city level and mutual surveillance arrangements at the state level.

COMMERCIAL BANK CLEARINGHOUSES

Starting in the 1850s, banks in a number of major cities formed voluntary associations known as clearinghouses.[17] Their purpose was partly to make the processing of each other's checks more efficient, but the associations also strove to maintain public confidence in the banking system, to the member banks' benefit. Clearinghouses prevented free riding by requiring minimum ratios of reserves to assets and imposing restrictions on portfolio holdings.

To join New York City's clearinghouse, a bank had to have its capital adequacy certified and then submit to periodic audits. Failure to comply with clearinghouse regulations could result in a fine or, in the case of an extreme violation, expulsion. Expulsion sent a strong signal to note holders and depositors that its liabilities were questionable. Banks consequently had a powerful incentive to remain in compliance.

The New York clearinghouse helped depositors gather reliable information in a second way. Every Tuesday morning, each of the city's banks was required by law to publish a statement of its average balances in various categories of assets and liabilities for the preceding week. In addition, the banks had to publish quarterly statements of their financial condition. The clearinghouse audits prevented banks from producing inaccurate statements or artificially dressing up their balance sheets just before the statement dates.

Clearinghouses demonstrated their value most dramatically during banking panics. Lacking the necessary information to distinguish between sound and unsound banks, depositors were tempted to pull their money out indiscriminately. When such a crisis arose, the clearinghouse's policy committee authorized the issuance of obligations known as clearinghouse loan certificates.

If a bank was experiencing withdrawals, it obtained a certificate by posting collateral and paying interest on the one-to-three-month obligation. It then substituted the certificate for currency that it had tied up in the clearing process for ordinary interbank transactions. With the currency thereby freed up, the bank satisfied depositors' withdrawals. This alleviated other depositors' fears that the bank might not have sufficient currency on hand.

The Federal Reserve System took over the function of lending to troubled banks on its establishment in 1914. Whatever the advantages of the new setup, the old clearinghouses provided an undeniable benefit: Banks watched one another, with both a strong economic incentive to ensure that all members remained sound and the high level of expertise needed to audit loan quality.

MUTUAL SURVEILLANCE ARRANGEMENTS

Banks in Indiana, Ohio, and Iowa operated successfully under systems of mutual surveillance during approximately the same years that deposit insurance schemes arose and collapsed under government auspices in New York, Michigan, and Vermont.[18] Mutual surveillance plans controlled the behavior of group members by such means as regulating dividend payments and loans to officers and directors.

Indiana's mutual surveillance arrangement demonstrated the power of banks watching one another. The system ran for 30 years without a single bank failure. Only once did the board of directors suspend a member bank for perceived irregularities in its loan portfolio. Over the same period, failures were frequent among Indiana banks that didn't join the mutual surveillance plan. A regional panic in 1854 and 1855 wiped out 55 of 94 recently formed, nonparticipating Hoosier State institutions. Another 14 failed in the Panic of 1857, out of 32 nonparticipants.[19]

Seeing a good thing, the federal government moved to do away with it. In 1863, Congress enacted the National Banking System as a way to finance the Civil War by increasing the demand for its debt. Nationally chartered banks were required to back their notes with government bonds. To encourage banks to obtain national charters, the federal government imposed a tax on state-chartered banknotes. Most of the participants in the mutual surveillance arrangements submitted to this financial pressure and obtained national charters. By 1866, all the states' mutual surveillance plans had ceased operations.

The disappearance of voluntary mutual surveillance plans opened the door to federally sponsored deposit insurance. Two-thirds of a century elapsed before Congress embraced the idea, however. When it did, it acted for reasons much different from those incorporated in the surrounding myth.

HOW THEY CHOSE THE PATH OF PROVEN FAILURE

Federal deposit insurance wasn't the brainchild of Franklin Roosevelt or even of the advisers who formed his famous Brain Trust. The Democratic platform on which FDR ran for president in 1932 didn't mention it. Economist and banking expert Carter Golembe has described deposit insurance as "the only important piece of legislation during the New Deal's famous 'one hundred days' which was neither requested nor supported by the new administration."[20]

Roosevelt wasn't oblivious to the losses incurred by depositors in the bank failures brought on by the Depression. But it was by no means obvious that deposit insurance offered the best means of nursing the banking system back to health, especially considering that state-sponsored insurance schemes had invariably flopped. The chairman of the Senate Banking Committee, Senator Carter Glass (D-VA), believed that the solution was to prohibit commercial banks from engaging in supposedly risky investment banking activities such as the underwriting and trading of securities. This wasn't any more self-evidently the magic bullet than federal deposit insurance, but Glass had Roosevelt in his corner.

With Glass resolutely opposed, proposals for federal deposit insurance went nowhere in the early days of the Depression. The impasse persisted even though Glass's counterpart on the House Banking Committee,

Representative Henry Steagall (D–AL), was a staunch advocate. Thanks to the Federal Reserve's horribly wrongheaded tight money policy, however, bank failures began to accelerate.

Between October 1932 and March 1933, 36 states responded to the widening panic by shutting down all their banks to prevent them from being bankrupted by withdrawals. Finally, newly inaugurated President Franklin Roosevelt declared a national bank holiday. In this atmosphere of crisis, Glass and Steagall struck a deal. The Banking Act of 1933, also known as the *Glass-Steagall Act,* gave Senator Glass the separation of commercial and investment banking that he craved, while Representative Steagall won his fight for deposit insurance.

From that day to this, deposit insurance has been popularly perceived as a response to the plight of savers devastated by bank failures. Curiously, Congress rejected calls for relief to depositors who had already lost their money. Yet in subsequent years, the lack of previous coverage was no impediment to the FDIC making uninsured depositors whole. This leads one to suspect that the true inspiration for establishing deposit insurance was not the loss of families' savings from 1930 through 1933. Heightening the skepticism is the fact that the scheme's proponents had been introducing bills in Congress for almost half a century before they finally succeeded.

THE HIDDEN PURPOSE OF DEPOSIT INSURANCE

In reality, the impetus behind deposit insurance was the preservation of small banks. These institutions were highly prone to failure. Not only were their financial resources limited, but the small banks' loan portfolios were heavily concentrated in their local economies. A single major employer's failure could financially devastate the small businesses to which a local bank had lent money. The small banks knew that they could survive any business downturn, however, if only the government would agree to insure their deposits. That way, depositors wouldn't withdraw their money, no matter how shaky the little banks became.

An alternative solution to the problem of small, precariously capitalized banks had been available for many years prior to the Depression. The government could have simply allowed banks to follow the tendency of other industries to achieve efficiency through expanded scale. A bank with branches throughout a state can amass enough assets and diversify its loan portfolio sufficiently to weather downturns more successfully than a bank with a single office in a small town.

Statewide branching wasn't merely a hypothetical solution to the banking system's weakness. Where it was allowed, its effectiveness had already been demonstrated by the time Franklin Roosevelt entered the White House. During the 1920s, plunging farm prices triggered a wave of bank failures. In the states hit hard by the crisis, one-office, or "unit," banks failed at about four times the rate of branch banks.[21] Among the 11,000 failures leading up to the introduction of federal deposit insurance in 1933, about 90 percent occurred at unit banks with less than $2 million of assets.[22] In stark contrast, there were no bank failures in Canada, which like the United States, suffered from the Depression but which unlike the United States, permitted branch banking on a nationwide basis.

Compared with Europe, the United States had a highly fragmented banking system. And because there were so many small banks in so many state legislature and congressional districts, they wielded immense political power. A number of states protected the economic interests of the small and inefficient banks by prohibiting branch banking. Senators and representatives from those states were particularly active in the introduction of 150 separate federal deposit insurance bills between 1886 and 1933.[23]

Naturally, the champions of the small banks didn't try to drum up support for deposit insurance by highlighting the self-interest of the small banks' shareholders. Instead, they conjured up the specter of excessive concentration of economic power. For example, Senator Arthur Vandenberg (R–MI) explicitly linked his support of the 1933 deposit insurance proposal to reversing a supposed trend toward "an America without small banks, an America whose credit would be controlled by a few men pulling the strings from New York."[24]

THE BOTTOM LINE

It would be hard to find any residue of this history in voters' present consciousness. The popular perception, conspicuously devoid of subtlety, runs something like this: *During the Depression, the common people lost their savings in bank runs. The New Deal put an end to that once and for all by instituting deposit insurance.* In this account, Uncle Sam ranks as a hero with all the populist instincts of James Stewart in *It's a Wonderful*

Life. To most voters, deposit insurance appears to be one of the government's more notable successes.

A fuller accounting would consider the massive cost of the S&L bailout, with no assurance that another deposit insurance program won't come knocking on taxpayers' doors in the future. The cost-benefit analysis should also include the inefficiencies of banks that could not survive— and in some cases might never have started up—if they could not offer insured deposits. Their continued operation is subsidized by payments to the FDIC by sound banks that would have little difficulty competing without the crutch of deposit insurance. With depositors having no incentive to monitor or discipline the institutions to which they have entrusted their money, some banks will inevitably abuse the system. They will take irresponsible risks, knowing that they can count on the deposit insurer to clean up the mess.

It doesn't have to be this way. The success of previous eras' clearing-houses and mutual surveillance arrangements suggest that less costly alternatives to deposit insurance are available. Savers could sleep every bit as soundly with their money in accounts backed by Treasury bills as they do with insured deposits. The costs of requiring banks to offer such accounts would be negligible compared with the FDIC's administrative budget and bailout costs.

Naturally, no vested interest is actively lobbying to change the status quo. Besides, replacing the present setup might force politicians to admit that they have put one over on the voters for decades. Their so-called insurance plan pays claims for which insurance was never written. It also fails to induce behavior that reduces the events that trigger claims.

In the private sector, this would be called bad business. Politicians instead call it one of the most successful social programs of all time. Sadder still, they have painted the picture so effectively that the public largely agrees with their assessment.

Epilogue

Can This Mess Be Fixed?

eflecting on the government's unwarranted intrusions in the marketplace is apt to unleash a variety of emotions. The tampering distorts economic relationships and consequently lowers the standard of living. That's a reason for sadness, yet the ridiculous rationales advanced for many subsidies and regulations are more likely to provoke laughter. At the same time, anger is an appropriate response to the misrepresentation at the heart of governmental interventions. Politicians promote their schemes in the name of the disadvantaged, but the true beneficiaries are interest groups that already have enough power to wield major influence in Congress.

This deception relies on the mistaken notion that ordinary folks invariably benefit when the government shields them from the merciless market. The reality is quite different for poor children and elderly sufferers of osteoporosis, whose diets are deficient in calcium as a consequence of price supports for dairy farmers. Neither does economic justice ring true to foreign farmers who are put out of business by subsidized exports of U.S. agricultural products.

In the final analysis, fairness has little to do with government intervention in the marketplace. The true, direct beneficiaries of public financing of sports stadiums hardly qualify as charity cases. They are ineligible for the giveaway unless they are already rich enough to own professional sports teams. Subsidies for homeowners and for savers disproportionately benefit the affluent. The burden of tariff protection is heavier on the poor than on the rich. A suitable response to such perverse wealth transfers is outrage.

Nonperverse wealth transfers, by the way, are in no way incompatible with reliance on the market to handle routine economic matters. Directly providing income to the disabled and the unemployed represents a sensible public policy. Certainly, straightforward income enhancement generates far lower administrative costs than providing assistance through an array of subsidies on everything from rents to ATM fees.

CHANNELING THE OUTRAGE

Once people understand the true effect of marketplace interference on income distribution, outrage follows. The anger only serves a useful purpose, however, if it is harnessed for constructive change. Effective action consists of more than replacing incumbents with challengers who are equally dedicated to the proposition of buying votes with taxpayer dollars. Neither will it solve the problem to support Republicans over Democrats, or vice versa. Exchanging economic favors for votes is a strategy that cuts across party lines and runs the full spectrum from conservative to liberal.

Fresh faces are no guarantors of reform, even when accompanied by idealistic rhetoric. Realistically, politics will always attract power seekers with a knack for cutting deals. It is as predictable as certain people gravitating toward show business because they crave the adoration of the crowd. Politicians aren't going to change their personalities, but the voters can force them to change their behavior.

Voters must challenge the rationales that elected officials offer for their meddling in the marketplace. When office holders uphold ethanol subsidies as a way to reduce energy consumption, the electorate must confront them with the facts about the energy consumed in producing ethanol. When corporations play one city off against another to wangle tax breaks, voters in all cities must protest that they are collectively getting fleeced.

By insisting on solid evidence of market failure to support a subsidy or regulation, voters can make a difference. Even the politicians most in thrall to interest groups are rational enough to alter their strategies under threat of being booted out of office. To cling to power, they will adopt new tactics, even if it means actually having to work at providing honest and efficient administration.

Citizens who hold their elected officials to a higher standard will have to manage their expectations carefully and exercise patience. Unwarranted intrusions operate on such a vast scale that there is no chance of immediately dismantling them all. The good news is that one small victory can represent a huge gain in public well-being given the government programs' massive drag on economic performance.

There is no permanent victory against unjustified intervention in the marketplace and that makes the task more arduous. The interest groups that derive the biggest benefits from subsidies are well organized and tenacious. If they lose one of their privileges to the indignation generated by a major scandal, they will work to restore it in a different guise. Politicians always stand ready to capitalize on the demand for unfair advantages. Therefore, citizens will have to be unwavering if they hope to eliminate the monkey business. They will have to object to every instance, large or small, of government interference that isn't truly justified by market failure.

It is a big job. That is all the more reason to get started right away. The first step is to shine a light on the ugly realities of unwarranted intrusions and open minds to the possibility of a new path.

Notes

Chapter 1: The Politics of Market Intervention

1. The two relevant articles are reprinted in Daniel F. Spulber, ed., *Famous Fables of Economics: Myths of Market Failures* (Malden, MA: Blackwell Publishers, 2002). Original citations are Stan J. Liebowitz and Stephen E. Margolis, "Beta, Macintosh and Other Fabulous Tales," *Winners, Losers and Microsoft* (Oakland, CA: Independent Institute, 1999), chap. 6, pp. 119–234; and Stan J. Liebowitz and Stephen E. Margolis, "The Fable of the Keys," *Journal of Law and Economics,* vol. 33, no. 1 (1990), pp. 1–25.

Chapter 2: Here They Come to Save the Day!

1. Bob Davis and Jacob M. Schlesinger, "Republicans, Democrats Divide on How to Encourage Saving," *Wall Street Journal* (November 16, 2003), p. A4.
2. Charles Lane, "TRB from Washington: Wrong Roth," *New Republic* (May 18, 1998), p. 6.
3. N. Gregory Mankiw, *Principles of Economics,* 2nd ed. (Fort Worth: Harcourt College Publishers, 2001) p. 806.
4. Eric M. Engen and William G. Gale, "The Illusory Effects of Savings Incentives on Saving," *Journal of Economic Perspectives* (Fall 1996), pp. 113–138.
5. James M. Poterba and Steven F. Venti, "How Retirement Savings Programs Increase Saving," *Journal of Economic Perspectives* (Fall 1996), pp. 91–112.
6. Glenn R. Hubbard and Jonathan S. Skinner, "Assessing the Effectiveness of Savings Incentives," *Journal of Economic Perspectives* (Fall 1996), pp. 73–90.
7. Alan Beattie and James Harding, "Savers Need More Incentives, Says White House Aide," *Financial Times* (November 6, 2003), p. 3.
8. See note 7, p. 3.

9. Ethan S. Harris and Charles Steindel, "The Decline in U.S. Saving and Its Implications for Economic Growth," *Quarterly Review* (Federal Reserve Bank of New York, Winter 1990/1991), p. 1.

10. David Francis, "The Low U.S. Savings Rate? No (Immediate) Problem," *Christian Science Monitor* (February 4, 1998), p. 19.

11. Bureau of Labor Statistics, http://data.bls.gov/PDQ/servlet/SurveyOutputServlet.

12. "The Savings Paradox?" *Facts from EBRI* (June 1999), http://www.ebri.org/facts/0699factb.htm.

13. Bureau of Economic Analysis, http://research.stlouisfed.org/fred2/data/PSAVERT.txt.

14. "Savings Rate Slides as Population Ages," *Daily Yomiuri* (October 28, 2003).

15. "Treasury Secretary Robert E. Rubin Makes U.S. Savings Bond Announcement," Bureau of the Public Debt, press release, April 30, 1997.

16. Jack Bobo, "Les Miserables," *National Underwriter/Life & Health Financial Services* (July 26, 1999), p. 17.

17. Vineeta Anand, *Pensions & Investments* (February 5, 2001), p. 8.

18. See note 15, p. 1.

19. "Best Minds Will Meet," *Pensions & Investments* (April 6, 1998), p. 37.

20. The Center for Responsive Politics, www.opensecrets.org.

21. See note 2, p. 6.

22. Lee Ann Gjertsen, "Looming Pension Crisis Seen as Threat to 401(k) Vendors," *Money Management Executive* (October 20, 2003), p. 12.

Chapter 3:   Be It Ever So Deductible

1. Kudzu is a vine introduced to the United States from Japan in 1876 and promoted as forage in the 1920s and for erosion control in the 1930s. Unfortunately, kudzu grows too well—up to 60 feet a year under ideal conditions. It now covers over seven million acres in the southern United States. Kudzu can destroy valuable forests by blocking trees' access to sunlight. The U.S. Forest Service has shifted its attention to controlling the vine's proliferation, but many herbicides have little effect on kudzu and one actually makes it grow better, *The Amazing Story of Kudzu,* http://www.alabamatv.org/kudzu.

2. Peter Dreier and John Atlas, "Reforming the Mansion Subsidy," *Nation* (May 2, 1994), pp. 592–595.

3. Lea Donosky "House Passes Historic Tax Bill," *Chicago Tribune* (September 26, 1986), p. 1.

4. See note 2, p. 594.

5. "Going Through the Roof," *Economist* (March 30, 2002), p. 77.

6. See note 2, p. 593.

7. *Assessing the Public Costs and Benefits of Fannie Mae and Freddie Mac,* Congressional Budget Office (May 1996).

8. *Federal Subsidies and the Housing GSEs,* Congressional Budget Office (May 23, 2001).
9. David S. Hilzenrath, "Lenders' Subsidy Grows," *Washington Post* (April 13, 2004), p. E1.
10. For a summary of this debate, see W. Scott Frame and Larry D. Wall, "Financing Housing through Government-Sponsored Enterprises," *Economic Review—Federal Reserve Bank of Atlanta* (First Quarter 2002), pp. 29–43.
11. See note 10, p. 32.
12. "Shuttered Dreams: How Fannie Mae and Freddie Mac Misspend the GSE Housing Subsidy," *FM Watch* (June 2001), p. 4.
13. See note 12, p. 5.
14. See note 12, p. 5.
15. Benjamin Wallace-Wells, "There Goes the Neighborhood," *Washington Monthly* (April 2004), pp. 30–36.
16. William Norman Grigg, "Will the Housing Bubble Burst?" *New American* (May 17, 2004), pp. 20–23.
17. Jennifer Lee and Eric Dash, "Long Insulated, Fannie Mae Feels Political Heat," *New York Times* (October 6, 2004), p. C1.
18. Patrick Barta, Greg Ip, and John D. McKinnon, "Out the Door: Freddie Mac Ousts Top Officials as Regulators Prepare Inquiries," *Wall Street Journal* (June 10, 2003), pp. A1, A14.
19. Jennifer Lee, "Overseer Says Fannie Mae May Be Due for Shake-Up," *New York Times* (September 24, 2004), p. C1.
20. James E. Murray, "Fannie and Freddie Grow Up," *Wall Street Journal* (March 25, 2005), p. A8.
21. "Administration Opposes House GSE Regulatory Bill," *CongressDaily* (October 26, 2005), pp. 9–10, http://web30.epnet.com/citation.asp?tb=1&_ug=sid+002AB61C%2D98F1%2D44C5%2DB5E19A1385E2%40sessionmgr5+dbs+aph+cp+1+352D&_us=frn+1+hd+True+hs+True+cst+0%3B1%3B2%3B3+or+Date+ss+SO+sm+KS+sl+0+dstb+KS+mh+1+ri+KAAACB1C00023080+062D&_uso=tg%5B0+%2D+db%5B0+%2Daph+hd+False+op%5B0+%2D+st%5B0+%2Dfannie++mae+ex%5B0+%2Dproximity+mdb%5B0+%2Dimh+FFBD&fn=1&rn=3.
22. Charles Percy, "A New Dawn for Our Cities," *Congressional Record* (October 17, 1966), pp. 2725B–2726B.
23. William M. Rohe and Leslie S. Stewart, "Homeownership and Neighborhood Policy Debate," *Housing Policy Debate* (Fannie Mae Foundation, 1996), pp. 37–80.
24. Edwin S. Mills, "Dividing Up the Investment Pie: Have We Overinvested in Housing?" *Federal Reserve Bank of Philadelphia Business Review* (March/April 1987), pp. 13–23.
25. In later years, economists tended to focus on gross domestic product (GDP), rather than GNP.
26. See note 24, p. 20.

27. See note 24, p. 22.
28. Lori L. Taylor, "Does the United States Still Overinvest in Housing?" *Federal Reserve Bank of Dallas Economic Review* (Second Quarter 1998), pp. 10–18.
29. See note 28, p. 11.

Chapter 4:   Protection Racket

1. John R. Paxton and William N. Eschmeyer, Consultant eds., *Encyclopedia of Fishes,* 2nd ed. (Sydney, Australia: Weldon Owen Pty Limited, 1998), pp. 106–112.
2. "Vietnamese Frozen Fish Pose Threat of Material Injury to U.S. Catfish, ITC Says," U.S.-Vietnam Trade Council web site, http://www.usvtc.org.
3. Margot Cohen and Murray Hiebert, "Muddying the Waters," *Far Eastern Economic Review* (December 6, 2001), pp. 67–69.
4. See note 2, p. 2.
5. See note 3, p. 67.
6. Tim Shorrock, "Catfish Wars: Vietnam versus United States," *Asia Times* (February 20, 2003), http://www.atimes.com/atimes/Southeast_Asia/EB20Ae01.html.
7. See note 6, p. 3.
8. See note 6, p. 2.
9. See note 3, p. 69.
10. Nguyen Hahn, "U.S. Embassy Rejects Catfish State Subsidy Claims: McCain," U.S. Vietnam Trade Council (January 3, 2003), http://www.usvtc.org.
11. "Harvesting Poverty," *New York Times* (July 22, 2003), p. A18.
12. See note 6, p. 2.
13. Daniel W. Drezner, "The Outsourcing Bogeyman," *Foreign Affairs* (May/June 2004), pp. 22–34.
14. James K. Glassman, "Exporting Lou Dobbs and John Kerry," *Tech Central Station,* http://www.techcentralstation.com/021104F.html.
15. Lisa DiCarlo, "The Politics of Outsourcing," *Forbes.com,* http://www.forbes.com /2004/02/18/cx_ld_0218outsourcing.html.
16. N. Gregory Mankiw, *Principles of Economics,* 3rd ed. (Mason, OH: Thomson South-Western, 2004).
17. Douglas A. Irwin, " 'Outsourcing' Is Good for America," *Wall Street Journal* (January 28, 2004), p. A16.
18. Michael Hirsh, "The Great Debunker," *Newsweek* (March 4, 1996), pp. 40–41.
19. Paul Krugman, "The Trade Tightrope," *New York Times* (February 27, 2004), p. A27.
20. Edmund L. Andrews, "Economics Adviser Learns the Principles of Politics," *New York Times* (February 26, 2004), p. C4.
21. See note 13, p. 22.
22. See note 13, p. 30.
23. See note 13, p. 22.

24. Charles Schumer and Paul Craig Roberts, "Second Thoughts on Free Trade," *New York Times* (January 6, 2004), p. A23.

25. See note 19, p. A27.

26. See note 24, p. A23.

27. See note 19, p. 25.

28. Steve Lohr, "Evidence of High-Skill Work Going Abroad," *New York Times* (June 16, 2004), p. C2.

29. See note 13, p. 26.

30. Walter B. Wriston, "Ever Heard of Insourcing?" *Wall Street Journal* (March 24, 2004), p. A20.

31. Jon E. Hilsenrath, "Behind Outsourcing Debate: Surprisingly Few Hard Numbers," *Wall Street Journal* (April 12, 2004), pp. A1, A7.

32. See note 13, p. 26.

33. Ben Bernanke, *Trade and Jobs,* remarks at the Distinguished Speaker Series, Fuqua School of Business, Duke University, Durham, North Carolina (March 30, 2004).

34. Geoffrey Colvin, "Bush vs. Kerry: Who's Stupider on Jobs?" *Fortune* (May 3, 2004), p. 76.

35. Richard Alston, J. R. Kearl, and Michael B. Vaughn. "Is There Consensus among Economists in the 1990s?" *American Economic Review* (May 1992), pp. 203–209; cited in note 16, p. 32.

36. "Linking with Foreign Workers: A Brief History," http://www.ueinternational .org/SolidarityWork/history.html.

37. John McQuaid, "Anti-Dumping Law Allows Windfalls," *Times-Picayune* (June 19, 2004), http://www.nola.com/news/t-p/index.ssf?/base/news-0/108763018043160.xml.

38. Estimate of the Consuming Industries Trade Action Coalition, a free-trade group opposed to anti-dumping duties on shrimp. Cited in McQuaid, "Anti-Dumping Law," p. 2.

39. Neil King Jr., "Catch of the Day: Battle over Shrimp," *Wall Street Journal* (June 11, 2004), p. A4.

40. Edward Gresser, "Toughest on the Poor," *Foreign Affairs* (November/December 2002), pp. 9–14.

41. *Harmonized Tariff Schedule of the United States (2004),* U.S. International Trade Commission (July 1, 2004), http://hotdocs.usitc.gov/tariff_chapters_current/toc.html.

42. See note 40, p. 12.

43. See note 40, p. 13.

44. See note 40, p. 11.

Chapter 5:   How Are You Going to Keep Them Down on the Farm?

1. "Dean Says Government Should Work for Family Farmers," ElectionBeat.com (January 4, 2004).

2. "Dennis Kucinich for President, 2004—Farm Policy," www.kucinich.us.issues /farmpolicy.php.
3. "Senator John Edwards Joins N.C. Young Farmers for Frank Discussions on Their Future Survival," *NCFB Home,* no. 1437 (August 23, 1999).
4. "Aid to Farmers—Memorial to Congress," Joint Resolution of the Georgia General Assembly, February 13, 1956, *Georgia Laws 1956,* pp. 131–132, Carl Vinson Institute of Government, University of Georgia.
5. "HR 922—Georgia Future Farmers of America Association; commend," Office of the Clerk of the House, www.legis.state.ga.us/legis/1995_96/fulltext/hr922.htm (last updated January 2, 1997).
6. Hancock Agricultural Investment Group, "A Chronological History of Agriculture in the United States," http://haig.jhancock.com/haig/farmland/history.html and U.S. Census Bureau, "Population Housing Units, Area Measurements, and Density: 1970 to 1990," www.census.gov/population/censusdata/table2.pdf.
7. "The Farmer Is the Man," *Plains Folk,* www.plainsfolk.com/songs/song15.htm.
8. "Agricultural Facts—History of Agriculture," www.norbest.com/a_agricultural _facts_02.cfm.
9. See note 8.
10. Northeast-Midwest Institute web site, http://www.nemw.org/poprural.htm.
11. See note 7.
12. The history of the dairy support program is drawn from Bill Winter, "What the Federal Government Did to the Dairy Industry (And How We Can Fix It)," *LP News,* www.lp.org.
13. James Bovard, "Our Next Criminal Class: Milk Bootleggers," *Cato Institute Briefing Paper No. 13* (June 14, 1991), http://www.cato.org/pubs/briefs/bp-013.html.
14. See note 13, p. 7.
15. Lewis Lord, "For Farmers, a Glut of Misery," *U.S. News & World Report* (November 3, 2003) p. 14.
16. J. Bishop Grewell, "Farm Subsidies Are Harm Subsidies," *American Enterprise* (October 16, 2002), pp. 47–48.
17. See note 13, p. 3.
18. See note 13, p. 4.
19. See note 13, p. 5.
20. Jeffrey D. Sachs, "Spring Broke," *New Republic* (September 29, 2003), p. 12.
21. "The Unkept Promise," *New York Times* (December 30, 2003) p. A20.
22. Michael Pollan, "The (Agri)Cultural Contradictions of Obesity," *New York Times* (October 12, 2003), pp. 41–47.
23. See note 22, p. 41.
24. "Veterans Tout Ethanol Benefits," *Rapid City Journal,* www.rapidcityjournal.com (January 25, 2004).
25. "The Magic of Arm & Hammer Baking Soda," www.armandhammer.com.
26. "Blueberries for Health," U.S. Highbush Blueberry Council, http://www.ushbc .org/health.htm.

27. James Bovard, "Archer Daniels Midland: A Case Study in Corporate Welfare," *Cato Institute Policy Analysis No. 241* (September 26, 1995), http://www.cato .org/pubs/pas/pa-241.html.

28. See note 27, p. 6.

29. "Dirty as Well as Dear?; Ethanol" *Economist* (January 17, 2004), p. 24.

30. See note 27, p. 9.

31. See note 27, p. 12.

32. See note 29, p. 24.

33. Mary Losure, "Ethanol Industry Steamrolls Opponents," *Minnesota Public Radio News,* http://news.mpr.org/features/200211/12_losurem_ethanol (November 12, 2002).

34. Eric Hymel, "Ethanol Producers Get a Handout from Consumers" (Heritage Foundation, October 16, 2002), http://www.heritage.org/Research/EnergyandEnvironment /bg1603.cfm.

35. See note 27, p. 12.

36. See note 33.

37. See note 27, p. 7.

38. See note 27, p. 8.

39. "Fuel's Gold: ADM's Million-Dollar Soft Money Donations Help the Ethanol Tax Break Survive," Common Cause (1998), http://www.commoncause.org.

40. See note 27, p. 1.

41. See note 39, p. 2.

42. See note 39, p. 2.

43. Peter Huber, "Crude Awakening," *Wall Street Journal* (February 3, 2006), p. A12.

44. See note 13, p. 3.

45. See note 13, pp. 4–5.

Chapter 6:   Location and Misallocation

1. Harvard economist Edward L. Glaeser downplays the importance of this sort of redistribution. If it is seen as a problem, he argues, it can be overridden by a central government redistribution policy (Edward L. Glaeser, "The Economics of Location-Based Tax Incentives," discussion paper no. 1932, Harvard Institute of Economic Research, November 2001). Readers are justified in doubting the wisdom of authorizing new government powers to fix a problem created by an earlier, questionable exercise of government powers.

2. See Michael Greenstone and Enrico Moretti, "Bidding for Industrial Plants: Does Winning a 'Million Dollar Plant' Increase Welfare?" (working paper no. 04-39, MIT Department of Economics, November 2004).

3. Shifting the tax burden won't entirely neutralize the economic impact of tax-induced corporation relocations. Companies add some deadweight costs to the economy when they pull up stakes. Most directly, they incur certain expenses that produce neither increases in output nor operating (aside from tax-related)

efficiencies. Perhaps, as well, the uprooting of families causes strains that municipalities must respond to with social services. When everything is accounted for, location-based tax incentives may have negative, rather than neutral effects on the economy.

4. The body that selects the Economics honoree is officially called the Prize Committee for the Bank of Sweden Prize in Economic Sciences in Memory of Alfred Nobel.

5. Dick Netzer, "Discussion," *New England Economic Review* (March/April 1997), pp. 131–135 (comment on Fisher and Peters in footnote 8, of this chapter), http://web8.epnet.com/citation.asp?tb=1&_ug=sid+96CF8D03%2D9F49%2D4281 %2D9D60%2DF1832057D870%40sessionmgr3+dbs+aph+cp+1+0652&_us=frn+1 +hd+True+hs+True+cst+0%3B1+or+Date+ss+SO+sm+KS+sl+0+dstb+KS+mh+1+ri +KAAACB3A00107276+5E16&_uso=tg%5B0+%2D+db%5B0+%2Daph+hd+False +op%5B0+%2D+st%5B0+%2Dnetzer++discussion+ex%5B0+%2Dproximity+mdb %5B0+%2Dimh+7BDD&cf=1&fn=1&rn=2. Original quotation in *Economist* (March 3, 1990).

6. Use of tax incentives to lure businesses got started in the 1930s with property tax abatements by several southern states. These incentives became widespread by the 1960s. The revival and expansion of federal investment tax credits, coupled with the emergence of supply-side economic theory, dramatically increased the use of location-based tax incentives in the 1970s and 1980s. See Peter D. Enrich, "Saving the States from Themselves: Commerce Clause Constraints on State Tax Incentives for Business," *Harvard Law Review* (December 1996), pp. 377–468.

7. See note 5, pp. 131–135.

8. See Peter Fisher and Alan Peters, "Tax and Spending Incentives and Enterprise Zones," *New England Economic Review* (March/April 1997), pp. 109–137.

9. James Surowiecki, "It Pays to Stay," *New Yorker* (December 13, 2004), p. 40.

10. See note 6, pp. 380, 422–424.

11. *U.S. Constitution,* Article I, Section 8, Clause 3.

12. "Professor Peter Enrich Turns Theory into Practice with Triumph over Corporate Welfare," *NUSL News and Events* (November 2004), http://www.slaw.neu.edu /news/enrich.htm.

13. For an overview of the record on economically targeted investments, see Cassandra Chrones Moore, "Whose Pension Is It Anyway?" *Cato Policy Analysis No. 234* (September 1, 1995), http://www.cato.org/pubs/pas/pa-236.html.

14. W. Wayne Marr, John R. Nofsinger, and John L. Trimble, "Economically Targeted Investments: A New Threat to Private Pension Funds," *Journal of Applied Corporate Finance* (Summer 1993), pp. 91–95.

15. "Colt's Patent Fire Arms Manufacturing Company 193," description of stock certificate for sale by Scripophily.com, with company history, 2005, http://www .scripophily.net/colpatfirarm2.html.

16. Craig Garthwaite, "Playing Politics with Retirement Accounts," *American Legislative Exchange Council Issue Analysis* (August 1999).

17. John Entine, "U.S. Pension Funds, Social Investing and Fiduciary Irresponsibility," *Ethical Corporation* (January 2004), pp. 24–27, http://www.jonentine.com/ethical_edge/2004_01_SRI_Funds.htm.

18. Alicia H. Munnell, "The Pitfalls of Social Investing: The Case of Public Pensions and Housing," *New England Economic Review* (September/October 1983), pp. 20–40.

19. M. Wayne Marr, John L. Trimble, and John R. Nofsinger, "Economically Targeted Investments," *Financial Analysts Journal* (March/April 1994), pp. 7–8.

20. See note 13, p. 5.

21. It would be inaccurate to say that politicians *fail* to satisfy the requirement of presenting their economic programs honestly. The fact is, they don't try very hard.

Chapter 7: Getting the City to Play Ball

1. James Quirk and Rodney D. Fort, *Pay Dirt: The Business of Professional Sports* (Princeton, NJ: Princeton University Press, 1992, 1997), p. xxiv.

2. Kevin J. Delaney and Rick Eckstein, "The Devil Is in the Details," *Criminal Sociology,* vol. 29, no. 2 (2003), pp. 189–210.

3. Robert A. Baade, "Stadiums, Professional Sports, and Economic Development: Assessing the Reality," *Heartland Institute Policy Study No. 62* (April 4, 1994), p. 3.

4. See note 3, p. 4.

5. See note 3, p. 4.

6. See note 3, p. 15.

7. Mark S. Rosentraub, *Major League Losers: The Real Cost of Sports and Who's Paying for It* (New York: Basic Books, 1997), p. 97.

8. Daniel Gross, "A Team Makes a City a High-Rent District," *New York Times* (May 2, 2004), sec. 3, p. 8.

9. Dean V. Baim, "Sports Stadiums as 'Wise Investments: An Evaluation,'" *Heartland Institute Policy Study No. 32* (November 26, 1990), p. 12.

10. Michiko Kakutani, "A Texas-Style Bashing: Double-Teaming 'Dubya'" (Review), *New York Times* (February 18, 2000), sec. E, p. 2.

11. See note 7, p. 20.

12. See note 7, p. 20.

13. See note 7, pp. 93, 111.

14. Except where noted, the figures cited in the account of the Texas Rangers affair are from Joe Conason, "Notes on a Native Son," *Harper's Magazine* (February 2000), pp. 39–53.

15. Joseph L. Bast, "Sports Stadium Madness: Why It Started, How to Stop It," *Heartland Institute Policy Study No. 85* (February 23, 1998), p. 20.

16. Dennis Zimmerman, "Subsidizing Stadiums: Who Benefits, Who Pays?" in Roger G. Noll and Andrew Zimbalist, eds., *Sports, Jobs, and Taxes: The Economic Impact of Sports Teams and Stadiums* (Washington, DC: Brookings Institution Press, 1997), pp. 119–145.

17. Mark Hyman, "Did the Bengals Claw Taxpayers?" *BusinessWeek* (October 6, 2003), p. 96.

18. Dennis Zimmerman, *Tax Exempt Bonds and the Economics of Professional Sports Stadiums*. CRS Report for Congress (Washington, DC: Congressional Research Service, May 29, 1996), p. 7.

19. See note 2, p. 195.

20. See note 2, p. 196.

21. See note 2, pp. 197–198.

22. See note 15, p. 16.

23. See note 15, pp. 15–16.

24. See note 2, p. 201.

25. John Crompton, "Beyond Economic Impact: An Alternative Rationale for the Public Subsidy of Major League Sports Facilities," *Journal of Sports Management* (2004), pp. 40–58.

26. See note 25, p. 53.

27. See note 15, p. 26.

Chapter 8: Art of the State

1. Beth Potier, "Karen Finley Provokes, Reveals in Lecture," *Harvard University Gazette* (February 14, 2002), http://www.news.harvard.edu/gazette/2002/02.14/06-finley.html.

2. "RJN: Karen Finley, the Ultimate Black Sheep," http://www.geocities.com/WestHollywood/2399/KAREN.HTML?20055.

3. C. Carr, "The Karen Finley Makeover: A Persecuted Performance Artist Gets Past Her Suffering," *Village Voice* (July 16, 2000), http://www.villagevoice.com/news/0045,carr,19637,1.html.

4. See note 1.

5. John Biskupic, " 'Decency' Can Be Weighed in Arts Agency's Funding," *Washington Post* (June 26, 1998), p. A1.

6. George F. Will, "The Art of Funding," *Newsweek* (July 6, 1998), p. 78.

7. Julie C. Van Camp, *Freedom of Expression at the National Endowment for the Arts,* An Interdisciplinary Education Project Partially Funded by the American Bar Association, Commission on College and University Legal Studies (last updated: October 16, 1993), p. 3, http://www.csulb.edu~jvancamp/freedom2.html.

8. Jeff Jacoby, "Don't Cave in to the NEA," *Boston Globe* (March 4, 1999), p. A19.

9. Naturally, the standard for declaring a failure would need to be more substantive than a particular artist's claim that his unsold works demonstrate that the world has failed to recognize his genius.

10. John Simon, *New York Magazine* (December 20, 2004), http://www.newyorkmetro.com/nymetro/arts/theater/reviews/10655.

11. Joseph Nocera, "Now Playing on Broadway: The Money Pit," *New York Times* (June 4, 2005), pp. C1, C4.

12. See note 11, p. C4.

13. Noël Carroll, "Can Government Funding of the Arts Be Justified Theoretically?" *Journal of Aesthetic Education* (Spring 1987), pp. 21–35.

14. As an adjunct to *Time*'s 2005 list of 100 best feature-length films of all time, critic Richard Corliss presented a list of short subjects with "grand achievements." *Andalusian Dog* was one of the 10 listed titles, http://www.time.com/time/2005 /100movies/0,23220,short_subjects,00.html.

15. See note 13, p. 28.

16. Cécile Aubert, Pranab K. Bardhan, and Jeff Dayton-Johnson, "Artfilms, Handicrafts and Other Cultural Goods: The Case for Subsidy" (working paper no. E04-340, University of California at Berkeley, November 2003).

17. The *auteur* theory, closely associated with French cinema of the 1960s, places primary emphasis on the director's role in creating a film. Director François Truffaut introduced the idea in a celebrated 1954 article. According to Answers.com, "Truffaut and his colleagues at the magazine *Cahiers du Cinema* recognized that moviemaking was an industrial process. However, they proposed an ideal to strive for: using the commercial apparatus just the way a writer uses a pen," http://www.answers.com/topic/auteur-theory.

18. Edward C. Banfield, "Arts and the Public Interest," in *Public Policy and the Aesthetic Interest: Critical Essays on Defining Cultural and Educational Relations,* Ralph A. Smith and Ronald Berman, eds. (Urbana: University of Illinois Press, 1992), pp. 29–39.

19. Ernest van den Haag, "Should the Government Subsidize the Arts?" In *Public Policy and the Aesthetic Interest: Critical Essays on Defining Cultural and Educational Relations,* Ralph A. Smith and Ronald Berman, eds. (Urbana: University of Illinois Press, 1992), pp. 52–60.

20. Michael Brenson, *Visionaries and Outcasts: The NEA, Congress, and the Place of the Visual Artist in America* (New York: The New Press, 2001), p. 1.

21. See note 18, p. 33.

22. Frank Rich, "The Armstrong Williams NewsHour," *New York Times* (June 26, 2005), sec. 4, p. 13.

23. *On the Issues,* http://www.ontheissues.org.

24. Polyconomics.com, http://.wanniski.com/showarticle.asp?rticleid=4438.

25. Granted, it could prove difficult in practice to segregate cash in such a way. Dollars received for educational programming would enable stations to divert dollars generated through telethons to public affairs programming. This is by no means a unique problem in government funding. Suppose the government funds a social program administered by a religious institution, which the institution would continue to provide if the government funding were not available. The government dollars free up funds to be used for strictly religious purposes. Few would resolve this problem by disqualifying religious institutions from administering

government-funded programs. Neither would it sit well, in view of the Constitution's church-state separation provision, for the government to give money to religious institutions with no strings attached. Similarly, government funding of public television should be directed to educational programs, despite impediments to perfect execution of that design.

26. James D. Ryan, "Analysis of the National Endowment of the Arts Using SAS®/STAT Software," presented at the Twenty-Third Annual SUGI International Conference, Nashville, Tennessee (March 22–25, 1998).
27. See note 7, p. 3.
28. See note 13, p. 23.
29. Frédéric Bastiat, "Theaters and Fine Arts," in *Selected Essays on Political Economy.* Seymour Cain, trans., George B. de Huszar, ed. (Irvington-on-Hudson, New York: The Foundation for Economic Education, 1995), pp. 7–11, http://www .econlib.org/library/Bastiat/basEss1.html.

Chapter 9:   Stock Arguments

1. Economagic.com.
2. Bloomberg.com. Total return consists of principal gain or loss, dividends, and reinvestment of dividends. Calculation assumes reinvestment of dividends in the index. Over the period in question, the value of the index rose at an annualized rate of 10.18%.
3. See note 2.
4. All quotations in this paragraph are from the U.S. Securities and Exchange Commission web site, http://www.sec.gov/about/whatwedo.shtml.
5. "2000 NASDAQ Decline Led to $3 Trillion Loss in Market Value by January 2001," press release #107-105, Congress of the United States Joint Economic Committee, (October 11, 2002).
6. See note 5.
7. Owen A. Lamont, "Go Down Fighting: Short Sellers vs. Firms" (working paper, January 9, 2003), p. 19.
8. This requirement is embodied in Rule 10a-1 of the Securities and Exchange Act of 1934. A short sale is also permitted at a price equivalent to the last sale price if *that* price is higher than the last different reported price.
9. "Short Sale Restrictions," U.S. Securities and Exchange Commission (modified August 19, 2003), http://www.sec.gov/answers/shortrestrict.htm.
10. "October 29, 1929—'Black Tuesday,'" CNN.com/U.S. (March 10, 2003), http://www.cnn.com/2003/US/03/10/sprj.80.1929.crash. Dustin Woodard, "Black Tuesday—1929," *About,* http://mutualfunds.about.com/cs/1929marketcrash/a/black _tuesday.htm.
11. For an explanation of margin buying, see "The Impotence of Margin Requirements," later in this chapter.

12. The statistics in the paragraphs dealing with the 1929 Stock Market Crash and its aftermath are from Edward Chancellor, *A Short History of the Bear,* Prudent Bear Funds, press room (October 29, 2001), http://www.prudentbear.com/press_room_short_selling_history.html.

13. See note 12, p. 3.

14. If the value of a stock bought on margin falls by a certain amount, the margin buyer must either put up additional cash or sell his position to repay his margin loan.

15. See note 12, p. 4.

16. Kathryn F. Staley, *Art of Short Selling* (New York: Wiley, 1997), pp. 235–238.

17. Shares of the energy trading company soared from $33 in January 1999 to $87–5/8 in September 2000. After massive financial reporting irregularities came to light during 2001, the stock finished the year at 60 cents a share.

18. See note 7.

19. See note 7, p. 1.

20. See note 7, p. 17.

21. See note 7, p. 9.

22. James Surowiecki, "Get Shorty," *New Yorker* (December 1, 2003), p. 42.

23. See note 7, p. 18.

24. David Armstrong, "Short-Seller Rocker Partners Was Mauled by Bull Market," *Wall Street Journal* (January 23, 2004), p. C1.

25. On "Black Monday," the Dow Jones Industrial Average fell 508.32 points, a one-day drop of 22.6 percent.

26. Jeffrey Keegan, "SEC: 1997 Circuit Breakers May Have Accelerated Declines," *Investment Dealers Digest* (September 21, 1998), p. 7.

27. Charles M. C. Lee, Mark J. Ready, and Paul J. Seguin, "Volume, Volatility, and New York Stock Exchange Trading Halts," *Journal of Finance* (March 1994), pp. 183–214.

28. Lucy F. Ackert, Bryan K. Church, and Narayanan Jayaraman, "Circuit Breakers with Uncertainty about the Presence of Informed Agents: I Know What You Know . . . I Think" (working paper, Federal Reserve Bank of Atlanta, December 2002).

29. John Kenneth Galbraith. *Great Crash: 1929* (New York: Houghton Mifflin, 1929).

30. Nicholas F. Brady et al. *Report of the Presidential Task Force on Market Mechanisms* (Washington, DC: U.S. Government Printing Office, January 1988). Also, U.S. Securities and Exchange Commission. *October 1987 Market Break: A Report by the Division of Market Regulation, U.S. Securities and Exchange Commission* (Washington, DC: U.S. Government Printing Office, February 1988).

31. Continuing with the text example previously introduced, suppose that after Bob buys 200 shares of Idiotronic on margin at $25 a share, the price falls to $18. On paper, he has lost $7 a share, reducing the equity in his account by $1,400. The remaining equity, $1,100, represents only 31% of the value in his account ($18 × 200 = $3,600). If Bob's broker requires a *maintenance margin* of 33 percent, he faces a margin call.

32. This account draws from Fred Vogelstein, Paul Sloan, and Anne Kates Smith, "In Hock for Hot Stocks," *U.S. News & World Report* (April 17, 2000), pp. 36–40.

33. The initial margin rate percentage of equity that the investor must put up when buying a stock. If the maximum amount that an investor can borrow on a purchase of $5,000 worth of shares is $2,500, then the initial margin rate is the required equity ($5,000 − $2,500 = $2,500) divided by the purchase amount ($5,000), or 50%.

34. See note ,132 p. 37.

35. See note 32, p. 40.

36. Peter Fortune, "Margin Lending and Stock Market Volatility," *New England Economic Review* (July/August 2001), pp. 3–25.

37. Kenneth A. Kim and Henry R. Oppenheimer, "Initial Margin Requirements, Volatility, and the Individual Investor: Insights from Japan," *Financial Review* (February 2002), pp. 1–16.

38. This explanation is proposed in Peter Coy, "Margin Debt Isn't the Problem," *BusinessWeek* (April 24, 2000), p. 162.

39. Jack L. Treynor and Dean LeBaron, "Insider Trading: Two Comments," *Financial Analysts Journal* (May/June 2004), pp. 10, 12.

40. CFA Institute web site, http://www.cfainstitute.org.

41. See note 39, p. 10.

42. Utpal Bhattacharya and Hazem Daouk, "The World Price of Insider Trading," *Journal of Finance* (February 2002), pp. 75–108; Laura Nyantung Beny, "Do Insider Trading Laws Matter? Some Preliminary Comparative Evidence," *American Law & Economics Review* (Spring 2005), pp. 144–183; Robert M. Bushman, Joseph D. Piotroski, and Abbie J. Smith, "Insider Trading Restrictions and Analysts' Incentives to Follow Firms," *Journal of Finance* (February 2005), pp. 35–66.

Chapter 10:   What Is Wrong with Payola?

1. Joshua Chaffin, "Spitzer to Make Radio Waves," *Financial Times* (July 26, 2005), p. 24.

2. Kerry Segrave, *Payola in the Music Industry: A History, 1880–1991* (Jefferson, NC: McFarland & Company, 1994), p. 109.

3. See note 2, p. 164.

4. R. H. Coase, "Payola in Radio and Television Broadcasting," *Journal of Law & Economics* (October 1979), pp. 269–328. Possibly as a result of plea-bargaining, the Brunswick executives were not found guilty of payola, but rather of conspiracy to sell records for cash without reporting the income and defrauding songwriters and recording artists of their royalties. But radio station music directors, who had been granted immunity, testified that they had received cash payments from representatives of Brunswick.

5. See note 2, p. 188.

6. See note 1, p. 24.

7. Some sources indicate that the term is derived from "pay" and the Victrola brand phonograph. Segrave, *Payola in the Music Industry,* p. 1, however, states that at the time *Variety* originated the term, it was enamored of coining industry slang terms by adding the suffix "-ola" to various words.

8. The 1958 hearing dealt primarily with issues such as corruption within the FCC and alleged conflicts of interest arising from the holding of broadcasting licenses by music publishers and record companies. Payola was a tangential item, but became central to the 1959 probe.

9. Murray N. Rothbard, "The Problem of Payola," *Free Market* (May 2001). This was the first publication of the piece, written by Rothbard in 1956. Ludwig von Mises Institute web site, http://www.mises.org/freemarket_detail.asp?control=359.

10. Note that Rothbard generalizes this portion of his argument, introducing a hypothetical case involving an out-of-town buyer for a clothing store who accepts payment for placing an order with a particular garment manufacturer.

11. The hypothetical figures in this paragraph are the author's, not Rothbard's.

12. Bear in mind that if all record companies were engaged in payola, the disc jockey's rational course was *not* to allow his judgment to be swayed by any single company's financial consideration.

13. Rothbard indirectly anticipated the more recent introduction of subscription-based satellite radio. In his argument, the deceived radio listeners' case would be stronger if they paid for the programs.

14. Rothbard taught at the University of Nevada, Las Vegas. He also served as vice president for academic affairs at the Mises Institute, a research and educational center.

15. The history of pay-for-play schemes is drawn from Coase, "Payola," Segrave, *Payola in the Music Industry,* and Tony Palmer, *All You Need Is Love: The Story of Popular Music* (New York: Grossman Publishers, a Division of the Viking Press, 1976), pp. 104–106.

16. Naturally, it would be a different matter if the retailing executives were demanding side payments. Instead, they are seeking concessions on the lease on behalf of the corporation that employs them. The benefits they extract therefore accrue to the entity that creates the value, just as the sheet music publishers' gifts and cash went to the artists who made the songs hits by performing them.

17. Jacob Slichter, "The Price of Fame," *New York Times* (July 29, 2005), p. A23. Slichter detailed his experiences with the band Semisonic in a book entitled, *So You Wanna Be a Rock & Roll Star: How I Machine-Gunned a Roomful of Record Executives and Other True Tales from a Drummer's Life.*

18. At least, only one possible *rational* objection remains. Some music fans contend that potentially successful records never get heard because no payola is pushing them onto the airwaves. But they fail to explain why record companies would deliberately refrain from promoting records with large sales potential. These allegations tend to confuse aesthetic quality (as determined by the objectors to the payola system) with popularity. It is hardly surprising that record companies choose not to allocate their payola dollars to records with lots of artistic merit but little sales potential. The failure of such

records to receive much airtime is a function of appealing to rarefied tastes, not the conspiracies imagined by some music fanatics.

19. Note that Rothbard effectively rejects this argument by emphasizing that the listeners are not harmed by payola, as they have no contract with the radio station that entitles them to hear records selected on the basis of artistic merit.

20. See note 4, pp. 311–312.

21. Note that the station would actually seek not only to attract a large number of listeners, but also to achieve the optimal demographic mix within its audience.

22. Record hops are informal dances where popular music is played.

23. See note 4, p. 319.

24. Billboard Hot 100, reported by Answers.com, http://www.answers.com /Hot%20100 %20No.%201%20Hits%20of%201959.

25. Peter W. Bernstein, "The Record Business: Rocking to the Big-Money Beat," *Fortune* (April 23, 1979), pp. 59–68.

26. See note 4, p. 276.

27. Songfacts, http://www.songfacts.com/detail.lasso?id=1429.

28. See note 4, pp. 275–278.

29. See note 4, p. 317.

Chapter 11:   What Is Big Brother Watching?

1. Brooks Barnes, "TV Drama: For Nielsen, Fixing Old Ratings System Causes New Static," *Wall Street Journal* (September 16, 2004), p. A1.

2. *Accountability of Audience Measurement: A Global Examination,* summary of a January 31, 2005, special meeting of the Advertising Research Foundation (ARF, March 2005).

3. Michele Greppi, "Burns Wants FTC to Oversee TV Ratings Fairness," *Television Week* (October 11, 2004), p. 29.

4. "Congressmen Urge Colleagues Not to Intervene in Television Ratings Business," *Entertainment Magazine* (March 17, 2005), p. 1, http://emol.org/emclub /?q=tvratings.

5. See note 4, p. 3.

6. According to "TV's Phony Ratings Game," *Week* (February 21, 2003), http:// theweekmagazine.com/briefing.asp?_id=349, the ratio of unusable diaries is 70%.

7. See note 6, p. 2.

8. Big Brother is the leader of a totalitarian society depicted in George Orwell's novel *Nineteen Eighty-Four,* published in 1949. In its entry for Big Brother (1984), *Wikipedia* states, "Since the publication of *Nineteen Eighty-Four,* the phrase "Big Brother" has entered general usage, to describe any overly-inquisitive or overly-controlling authority figure or attempts by government to increase surveillance," http://en.wikipedia.org/wiki/Big_Brother_(1984).

9. The discussion of the history and the technical challenges of television ratings draws on Lynn Schafer Gross, *Ratings.* Museum of Broadcast Communications, http://www.museum.tv/archives/etv/R/htmlR/ratings/ratings.htm.

10. "MRC History," Media Rating Council web site, http://www.mrc.htsp.com /history.jsp.

11. See note 9, pp. 3–5.

12. "The Revolution Will Not Be Televised," *New Republic* (April 26, 2004), p. 8, http://www.tnr.com/doc.mhtml?i=20040426&s=notebook042604twp.

13. Marian Zapata-Rossa and Christopher Jaquez, *Latinos and the Nielsen Ratings.* Congressional Hispanic Caucus Institute, Inc. (Undated; authors were 2002–2003 CHCI Fellows), p. 4.

14. See note 13, p. 4.

15. Raymond Hernandez and Stuart Elliott, "The Odd Couple vs. Nielsen," *New York Times* (June 14, 2004), p. C1.

16. Anthony Bianco and Ronald Grover, "How Nielsen Stood Up to Murdoch," *BusinessWeek* (September 20, 2004), p. 89, http://businessweek.com/magazine /content/04_38/b3900100_mz017.htm.

17. See note 16, p. 89.

18. See note 16, p. 89.

19. Randall Rothenberg, "Ruckus over People Meters Points Up Accountability Issue," *Advertising Age* (June 21, 2004), p. 16, http://web11.epnet.com /citation .asp?tb-1&_ugsid+626FAB77%2D5C59%2D4FF9%2D9.

20. See note 1, p. A8

21. See note 16, p. 89.

22. See note 16, p. 89.

23. See note 15, p. C1.

24. Herb Boyd, "Nielsen Still Unsettled," *New York Amsterdam News* (June 17, 2004), p. 6, http://web11.epnet.com/citation.asp?tb=1&_ug=sid+626FAB77%2D5C59% 2D4FF9%2D9.

25. Stuart Elliott, "Nielsen Media's Revised Ratings System Is Denied Accreditation by Industry Group," *New York Times* (May 29, 2004), p. C3.

26. "Counting the Money," *Economist* (June 12, 2004), p. | nb62

27. "The Testimony of Mr. Tom Arnost, President, Univision Television, Inc," Senate Committee on Commerce, Science and Transportation (July 15, 2004), http://commerce.senate.gov/hearings/testimony.cfm?if-1269&wit_id =3653.

28. Gale Metzger, Testimony before the Senate Committee on Commerce, Science and Technology (July 27, 2005), p. 7.

29. National Urban League web site, http://www.nul.org/mission.html.

30. Katy Bachman, "ANA Opposes FAIR Ratings Act," *MediaWeek* (July 26, 2005), http://www.mediaweek.com/mw/news/networktv/article_display.jsp?vnu _content_id=1000991999.

31. See note 16, p. 89.

32. Jay Sherman, "Nielsen Agrees to Task Force Plans," *Television Week* (March 28, 2005), p. 28.

33. See note 25, p. C3.

34. Toni Fitzgerald, "MRC on Its Mission as Media Overseer," *Media Life* (April 26, 2005), p. 4, http://www.medialifemagazine.com/News2005/april05/apr25/2_tues /news4tuesday.html.

35. See note 25, p. C3.

36. Katy Bachman, "Univision Sues Nielsen," *MediaWeek* (June 14, 2004), pp. 7–8, http://www.adweek.com/aw/national/article_display.jsp?vnu_content_id =1000528666.

37. Stuart Elliott, "Nielsen Responds to Univision Suit," *New York Times* (June 23, 2004), p. C5.

38. See note 1, p. A8.

39. Katy Bachman, "Senators Introduce FAIR Ratings Bill," *Media Week* (July 1, 2005), http://www.mediaweek.com/mw/news/recent_display.jsp?vnu_content_id =1000972720.

40. "News Corp. Courts Democrats," *CNN.money* (August 9, 2005), http://money.cnn .com/2005/08/09/news/fortune500/newscorp_dems.

41. Jim Snyder, "NewsCorp. Marshals Lobbyists," *Hill* (August 15, 2005), http://www .hillnews.com/thehill/export/TheHill/News/Frontpage/081005/news.html.

42. See note 41.

43. See note 39, p. 000.

44. Katy Bachman, "Not FAIR, Pleads Nielsen," *Media Week* (July 11, 2005), p. 6, http:// mediaweek.com/mw/news/tvstations/article_display.jsp?vnu_content_id=1000.

45. See note 2, p. 8.

46. Erwin Ephron, "The Law Is an Ass, but Flowers Might Help," *Ephron on Media* (February 4, 2005), http://www.ephrononmedia.com/article_archive/articleViewerPublic .asp?rticleID=137.

47. See note 9, *Ratings,* p. 3.

48. Jon Lafayette, "New Challenger Taking on Nielsen," *Television Week* (July 12, 2004), p. 29.

49. Theodore Levitt, "Marketing Myopia," *Harvard Business Online* (republished July 1, 2004), http://harvardbusinessonline.hbsp.harvard.edu/b01/en/common/item _detail.jhtml?id=R0407L.

50. Michele Greppi, "Nielsen Unveils Updated Diaries," *Television Week* (May 9, 2005), pp. 6–7.

51. Lee Alan Hill, "A Fine Line for Nielsen," *Television Week* (August 9, 2004), pp. 12–13.

52. At a January 31, 2005 meeting of the Advertising Research Foundation (ARF), Attorney Stephen Smith of Morrison & Foerster LLP stated that a JIC would not inherently violate antitrust laws. Agreements involving coordination among firms are lawful, he said, if they create efficiency and enhance competition, on balance. Attorney Phil Verveer of Willkie Farr & Gallagher LLP and others argued, in contrast, that creating a lawful JIC would be impossible in practice. For further details, see "MRC History," pp. 11–12.

53. Richard Fielding, *MediaWeek* (October 11, 2004), p. 22, http://web11.epnet.com /citation.asp?tb=1&_ug=sid+626FAB77%2D5C59%2D4FF9%2D9.

54. Brooks Barnes, "Where're the Ratings, Dude?" *Wall Street Journal* (March 7, 2005), p. B1.

Chapter 12:   Getting Cash and Making the Rent

1. America's War of Independence lasted from April 1775 to September 1783. The Bill of Rights was passed by Congress in September 1789 and finally ratified by the states in December 1791.

2. Dean Foust and Seanna Browder, "Mad as Hell at the Cash Machine," *Business Week* (September 15, 1997), p. 124.

3. *Double ATM Fees, Triple Trouble: A Fifth PIRG National Survey of ATM Surcharging Rates.* U.S. Public Interest Research Group (April 1, 2001), http://www.stopatmfees.com/report01/report01.pdf.

4. At least, they had not been charged at the ATM by the bank that owned it. Their own banks might already have been charging them as a means of recovering interchange fees.

5. "Fast Cash," *Public Campaign: A New Kind of Reform Politics* (September 23, 1998), http://www.publiccampaign.org/publications/ouch-cpi/001-020/ouch010.htm.

6. See note 5, p. 1.

7. *Marketplace: News Archives.* American Public Media (June 11, 1997), http://marketplace.publicradio.org/shows/1997/06/11_mpp.html.

8. Larry Elder, "Al D'Amato: Automatic Regulator Machine," *FrontPageMagazine.com* (July 31, 1998), http://frontpagemag.com/articles/ReadArticle.asp?ID-2881. This gleeful lampoon of D'Amato's crusade facetiously urges him to attack other consumer "wallops" such as McDonald's refusal to allow substitution of a soft drink for coffee in its standard breakfast.

9. See note 5, p. 1.

10. Richard M. Alston, J. R. Kearl, and Michael B. Vaughn, "Is There Consensus among Economists in the 1990s?" *American Economic Review* (May 1992), pp. 203–209.

11. Campbell R. McConnell, *Economics: Principles, Problems, and Policies,* 8th ed. (New York: McGraw-Hill, 1981), p. 714.

12. *Rent Control Library.* Fair Rental Policy Organization, http://www.frpo.org/RentControlLibrary.asp?wid=178.

13. Peter Salins and Gerard Mildner, "Does Rent Control Help the Poor?" *City Journal* (Winter 1991), pp. 39–45.

14. Peter D. Salins, "Scarcity by Design: New York's Failed Housing Policies," *City Journal* (Winter 1993), pp. 70–76, http://www.manhattan-institute.org/cfml/printable.cfm?id=1153.

15. See note 13, p. 43.

16. Patrick O'Gilfoil Healy, "The Art of Persuading Tenants to Move," *New York Times* (August 28, 2005), sec. 11, pp. 1, 7.

17. Christine Haughney and Ryan Chittum, "Plots & Ploys: What's Brewing in the Real Estate Market," *Wall Street Journal* (August 3, 2005), p. B6.

18. The account of Cyndi Lauper's rent dispute is drawn from (1) "Lauper Sues Landlords over 'Rent Scam,'" contactmusic.com (May 30, 2005), http://www.contactmusic .com/new/xmlfeed.nsf/mndwebpages/lauper%20sues%20landlord; (2) Julie Keller, "Cyndi Lauper for Cheap Rent," Eonline (May 31, 2005), http://www .eonline.com/News/Items/0,1,16660,00.html; and (3) "Cyndi Lauper's Rent," *New York Sun* (July 8, 2005), p. 14, http://www.nysun.com/article/16680.

19. This is presumably a reference to Columbia recording artist Barbra Streisand.

20. Scott Lyle, posted on "Cyndi Lauper—Forum Topic Messages," cyndilauper.com (June 5, 2005), http://www.cyndilauper.com/forum_topic_det.php?forum_id =6&topic_id=413.

21. Steven Wishnia, "Vacancy Decontrol: A Disaster Then, a Disaster Now" (May 1997), http://www.tenant.net/Tengroup/Metcounc/May97/vacancy.html; and Peter Dreier and Winton Pitcoff, "I'm a Tenant and I Vote!" NHI Shelterforce Online (July/August 1997), http://www.nhi.org/online/issues/94/dreier.html.

22. To put this figure in perspective, the New York State median household income in 1997 was about $31,000 (based on U.S. Census Bureau historical data reported in 2003 dollars, adjusted by the Consumer Price Index-Northeast Urban series).

23. "The Great Manhattan Rip-Off," *Economist* (June 7, 2003), p. 25–26.

24. "Housing First! Affordable Housing for All New Yorkers," Mayor Michael Bloomberg on Housing, http://www.housingfirst.net/on-bloombergonhousing.html.

25. "Mayoral Issue Grid: Housing," *Gotham Gazette* (August 25, 2005), http://www .gothamgazette.com/article/Housing/20050815/10/1525.

26. "Housing Advocates Endorse Miller for Mayor," press release, Gifford Miller for Mayor (August 10, 2005), http://www.millerfornewyork.com/press/081005 _pressrelease.html.

Chapter 13:   Honesty Is the Worst Policy

1. National Bureau of Economic Research, http://www.nber.org/cycles/cyclesmain.html.

2. John Maynard Keynes, *The General Theory of Employment, Interest, and Money.* (New York: Harcourt, Brace, 1936).

3. Steve H. Hanke, "We're All Keynesians—Still?" *Forbes Magazine* (February 22, 1999), http://www.forbes.com/forbes/1999/0222/6304078a.html.

4. For a fuller discussion, see *Cyber-Economics: An On-Line Textbook for Introductory Economics,* http://ingrimayne.saintjoe.edu.

5. Bruce Bartlett, "The Difficult Business of Forecasting," National Center for Policy Analysis (February 16, 2004), http://www.ncpa.org/edo/bb/2004 /20040216bb.htm.

6. Drawn from Martin Feldstein, "Commentary: Is There a Role for Discretionary Fiscal Policy?" *Proceedings* (2003), pp. 151–162. Federal Reserve Bank of Kansas City, http://ideas.repec.org/a/fip/fedkpr/y2003p151–162.html.

7. Alan J. Auerbach, "Is There a Role for Discretionary Fiscal Policy?" *Proceedings* (2003), pp. 109–150. Federal Reserve Bank of Kansas City, http://ideas.repec .org/a/fip/fedkpr/y2003p109–150.html.

8. Laura D'andrea Tyson, "Bush's New Tax-Cut Logic Is No Better Than the Old," *BusinessWeek Online* (January 15, 2001), http://www.businessweek.com/2001 /01_03/b3715033.htm.

9. See note 8.

10. "Kerry Measures 'Middle-Class Misery,'" *CNN.Money* (April 12, 2004), http://money.cnn.com/2004/04/12/news/economy/election_misery. Economic statistics are subject to subsequent revision. A later check showed the February 2004 unemployment rate at 5.7 percent.

11. "Kerry's 'Misery Index' Accentuates the Negative," FactCheck.org., Annenberg Political Fact Check (April 13, 2004), http://www.factcheck.org/article170.html. In December 2000, unemployment was 3.9 percent and inflation was running 3.4 percent, producing a misery index of 7.3 percent.

12. Gregg Easterbrook, *Easterblogg, New Republic Online* (March 13, 2004), http://www.tnr.com/easterbrook.mhtml?week=2004-04-13.

13. See note 12.

14. "Kerry Measures 'Middle-Class Misery,'" *CNN.Money* (April 12, 2004), http://money.cnn.com/2004/04/12/news/economy/election_misery.

15. "Overall Unemployment in the Civilian Labor Force, 1920–2004," *Infoplease,* http://www.infoplease.com/ipa/A0104719.html. For the record, the Consumer Price Index *declined* by 10.3 percent in 1932, according to the Bureau of Labor Statistics. That would have produced a misery index of 13.3 percent, had anyone been calculating the series at the time.

16. *NBER's Recession Dating Procedure.* Business Cycle Dating Committee, National Bureau of Economic Research (October 21, 2003), http://www.nber.org /cycles/recessions.html.

17. The account of the controversy over the dating of the beginning of the 2001 recession derives from Michael J. Mandel, "Inventing the 'Clinton Recession,'" *BusinessWeek* (February 23, 2004), p. 48.

18. George Hager, "Gloom and Doom on the Campaign Trail," *Washington Post* (June 8, 1999), p. E1.

19. Peter G. Gosselin, "Campaign 2000: Tax Cuts Seen as Spoiler—in Boom Times," *Los Angeles Times* (August 26, 2000), p. 1.

20. See note 8.

21. Lee Walczak and Howard Gleckman, "Tax Cuts: Where's the Old Magic?" *BusinessWeek Online* (January 31, 2000), http://www.businessweekasia.com/2000/00_05 /b3666102.htm.

22. See note 8.

23. *On the Issues.* Columbia Commonwealth University, http://www.issues2000.org/2004 /George_W__Bush_Tax_Reform.htm.

24. Thomas G. Donlan, "Rope-a-Dope," *Barron's* (February 28, 2005), p. 43.

Chapter 14: Campaign Finance Reform: The Permanent Campaign

1. John A. Garraty, *The American Nation: A History of the United States since 1865,* Vol. 2, 5th ed. (New York: Harper & Row, Publishers, 1983), p. 535.

2. Thomas Fleming, "The Long, Stormy Marriage of Money and Politics," *American Heritage* (November 1998), pp. 45–53, http://homepages.uc.edu/~lawsonb /teaching/pres/fleming.htm. At 4.

3. "In the Wake of the Armstrong Investigation," in *Voices from the Field,* National Association of Life Underwriters (August 1989), http://www.advisortoday.com /200411/OpenBook/vftf_armstronginv.html.

4. See note 1, p. 535.

5. Julia Malone, "Despite Reforms, Money Talks; Campaign Finance Has Long History," *Atlanta Journal-Constitution* (February 24, 2002), p. A6.

6. "Campaign Contributions," *Theodore Roosevelt Web Book,* Theodore Roosevelt Association, pp. 62–63, http://www.theodoreroosevelt.org/TR%20Web%20Book /TR_CD_to_HTML99.html.

7. Daniel Yergin, *Prize: The Epic Quest for Oil, Money, and Power* (New York: Simon & Schuster, 1991), p. 107.

8. See note 2, At 6.

9. See note 2, At 6.

10. "Historical Context" (Chapter 1), in *History of Campaign Finance,* Annual Report of the Federal Election Commission (April 1995), www.fec.gov.

11. See note 2, At 6.

12. See note 2, At 8.

13. See note 2, At 8.

14. Scott E. Thomas and Jeffrey H. Bowman, "Obstacles to Effective Enforcement of the Federal Election Campaign Act," *Administrative Law Review* (Spring 2000), pp. 575–608.

15. *No Bark, No Bite, No Point.* Case for Closing the Federal Election Commission and Establishing a New System of Enforcing the Nation's Campaign Finance Laws, Project FEC (2002), p. 72.

16. See note 15, pp. 87–88.

17. Ruth Marcus, "GOP Hits Gore on Temple Fund-Raiser," *Washington Post* (February 10, 1998), p. A1.

18. Charles Lewis and the Center for Public Integrity, *Buying of the President 2000.* (New York: Avon Books, 2000), p. 26.

19. See note 15, p. 91.

20. "Bipartisan Campaign Reform Act," *Wikipedia,* http://wikipedia.org/wiki /Bipartisan_Campign_Reform_Act_of_2002.

21. John McCain, "Paying for Campaigns: McCain Eyes Next Target," *USA Today* (November 4, 2004), p. A27, http://www.campaignlegalcenter.org/press-1375.html.

22. See note 15, p. 95.

23. Carol D. Leonnig, "Judge Strikes Down 15 FEC Rules on Campaign Finance," *Washington Post* (September 21, 2004), p. A1.
24. See note 23, p. A1.
25. "Media Fund, 2004 Election Cycle," Opensecrets. Org, http://www.opensecrets.org/527s/527events.asp?orgid=15.
26. "Swift Veterans Quotes," Swift Vets and POWs for Truth, http://swift1.he.net/~swiftvet/index.php?topic=SwiftVetQuotes.
27. Kimberley A. Strassel, "The Cash That Dare Not Speak His Name," *Wall Street Journal* (July 30, 2004), p. A10.
28. Albert R. Hunt, "McCain-Feingold Did Its Job," *Wall Street Journal* (November 18, 2004), p. A19.
29. "Kerry Stumbled on a Heap of Dollars," *Financial Times* (December 13, 2004), p. 4.
30. See note 27, p. A10.
31. "527 Group," *Wikipedia,* http://en.wikipedia.org/wiki/527_committee.
32. John F. Harris and Peter Baker, "Clinton Defends Fund-Raising," *Washington Post* (March 8, 1997), p. A1.
33. See note 2, At 5.
34. See note 15, p. 88.
35. See note 2, At 12.
36. See note 2, At 10.
37. See note 2, At 10.
38. Peter Beinart, "TRB from Washington: Golden," *New Republic* (January 24, 2005), p. 6.
39. See note 2, At 10.

Chapter 15: Here's That Rainy Day

1. From "Here's That Rainy Day," by Johnny Burke and Jimmy Van Heusen. Perhaps fittingly, in view of this chapter's focus on a failed system, the show for which the song was composed was a flop. The 1953 Broadway musical *Carnival in Flanders* (book by Preston Sturges) closed after only six performances.
2. Peter A. Diamond and Peter R. Orszag, *Reforming Social Security: A Balanced Plan* Policy Brief #126, The Brookings Institution (December 2003), p. 1.
3. David M. Walker, *Social Security Reform: Analysis of a Trust Fund Exhaustion Scenario Illustrates the Difficult Choices and the Need for Early Action,* testimony before the Special Committee on Aging, U.S. Senate (U.S. General Accounting Office, July 29, 2003), p. 2.
4. David C. John, *Answering the Top 10 Myths about Social Security Reform,* Backgrounder #1613 (Heritage Foundation, November 19, 2002).
5. Michael Tanner, "Social Security Reform Can No Longer Be Ignored," *Fox News* (March 10, 2004), http://www.foxnews.com/story/0,2933,113860,00.html.
6. "A Shock to the System," *Uncommon Knowledge,* Transcript 808. Segment filmed on June 23, 2003.

7. See note 3, p. 5.

8. See note 3, p. 8.

9. *Social Security's Future—FAQs.* Social Security Online, p. 3, http://www.ssa.gov/qa.htm.

10. Milton Friedman, "Speaking the Truth about Social Security Reform," *Cato Institute Briefing Paper No. 46* (April 12, 1999), p. 2.

11. *Statement of Rep. Harold Ford on Social Security Reform, 9/15/03,* Social Security Choice.org (September 15, 2003), http://www.house.gov/ford/press_archives/20030916socialsecurity.html.

12. David Wessel, "Debate on Social Security Looks Promising," *Wall Street Journal* (March 4, 2004), p. A2.

13. See note 9, p. 4.

14. Richard A. Ryan, "Social Security Reform Stalls," *Detroit News,* http://www.socialsecuritychoice.org/archives/2005/01/democrats_on_pe.php.

15. "Life Expectancy for Social Security," *Social Security Online,* http://www.ssa.gov/history/lifeexpect.html (as of September 2004).

16. Amie Jamieson, Hyon B. Shin, and Jennifer Day, *Voting and Registration in the Election of November 2000* (U.S. Census Bureau, February 2002), p. 6.

17. Jerome Tuccille, *Alan Shrugged: The Life and Times of Alan Greenspan, the World's Most Powerful Banker* (Hoboken, NJ: Wiley, 2002), pp. 137–138. The ensuing discussion of the National Commission on Social Security Reform also draws on this source.

18. See note 17, p. 151.

19. See note 14.

20. "Transcript of Debate between Bush and Kerry, with Domestic Policy the Topic," *New York Times* (October 14, 2004), pp. A22–A25.

21. See note 20, p. A23.

22. See note 20, p. A23.

23. See note 20, p. A23.

24. Michael Tanner, "Social Security Reform Can No Longer Be Ignored," *Fox News.com,* http://www.foxnews.com/story/0,2933,113860,00.html.

25. John Geanakoplos, "Generation X: Does Bush Understand His Social Security Plan?" *New Republic* (October 23, 2000), pp. 18–20.

26. See, for example, Peter Diamond, "Social Security," *American Economic Review* (March 2004), pp. 1–23.

27. Laurence J. Kotlikoff, "Privatizing Social Security the Right Way," *Independent Review* (Summer 2000), pp. 55–63.

Chapter 16: A Case of Insurance Fraud

1. This discussion draws on George G. Kaufman, "Too Big to Fail in U.S. Banking: Quo Vadis?" *Quarterly Review of Economics and Finance* (Summer 2002), pp. 423–436; and "Continental Illinois and 'Too Big to Fail,'" in *History of the*

Eighties—Lessons for the Future. Federal Deposit Insurance Corporation Division of Research and Statistics Federal Deposit Insurance Corporation (revised June 5, 2000), http://www.fdic.gov/bank/historical/history, http://www.fdic.gov/bank/historical/235_258.pdf.

2. This saying has been attributed to and claimed by a number of businesspeople, but its true origin is obscure.

3. See note 1, p. 15.

4. See note 1, p. 15.

5. All figures in this discussion of health care costs are from Don R. Powell, "Characteristics of Successful Wellness Programs," *Employee Benefits Journal* (September 1999), pp. 15–21.

6. Eugene White, "Deposit Insurance," in Gerard Caprio Jr. and Dmitri Vittras, *Reforming Financial Systems: Historical Implications for Policy* (Cambridge: Cambridge University Press, 1997), pp. 85–100. At 91.

7. Mary Williams Walsh, "Bailout Feared if Airlines Shed Their Pensions," *New York Times* (August 1, 2004) section 1, p. 1. Also, consultant Bert Ely provides an estimate of $175 billion in "Savings and Loan Crisis," *Concise Encyclopedia of Economics,* http://www.econlib.org/library/Enc/SavingsandLoanCrisis.html.

8. The case against characterizing deposit insurance as genuine insurance can't rest exclusively on its failure to reduce the incidence of claim-triggering events. After all, there are other examples of insurance that has no such effect. Earthquake insurance, for example, does nothing to reduce the frequency of earthquakes.

9. Chris Farrell, "FDIC Reform: Use the Market to Monitor Big Banks," *Federal Reserve Bank of Minneapolis—The Region* (June 2000). Note that the legislation establishing deposit insurance was actually signed in 1933, with the Temporary Deposit Insurance Fund commencing operations on January 1, 1934.

10. Eugene N. White, *Legacy of Deposit Insurance: The Growth, Spread, and Cost of Insuring Financial Intermediaries* (working paper no. 6063, National Bureau of Economic Research, June 1997), p. 34.

11. See note 6.

12. The sources for the historical accounts of deposit insurance and clearinghouses include Charles W. Calomiris, "Deposit Insurance: Lessons from the Record," *Economic Perspectives of the Federal Reserve Bank of Chicago* (May/June 1989), pp. 10–30; and Charles W. Calomiris, "Is Deposit Insurance Necessary? A Historical Perspective," *Journal of Economic History* (June 1990), pp. 283–295.

13. See note 12, p. 21.

14. Calomiris, "Deposit Insurance," pp. 22–24. Texas slowly paid off its outstanding claims through special assessments on banks that remained in the insurance system.

15. See note 12, p. 10.

16. In the failed state systems, the strong banks quite sensibly opted out of the system, if they were allowed to, instead of being exploited by the free-riding risky banks. As a result, participation in the voluntary programs was subject to the "adverse selection" problem to which many kinds of insurance are prone. For example, people

with undisclosed health problems are the most likely to apply for health insurance. As a consequence, the insurance company doesn't get to make a fair bet on the likelihood that the policyholder will have a claim.

17. This section draws on Gary Gorton and Donald J. Mullineaux, "The Joint Production of Confidence: Endogenous Regulation and Nineteenth Century Commercial-Bank Clearinghouses," *Journal of Money, Credit, and Banking* (November 1987), pp. 457–468.

18. *Mutual surveillance arrangement* is a term introduced by the author. Previous writings on the subject have not generated a standard term to describe these state-level programs, which differed fundamentally from the ill-starred deposit insurance schemes.

19. See note 12, p. 16.

20. Carter H. Golembe, "The Deposit Insurance Legislation of 1933: An Examination of Its Antecedents and Its Purposes," *Political Science Quarterly* (June 1960), pp. 181–200. At 182.

21. Charles W. Calomiris, "Is Deposit Insurance Necessary? A Historical Perspective," *Journal of Economic History* (June 1990), pp. 283–295.

22. "Understanding How the Glass-Steagall Act Impacts Investment Banking and the Role of Commercial Banking," *Brain Bank* (Cool Fire Technology), http://www.cftech.com/BrainBank/SPECIALREPORTS/GlassSteagall.html. According to studies that rely on state-level data, states that allowed branch banking experienced lower failure rates, while studies of individual banks show that branch banks were more likely than unit banks to fail. Mark Carlson of the Federal Reserve Board and Kris James Mitchener of Santa Clara University suggest that the seemingly contradictory findings can be reconciled. They argue, citing data on national banks in the 1920s and 1930s, that branch banking increased competition and forced weak banks to exit the banking system. The consolidation, Carlson and Mitchener maintain, strengthened the overall banking system without necessarily strengthening the branch banks themselves. See Mark Carlson and Kris James Mitchener, "Branch Banking, Bank Competition, and Financial Stability," working paper, http://ideas.repec.org/p/nbr/nberwo/11291.html.

23. White, "Deposit Insurance," p. 90 and Golembe, "Deposit Insurance Legislation," p. 196.

24. See note 20, p. 197.

Index

The Bottom LINE diet

The Bottom LINE diet

HOW I LOST WEIGHT, KEPT IT OFF . . .
AND YOU CAN TOO!

Jessica Irvine

ALLEN&UNWIN
SYDNEY·MELBOURNE·AUCKLAND·LONDON

First published in 2014

Allen & Unwin
83 Alexander Street
Crows Nest NSW 2065
Australia
Phone: (61 2) 8425 0100
Email: info@allenandunwin.com
Web: www.allenandunwin.com

Cataloguing-in-Publication details are available
from the National Library of Australia
www.trove.nla.gov.au

ISBN 978 1 74331 783 9

Internal design by Liz Seymour
Photos by Lucy Parakhina
Set in 10.5/16 pt Palatino by Bookhouse, Sydney
Printed in Australia by McPherson's Printing Group

10 9 8 7 6 5 4 3 2 1

The paper in this book is FSC® certified.
FSC® promotes environmentally responsible,
socially beneficial and economically viable
management of the world's forests.

Contents

USEFUL RESOURCES AND BITS OF INFORMATION

Introduction

All books are written with a particular reader in mind. You and I have never met, although I'm sure we'd get along famously if we did. In the meantime, I'm assuming if you bought this book—thanks for that, by the way—you'd like to lose some weight, and keep it off. (And believe me, keeping it off is the hardest bit. We'll get to that.) This book is written for the twenty-year-old version of myself. It is the tough love talk I wish someone had given me all those years ago about my body and how I was supposed to look after it. Before I started buttering my toast on both sides because, hey, it tastes better that way. Before I started driving to McDonald's on my lunch break, parking away from work and secretly devouring an entire Big Mac meal, with fries and coke, plus an extra cheeseburger because one burger never quite filled me up. Before I started ordering takeaway Thai curries for dinner every night. (They've got vegetables in them so they must be healthy, right?) Before I decided that exercise wasn't for me. (It was too time-consuming, or work was too stressful.) Before I started going to nice restaurants and eating entree, main and dessert. Oh, and a bottle of wine, please. Wait a minute; make that two. Before I put on 20 kilograms and had to work hard—am still working hard—to get it off and keep it off.

I have never been obese. But throughout my twenties I consistently gained 1 or 2 kilograms a year until, six months before my 30th birthday, I weighed in at 87 kilograms, which, for my height of 179 centimetres, put me officially in the overweight category. I was a 'creeper'. Left to my own eating and exercise habits, I have no doubt I would have made my way into the obese category—too stunned to even begin figuring out how to stop myself.

I'm a university-educated journalist. I'm supposed to be able to figure this stuff out. But I couldn't. Every year I'd write a New Year's resolution column telling readers my latest idea about how I would lose weight that year. I'd go to the gym three times a week. (I didn't.) I'd do one minute of exercise for every dollar I spent. (The plan was derailed when my fifteen-year-old Corolla required an expensive timing belt change.)

In 2010 I found out I had polycystic ovarian syndrome, a hormonal imbalance that affects one in ten women and is associated with weight gain. There you go then, I thought. It's not that I'm eating too many pies; I have a terrible disease.

•

Everyone has a moment when they realise they're overweight. For me, it was seeing a photo of myself taken at a friend's party on New Year's Eve 2010. You see, the weight creeps on so slowly, you don't notice it from day to day. But it all adds up. And the camera never lies.

When I look at that photo, I still remember the agony of getting ready that evening. It was summer—too hot to wear my usual uniform of stretchy denim jeans and a black T-shirt. So, reluctantly, I pulled on some shapeless knee-length black shorts and a billowy top that could have hidden any pregnancy. But, I reasoned, the top was low cut, and cleavage—as any woman who has been overweight can attest—is the refuge of the larger woman, the ultimate accessory to distract from, well, the rest. I didn't feel fashionable. I didn't care. I had numbed myself to the possibility of ever looking particularly cute. If I could just pass for bland, sink into the background, that'd be great.

A few months later my best friend from childhood mentioned she had signed up to an online 12 Week Body Transformation program run by *The Biggest Loser* trainer Michelle Bridges. With the image of me from that photo seared into my retinas, I signed up at the last minute. I had never tried dieting before. But this seemed different. The program has since expanded into a business empire for Bridges, reportedly employing more than 50 people. But back then it was relatively unknown. The essence of the program—although they don't tell you specifically before you sign up—is a combination of calorie restriction and exercise. Women eat 1200 calories a day, men a bit more, and everyone exercises for about an hour six times a week. And guess what? It works. For a while, at least. The results were immediate.

For twelve weeks I stuck to the 1200 calories a day meal plan and exercised six days a week. Boy, was I hungry. But a steely determination came over me. I dropped a kilogram a week. By the end of the year I was 20 kilograms lighter and boasting about my weight loss in columns in the newspaper.

A year later, however, I was 10 kilograms heavier again. I had regained half my weight loss and was well on my way to putting it all back on. My steely determination to eat 1200 calories a day had somehow melted when I felt 'skinny' again. The gym sessions and jogging, which had never really been my thing, soon became routines of the past. Little by little, mouthful by mouthful, I undid all my hard work. I had fallen into the same trap as 95 per cent of people who lose weight.

But I was determined to be part of the other 5 per cent. Of all the things I had learnt on the Bridges program—and I learnt a lot—one fact stood out, a fact I had never known before. It was a rule of thumb commonly advocated in the United States that a calorie deficit of about 3500 calories will lead to weight loss of 1 pound. Converting that to metric, it means a calorie deficit of roughly 7700 calories (or 32,000 kilojoules) to lose 1 kilogram. Could it really be as simple as that? Calories in and calories out? It had worked for me on the Bridges program. Could I apply the equation to my everyday life, rather than following a regimented food and exercise plan?

I decided to go it alone. I made a New Year's resolution to drop the 10 kilograms I had regained in time for the federal budget in May 2013. (I'm an economics journalist, so the date meant a lot to me.) I've always been a numbers geek, so I did it the only way I knew how: I started a spreadsheet. In one column: calories in. In another: calories out. I crunched the numbers for almost five months.

And it worked. I dropped only 5 kilograms rather than my goal of 10 kilograms, but I could see exactly why. I had eaten more calories than I had set out to eat and had done slightly less exercise. But the 7700 calories in a kilo equation worked. With some rounding errors, I lost almost exactly the amount of weight the equation predicted, and this time I've kept it off. Three years after embarking on my weight-loss journey, I'm still 15 kilograms down from my initial weight. As I write this, I weigh 72 kilograms, putting me smack-bang in the middle of my healthy-body weight range for my height. I have beaten the odds. I am a successful loser.

And so I want to share with you, for no more than the price of this book, the secret to enduring weight loss. Here it is (and it's only the introduction!). Weight loss comes down to one simple equation: energy in minus energy out. Weight loss, for all its emotional and mental struggle, is a straightforward numbers game. Get the numbers right, and anyone can lose weight.

Of course if it really were that simple no one would be fat, right? Well, no. As it turns out, weight loss, while uncomplicated in theory, is difficult to achieve in real life. It's a struggle to make good food and exercise choices in our obesogenic environment. There are measurement issues, too. Our bodies are not walking calorie calculators. It can be hard to work out the calories in your food. It's harder still to measure exactly how many calories you burn in a day.

I'm not saying it's easy. What I *am* saying is that reducing your energy intake so that it is below your energy expenditure each day is the only proven way to lose weight in the long term. The only weight-loss secret you will find in these pages is knowledge of how your body works. Knowledge is power. I now know that it *is* possible to both lose weight and keep it off. I want to share that knowledge with you.

I want you to know what I know.

I have always been a details person. Give me the specifics. This is a book that will give you all the information you need to shift the weight and keep it off. There are facts in this book that, once you know, you cannot un-know. They will change the way you look at food and exercise forever. As they have for me, they will guide you to make better decisions about food and exercise at every turn. You will learn the basic framework for healthy and sustainable eating. Whether you can stick to it is up to you. If you do, that's great. If you can't, at least you'll know why you're not losing weight. Perhaps you can stop beating yourself up about it. Perhaps you'll get to know your body a bit better and be kinder to it. Because it's never too late. Every day is a new day and a chance to make better decisions, to eat less and move more.

•

Before we start, I need to tell you what I am and what I am not. What I am not: a scientist, a nutritionist or an exercise physiologist. What I am: a professional journalist and a person who has lost a substantial amount of weight. I know it's not enough to say, 'It worked for me so it will work for everyone.' I may be a freakish creature who burns calories faster than most and absorbs fewer calories from food. Maybe. But I doubt it.

In writing this book, I have interviewed many of Australia's and indeed the world's leading experts on weight-loss science. I've spoken to endocrinologists, nutritionists, obesity experts, biologists and exercise physiologists. They each have an interesting story to tell about how the body works—about the impact of hunger hormones, gut bacteria and genes. But on the basic science, they are unanimous: it is impossible to lose weight without eating fewer calories than you expend in a day.

I'm not going to lie to you. To lose weight you will have to change your life, your habits. But that's okay; chances are your current lifestyle is making you not only fat, but unhappy. Am I right? Perhaps you suffer energy slumps after eating, or a racing heart after climbing the stairs. Perhaps you just can't find anything to wear. Losing weight is hard work, believe me. But I know being overweight is even harder.

You might think losing weight is impossible. But I'm here to tell you it is possible. Anyone can do it if they know how. And I'm going to tell you how. But before I do, there's some other stuff I think you need to know.

PART 1
WHY ARE
WE FAT?

1

Why we're losing the fight against the flab

I know why you're fat, and it's not your fault. Australians are, as a nation, suffering a kind of reverse body dysmorphia. The image we have of ourselves—a country of rugged, bronzed, athletic, sporty men and women—has never been further from the truth. Australians rightly celebrate the success of our elite athletes in the international sporting arena, but we do so from the comfort of our couches. With a bucket of KFC at our side.

Australia's collective waistline has been expanding steadily for decades. Only one-third of Australians are now of a weight considered by doctors to be healthy, or what the medical profession still somewhat erroneously categorises as 'normal'. In reality, a healthy weight is anything but normal these days. Two-thirds of Australians are either overweight or obese on the standard test of body mass index (see box opposite, 'How fat are you, anyway?'). Getting a grip on the exact size of our obesity epidemic is difficult because researchers have found we all habitually underestimate our weight. It's just the first of many ways in which we are totally clueless about our own bodies.

To overcome this, the most up-to-date survey of the weight of the nation as I write, the Australian Health Survey, conducted by the Australian Bureau of Statistics in 2011–13, went one step further. Instead of asking people for their weight, they actually got them on the scales. The verdict? According to the first results released from the survey in October 2012, 63 per cent of Australian adults are either overweight or obese. This is up dramatically from 61 per cent in 2007–08. A 2 percentage point change might seem small at first, but equates to nearly half a million Aussies moving into the unhealthy weight range in just five years.

Women are the target for most fad diets. But, surprisingly, the figures reveal men have by far the bigger problem when it comes to weight. Of Australian men, 70 per cent are either overweight or obese. For women, the figure is much lower, at 56 per cent. Men of Australia: it's time to take control of that beer gut. Chances are, if you don't, it's only going to get worse. The health survey results confirm weight problems increase over the course of your life. A worrying 25 per cent of children are overweight or obese, but 75 per cent of people are overweight or obese by the time they hit their late sixties.

Aussies are not alone in their fight against the flab. Obesity rates are rising in every developed nation in the world, and in developing nations too. Globally, it is estimated that 1.5 billion adults are overweight and another half a billion are obese. Worryingly, 170 million of the world's children are also overweight or obese.

HOW FAT ARE YOU, ANYWAY?

Doctors have come up with many different ways to test whether a person is carrying too much weight. Measuring your waist is a pretty easy test. A waist circumference of more than 80 centimetres for women and more than 94 centimetres for men is considered to put you at higher risk of health problems. Body fat percentage is another indicator, but it is harder to measure accurately. There are expensive tests you can do that involve X-rays, and some bathroom scales will also estimate your body fat percentage by sending a small electrical current through you. But the results can fluctuate wildly.

Most doctors are still happy to go with body mass index as an indicator—a calculation of your body weight divided by the square of your height. There are many online calculators you can use to calculate your body mass index. A healthy range is anything between 18.5 and 25. Anything between 25 and 30 is overweight, and over 30 is obese. Or you can use the chart on the next page.

People furiously debate whether body mass index is a good measure of a healthy weight. Muscle-bound athletes, while healthy, often tip the body mass index chart as overweight because of their higher muscle mass. If you show up as overweight on the chart below, it is possible that, unbeknown to you, you have the muscle structure of Arnold Schwarzenegger in his prime. Chances are, however, you are just overweight. Sorry. But isn't it better to know?

BODY MASS INDEX CHART FOR ADULTS

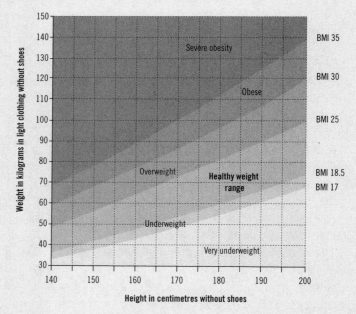

Source: National Health and Medical Research Council, *Australian Dietary Guidelines*, 2013.

The spiralling costs of obesity

Obesity is increasingly recognised around the world as one of the single biggest threats to human health and wellbeing.

Carrying excess weight is an established risk factor for type 2 diabetes, cardiovascular diseases, high blood pressure and many cancers. Scientists estimate that the first generation in history of children who will die earlier than their parents has already been born. How's that for progress?

In addition to increased mortality, obesity also imposes substantial costs on the living. Obese people suffer greater physical ill health throughout their lives, not to mention the unhappiness they may feel about their body. Trust me; I know. People carrying excess weight also suffer financially. Women, in particular, tend to suffer a weight-related wage penalty at work. Obese women earn about 12 per cent less than women of healthy weight, according to a 2004 paper titled 'The impact of obesity on wages' by Cornell University economist John Cawley. Overweight women earn 4.5 per cent less than healthy weight women. At a social level, there are substantial costs too, including direct medical costs and more indirect costs through job absenteeism and lower productivity.

We're fat. We're miserable. And we're dying sooner. Crisis? You bet. The problem is so large—and so costly—it has finally grabbed the attention of economists. In December 2012, *The Economist* magazine ran a special feature on the causes and consequences of the obesity epidemic. It reported that the health costs of obesity account for one-fifth of the United States' total healthcare bill. National productivity, too, is compromised by poor health. But even *The Economist*—usually a bastion of economic rationalism and individual responsibility—is not prepared to lay blame for the problem entirely on individuals:

❝ Obesity is, at its heart, the result of many personal decisions. But the rise of obesity—across many countries and disproportionately among the poor—suggests that becoming fat cannot just be blamed on individual frailty. Millions of people, of all cultures, did not become lazy gluttons at the same time, en masse. Broader forces are at work. **❞**

So, what changed?

The economy is making you fat

I think it's really important for you to know that the reason you are fat is not because you are a bad or lazy person. You are fat because of the world you live in. If you lived on the savannah, ate buckwheat and walked all day in search of water, guess what? You would not be fat.

Our obesity epidemic is, in fact, a recent phenomenon, having emerged only in the last three or four decades. You are struggling with your weight in a way your grandparents never did. Did humans, as a species, suddenly evolve to start eating more or moving less? No, of course not. Human evolution doesn't work that quickly. But changes in the economy can happen rapidly and these changes exert a powerful influence on the way we work, eat and play. The economy you live in is very different to the economy your grandparents lived in. If you're looking for someone to blame for your ever-expanding waistline, the economy is a good place to start. The economy is making you fat.

A person's weight is a natural result of the amount of energy they consume and the amount of energy they expend. At a population level, as well as an individual level, that balance has been thrown totally out of whack. 'Obesity is a normal response by normal people to obesogenic environments,' concluded the respected medical journal *The Lancet* in 2011, in the executive summary of a special series which called for urgent action from governments to address the obesity epidemic. The series identified several economic drivers of the obesity crisis. 'Changes in the global food system are driving up population energy intakes; many other environmental factors such as urban environments, transport systems, socio-economic conditions, and cultural factors also influence energy intake and levels of physical activity.' Too many calories in and fewer calories out. It's a recipe for dietary disaster.

And we're not winning the battle. 'We're at a standstill.' That's the judgement of Stephan Rössner, a respected Swedish physician and the former head of the International Association for the Study of Obesity. Speaking at a medical congress in Stockholm in October 2011, Rössner confessed that, despite decades of research and efforts to understand and reverse the rising tide of obesity, progress has stalled. 'People don't want to hear this, but a sound diet and physical activity is still what's needed,' he said. When I emailed him later about his speech, which was reported in the Swedish newspaper

Nordstjernan, Rössner agreed that his assessment is 'rather pessimistic'. And yet, even small amounts of weight loss would help: 'A weight loss of about 5 per cent doesn't sound like much, but it has been proven that it is enough to improve blood sugar, blood lipids and blood pressure. You feel better and move with more ease.' Most people try to lose too much too fast, says Rössner. 'Many start out too hard, and then they get tired.'

The despair that has struck the hearts of so many failed dieters has also struck many of the world's obesity researchers. Garry Eggers is one of Australia's leading obesity researchers. In 1991 he founded the first weight-loss program designed specifically for men—Gutbusters—which was later bought out by Weight Watchers. Having devoted his entire life to finding a way to fight the flab, Eggers tells me that while he has had some success with individuals, 'I regard myself as a failure at the population level because I have worked in this area for 25 years and we're still getting fat.' And if current trends continue, it is only going to keep getting worse.

Indeed, the statistics on weight regain after weight loss are sobering. It is estimated that 95 per cent of people who lose weight will put it back on within five years. One of Australia's leading epidemiologists, Joseph Proietto, has seen it all in his obesity clinic at Austin Health in Melbourne. He tells me he is convinced only drugs can help us solve the crisis. 'We have a cohort of people who are able to tolerate appetite suppressants and are maintaining weight loss,' he tells me over the phone.

But many more have put all the weight back on. 'It's tough treating obesity at the moment,' he sighs.

From Bradman to *The Biggest Loser*

If we are to reverse the trend of growing obesity, we need a better understanding of what is causing our expanding waistlines. It would be too simplistic to blame the obesity crisis on cheeseburgers and chairs. But it's a pretty good place to start. The last 100 years have brought such rapid technological and social change that it's easy to forget how differently we live today from those born even just a few generations ago. But one thing is for sure: we are moving less and eating more. You know those stories Grandma is always telling you about how she had to walk 15 miles in the rain to get to school? Well, she's not lying. At the turn of the twentieth century, walking accounted for more than a third of all urban trips in Australia, making it the most popular way to get around at the time.

These days, we are walking far less. In 2011–12, less than one in five Australian adults walked the recommended 10,000 steps per day, according to the Australian Bureau of Statistic's data. Why? Again, it's our lifestyles. A 2004 US study led by David R Bassett of steps walked each day by the Amish people, who live in communities which have not adopted the technologies of the 20th and 21st centuries like cars, televisions and iPhones, found that Amish men walked 18,000 steps a day, while Amish women walked 14,000 steps a day. Another obesity researcher,

James Hill, discovered in 2006 that the average American man walked 5940 steps in a day and the average American woman just 5276. Amish people walk more and have much lower levels of obesity than the average American. Coincidence? No. It is estimated that the difference between these two lifestyles—one representing an older, agriculture-based society and one the modern life most people now lead—could account for a loss in energy output of between 400 and 600 calories a day. That's big. And it all adds up.

In 1904 the first Ford motor car was imported to Australia. By 1914 the Model T Ford was Australia's biggest-selling car. Almost exactly a century later, when Ford Australia boss Bob Graziano announced the closure of the company's Australian manufacturing facilities due to a high dollar and high labour costs, he observed that Australians can today choose from 365 different models of car—one for every day of the year. We love our cars. According to the Bureau of Statistics, in 2013 there were 7.5 motor vehicles for every ten people. That's almost one each. The graph on the next page gives a fairly clear picture of how car use has replaced walking.

But our love of machines does not stop at the driveway. On a September evening in 1956, Australians heard these words for the first time: 'Good evening and welcome to television.' We haven't switched off since. The average Australian adult watches just shy of two hours of television a day.

In a paper released in 2010 titled 'Television viewing time and mortality', a team of Australian researchers led by David Dunstan found a link between increased screen time and

USE OF CAR VERSUS WALKING, 1900–2011

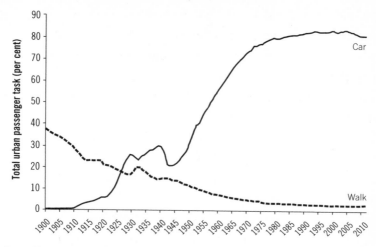

Source: 'Modal shares for urban passenger transport in Australia, 1900–2011', Major Cities Unit, *State of Australian Cities 2012*, Department of Infrastructure and Transport, Canberra, 2012.

increased risk of cardiovascular death. Each hour of television viewed was associated with an 11 per cent increase in all-cause mortality and an 18 per cent increase in cardiovascular mortality. When compared with those who watched less than two hours a day (light viewers), those watching more than four hours a day (heavy viewers) had a whopping 46 per cent increased risk of all-cause mortality and an 80 per cent increased risk of cardiovascular mortality. Not only is the idiot box making you dumber; it's making you fatter.

At the same time we began sitting in front of the television for longer, we also began spending less time participating in sport. A survey of time use by the Australian Bureau of Statistics found Australians spent an extra hour a week watching television and using the internet in 2006 than they did in 1997. Over the same period, time spent on sport and outdoor activity decreased by nearly an hour per week. If only being a couch potato was an Olympic sport, we'd be champions.

Calories, calories everywhere, but not a nutrient in sight

Whether obesity is caused primarily by moving less or by eating more is the subject of much debate. Likely it's both. But recently, researchers have begun to target overeating as the major cause of rising obesity levels. In *The Lancet*'s 2011 series on obesity, Boyd Swinburn and his colleagues identified the passive overconsumption of cheap calories as the problem's main driver:

" The simultaneous increases in obesity in almost all countries seem to be driven mainly by changes in the global food system, which is producing more processed, affordable, and effectively marketed food than ever before. This passive overconsumption of energy leading to obesity is a predictable outcome of market economies predicated on consumption-based growth. **"**

According to Boyd et al., an 'energy balance flipping point' seems to have been reached sometime in the 1960s or 1970s, after which we could no longer compensate for our increasingly sedentary behaviour by simply eating less. Instead, the world emerged from the ravages and rations of two world wars into a golden era of abundance and growth. In fact, the only countries that have ever managed to successfully reverse obesity are Cuba and Nauru, and it took economic recessions in both countries to accomplish it. But in the prosperous post-war era in Australia, we fled to the suburbs and set up house with a fridge and a washing machine, and a car or two in every driveway. The age that gave us baby boomers also gave us obesity.

As our economy grew, food became more abundant. As we got richer, food got relatively cheaper. As a result, we have been able to spend more of our income paying other people to prepare our food. According to official retail sales data, Australians spend about $9 billion a month buying food to consume at home and another $3 billion on calorie-laden meals at cafes, restaurants and takeaway food outlets. The paradox of the success of shows like *MasterChef* is that they haven't encouraged us to cook more, but to eat out more.

In 1970 Germaine Greer published *The Female Eunuch* and women began storming the workforce. Time spent on food preparation at home decreased, meaning more takeaways. In 1971 McDonald's Australia opened its first restaurant, in the Sydney suburb of Yagoona. By 2013 the company had more than 780 restaurants across Australia. According to their website, more than a million Aussies now suffer a Mac attack each day.

I'm not saying that working women or McDonald's caused the obesity epidemic. If anything, men are to blame for not picking up the slack at home when their womenfolk started earning the big bucks. What I am saying is that McDonald's and being a working woman were instrumental in my own weight gain.

Obesity is the natural result of the human desire to eat more and move less, according to James Hill, the director of the Center for Human Nutrition at the University of Colorado.

&& It is important to realize that at some level we intentionally created the environment that is making us fat and we are not unhappy with it. We have achieved much of mankind's desire to have a consistent, reliable food supply and to reduce the amount of work required for daily living. Although weight gain may best be seen as an unintended consequence of aspiring to the 'good life', it is not going to be easy to give up some of the things in the environment that are helping sustain high obesity rates. **"**

Get it? Humans have been trying for millennia to create exactly this environment: lots of food and little need for physical activity. This is what we've wanted all along. Or is it? Now that our capitalist nirvana has arrived, it seems we're slowly realising it's not quite what we wanted after all. We've gone too far and it's making us sick. We need to cut back a bit of the eating and reintroduce a bit of the moving. But we'll have to make a conscious decision to do that, because the economy is pushing us in the opposite direction. To lose weight, we have to resist the economic incentives all around us. And perversely, as I'm about to show you, we might even have to pay more to eat less.

Money talks at the kitchen table

Economics is founded on the observation that people respond in profound ways to prices. The fact that poorer people get fatter in bigger numbers suggests that food prices play a key role in the obesity epidemic. Is it simply cheaper to eat bad food? Or, put another way, is it too expensive to eat good food?

A study conducted in 2004 and 2006 of 372 food and drink prices in two major supermarket chains in Seattle by American obesity researchers Pablo Monsivais and Adam Drewnowski found that there is indeed a financial penalty to choosing lower energy foods like fruit and vegetables. Their paper 'The rising cost of low-energy-density foods' contained two important findings. First, the results showed that low-energy-density foods are, indeed, more costly per calorie. The average cost of foods in the bottom fifth of foods by energy density—things like blueberries and seafood—were found to be US$18.16 per 1000 calories. For the top one-fifth of foods by energy density—things like oils and cookies—the average cost was just US$1.76 per 1000 calories. 'High-energy-density foods provided the most dietary energy at least cost,' the researchers found.

The following graph makes the point vividly. Foods that appear higher on the vertical axis are more energy dense—they have more calories per gram. Foods like margarine and olive oil are the most energy dense. And guess what? They're also the cheapest, as we can see from where they are positioned along the horizontal axis. Foods that appear on the left-hand side of the horizontal axis are cheaper per calorie. Olive oil is energy dense, but it only costs about US$1 per 1000 calories. It's also highly delicious. Is it any wonder that restaurant and takeaway foods are smothered in it?

ASSOCIATION OF ENERGY COST AND ENERGY DENSITY

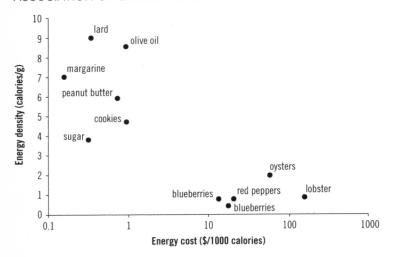

Source: P Monsivias and A Drewnowski, 'The rising cost of low-energy-density foods', *Journal of the American Dietetic Association*, vol. 107, no. 12, December 2007, pp. 2071–6.

Foods situated towards the bottom right of the graph are less energy dense (less likely to make you fat!) but also more expensive. Blueberries have less than 1 calorie per gram, compared to olive oil's 9 calories per gram, but blueberries cost ten times as much per calorie. Margarine and sugar are energy dense and cheap. Blueberries, red peppers (capsicums) and seafood are calorie sparse, but expensive.

Monsivais and Drewnowski's second important finding was that the price of low-energy-density foods had increased faster than the price of high-energy-density foods. Over the two years studied, the least-energy-dense foods became 19.5 per cent more expensive, whereas the most-energy-dense foods actually became 1.8 per cent more affordable. So calorie-sparse, healthy foods are more expensive, and their cost rises more quickly than calorie-dense foods.

❝ The finding that energy-dense foods are not only the least expensive, but also most resistant to inflation, may help explain why the highest rates of obesity continue to be observed among groups of limited economic means. The sharp price increase for the low-energy-density foods suggests that economic factors may pose a barrier to the adoption of more healthful diets and so limit the impact of dietary guidance. **❞**

Pretty soon I'm going to be telling you that you need to consume fewer energy-dense foods and more energy-sparse foods. I'll do so knowing that this may well turn out to be more expensive. Losing weight can be expensive. But you know what? Being overweight is expensive too, in lost wages, ill health, medical costs and premature death. It's a false economy to pretend otherwise. There are no easy answers here.

The weight-loss industry is making a motza out of you

Of course, the desire for easy answers springs eternal. Many people are making their fortunes out of our attempts to lose weight. It's ironic. The economy grew by overfeeding you, and now it's growing further by exploiting your attempts to get thin. Throwing a brick through a window adds to economic growth because a builder must be employed to fix it. Getting fat and then spending lots of money on diets also makes the money go round. Fighting the flab is big business in Australia and around the world. According to research group IBIS World, Australians were set to spend almost $650 million in 2013–14 on weight-loss counselling services, low-calorie foods and dietary supplements.

There's no shortage of people willing to tap into this new market to sell you stuff: gym memberships, home gym equipment, weight-loss programs, neon workout clothes, antacids and other drugs. A report released by Bank of America Merrill Lynch in 2012 identified over 50 global stocks likely to benefit from this new wave of spending on health products. They include food companies such as PepsiCo,

Nestlé, Heinz, Kellogg's and Kraft Foods; sports apparel retailers Adidas, ASICS, Foot Locker, Lululemon Athletica and Nike; vitamin and pharmaceutical companies including Novo Nordisk, which has a global market capitalisation of US$73 billion; and weight management program companies like Herbalife and Weight Watchers. Weight Watchers was owned for many years by food company Heinz. In 2006, Nestlé—the makers of Milo, Kit Kats and Peters Ice Cream—gobbled up the global operations of Jenny Craig (and in 2010 secured the Australian franchise). It's just a fact of life that the same companies that made a profit out of your binge have also been seeking to profit from your attempts to lose weight. That's smart business. In an interview with ABC Radio in December 2010, the nutritionist Rosemary Stanton described it as the 'perfect circle': 'You create the problem and then you create the solution and you've gone full circle and you could have avoided the entire problem by not eating these products in the first place.'

I don't want to make you paranoid (okay, maybe just a bit), but the economy is out to get you. A certain amount of paranoia is justified when it comes to our food environment. The commercialisation of farming and the replacement of farmers' markets with big supermarkets have put greater distance between food producers and food consumers. An agency problem arises because there are more links in the food supply chain. Producers are no longer as accountable to food consumers. They don't mind altering your food to make it saltier, sweeter, better tasting. Even if it makes you fat.

Governments are desperately looking for ways to align food prices with good social outcomes. But in the meantime, you're on your own. It's up to you to beat the system. You can't just go with the flow. Going with the flow these days means getting fat. And often paying big bucks in your attempts to get slim again.

It's time to fight economics with economics

You might still be wondering why an economics journalist has written a book about how to lose weight. It's a fair question, so let's deal with it now. Most people think economics is just about money—how to get it and how to spend it. But economics is bigger than that. At its heart, economics is the study of how we, as a society, make decisions about how to allocate our scarce resources, such as time and money. The central problem in economics is that there's never enough time and there's never enough money.

Life, as it turns out, is a series of trade-offs—of roads taken and roads not taken. At every point in our lives, daily and hourly, we are forced to make decisions. Some we make consciously. Most we make subconsciously. But they are all decisions, because, if we thought about it, we could choose differently. According to Swinburn and colleagues in *The Lancet*, 'Undoubtedly, the final decision to consume a particular food or beverage, or to exercise or not, is an individual decision. However, to negotiate the complexity of the environment and the choices it poses, many of these decisions are automatic or subconscious.'

The trick is to become aware of the subconscious decisions we make, and choose, as best we can, to make better conscious decisions. That's where economics comes in. Economics is about helping you to identify the benefits and costs of competing courses of action.

Consider the decision to take on an extra shift at work. An extra hour of work will earn you extra income, and you could use that income to buy things you like. But it also means an hour lost that could have been spent with your family. Perhaps that hour of family time would bring you more pleasure (economists call it 'utility') than the item you could buy with the income you would earn from work. A real economist wouldn't necessarily choose the option that maximises their money; they would aim to maximise their total happiness in life.

The economic decision-making process can be applied to other parts of our lives too. Learning to think like an economist can help you not only make more money, but also lose weight. Just as we must decide how to split our time between work and home life, we must also make decisions at home. It is a decision to sit on the couch or go the gym. It is a decision to eat an apple instead of a chocolate bar. Economics says eating is a decision we make, weighing up the utility, or pleasure, of eating against the disutility of future ill health if we eat too much. Turns out we're terrible at this calculation. Just like with the decision to spend or save money, we struggle to forgo current pleasure from eating food or sitting on the couch in order to obtain future gain (losing weight). We're fat for the same reason we rack up big credit card bills or fail to save enough for retirement.

A new field of economics called behavioural economics is studying the way we actually make decisions. Researchers have discovered that many of the decisions we make about food are not very well informed. We consistently underestimate the calories in our food. Surveys suggest people of normal weight underestimate their calories by around 20 per cent and obese people by 30 or 40 per cent. And the bigger the meal, the worse we are at estimating the energy content, according to consumer psychologist Brian Wansink. In an experiment for his book *Mindless Eating*, Wansink found people who ate a 300-calorie burger underestimated its calories by 10 per cent. Those who ate a 900-calorie burger underestimated by 40 per cent. We are almost oblivious to the actual calorie content of our food.

The food decisions we make are also influenced heavily by the way choices are framed. We will, for example, eat more food off a bigger plate. In another experiment, Wansink gave people either a 480-gram bowl or a 960-gram bowl and then asked them to serve themselves ice-cream. People with the bigger bowl took, on average, 31 per cent more, equal to an additional 127 calories. It gets worse. Those given both a bigger bowl and a bigger serving scoop helped themselves to 57 per cent more than the people with a smaller bowl and a smaller scoop.

Even the colour of cutlery can impact food consumption, according to Oxford University researchers Vanessa Harrar and Charles Spence. The people they studied reported that food tasted saltier when eaten from a knife, and denser and more expensive from a light plastic spoon. White yoghurt eaten from a white spoon tasted sweeter than the same yoghurt eaten from a black spoon. Still think we're rational? The Nobel Prize–winning economist Daniel Kahneman thinks we are, but imperfectly so. In his book, *Thinking, Fast and Slow*, he has some fun with classical economics' idea that humans are perfectly rational, always weighing the costs and benefits to arrive at an optimal outcome: 'I once heard Gary Becker . . . a Nobel laureate of the Chicago school, argue in a lighter vein, but not entirely as a joke, that we should consider the possibility of explaining the so-called obesity epidemic by people's belief that a cure for diabetes will soon become available.'

It is clear we are making terrible decisions when it comes to food and exercise. The question is, if we were better informed of the consequences of our decisions, would we make better decisions? I think so. I have. Being aware of your choices in life—the trade-offs you face—is the first step towards making better choices.

The whole point of this book is to help you make better decisions when it comes to food and exercise. Your weight is a reflection of all the decisions you have made in the past about diet and exercise. The good news is that the future is unknown. It's not too late to change. But to do so you must fight not only the economy, but your own biology. It's time to meet the enemy within.

2

Why our bodies are working against us

It is abundantly clear that changes in our food supply and energy expenditure levels are major drivers of increasing obesity. So the answer is obvious, right? We should just eat less and move more. And yet, if it is that easy, why do so many of us struggle to lose weight and why do 95 per cent of us put it back on? It's actually not so surprising, once you understand a bit about the body and the way it has evolved to regulate energy in and energy out.

You see, your body wants you to get fat. It's a primal instinct honed over millennia. Our lifestyles and our economy may have moved on, but our bodies haven't. Our bodies are not designed for this world. In days gone by, the defining feature of humans' lives was not abundance, as it is now, but scarcity. In such a world, we became calorie homing pigeons.

We learnt to seek out and conserve energy. We roamed the desert looking for berry bushes. (Okay, I'm exaggerating here, but you get what I mean.) Now there are berry bushes everywhere! In your freezer, in your pantry, under your pillow. Berries, berries everywhere, and they taste so sweet!

Just as we respond to economic signals by purchasing more cheap, sweet, fatty food, we also follow a primal urge to seek sufficient nutrition. We did this historically by eating everything in sight and hoping for the best. And we haven't changed a bit. It's just that today we are surrounded by cheap, delicious, calorie-dense food. Did somebody say Mars Bar?

It's almost like we can't rely on the signals our bodies are sending us anymore. We're a Commodore 64 version of ourselves when what we need to be is the latest Apple Mac to process all the incoming information and make better decisions.

So I guess you just need greater discipline, hey? You undisciplined chocoholic, you. Well, yes, in a sense. But if you're going to try to fight both your environment and your body, to be forewarned is to be forearmed.

The hunger games

We need to talk about hunger. Hunger is the most primal of sensations. Try to think back to the last time you were hungry. Remember how your resolve to lose weight melted just as fast as that chocolate on your tongue? That overpowering hunger wasn't just a mental thing; hunger is a physical reaction to a perceived need for food.

The physical symptoms of hunger include a churning stomach, excess saliva production (it's getting ready to slide down all that lovely food), feelings of weakness, dizziness and trouble concentrating. Hunger is not a psychosomatic state conjured up by the weak-willed dieter. It is, in fact, a physical expression of our natural systems for regulating appetite and satiety.

When you get hungry, something happens to the hormones in your body. Increased hunger is associated with greater circulation of the hormone ghrelin, which scientists call the hunger hormone. I call it the gremlin. It's that nasty voice inside your head that makes you abandon all hope of losing weight and devour an entire pizza.

MEET THE HUNGER HORMONES

There are many hormones in your body that regulate appetite. These circulate in the blood and send signals to the hypothalamus—a part of your brain—telling you whether you're hungry or full. More specifically, the signals are registered in a part of the hypothalamus called the appestat. Get it? Your appestat is like a temperature thermostat, only to control your appetite.

Hunger hormones play an important role in prompting you to initiate meals and in determining how much you eat by affecting how quickly you feel full. The bad guys tell you you're hungry. Watch out: they make you cranky as hell. The main bad hunger hormone is gremlin (oh, okay, ghrelin). Then there are the good hunger hormones, which tell your brain you're full. And there are plenty of those good guys. They include leptin, insulin, glucagon-like peptide-1 (GLP-1, or the 'good little peptide' for short), peptide YY, cholecystokinin, pancreatic polypeptide and amyline. All of these are released from your digestive tract and pancreas when you eat, and send signals to your brain when you've had enough. Leptin is a protein produced in adipose fat tissue (the fat that sits around your organs) that, when present in the bloodstream, tells the brain that you have enough fat stored, reducing hunger. No more please, we're full.

Studies of overweight people have shown they suffer a double whammy when it comes to the hunger hormones. Not only do they get more excited by the sight of food, but they are also less satisfied when they eat it. Pretty mean, huh? Overweight people can eat so much they screw up the leptin receptors in their brain. They can become leptin resistant. And some people are born with a dodgy appestat. The bad news for those who put on excess weight and then try to lose it is that it can take time for the appestat to adjust to the reduced production of leptin from the fat cells. If, indeed, it ever responds at all.

Will I be hungry forever?

Do you want to hear something really, truly depressing? Probably not, but I think you need to know. It's a basic law of body physics that to stay thin after weight loss, you have to keep eating less than you did before you lost the weight. So a hormonal hunger mechanism that told you to keep craving food at your previous level of eating would be problematic indeed. And yet some scientists believe it may be possible that someone who has lost weight may always—or at least for a very long time—maintain the appetite level they had when they overate.

Remember Joseph Proietto, the epidemiologist from Melbourne I mentioned in chapter 1? I interviewed him on the phone one morning before having breakfast. I was hungry. In fact, I had been struggling a bit with hunger all week. I asked him whether I would always crave the same amount of calories as I used to consume when I was at my peak weight.

Possibly, was his crushing reply. 'Following weight loss, the hormones that control weight loss change in a direction to make you more hungry, and those changes are persistent even after one year.' That, says Proietto, is why people regain weight. It's just too hard to fight the hunger hormones over such a long period.

How do we know people are still hungry after a year? Well, with his colleagues, Proietto has studied them and written up the results in a fascinating (and horrifying) paper published in 2011. The study took 50 overweight or obese people and put them on a ten-week, very low-energy diet to induce weight loss. The diet consisted of a very low-calorie weight-loss drink plus two cups of low-starch vegetables, providing 500 to 550 calories a day. At the end of the ten-week weight-loss period, the participants were given individual advice by a dietitian about appropriate food consumption to match their calculated energy expenditure. However, they received no guidance on exactly what to eat beyond recommendations to eat carbohydrate with a low glycaemic index and to reduce their fat intake. (A low glycaemic index reading is given to foods from which the body takes longer to access energy, thereby avoiding sharp energy spikes and slumps.) They were encouraged to do 30 minutes of moderately intense physical activity on most days of the week. They were monitored physically every two months and were also contacted by phone for check-ups.

One year later the remaining participants were brought in for retesting. Not everyone made it through the study. Four people withdrew in the first eight weeks, seven didn't achieve the 10 per cent weight loss required to continue and a further five withdrew in the follow-up year. Of those who made it through and were available for testing after a year, the average weight loss was 13.5 kilograms (or 14 per cent of the participants' initial weight).

For the retesting, after an overnight fast the participants were fed a 550-calorie meal of one boiled egg, toast, margarine, orange juice, wholegrain cereal biscuits and whole milk. Blood samples were taken at 30-minute intervals for up to four hours. Proietto and his team then compared levels of circulating hunger hormones with those recorded at the start of the study to see if hunger had reduced along with weight.

Did the hunger wear off? Unfortunately, no. The scientists found that even after a year, participants' blood had higher circulating levels of the hunger hormone ghrelin. The blood levels of the hormone leptin—the hormone that tells you you're full—had fallen by a whopping 65 per cent during the ten-week period. The levels had then risen during the follow-up year, but by the end of the year were at 35.5 per cent below the original levels. There were also significant reductions in other satiety hormones, including peptide YY, cholecystokinin, insulin and amylin.

Furthermore, the participants were found to have experienced a 'significant increase in subjective appetite' during the test period: 'mean ratings of hunger, desire and urge to eat, and prospective consumption were significantly higher at week 10 and 62 than at baseline.' Critically, patients were as hungry at week 62 as they were at week 10. In fact, 'one year after initial weight reduction, levels of the circulating mediators of appetite that encourage weight regain after diet-induced weight loss do not revert to the levels recorded before the weight loss.' Read it and weep:

" Caloric restriction results in acute compensatory changes, including profound reductions in energy expenditure and levels of leptin and cholecystokinin and increases in ghrelin and appetite, all of which promote weight regain . . .

Although short-term weight loss is readily achieved through dietary restriction, only a small minority of obese people maintain diet-induced weight loss in the long term.

A multitude of hormones, peptides, and nutrients are involved in the homeostatic regulation of body weight, many of which are perturbed after weight loss. Whether these changes represent a transient compensatory response to an energy deficit is unknown, but an important finding of this study is that many of these alterations persist for 12 months after weight loss, even after the onset of weight regain, suggesting that the high rate of relapse among obese people who have lost weight has a strong physiological basis and is not simply the result of the voluntary resumption of old habits. **"**

I told you your body's fighting you, didn't I? The real question is will it fight you forever? According to Proietto and colleagues, perhaps so:

" Taken together, these findings indicate that in obese persons who have lost weight, multiple compensatory mechanisms encouraging weight gain, which persist for at least one year, must be overcome in order to maintain weight loss. These mechanisms would be advantageous for a lean person in an environment where food was scarce, but in an environment in which energy-dense food is abundant and physical activity is largely unnecessary, the high rate of relapse after weight loss is not surprising. Furthermore the activation of this coordinated response in people who remain obese after weight loss supports the view that there is an elevated body-weight set point in obese persons and that efforts to reduce weight below this point are vigorously resisted. **"**

It is possible, the researchers noted, that our bodies eventually become less sensitive to circulating hunger hormones and simply ignore them. But I can tell you that this didn't happen to me. In the year in which I regained 10 kilograms after the initial rapid weight loss, I was as hungry as hell.

I still struggle with my appetite most days. But I do believe it has become easier for me to eat less and feel fuller. I have to believe that my appetite can reset to a lower level, but we don't know for sure. It's an area for further study. Proietto and his colleagues are conducting further research to find out whether the hunger hormone response is different if you lose the weight quicker or slower, and if you lose 5 per cent or 10 per cent of your body weight.

Given that there is a physical hunger mechanism, Proietto is hopeful that, one day, effective drugs will be developed to help us fight hunger. Surgery is a radical option for people who decide they simply cannot eat less of their own volition. Different types of surgery successfully reduce hunger in different ways—for example, by squeezing a nerve that sends hunger signals to the brain, reducing the level of ghrelin, or by increasing hormones that suppress hunger. But we have some way to go to develop safe and effective non-surgical appetite suppressants. 'All the ones you buy over the counter are a waste of money,' warns Proietto.

There are trials underway for ghrelin suppressants and leptin supplements. Maybe one day reducing hunger will be as easy as popping a pill. Until then, you're going to have to fight hunger alone.

Learning to live with the hunger monster

It's a catch-22. Consuming fewer calories than you expend has been shown to produce an immediate hunger hormone response. And yet consuming fewer calories than you expend is the *only* way to lose weight.

In search of hope, I speak to Jennie Brand-Miller, a nutrition researcher at the University of Sydney. Is it possible to restrict calories without feeling hungry?

Unlikely, is the reply. 'If the difference between daily calorie intake and calorie need is small, you mightn't notice less than 50 calories. If your difference is around the 500 calories mark—that is often the case with weight loss—I think you have to exercise a great deal of self-discipline. It's hard. Hunger is such a primitive signal. Our body has lots and lots of ways to make us eat.' Brand-Miller says we have to retrain our minds to react differently to the hunger sensation. 'Hunger is everything. Say to yourself, This hunger means that I'm losing weight.'

Factors in our modern lives also drive hunger. Stress, anxiety and lack of sleep can all increase appetite, says Brand-Miller. 'What kicks the energy appestat off the balance level are things like significant depression and stress, which both kick up appetite, and that spells trouble. Doing certain things, like sitting for a very long period of time or getting stressed or not sleeping enough could actually do something to your appestat, which means you're more likely to have that extra mouthful of food, more likely to have a delicious calorie-laden croissant, not toast, or a couple of extra spoonfuls of muesli—really small but important changes in calories in.' An important discovery for me has been the realisation that the gnawing feeling of hunger I often feel in my stomach sometimes isn't hunger at all. It's stress. The knot in your belly that stress causes can feel uncannily like hunger. I know I frequently get confused and reach for a chocolate bar when what I really need is a bubble bath or a nap.

Embracing hunger, but giving in a little

So you've decided to learn to identify and embrace hunger. Hunger pangs are literally weight loss in action. And then you eat a pizza. Back to square one? Hardly. Sometimes it's best to give in to temptation. Instead of pushing on through hunger with the diligence of a monk, you can yield to it occasionally and live to fight another weight-loss day.

I'm pretty sure that fasting diets, such as the 5:2 Diet, which requires users to consume just 500 to 600 calories on two days of the week, work primarily because it's hard to fight hunger every day. Better to fight it on just two days of the week, and give in for the rest. As long as you don't just use your non-fasting days to consume all the calories you missed on your fasting days, you can successfully restrict your calories to achieve weight loss.

Amanda Salis, an obesity researcher at the University of Sydney, told me that the body has both a 'famine response' to underfeeding and a 'fat brake' to overfeeding. The latter responds to slight overfeeding by prompting us to increase incidental activity, like fidgeting. But severe overeating can overwhelm the fat brake.

And severe calorie restriction only inflames the famine response, according to Salis. 'The more restrictive you are, the stronger the famine reaction is.' This is why so many diets fail. 'Without understanding what their body is going to do in response to that, people start a diet and then they get really hungry and eat pizza. They can't help it. And then they feel guilty. And then they eat a Crunchie bar. They think, I'm just weak, I'm helpless, I might as well give up. They're trying to fight their bodies.'

Salis herself has lost nearly 30 kilograms and has kept it off. She says it took four years to lose the first 24 kilograms and another two years to lose the rest—a pace that many would consider quite slow. 'I love my food too much,' she explains. 'And the more weight you lose, the harder it gets to keep losing it: Your body is fighting more the closer you get to the goal that's right for you. The weight that you want to be, your body fights.'

Salis's advice is simple: slow down. She says it's best to make sporadic attempts at weight loss, then consolidate with long periods of plateauing. 'I think take a really patient, long-term view on it. It does seem that with time, that famine response subsides. If you can, lose half a kilogram in a month and then have a break for a month or two or three. People always think that's so slow, but they don't realise the cycle of binge and gain is so bad.'

I ask again: Can we change our set points? Can our hunger reset?

Salis's answer is more comforting than Proietto's. 'I sense we might be able to. If you have kept the weight off for two years, then the likelihood you'll gain it back is quite a lot less.'

Genetics and epigenetics

But what if you just can't shake that gnawing feeling that you're hungry all the time? Could there be something wrong with you? Well, yes. It is always worth consulting a doctor if you struggle with weight loss. Genes can play a role. And an emerging field of science called epigenetics has suggested that our environment can also play a key role in weight control by permanently switching on or switching off genes that control certain hormonal responses.

Leptin resistance is an example of a genetic condition that can affect weight. A child born with a mutation in the leptin gene will always crave food and prefer foods with more energy per gram. Brand-Miller explains that 'those people that manage to keep a good weight all their lives—their leptin is doing the job that it should do. It tells them when they're eating too much and when they're eating too little and should correspondingly eat more. But a child with a leptin mutation will just eat and eat and eat.'

Scientists have been scouring what are known as gene sentence structures, looking for an association with obesity. In 2007 they discovered the FTO gene and subsequently found that a mutated FTO gene leads to increased ghrelin, the hormone that induces feelings of hunger. When a person inherits a mutated FTO gene from one parent (which happens to around half of the population), they are 30 per cent more likely to be obese than someone without a mutation. Inheriting a mutated gene from both parents increases the likelihood to 70 per cent.

The impact of parents on their children's weight is also emerging as an important new field of study. Indeed, studies of twins who have been separated at birth and raised by different parents have found that the twins' weight will, even after years of meals eaten apart, more closely resemble the birth parents' weight than the adoptive parents'. 'What a lot of our research shows is that the mother's weight during pregnancy has a huge influence on the child's weight at birth and their subsequent weight gain as children,' explains Brand-Miller. 'A lot of our obesity epidemic can be traced back to the fact that mothers have higher and higher weights during pregnancy, and it's a vicious cycle.' A mother with a body mass index of 30 or above can leave marks on her child's genes that could influence that child's appetite for life. Studies have also shown that babies born to women who suffer malnourishment and a lack of calories may develop weight problems later in life.

It is entirely possible to draw the genetic short straw when it comes to weight control. Inherited genes may cause you to absorb more calories from food than other people (although the difference is only marginal). They may also make you feel hungrier or less satisfied by food. But before you conclude you are overweight because your mum ate a chocolate cake during pregnancy and decide to give up, ask yourself this: How do you know? While it is possible that you have a gene problem, maybe, just maybe, you're eating too much. Until you try to lose weight, perhaps by following the formula I will show you in part 2 of this book, you won't know if it's genetics or just overeating. And even if genes *are* playing a role in your weight gain, you still have to eat the food to gain the fat. If you don't eat the food, you don't put on the weight. And if you eat fewer calories each day than your body needs to power its daily activities, you lose weight.

The question is whether you can fight your body in the long term to eat within its requirements. I'm not giving up on you yet. And nor should you.

3

Why it's time to end the food wars

A lot of ridiculous things get written and reported about what you should and should not put in your mouth. We are constantly bombarded with conflicting messages about food. When was the last time you heard a report telling you to cut out an entire food group? Cut out carbs. Scrap full-fat food. Quit sugar. There is a profusion of food confusion. What on earth are we supposed to eat? How did we manage to turn something as simple as eating into an intellectual battlefield?

The food wars have been raging among researchers for a century now. And thanks to an ever more energetic 24-hour news cycle (if only our bodies were that active!), their battles have spilled out onto the street.

The debate about nutrition has, at times, focused on the overall quantity of food consumed and, at others, on the composition of food. In the late 1800s a serious-looking fellow called Wilbur Atwater, born in New York in 1844, invented the first calorimeter, a machine for measuring the energy content of food. He also devised the Atwater system, a way of assigning units of energy—calories—to the three macronutrient food groups of carbohydrate, protein and fat. It was Atwater who determined that fat is more energy dense than carbohydrate or protein. He also claimed that Americans in general ate too much sugar and did not do enough exercise. Sounds to me like not much has changed.

Take a look at the 1930s poster opposite, from the US Department of Agriculture. It was designed to help people understand what a 100-calorie portion of different foods looks like. Recently, things have come full circle and the web has exploded with blogs and YouTube clips attempting to picture for people how many calories are in common foods.

But sometime in the mid twentieth century, talking about calories fell completely out of fashion. Debate began to focus instead on which macronutrients we should eat more or less of. Was it just too hard to count calories, or too boring? Or was the search for the quick fix too powerful—the promise that by eliminating one food group you could then give in to all other food temptations and the hunger monster within, and eat as much of everything else as you liked? The human desire for a quick fix to our weight problem seems to be overpowering. And so the past few decades have seen the flourishing of fad diets based on what you should eat, rather than how much.

100-CALORIE PORTIONS OF A FEW FAMILIAR FOODS

ESTIMATES BASED ON AVERAGE FOOD VALUES

Source: Bureau of Home Economics, United States Department of Agriculture, [1927–31], copy at ARC no. 5838434, US National Archives, College Park, MD.

MEET THE MACRONUTRIENTS

It's a scientific fact that all food is made up of two or more of the three fundamental macronutrients: carbohydrate, protein and fat. (There's also dietary fibre, which your body can't absorb, and micronutrients, like vitamins and minerals, but let's just focus on macronutrients for now.) Pretty much all of the debate in modern dieting revolves around differing opinions on what is the optimal mix of macronutrients. As things stand, most of us consume a diet of around 15 per cent protein, 30 per cent fat and 55 per cent carbohydrate. Diet advocates want to tinker with that mix.

MACRONUTRIENT PROFILES OF POPULAR DIETS

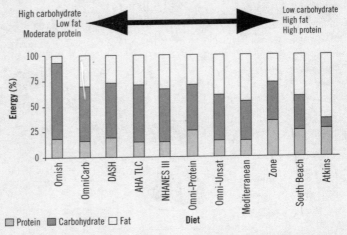

High carbohydrate
Low fat
Moderate protein

Low carbohydrate
High fat
High protein

☐ Protein ■ Carbohydrate ☐ Fat

Diet

Notes: Three diets are shown with the prefix 'Omni'. These were diets developed by Harvard Medical School. DASH stands for Dietary Approaches to Stop Hypertension. AHA TLC stands for American Heart Association Therapeutic Lifestyle Changes diet. And NHANES III is the typical US macronutrient intake as reported in the third Health and Nutrition Examination Survey. It is useful for comparison to note that the CSIRO's Total Wellbeing Diet has a split of 26 per cent fat, 33 per cent protein and 39 per cent carbohydrate, meaning it is a relatively low-fat, high-protein, low-carbohydrate diet.

Source: R de Souza et al., 'Alternatives for macronutrient intake and chronic disease: A comparison of the OmniHeart diets with popular diets and with dietary recommendations', *American Journal of Clinical Nutrition*, vol. 88, no. 1, July 2008, pp. 1–11, figure 1.

Easy, you say. I know all this. Bread is carbs, meat is protein and dairy is fat, right? But macronutrients do not live only where you think they live. All foods contain varying proportions of at least two of the macronutrients. Meat, for example, is not all protein; it also contains fat, but no carbohydrate. And milk is not, despite what you may think, all fat, but a mix of carbohydrate, protein and fat. Bread has protein in it, although it is mostly carbohydrate. Fruit contains no protein and is also mostly carbohydrate.

Fat is pretty hard to avoid and seems to live everywhere—and in surprising quantities in meat. The industrialisation of farming has seen a rise in the percentage of fat in meat. Even our cows got fat! Have a browse of the following table to get a sense of where the macronutrients live.

MACRONUTRIENT COMPONENTS OF DIFFERENT FOODS

FOOD	CALORIES	FAT (G)	CARBOHYDRATE (G)	PROTEIN (G)
Full Cream milk, Dairy Farmers (250 ml)	158	8.5	12.2	8.0
Lite White milk, Dairy Farmers (250 ml)	120	3.5	13.0	9.0
Shape No Fat milk, Dairy Farmers (250 ml)	98	0.2	13.5	10.0
Tasty natural cheese slice, Bega (21 g)	86	7.3	0.0	5.2
Feta cheese (20 g)	37	4.0	1.0	4.0
Cottage Cheese, Weight Watchers (20 g)	18	0.5	0.8	2.5
White bread, Wonder White (slice)	70	1.0	14.0	2.0
Wholegrain Quinoa & Flaxseed bread, Helga's (slice)	100	1.8	14.8	4.4

FOOD	CALORIES	FAT (G)	CARBOHYDRATE (G)	PROTEIN (G)
Thin beef sausage, Woolworths (85 g)	221	17.9	5.0	10.6
Beef rib eye steak (85 g)	170	10.5	0.0	18.0
Chicken breast (85 g)	86	1.9	0.0	16.0
Smoked salmon (85 g)	163	8.5	0.0	19.5
Granny Smith apple (medium)	72	0.2	19.0	0.0

Source: www.myfitnesspal.com

The most striking thing about this table for me is the way in which the macronutrients are distributed across a wide variety of foods. If you were really serious about not eating a single carbohydrate, for example, you couldn't eat milk, feta cheese or sausages—not to mention fruit and vegetables! The fact that the macronutrients are distributed throughout all common foodstuffs is significant. It's almost as if Mother Nature intends for us to eat a variety of macronutrients in every bite . . . Which, of course, she does.

A brief history of the food wars

Once upon a time there was an American scientist named Ancel Keys. Born in 1904, he lived to the ripe old age of 99. He remains one of the most influential diet researchers that has ever lived. His ideas about what we should eat are still influencing what is in your fridge.

When war broke out in 1939, the US government called on Keys to design a portable, non-perishable and calorie-controlled diet for soldiers, which became known as K-rations. In the late 1950s and the 1960s, Keys oversaw the now famous Seven Countries Study, which looked at the diet and mortality rates of men in the United States, Finland, the Netherlands, Italy, Greece, Japan and what was then Yugoslavia. The figures threw up some seemingly confusing results.

American men, for example, were the best fed in the world, but died of cardiovascular disease more often than men from the other countries. Italy, on the other hand, was home to the highest concentration of 100 year olds in the seven countries. The dietary difference? Italians ate a diet low in animal fat. US health authorities soon seized upon this finding to encourage Americans to eat a diet low in animal fat to guard against heart disease. Lo and behold, the Mediterranean Diet was born. From a calorie point of view, a diet low in fat makes sense. Chemically, of the three macronutrients, fat is the most energy dense, packing about 9 calories per gram, compared to the 4 calories per gram in carbohydrate and protein.

Keys later refined his results, discovering that saturated fat was the main problem for hearts, rather than healthier vegetable-based and unsaturated fat. But the fat cat was out of the bag. 'Save me your complicated science mumble talk; give me low fat!' consumers demanded. Food manufacturers around the world responded by reducing the fat content of foods like milk, cheese and yoghurt and slapping 'low fat' labels on them. But they didn't stop there. To make the food more palatable to consumers, they started packing it full of sugar. The irony of the low-fat movement was that without actually reducing the amount of fat we ate—we just ate more food overall—it increased the amount of added sugar in our diet. Americans, and the world, kept getting fatter.

Then, sometime in the 1960s, an overweight man read a study that suggested a diet low in carbohydrate would result in weight loss. He tried it. It worked. In 1972 he published a book about his journey called *Dr. Atkins' Diet Revolution*. The Atkins Diet was born. Fat-starved consumers were now told that fat had never been the real enemy. Carbohydrate was the real enemy. All you had to do was eat a diet high in protein and fat, and cut out carbohydrate altogether, and you'd be skinny for life. Yippee!

The demonisation of carbohydrate continues unabated in more recent diets like the Paleo Diet, which encourages you to eat like a caveman: meat, fat and non-starchy vegetables alone. Forget, for the moment, that cavemen died at about the age of 30 and had IQs you could count on one hand (if you could count at all, that is).

In 2007 a charismatic American science writer, Gary Taubes, wrote a book called *Good Calories, Bad Calories*, which argued that the main driver of obesity is not excessive overall calorie consumption, but excessive consumption of 'bad calories'. By bad calories he means mostly highly refined carbohydrate. Stop eating bad calories and you can eat as many good calories (protein and vegetables) as you like and not get fat.

Following that, attention turned to sugar as the dietary devil. In May 2009 paediatric endocrinologist Robert Lustig delivered an excellent lecture called 'Sugar: The Bitter Truth', which is available on YouTube. (Watch it; it's great.) In it, Lustig argues that increasing consumption of added sugar is the main driver of the obesity epidemic.

Sugar is a naturally occurring substance that is part of the carbohydrate macronutrient group. It occurs in nature in fruits and vegetables, and has a deliciously sweet taste that humans find irresistible. Berries, berries everywhere, remember? Because we love sugar so much, food producers have begun packing our food with concentrated versions in the most unlikely sources: yoghurt, bread and fruit juices, and condiments like tomato sauce, which is one-quarter sugar. (I know. Shocking, right?) Throughout history, sugar has been an excellent source of instant energy for humans to fuel the brain and activity; you aren't imagining your sugar highs. But after the sugar high comes the sugar low. When the liver senses increased sugar in the blood it begins to release an enzyme called insulin, which essentially acts as a doorman, opening the doors of cells so they can absorb the sugar from the blood. A large amount of ingested sugar can overload the insulin response, and if not enough insulin is released, too much sugar remains in the blood or is excreted in the urine, and, bingo, diabetes.

The amount of sugar in our diet has increased rapidly over quite a short period of time. Everyone agrees that we should eat less sugar than we do. Australian dietary guidelines released in 2013 gave the strongest warning yet about the need to reduce excessive sugar consumption, advising Australians to 'limit intake of foods and drinks containing added sugars, such as confectionary, sugar-sweetened soft drinks and cordials, fruit drinks, vitamin waters and energy and sports drinks'. While the Australian guidelines make no recommendation on exactly how much sugar you should consume a day, the American Heart Foundation advises women to limit themselves to around 5 teaspoons of added sugar a day and men to around 9 teaspoons. One can of cola alone, contains around 40 grams, or 10 teaspoons, of sugar. Clearly, we need to cut back.

But once again, some want to take it to extremes. Not content with telling people to cut back, the quit sugar movement began. In Australia a former lawyer, David Gillespie, became a bestselling author with his book *Sweet Poison*, about his journey to lose 40 kilograms with no exercise, just by quitting sugar. Gillespie has become something of a superstar with his followers, who have successfully lost weight by cutting out sugar. His promise is simple: cut out sugar from your diet and you will never be hungry enough to overeat again. Another Australian author, Sarah Wilson, has also published a step-by-step guide to eliminating sugar from your diet called *I Quit Sugar*.

Maybe Gillespie and Wilson are right. I haven't tried quitting sugar. Perhaps I lack the discipline. Maybe I just like sugar too much. I'm certainly not about to stop eating fruit. But while I haven't given up sugar altogether, I definitely have cut back. Not because sugar per se is evil, but from a practical point of view: sugar is so energy dense that if you give yourself a limited food calorie budget, you can't afford much of it—particularly added sugars. Once you start to follow a calorie-conscious diet, which I'll describe in part 2, you'll soon find there's not much room for added sugar in your daily food allowance.

I have a lot of time for advice that says we should be eating less added sugar, less fat and less highly refined carbohydrate, like white bread, than we do. Clearly, we are consuming way too much of all these foods, and sugar in particular. But given the temptations we face in daily life, I don't think it's sensible to tell people to exclude entire food groups altogether. One slice of chocolate and you're off the wagon, eating yourself into those size 18 pants again. I am also deeply suspicious of any diet that says you can exclude one food group and eat as much as you like of the others, regardless of total calorie intake. If it sounds too good to be true, it probably is. Which is not to say there isn't a kernel of truth to all these diets, just that there are no magic tricks.

'People are so all or nothing,' sighs nutritionist Joanna McMillan, founder of the website www.getlean.com.au and a regular media commentator on weight loss. 'I'm really fed up with providing comment on the latest fad diet,' she tells me. The truth, according to McMillan, is that the body can accept a wide range of diets with different macronutrient splits. 'The answer is that humans are highly adaptable. There is no one diet. There's no one approach for everyone.'

Putting food theory to the test

What scientific evidence do we have that any one diet is better than the others? The answer to that is plenty. The problem is, most of the evidence is contradictory. Advocates of particular diets can always find an academic study to back them up. But there is a real lack of surveys with large enough sample sizes and long enough time scales to make a clear call. This doesn't mean we won't one day find the perfect macronutrient mix for weight loss and maintenance; we simply haven't found it yet. Scientists are always torturing poor little rats, and many experiments have been conducted to manipulate the macronutrient mix of their diets and convert the poor creatures into yo-yo dieters. But it is hard to replicate the studies on humans. People make food and exercise decisions every moment of every day. They are notoriously bad at giving researchers an accurate account of what they eat and do. And there are precious few people willing to lock themselves up in a laboratory for observation for years on end so that scientists can accurately monitor their weight and diet.

The biggest and most comprehensive survey I have been able to find on the impact on weight loss and weight main-tenance of different macronutrient splits was conducted between October 2004 and December 2007 by American researchers. The results appeared in a 2009 article of *The New England Journal of Medicine*, in which the problem was set out clearly:

ff There is intense debate about what types of diet are most effective for treating overweight [people]—those that emphasize protein, those that emphasize carbohydrates, or those that emphasize fat . . . The crucial question is whether overweight people have a better response in the long term to diets that emphasize a specific macronutrient composition. **JJ**

And so the researchers set about finding out, enlisting 811 participants and randomly assigning them to one of the four diets listed in the table below. The diet groups allowed them to test which levels of fat, protein and carbohydrate in a diet were best for weight loss.

NUTRIENT GOALS FOR THE FOUR DIET GROUPS OBSERVED IN THE NEW ENGLAND STUDY

DIET	FAT	PROTEIN	CARBOHYDRATE
Low fat, average protein	20	15	65
Low fat, high protein	20	25	55
High fat, average protein	40	15	45
High fat, high protein	40	25	35

Note: Amounts are given as percentages.
Source: Adapted from FM Sacks et al., 'Comparison of weight-loss diets with different compositions of fat, protein and carbohydrates', *New England Journal of Medicine*, vol. 360, no. 9, 26 February 2009, pp. 859–73.

Participants enlisted were aged between 30 and 70 years and had body mass indexes of between 25 and 40, making them a mix of overweight and obese. Forty per cent were men. (Many studies have difficulty recruiting men for weight-loss research, so this was quite a good turnout.) All were assessed as having sufficient motivation to lose weight and to attempt to keep it off. Participants were not told which diet group they were in. Each person had a diet specially designed so they would be 750 calories a day short of their energy requirement. Group and individual counselling sessions were held throughout the study. Participants prepared their own food, kept a food diary and used an online tool to find out how close they were to meeting their goal diet. They were told to do 90 minutes of moderate exercise per week.

Of the 811 people that started, 645 completed the study, which is a pretty high proportion for this type of research. At the end of the study roughly 35 per cent of the participants weighed at least 5 per cent less than they had at the start, and in each diet group about 15 per cent weighed less by at least 10 per cent. Around 3 per cent of the participants had lost 20 kilograms or more.

Do those results sound a bit low to you? Importantly, the researchers found that participants did not stick to their diets. Left to their own devices, they ate more of every macronutrient than they were asked to, particularly carbohydrate. Instead of creating the required daily 750-calorie deficit, the participants managed a deficit of only about 225 calories a day. 'Overall, these findings with respect to adherence to macronutrient goals suggest that participants in weight-loss programs revert to their customary macronutrient intakes over time, but may nonetheless be able to maintain weight loss.'

But while adherence was not complete, the participants did manage to swing their diets towards the four prescribed patterns. Those who attended the group sessions were found to achieve better results, equivalent to about 200 grams extra loss for every session attended, regardless of which diet they were on. Because high-protein and low-fat diets were more radical departures from people's ordinary diets, participants on those meal plans were more likely to attend group sessions. The researchers said, 'We view attendance at counseling sessions as a proxy for commitment to achieving weight loss and for engagement in the program . . . These findings together point to behavioral factors rather than macronutrient metabolism as the main influences on weight loss.'

There were benefits from weight loss for all diet groups, including reduced risk factors for cardiovascular disease and diabetes. However, twelve months in to the study, participants from all the diet groups began to slowly regain weight. Only 185 people, or 23 per cent, continued to lose weight from six months through the study to its end, with no significant difference between the diet groups.

Perhaps unsurprisingly, participants who completed the study lost more weight than those who didn't. Of all participants who started the study, weight loss after two years was virtually the same for those assigned to high- and average-protein diets (3.6 kilograms and 3 kilograms, respectively). But those who completed the study on the high-protein diet lost a higher average of 4.5 kilograms. Those who completed the average-protein diet lost an average of 3.6 kilograms. As for variations in fat, all participants who started the study on the high-fat and average-fat diets lost an average of 3.3 kilograms—exactly the same. For those who completed the study, again the results were higher than for those who did not complete it. But at 3.9 kilograms, weight loss for the high-fat diet and 4.1 kilograms for the average-fat diet, there was little apparent difference from varying fat percentage in the diet. The researchers also found no effect on weight loss of a high- or low-carbohydrate diet.

So what have we learnt? First, people are crap at sticking to diets. Second, even so, people can lose weight successfully on a calorie-controlled diet. And third, it's hard to maintain weight loss—most of us will begin putting weight back on after about a year. But what about the main question? Did one diet produce more or less weight loss and maintenance than the others? On the surface, the results suggest a higher protein diet produced slightly more weight loss, particularly among those who completed the study. However, according to the researchers:

❝ The principal finding is that the diets were equally successful in promoting clinically meaningful weight loss and the maintenance of weight loss over the course of two years . . .

These divergent results suggest that any type of diet, when taught for the purpose of weight loss with enthusiasm and persistence, can be effective. When non-nutritional influences are minimized, as they were in our study, the specific macronutrient content is of minor importance, as was suggested many years ago.

In conclusion, diets that are successful in causing weight loss can emphasize a range of fat, protein, and carbohydrate compositions that have beneficial effects on risk factors for cardiovascular disease and diabetes. Such diets can also be tailored to individual patients on the basis of their personal and cultural preferences and may therefore have the best chance for long-term success. **"**

So even this most rigorous study failed to produce a finding that diets of one macronutrient split have any more impact on lasting weight loss than diets of a different split. This is not to say that future studies will be unsuccessful in proving a link. Maybe researchers will find better ways to persuade participants to adhere to the strict diets required. The most recent review of all the available scientific research comparing calorie-restricted diets of varying macronutrient splits was undertaken by obesity researchers led by Tom Wycherley, in Adelaide in 2012. Comparing the results of 24 separate studies, they found 'modest' benefits from a high protein diet (25 to 35 per cent of calories) versus a standard protein diet (about 15 per cent of calories) in terms of weight loss, fat loss, maintenance of lean muscle mass and boosted resting energy expenditure. The difference, they estimate, was equal to about

1 kilogram of additional weight loss over eight weeks on a strict calorie-controlled diet. But with only one study in their sample measuring results over a year, they also concluded that more long-term evidence is needed on the health impact of high-protein diets.

For now, there is as yet no conclusive scientific proof that any of the macronutrient splits is better than another for sustained weight loss. By far the best chance of weight loss is found in adherence to a calorie-controlled diet, irrespective of its composition.

Perhaps the most infamous example of this is the Twinkie Diet. In 2010 a professor at Kansas State University, Mark Haub—a.k.a. the Twinkie guy—lost 12 kilograms by restricting himself to 1800 calories a day for ten weeks. He ate a diet consisting of Twinkies, cakes, Doritos and Oreo biscuits. He also took a vitamin supplement, drank a protein shake and ate some vegetables each day. His body mass index fell from 28.8 (overweight) to 24.9 (within the normal range). His cholesterol and triglyceride levels fell. I emailed him in June 2013 to find out how things were going, and he told me that although he no longer weighed regularly, he had regained about 3 kilograms in the twenty months after his experiment.

So getting weight off seems to have health benefits, no matter how you go about it. Of course, nutrition is important too. A diet comprised entirely of fat would be just as unhealthy as a diet composed entirely of protein. The body requires all of the three macronutrients to function. It also requires a diet rich in micronutrients, like calcium, vitamins, iron and zinc, which are obtained by eating a varied diet including leafy and colourful vegetables. I'm not recommending the Twinkie Diet for long-term health, just observing that it works for short-term weight loss. When it comes to sustained weight loss, it's about finding the combination of foods that satisfy you enough to mean you can stick to a lower calorie diet than you're used to.

The good news is that diets can be tailored to suit individual preferences, cultural backgrounds and lifestyles. That was the conclusion of another Harvard School of Public Health study into the health benefits of different popular diets conducted by Russell de Souza and colleagues:

❝ Although the optimal macronutrient profile of the diet remains unknown, data are emerging that compliance, rather than a specific macronutrient distribution, may be the most important determinant of whether or not a diet achieves its intended effect (eg, weight loss and chronic disease risk reduction). To maximize adherence to any diet plan, it is imperative to consider an individual's food preferences, culture, lifestyle, and religious beliefs. Advocating a single dietary pattern to reduce chronic disease risk for a diverse population is unlikely to be an effective approach to promote health. **❞**

And yet, advocating a single dietary pattern is exactly what we've been trying to do for decades. No wonder we're still fat.

The importance of protein

I want to spend some time at this point filling you in on a recent and potentially revolutionary theory in weight-loss science. Pioneering research by Sydney-based biologist and obesity researcher Stephen Simpson has pinpointed the critical role of protein in our diet. Simpson heads the study of obesity at the University of Sydney's Charles Perkins Centre. Having cost half a billion dollars to build, and with its links to more than 900 researchers, it is likely the biggest obesity research centre anywhere in the world.

During an interview with Simpson I mentioned my weight-loss idea that 'it's all calories in, calories out', but got the feeling he wasn't too impressed with my simplistic approach. 'At one level, the simple energy in and energy out equation has to be true. But the key question is: are calories all the same, and how easy is it to sustain a limitation of energy in?'

But, I pleaded, surely calories are just calories, no matter where they come from?

'Not in terms of their impact on appetite, metabolic and cardiovascular health, the gut microbiome [the microbes living in your gut], immune function and body fat percentage; in all these cases calories ain't calories. The types of calories—the balance of different macronutrients—is critical. So if you presume calories are the same, in a fundamental way, you're fundamentally wrong.' Perhaps reacting to the somewhat crushed and confused look on my face, he went on, 'What we know, and the laws of physics dictate, is if you reduce your calorie intake below your calorie expenditure you will lose weight. But whether you lose that weight from body fat or lean muscle depends on the types of calories—the balance of protein, carbs and fat—in the diet.'

Simpson arrived at the study of obesity in a roundabout kind of way. An insect enthusiast from a tender age, his central research interest was locust swarms. Why do locusts swarm? Turns out locusts are a nasty bunch. They swarm in search of food—specifically protein. And where do they find it? They cannibalise each other. Once their need for protein is satisfied, they stop swarming.

It seems that humans are a bit like locusts, just more polite and further up the food chain. Instead of cannibalising each other in search of the protein we need, we get it from eating other animals or, in the case of vegetarians, eating a hell of a lot of beans. According to Simpson's research, this appetite for protein is the central driver of our consumption of food. Basically, we keep eating until we get enough protein. The finding was backed up through studies of spider monkeys, moths, locusts and mice. All these animals, when denied enough protein, will overeat other, less dense sources of protein to get their fix. The result? They eat too many calories overall, end up in 'positive energy balance' and gain weight.

In 2004 Simpson and his colleague David Raubenheimer gave the phenomenon a name: the protein leverage hypothesis. In a groundbreaking paper, they observed how the focus of most obesity research to that point had dwelt on the role of carbohydrate and fat in the diet. Protein makes up only a small part of our diet, about 15 per cent of total calorie intake, and it has remained a relatively stable proportion of our diet, leading it to be overlooked in much of the academic research. But, Simpson and Raubenheimer asked, what if this stability of consumption were actually an indicator that protein plays a crucial role in our diet? 'Paradoxically, it may be precisely because protein comprises a small component of the diet and is tightly regulated that it could have sufficient leverage over human ingestive behaviour to explain obesity.'

In fact, according to their thesis, the search for protein is the number one driver of overconsumption in our modern environment of cheap carbohydrate and fat. Foods heavy in carbohydrate and fat have become relatively cheaper, and protein sources like meat have become more expensive. We tend to avoid more expensive, purer sources of protein and, as a result, overeat the cheap carby, fatty stuff just to get access to the low levels of protein they also contain. Food manufacturers are tricking us too, dressing up cheap carbohydrate and fat with salt to imitate the usual taste of protein-rich foods.

❝ The implications for body weight regulation are clear: unless the excess C + F [carbohydrate plus fat] ingested to maintain P [protein] intake is removed, for example, through increased physical activity or thermogenesis [the production of heat in our body], body weight will rise, predisposing towards obesity.

Taste stimuli naturally associated with protein-rich foods, such as sodium and umami stimulants, are extensively used in low-protein processed foods, and may as a result subvert protein regulatory systems and lead to over-consumption of fat and carbohydrates.

In combination, it is unsurprising that we should be prone in our modern environment to being misdirected onto diets containing a higher ratio of F + C : P than is optimal. The central argument in this paper is that if you add to this the protein leverage effect, it is also unsurprising that the regulatory systems controlling intake by modern humans are prone to becoming unstable, driving a catastrophic cycle of over-consumption and obesity. 🙶

And guess what? The proportion of protein in our diet is, indeed, falling. At least, it is in the United States. Simpson and Raubenheimer used United Nations data on the availability (not consumption) of nutrients to suggest that the proportion of protein in the average US diet dropped from 14 per cent in 1961 to 12.5 per cent in 2000. The following graph shows that while our intake of protein in kilojoules has risen only slightly over the past half-century, our intake of carbohydrate and fat has climbed by a disproportionately greater amount. Yep, we're carb loading—big time.

It looks like we're after a certain amount of protein each day, and we won't stop eating until we get it. If we have access

CONSUMPTION OF PROTEIN VERSUS CONSUMPTION OF CARBOHYDRATE PLUS FAT IN THE UNITED STATES

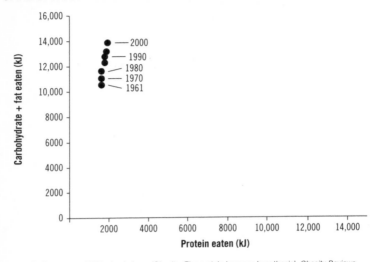

Source: SJ Simpson and D Raubenheimer, 'Obesity: The protein leverage hypothesis', *Obesity Reviews*, vol. 6, no. 2, May 2005, pp. 133–42, figure 3.

to the required amount of protein from high-protein foods, we don't eat so much carbohydrate and fat. It's eating all the unnecessary carbohydrate and fat in low-protein foods that makes us fat.

To back up the theory, Simpson and a team of researchers led by Alison Gosby conducted a human study of protein's effect on total calorie consumption. The participants consisted of sixteen females and six males; they were all lean, with an average age of 25. Uni students have more time on their hands, you see. The group stayed at a sleep study centre on three separate occasions, each lasting four days. On each occasion, the participants were given a diet containing a different proportion of protein: 10 per cent (low), 15 per cent (about average) and 25 per cent protein (high).

To ensure the participants didn't twig to what they were up to—by feeding them more meat, for example—the researchers designed all of the meals to look exactly the same, despite the variations in their protein content. Meals were carefully matched to taste the same and have the same palatability. They also contained the same number of calories. The proportion of fat in each diet was kept constant, at 30 per cent, meaning the carbohydrate amount varied, between 60, 55 and then 45 per cent of energy consumed. Participants were allowed to snack at will and were taken for a one-hour supervised walk each day.

Did varying the proportion of protein in the diet have an impact? It did. The researchers found that participants consumed an average of 12 per cent more energy over the four-day study period on the 10 per cent protein diet compared with the 15 per cent diet. Rather than eating more at meal times, participants on the low-protein diet suffered serial snack attacks, with 70 per cent of the increase in energy intake coming from snacking between meals.

Okay, so we should all start eating heaps of meat, right? Well, not exactly. 'Whereas reducing dietary protein from 15 per cent to 10 per cent evoked a significant increased energy intake, an increase from 15 per cent to 25 per cent protein did not lead to a reduction in energy intake.' Sorry, guys, no magic bullet. What this does suggest is that people eating a low proportion of protein in their diet could try upping it a bit.

In the study just mentioned, participants reported higher hunger levels one to two hours after breakfast on the 10 per cent protein diet than they did on the 25 per cent protein diet. Protein makes you feel fuller for longer. Other studies have also looked closely at the role of protein in our diets. The Diet, Obesity and Genes project, or Diogenes, was another major study conducted in 2007 across eight countries to find the most effective diet mix. Funded by countries in the European Union, it was headed by Arne Astrup from the Department of Human Nutrition at the University of Copenhagen. It focused on the relative impact on reducing hunger and spontaneous eating of diets high in protein and low glycaemic index carbohydrates. For a long time, nutritionists have recommended low glycaemic index foods as they are thought to curb hunger for longer.

The Diogenes study remains one of the world's biggest-ever diet studies, enlisting entire families. The goal was to identify the diet most effective in avoiding weight gain and regain. In an initial eight-week phase, adults were required to lose 8 per cent of their body weight. Participants in Copenhagen and Maastricht were given free food from a special supermarket for six months. Others, in the United Kingdom, Bulgaria, Crete, the Czech Republic and Spain, were given dietary advice only. Of the 763 families who began the study, 565 successfully lost weight—an average of 11.2 kilograms per person during the eight weeks—and these were then randomly put onto one of five different diets, including a control group. Families on a diet with higher protein showed better weight-loss maintenance. According to Astrup:

❝ The first results from the DioGenes dietary intervention study clearly show that an increased dietary protein content decreases weight regain after a weight loss, whereas the glycemic index did not play any detectable role. Consequently, we conclude that the efficacy of an increased protein content is important for prevention of weight regain, whereas a diet low in glycemic index possesses no advantage. **❞**

Fantastic news, Jess! you may be thinking. I'm going to start eating protein for breakfast, lunch and tea! Er, no, that's not what I'm trying to say. Simpson is quick to warn against interpreting his research as advocating a high-protein diet. Evidence from animal studies suggests that such diets are associated with shorter life spans. 'Lose weight; die early,' he quips. So what should you do? According to Simpson, 'If you want to lose weight, you should go on a higher percentage protein diet—which will help limit calories—increase exercise and remove highly processed foods from your diet—you've no idea what's in them. Once you have lost the weight you should continue with the last two, but normalise your protein intake.' So, if you're hungry while losing weight, eat some baked beans or chicken, rather than fruit—it will probably keep you feeling fuller for longer. But bacon for breakfast, lunch and tea? Warns Simpson, 'You need to immunise yourself against idiocy and not be influenced by fad diets—or at least try to understand what a particular fad diet means in terms of how many and what type of calories you are eating. There's a lot of nonsense and pseudoscience in this area, much of which stems from people wanting to make a lot of money out of people (this includes most of us nowadays) who want to lose weight and are unable to assess the quality of evidence.'

The bottom line is that there is no academic agreement about the appropriate split of macronutrients for the body, between protein carbohydrates and fat. But there is a growing consensus that getting enough protein will help you to limit your appetite and eat less. It may also help to maintain muscle mass and promote fat loss instead during weight loss. Turns out when I was on my spreadsheet diet, I was eating an average of 24 per cent protein (higher than population average), 35.5 per cent fat and 40 per cent carbohydrate. My protein percentage could vary between weeks from 19 per cent to 27 per cent. It does appear a high protein diet helps you adhere to a lower calorie plan, and that's why it matters. You can easily keep track of this with the smartphone app MyFitnessPal (see chapter 7).

Researchers will no doubt spend many years investigating the optimal mix of macronutrients. But for ordinary folk I think it's time we stopped worrying so much about what to eat and refocus on how much we are eating. The science about *what* to eat—the optimum split of macronutrients—is far from settled. But the science about *how much* to eat to lose weight is pretty clear cut: a little less than you need each day. Until the science is resolved on the former, why not just go for the scientifically proven advice that you need to balance your energy intake, wherever it comes from, with your energy expenditure.

4

Why Newton wasn't wrong

Little is known of the diet and exercise habits of the great seventeenth-century physicist and mathematician Isaac Newton. According to some accounts, he was a vegetarian. According to others, he consumed only bread, water and wine while working. Portraits of Newton suggest a slim man in youth, and an older man with something of a double chin. In one of his few surviving personal notebooks, now held in the Fitzwilliam Library in Cambridge, the great physicist kept a list of his sins. A devout Christian, Newton admits variously to 'neglecting to pray', exhibiting 'peevishness with my mother' and 'punching my sister'. The list also includes numerous food-related confessions, some of which may be familiar, some unfamiliar, to the modern dieter, including 'eating an apple at Thy house', 'making pies on Sunday night', 'stealing cherry cobs from Eduard Storer' and subsequently 'denying that I did so', 'robbing my mother's box of plums and sugar', 'gluttony in my sickness', 'peevishness at Master Clarks for a piece of bread and butter' and 'gluttony'.

So it may be wrong to hold Newton up as the greatest weight-loss guru of all time. Perhaps we can think of him as a case of 'do as I say, not as I do'. Because Newton, for all his personal foibles, was the pioneer of the idea of energy conservation. And if you want to lose weight, you need to know a bit about it.

The first law of thermodynamics

According to Newton's first law of thermodynamics, energy can be neither created nor destroyed. Energy into a system can't just disappear—it must go somewhere. Turns out this obscure physics equation has a real application in the world of weight loss and maintenance. The human body—for all its intricacies—conforms to the fundamental law of energy in and energy out. Energy consumed, in food and drink, must go somewhere. It can't just disappear. If the energy in food is not immediately used to power our daily activities, it must go somewhere else. And that somewhere is your butt. Or, more generally, wherever your body's fat cells reside.

In May 2011 the American Society for Nutrition convened a panel of six experts on energy balance in humans. The panel met for four days in Chicago and produced a consensus statement on the science of energy balance titled 'Energy Balance and Its Components: Implications for Body Weight Regulation'. Its conclusion was simple: 'A fundamental principle of nutrition and metabolism is that body weight change is associated with an imbalance between the energy content of food eaten and energy expended by the body to maintain life and to perform physical work.' To lose weight, you must put less energy in than your body needs each day. When you do this, your body will dig into its own energy stores to fuel itself. The result? You lose weight. So losing weight comes down to one simple equation: calories in minus calories out.

Or does it? Here's an upfront disclosure: pretty much every obesity researcher I interviewed for this book when I first asked, 'Doesn't it all come down to calories in and calories out?' tried to dissuade me from this seemingly naive belief. Obesity researchers have seen the message of calories in and calories out fail for decade after decade.

It's about gut bacteria, said one. Porous stomachs, said another. Hormonal imbalances, impaired leptin signals, whacked-out appestats, they continued. Obesity researcher Garry Eggers was particularly sceptical about reducing the message to something so basic. 'I don't think it's as simple as that. There is a tendency with people who do lose weight to instantly think that what they did is the one and only way to lose weight. Energy in and energy out is a general equation, but it's a physics equation; it doesn't necessarily apply to a biological organism.' According to Eggers, different people can do the exact same thing, but their weight may come off at different rates. 'I don't mind people talking about things in calories, but we have moved on a bit in the last ten years.

It is important you recognise that this is a general approach to weight loss. The actual specific results don't apply to individuals.'

The experts agree that results can vary from person to person, but they are unanimous on one thing. When pushed one final time by me saying, 'But for most people, if they consume fewer calories than they use in a day, they'll lose weight, right?' every obesity researcher I spoke to conceded the point.

'I'm not averse to what you're doing,' Eggers told me. 'I've become quite disillusioned . . . We did it in the 1990s and that was what we focused on all the time and it didn't work . . . The women's mags are famous for their calorie-counting approach.' According to Eggers, energy balance is just the tip of the iceberg. 'The top bit is physics, but below the surface is genes, biology, bacteria. This is a big picture issue. This is an economic issue and we can't just put the blame back on the individual.'

Joseph Proietto was more easily convinced by my approach. 'You are right, in my view. But it's not the end of the story. You are right that weight can only be the end result of energy in and energy out. The problem is why do people have too much energy in and why don't they then burn it off by having more energy out? It's energy in and energy out, but what drives there to be more energy in?'

There seems to be a widespread resistance among academics to reduce the problem to a simple calories in and calories out equation. Harry Rutter, a scientific advisor to the National

Obesity Observatory in the United Kingdom, put it this way in *The Lancet* in August 2011:

❝ There is a seductive simplicity to the conceptualisation of obesity as a straightforward problem of energy balance—calories in versus calories out. But the physiological, behavioural, and environmental influences on this relation are asymmetrical. Therefore, although the basic arithmetic holds true, in practice it is much easier for people, and populations, to gain weight than to lose it. ❞

You see, all I heard just then was 'the basic arithmetic holds true'. In the newspaper business, we call that burying the lead—the lead being the most important thing you really need to know. For all the complex factors that interplay to produce obesity—environment, psychology, economy and so on—the central element of the picture is still energy in and energy out. Too much of the former and not enough of the latter.

The elephant in the room

Everybody seems just a little bit hesitant to tell you this, so let me. You are eating way too much and moving much too little.

I get the feeling obesity researchers are, in some ways, trying to avoid people being disappointed. They want them to know that the body is a living organism, that results will vary. They don't want them to give up because they don't lose weight in one week.

But I think they risk missing the point: that it does come down to calories in and calories out. To lose weight you absolutely must create an energy deficit. You simply can't lose weight while eating more calories than you expend. It's not possible. Your body is a complex biological organism, one of the most miraculous machines ever built. But I get the feeling that most people have no idea how it works. I think that to lose weight people need to know a bit more about how their body uses the energy they ingest. We need to break it down a bit. Bear with me: I'm about to lay some science on you.

What makes you, well . . . you?

I know you are a wonderful creature full of emotions, hopes and dreams. But when you break it all down, you really are just a lump of fat, water, protein, bone, cell solids, glycogen and some non-soluble fibre just passing through, if you know what I mean. You might have heard that your body is 70 per cent water. Well, that's true, on average. But just as people's weight can vary, so too can their body composition. The following graph shows the body breakdown of a lean 70-kilogram man and an obese 120-kilogram man. What is immediately apparent is that fat makes up a greater proportion of the obese man's body.

The main difference between the two men is their differing levels of fat storage. The obese man also has slightly more

WHAT ARE YOU MADE OF?

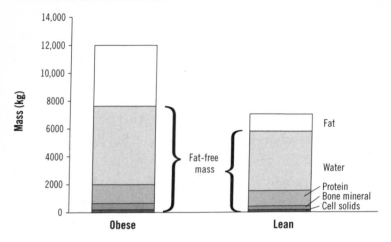

Source: KD Hall, 'Modeling metabolic adaptations and energy regulation in humans', *Annual Review of Nutrition*, vol. 32, 21 August 2012, pp. 35–54, figure a.

protein and bone mineral mass than the lean man. But by far the biggest difference between the two is the obese man's excessive stores of fat. This is what happens when you over-consume energy. The vast majority of it ends up in your fat cells. The aim of any dieter should be to target those fat stores by forcing the body to turn to them for energy. Unfortunately, the body is a bit less discriminating than that and will attempt to find energy wherever it can, including the body's stores of protein, found in muscle. More on that later. First, here's a question you might not have thought to ask before, but which is central to losing weight. Why do we eat?

Eating isn't just a nice thing we do with friends and family, or a boredom-busting way to while away the hours or to fill an emotional gap. There is, in fact, a specific biological purpose for eating. Food is fuel. Food is the vessel through which we deliver energy to our body to fuel our everyday activities. It is also the way we take in essential micronutrients that the body requires for life, but can't generate itself.

Food, essentially, is a bunch of molecules that we ingest so the body can break them down to rebuild its organs and tissue and access energy for movement. Our muscles, brain, heart and liver all need to be constantly replenished with new molecules. They also need energy to work. The process known as metabolism, breaking down long-chain molecules into smaller molecules, releases the energy necessary to fuel the range of activities needed for survival. That's why we eat.

IS THERE SUCH A THING AS A SLOW METABOLISM?

Many a frustrated dieter has blamed a slow metabolism for their weight gain. But according to the experts, there are no such things as slow and fast metabolisms, unless you have an illness like hyperactive thyroid syndrome, metabolic disease or Cushing's disease.

In fact, when scientists put people in metabolic chambers to measure their energy use and then adjust the energy expended to account for people's varying compositions of body fat, it turns out we all perform this process of breaking down foods to release energy at the same rate. In fact, if anything, bigger people are at an advantage because their bodies require more energy to move their larger mass around.

When you eat food, it travels into your stomach and small intestines. Like eager dance partners, there are specific molecules called enzymes waiting to embrace the three macronutrients and break them down for the body to use to build cells and release energy.

Carbohydrate is broken down into simpler sugars, like glycogen, and absorbed into the bloodstream. This is the body's main source of energy. But energy can also be obtained from breaking down the two other main macronutrients.

Fat is essential for the body, helping it to absorb nutrients and regulate body temperature. It is broken down into fatty acids by a substance called bile, which is produced in the liver and stored in the gallbladder. These fatty acids are also absorbed into the bloodstream and are sent to fat cells to be stored for later energy use.

Protein forms the building blocks for muscle and body tissue, which are constantly breaking down and must be rebuilt. Your muscles and organs are made mostly of protein. That's why maintaining a supply of protein into the body is essential. Ingested protein is broken down into amino acids, which are, in turn, reassembled by the body into protein that can be used for muscle repair and growth.

Micronutrients, essentially vitamins and minerals, are absorbed into the bloodstream too and sent around the body to where they are needed. Dietary fibre—stuff your body can't break down—goes all the way through your digestive tract and ends up in the toilet.

The human body really is the most marvellous recycling and garbage-sorting machine. In a 2012 paper called 'Modelling metabolic adaptations and energy regulation in humans', Kevin Hall, perhaps the world's leading researcher on the energy balance equation, used the analogy of a car that instead of running on just one type of fuel could run on an arbitrary mixture of whatever fuels were available:

" Such a flex-fuel vehicle would allow the driver to fill the tank with whatever fuel was cheaper or more readily available, regardless of what mixture is already in the tank. Although designing a flex-fuel vehicle would be a significant engineering challenge, imagine the additional complexity if the vehicle could have no fuel tank. Rather, the vehicle itself must be composed of its fuel and must continually break down and reconstruct its components. Furthermore, despite the daily turnover of its components and fluctuations of fuel delivery, the composition of the vehicle must remain relatively stable and maintain similar performance characteristics.

Exactly this remarkable engineering feat is accomplished by the human body through its use of the three dietary macronutrients (carbohydrate, fat and protein) to both fuel metabolism and provide substrates for body constituents. "

Despite the amazing amount of crap food we put in our body, it just keeps chugging along, breaking it down, using what it can, expelling what it can't and storing the rest. And all without a word of thanks from its owner. Take a moment to thank your poor body. You've put it through hell, and it just keeps doing its job.

So what happens when you consume less food than you need? In such an unlikely event (for most of us), the body has only three potential energy stores to tap: fat cells, protein (in lean muscle mass) and glycogen (which is stored mainly in the liver and muscles). When your body is deciding which one to use, it faces several constraints. The protein in muscle mass is fundamentally useful and cannot be depleted too much or you will, literally, die. So while the body may break down some of its muscle mass to access energy, it's not its preference. Fat stores are a much better energy reserve and, unlike protein stores, can be depleted to very low levels without much harm to you at all. Let's return to our obese 120-kilogram man and our lean 70-kilogram man. The graph on the next page shows their respective energy stores.

The obese man has more energy by far stored in fat than he has in protein. Glycogen makes up only a small amount of available energy in both men (about 2000 calories in total—roughly as much as you'd need for a day's worth of energy). The body of the obese man faces an obvious choice and will go for the fat. The body of the lean man faces a less obvious choice. Denied enough calories from food, it will likely attempt to access more energy from its protein stores than the

BODY ENERGY STORES IN AN OBESE PERSON VERSUS A LEAN PERSON

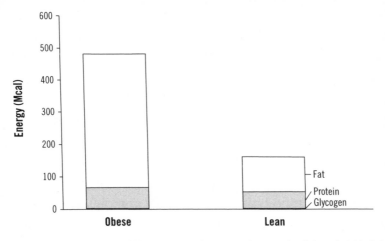

Note: 1 Mcal is 1 megacalorie (1000 kilocalories, or what most people commonly refer to, and what I refer to throughout this book, as 'calories').

Source: KD Hall, 'Modeling metabolic adaptations and energy regulation in humans', *Annual Review of Nutrition*, vol. 32, 21 August 2012, pp. 35–54, figure b.

obese man's body will. This might seem like an odd thing to mention, but it will become apparent in part 3 of this book why the changing composition of the body during weight loss influences where the weight is lost (from fat or muscle) the closer you get to your goal weight.

For now, let's assume that for most obese people, when the body goes looking for energy, it will mostly use fat. The process by which fat is burnt is simple. The fat is oxidised, which means the fat cells combine with oxygen to create a chemical reaction that gives off heat, or rather energy. The by-products of this process are mostly carbon dioxide and water, which you breathe, sweat or urinate out. Yes, all that huffing and puffing really is necessary.

A quick recap

So what have we learnt?

1   The body requires food for energy and also to obtain the building blocks it needs to constantly rebuild itself.
2   Excess food not used for these purposes is stored in fat cells.
3   The human body is a wondrously complex organism, with muscles, cells, hormones, skin and bones all working tirelessly to keep you together and functioning.
4   But it is not entirely wondrous and conforms to the first law of thermodynamics, that energy can be neither created nor destroyed.
5   Weight loss, for all the emotion, struggle and dreams of doughnuts, comes down to a simple equation: calories in minus calories out.
6   If you eat more energy than you expend, your body must store the excess, usually as fat.
7   If you eat less energy than you expend, your body must dig into its reserves of energy, stored in either fat cells or muscle, and you will lose weight.

I know what you're thinking. That's all really fascinating stuff, Jess. I'm sure thousands of researchers will spend millions of dollars and research hours investigating this stuff. Good on them. But you said you were going to tell me how to lose weight.

Well, okay, since you put it so nicely, I will.

PART 2
HOW TO
LOSE WEIGHT

5

How to find your bottom line

Everyone knows that to lose weight you have to eat less or move more, or both. The critical question is how much? For example, how many times do you need to go to the gym each week and for how long? Must you give up chocolate forever, existing entirely on lettuce leaves and air?

Many diets fail because we either overshoot or undershoot. Either we try to do things that are unsustainable and, let's face it, not terribly effective, like cutting our food intake so low that we unleash the hunger monster within. Or we walk around the block a few times in the vain hope that this will have a dramatic impact on our bottom line.

No, if you want to lose weight you have to get smart. Forget about isolating your deltoid muscle; the main muscle you need to engage is your brain. You have to learn how much energy your body needs you to consume. You have to figure out your number. You have to find your bottom line.

What's your number?

Perhaps you don't know it yet, but everyone on this earth has a number. It's a special number, unique to each person. And just as we change, so too does our number change over time and, indeed, from day to day. It is the number of calories, or units of energy, we need to consume each day to live, breathe and move.

You've probably heard and read a lot of advertisements trying to sell you the miracle diet, the secret to rapid weight loss, the foolproof way of slimming. You should be sceptical of them. You should be sceptical of anyone pushing a simple answer to weight loss. But I passionately believe there really is one scientifically proven, and relatively simple, way to lose weight. Here are three irreducible truths about the human body that no expert I have spoken to fundamentally disagrees with:

- Weight *gain* happens when energy consumed is greater than energy burnt.
- Weight *maintenance* happens when energy consumed is equal to energy burnt.
- Weight *loss* happens when energy consumed is less than energy burnt.

The only scientifically proven method of weight loss is to consume less energy than you burn, forcing your body to release the stores of energy in its fat and other cells. No diet works without this, and any diet that doesn't involve reducing energy in or increasing energy out, or both, is doomed to fail.

I know you don't have all day, so here it is. This entire book can be summarised in one sentence:

To lose weight you must consume fewer calories than you need (to fuel basic body functions, incidental movement, digestion and purposeful exercise), forcing your body to access and release energy stored in your fat cells.

And because I really like equations, here is another way of saying exactly the same thing:

Weight loss occurs when
energy in $<$ energy out

And because I really, really like graphs, you can also think about it like this:

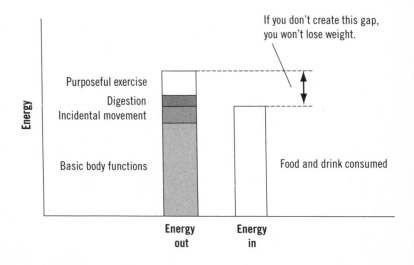

Before we move on, spend a moment looking at the graph (even if you hate graphs). Flip back to it as we proceed and as I discuss each component part. That graph is the crux of this book. It shows the four main ways the body uses energy: to fuel basic body functions, incidental movement, digestion and any extra 'purposeful' exercise you perform. Energy is ingested by eating food and drinking. If energy in is smaller than energy out, you create a gap that must be met from the body's existing stores of energy. Once you have this framework in your head, you'll have a template for life to guide you as you go about making choices to balance your eating and exercise habits. (And remember, they are choices.)

ENERGY MEASUREMENTS

Energy is measured in calories and kilojoules. While dollars are the unit of measurement for Australia's economy, calories and kilojoules are the units of measurement you need to be familiar with to lose weight.

Calories

One calorie is the amount of energy needed to raise the temperature of 1 kilogram of water by 1 degree Celsius. Scientists measure the calorie content of food by putting it in a machine called a bomb calorimeter. By incinerating food and measuring how much heat it gives off, they are able to calculate its energy content. When Wilbur Atwater performed these experiments in the late 1800s and designed his system of calorie counting, he found out that fat gives off more energy than carbohydrate and protein. Because we can measure calories only indirectly, calorie counts on food labels are always a best guess, but they provide a good guide.

Kilocalories

Most of the labels and literature you read discussing calories (including the definition I've just given above) are actually referring to *kilocalories*. Strictly speaking, 1 calorie raises only 1 *gram* of water by 1 degree Celsius, so to raise 1 *kilogram* by 1 degree you need 1000 of these calories: a kilocalorie. But in common usage the word kilocalorie has been replaced by the word calorie. Forget about kilocalories. If you see the word, it probably means what you think calories are. Sometimes the two types of calories are distinguished by calling them small calories and large calories, but in this book I use calorie to mean the same as kilocalorie. Confused? Don't be.

Kilojoules

I'm aware that some of you may be wanting to throw something at me, yelling, 'For goodness sake, woman, in Australia we eat *kilojoules*!' Indeed, all official information and food labelling in Australia is displayed in kilojoules. But in the United States, which is the centre of a lot of weight-loss research, information, food labels and gadgetry (gym machines will usually give calorie counts) has been developed using calories. I really wish Australia had decided to go with calories for its labelling. I think there would be a benefit to consumers in harmonising the measurements used.

I also prefer calories because it's easier to work with smaller numbers. There are 4.18 kilojoules to every calorie, which means if you count kilojoules you inevitably have to deal with bigger numbers. It's one thing to add up to 2000 (a typical daily calorie requirement); it's quite another to add up to 8700 (a typical daily kilojoule requirement).

Believe me; I agonised long and hard about which unit to use in this book. In the end, because I always work in calories, that's what I have used. You can easily convert any calorie measurements I give to kilojoules by multiplying the calorie amount by 4.18. Realistically, if you're serious about losing weight, you need to know how to count both calories and kilojoules. Sorry. I never said this would be easy, only that it would work.

The four types of 'energy out'

In chapter 7, I'll give you my tips on the 'energy in' side of the equation: how to make better food choices to maximise food enjoyment and nutrition while minimising calories consumed. For now I want to focus on the 'energy out' side. You need to know this first before you can decide how much energy to put in. There are four major components of energy use in the human body. It's time to discuss each, in turn, and start calculating your daily calorie burn. It's time to find your bottom line.

BASIC BODY FUNCTIONS

I realise I've loaded you up with a lot of bad news so far—there's no quick fix, losing weight is hard . . . yadda yadda. So, finally some good news. You're supposed to eat! This might sound dumb initially, but it strikes me as marvellously good news. When you're overweight, you see food as the enemy. You feel bad for eating. You know you're supposed to eat less, but surely you can't be expected to stop eating altogether, right? Yes, you're right. The body needs food. People who don't eat die.

That is because in every second of every day your body uses energy. Even if you lay perfectly still all day you would still be using energy—quite a lot, actually. Your body needs energy to breathe, blink, pump your heart, regenerate skin cells, even grow eyelashes. With every breath, every blink and every heartbeat, you are consuming calories. Indeed, for most of us (triathletes aside), most of the energy we require each day goes towards powering these basic functions.

In 1912 two American scientists, James Harris and Francis Benedict, came up with a way to calculate our approximate energy needs for when we are resting, which is called our basal metabolic rate. (Basal whatsamajiggy?) A person's basal metabolic rate is an estimate of how many calories a person would burn if they just lay completely still in bed all day. In truth, it can only ever be an estimate. Studies have found there is large variability in people's resting energy expenditures even if they are the same sex, height, weight, age and body composition. And that variability can be as big as 250 calories a day. More muscly people have a higher basal metabolic rate because lean muscle tissue uses a lot of energy.

But if you want to know how much to eat, you've got to start somewhere. And that somewhere is your basal metabolic rate. There are any number of online calculators, based on the Harris-Benedict equation, that will let you input your height, weight, age and sex to arrive at a basal metabolic rate estimate. Opposite are a couple of charts you can also check yourself against—one for the boys and one for the girls.

What should be immediately obvious from these charts is the wide variance between people in their daily resting calorie requirement. That requirement increases with height and weight. If you take two people of the same height but different weights, the lighter person will have a lower basal metabolic rate. The same individual can, at different stages of their life, also have a different basal metabolic rate depending on their weight. For example, a 40-year-old, 180-centimetre man who starts his weight-loss journey at 110 kilograms begins with a base energy requirement of 2210 calories. By the time he has dropped to 90 kilograms, that base requirement will have dropped to 1935 calories—he will need to eat almost 300 calories fewer a day. Because his body is smaller after weight loss, there is less stress on it, and it takes less energy to power the basic body functions.

Good news for young people

If you are 30, you can add an extra 50 calories a day to the figures shown in the charts. Twenty year olds, you lucky

BASAL METABOLIC RATE, OR BASE NUMBER OF CALORIES NEEDED EACH DAY, FOR A 40-YEAR-OLD MAN

HEIGHT (CM)	WEIGHT (KG)							
	60	70	80	90	100	110	120	130
155	1397	1534	1672	1809	1947	2084	2222	2359
160	1422	1559	1697	1834	1972	2109	2247	2385
165	1447	1584	1722	1859	1997	2134	2272	2410
170	1472	1609	1747	1884	2022	2160	2297	2435
175	1497	1634	1772	1909	2047	2185	2322	2460
180	1522	1659	1797	1935	2072	2210	2347	2485
185	1547	1684	1822	1960	2097	2235	2372	2510
190	1572	1710	1847	1985	2122	2260	2397	2535
195	1597	1735	1872	2010	2147	2285	2422	2560

BASAL METABOLIC RATE, OR BASE NUMBER OF CALORIES NEEDED EACH DAY, FOR A 40-YEAR-OLD WOMAN

HEIGHT (CM)	WEIGHT (KG)							
	50	60	70	80	90	100	110	120
145	1214	1310	1406	1501	1597	1693	1788	1884
150	1224	1319	1415	1511	1606	1702	1797	1893
155	1233	1329	1424	1520	1615	1711	1807	1902
160	1242	1338	1433	1529	1625	1720	1816	1912
165	1251	1347	1443	1538	1634	1730	1825	1921
170	1261	1356	1452	1548	1643	1739	1834	1930
175	1270	1366	1461	1557	1652	1748	1844	1939
180	1279	1375	1470	1566	1662	1757	1853	1949
185	1288	1384	1480	1575	1671	1767	1862	1958

devils, you can add an extra 100 calories. But how can I break this to you 50 year olds? You need to lop off about 50 calories from these figures. And 60 year olds? You need to take off about 100 calories. Age is a cruel mistress. She strips you not only of your youth, but of your food allowance. That's why so many of us gain weight with age. Our body slows down, but our appetite doesn't.

Bad news for short people

You get to eat less than tall people. Being the pint-sized bundle of joy that you are, it takes less energy for your body to move your mass around. Unfortunately for you, that means you have lower energy expenditure on basic body functions than your taller friends.

Bad news for women

You can't match your man forkful for forkful. In fact, even if you are the same height and weight as your man, you still have to eat about 200 calories less a day. This is because men have, on average, a higher muscle mass than women and muscle tissue is more metabolically active than fat. Women, by contrast, have evolved to store fat more easily so they can draw on it for breastfeeding. I'm as much of a feminist as anyone, but you can't fight nature on this one. I'm sorry. Ladies, eat less than your male dinner companions.

Good news for overweight or obese people

Having excess fat is like carrying around a set of dumbbells in your thighs. It takes more effort for your muscles to move you about the place, so your daily energy requirements are higher than someone who is skinnier than you. The bigger you are initially, the higher your basal metabolic rate. If you stick to the same diet as a thinner person, you will drop more weight, at least at first.

What about all the short, middle-aged women?

So short people need fewer calories than tall people. Husbands get to eat more than wives and young people get to eat more than older people. Tall young men, you've just hit the calorie jackpot!

If you're a short, middle-aged woman, however, you're probably feeling pretty jipped right now. You must eat less. Unfair? You betcha. But who told you life was fair? Perhaps when you get over the shock, you'll find some comfort in this news. It certainly helps to explain why there are so many middle-aged women who struggle with their weight. They're not imagining it; they have to eat less to avoid putting on weight than all those tall young men. If you keep eating the same size meals as your teenage boys, I guarantee you will put on weight.

But before you give up entirely, I have some good news up my sleeve: you can learn to make your calories go further by spending them on more satisfying, lower calorie foods. And you can earn more calories through exercise. We'll get to that.

STEP 1
Write your basal metabolic rate here: _____ calories

INCIDENTAL MOVEMENT

The sad—or happy, depending on your point of view—fact is that it's a rare day when we're allowed to just lie in bed. Every day we get up, have a shower, make breakfast, go to work, go to the toilet a few times, have lunch, travel back from work, make dinner and generally shuffle around a bit. As we discussed in chapter 1, we're all doing a whole lot less of this incidental sort of activity than our ancestors did. Some people do more than others, depending on their jobs. Bricklayers, for instance, will burn more calories in a day than desk workers. It's actually pretty hard to know how much energy you are burning with this incidental movement. As a rough guide, Harris and Benedict (why do I suddenly fancy some hollandaise sauce?) also came up with a formula for estimating the impact of this incidental movement on your daily calorie burn. The trick is to multiply your basal metabolic rate by an activity loading from the table opposite.

Before you estimate your activity level, you should know that most people dramatically overestimate how much activity they do each day and underestimate how much time they spend sitting. I catch a train to work and sit at my desk most days, so I choose to take the base loading for 'sedentary' as my usual loading. It's rare for me to be up on my feet for most of the day. Be honest with yourself. It's better to be a bit conservative and surprise yourself with more rapid than expected weight loss than to overestimate how active you are and then be disappointed later on.

INCIDENTAL MOVEMENT LOADINGS

ACTIVITY LEVEL	DESCRIPTION	INCIDENTAL MOVEMENT LOADING
Sedentary	You get little to no exercise (desk job)	Your BMR × 0.200
Light active	You exercise lightly (1 to 3 days a week)	Your BMR × 0.375
Moderately active	You exercise moderately (3 to 5 days a week)	Your BMR × 0.550
Very active	You exercise heavily (6 to 7 days a week)	Your BMR × 0.725
Extra active	Very hard exercise every day or physical job	Your BMR × 0.900

I also like to choose 'sedentary' because I calculate my exercise separately. If you play sports six to seven times a week, feel free to choose 'very active' here. But don't double count when we get to purposeful exercise. If in doubt, go 'sedentary'. Multiply your basal metabolic rate by 0.2 and record it below.

STEP 2
Write your incidental movement here: _____ calories

DIGESTION

Studies have shown that eating boosts your metabolism for several hours after each meal; that is, the body gives off heat and is using energy to digest the food you have taken on board. It makes sense, once you remember all that work your body has to do to sort digestible macronutrients from non-digestible fibre, break down the macronutrients and send them off to rebuild cells and organs.

The energy expended through this digestive process can vary from person to person and is thought to be equivalent to between 7 and 14 per cent of the calories consumed. Let's split that down the middle and say 10 per cent. So if you eat 2000 calories in a day, you can expect to burn around 200 calories a day just in digestion. This is called the thermogenic effect of food, or diet-induced thermogenesis.

The effect can vary in size depending on the food eaten. For example, the body requires more energy to digest protein than carbohydrate and, in turn, requires more energy to digest carbohydrate than fat. (So, not only is fat more calorific than the other macronutrients and less satiating, it also requires less energy to digest: three good reasons to avoid excess consumption.)

It will be up to you to decide for yourself how much to eat to meet your weight-loss goals. But assuming you will probably be eating between 1500 and 2000 calories a day, you could expect to burn between 150 and 200 calories a day through digestion. If in doubt, just pop in 150 calories for digestion (again, it's better to underestimate than overestimate).

STEP 3
Write your digestion burn here: _____ calories

PURPOSEFUL EXERCISE

By now you've probably got a pretty good idea of how many calories you burn on days when you do no additional, or what I call purposeful, exercise—gym sessions or sports matches you go out of your way to do. This daily calorie allowance comprises your basal metabolic rate (Step 1), calories burnt through incidental activity (Step 2) and calories burnt through digestion (Step 3). You may be shocked at how small it is. Particularly when you think that one BBQ Meatlover's pizza has around 1600 calories—an entire day's calories for many. (See chapter 7 for more shocking calorie counts.)

The good news is that you can increase your daily calorie allowance by doing extra chores—i.e. additional exercise. You can't include anything here that you have already factored into your incidental activity in Step 2 above. That would be double counting. But if you're up for it, you can really turbo-charge your weight loss and calorie burn with some extra exercise sessions. But you need to know what type of exercise will give you the biggest calorie bang for your buck.

Well, prepare to be shocked again. All those hour-long walks you're doing to lose weight? Look at the following chart and see how far they're getting you in the energy usage stakes.

The most striking thing I find about this table is the difference between walking and running for calorie burning. Even a fairly slow jog at about 8 kilometres per hour will burn twice the calories of a fast walk at 5.5 kilometres per hour. Run, don't

CALORIES BURNT DURING ONE HOUR OF EXERCISE

	FEMALE 40 YEARS, 165 CM		MALE 40 YEARS, 175 CM	
	60 KG	80 KG	80 KG	100 KG
Basketball	387	602	522	706
Bicycling: gentle	387	602	522	706
Bicycling: vigorous	645	1003	870	1177
Bushwalking	387	602	522	706
Dancing: nightclub	290	451	391	530
Fishing	193	301	261	353
Frisbee	193	301	261	353
Golf	277	431	374	506
Kayaking	322	501	435	588
Lawn bowling	213	331	287	388
Martial arts	664	1033	896	1212
Paddleboarding	387	602	522	706
Pilates	245	381	331	447
Rock climbing	516	802	696	941
Running/jogging	516	802	696	941
Rugby	535	832	722	977
Rollerskating	451	702	609	824
Skateboarding	322	501	435	588
Skiing	451	702	609	824
Snorkelling	322	501	435	588
Soccer	451	702	609	824
Surfing	193	301	261	353
Swimming	451	702	609	824
Table tennis	258	401	348	471
Tennis	451	702	609	824
Touch football	516	802	696	941
Volleyball	516	802	696	941
Walking: gentle	226	351	304	412
Walking: vigorous	245	381	331	447
Walking the dog	193	301	261	353
Weight lifting	193	301	261	353
Yoga	161	251	217	294

Note: Actual calories burnt will vary depending on individual exertion level, age, sex, height and weight. For individualised results, go to www.8700.com.au, or download the NSW government's '8700' smartphone app, and enter your details into the 'How to burn your kJs' calculator. There is also a kilojoules to calories converter.

Source: www.8700.com.au

walk! For those with injuries, water aerobics, swimming or the stair treadmill will also burn more calories than a simple walk. Another surprise, perhaps, is that heavier people burn more calories performing all exercise activities than leaner people. Again, a heavy body has to work harder than a lean body to carry its weight through whatever activity it is doing. There's a reason why you feel more tired and out of breath than your leaner friends: you're working harder.

When we get to chapter 8, I will spill the beans on all the ways I have found to exercise effectively and measure calories expended. You're going to meet a gadget that has changed my life—the heart rate monitor. For around $100 you can buy a watch and chest strap that will take all the guesswork out of exercise, telling you exactly how many calories you are burning in a session. You can learn what exercises really push you to your limits and which are less effective. I refuse to exercise without mine.

If you decide to use a heart rate monitor you will be able to include a very precise estimate of your purposeful exercise burn. If not, use the table on the opposite page to estimate the final component of your bottom line.

STEP 4
Write your purposeful exercise burn here: _____ calories

YOUR BOTTOM LINE

So, that's it. Taken together, these four types of energy use add up to your daily calorie burn. For example, this is what a typical day with no exercise looks like for me:

JESS'S DAILY CALORIE BURN

STEP	ENERGY USE	CALORIES BURNT
1	Basal metabolic rate (for a 179 cm, 72 kg, 32-year-old female)	1525
2	Incidental movement loading (sedentary): 1525 × 0.200	305
3	Digestion (based on intake of 2000 calories)	200
4	Purposeful exercise	0
	Total daily energy use	2030

Go on, fill in yours:

YOUR DAILY CALORIE BURN

STEP	ENERGY USE	CALORIES BURNT
1	Basal metabolic rate (for a _____ cm, _____ kg, ____-year-old _____)	____
2	Incidental movement loading (_____): ____ × ____	____
3	Digestion (based on intake of _____ calories)	____
4	Purposeful exercise	____
	Total daily energy use	____

Note: If in doubt, use my loadings for steps 2, 3 and 4.

At the very least, you should be aiming to consume no more than this amount of calories on average each day. Consume less and, over time, you will lose weight. That's the real bottom line.

Measurement issues

Of course, this is an estimate. The only reliable way to measure your daily calorie burn is to observe over time the food intake you can ingest without putting on weight. But doing the above calculation is a pretty good starting point. It will get you thinking about your body and how many calories it needs. You will be able to hone your calculation over time. For example, if you consistently put on weight eating a certain number of calories, it's possible you have overestimated your daily calorie burn. You can always go back and make a more conservative estimate. The proof, as they say, is in the eating.

Scientists have developed more precise ways of measuring your number, if you're up for it. They can lock you in a sealed room, pump it with fresh air and measure oxygen consumed and carbon dioxide produced. These 'whole room calorimeters' can measure a person's energy use with 1–2 per cent precision. If you want to know the calorie content of your food, you can let scientists feed you and then collect and measure your poo. Or you could just use my method!

Speaking of poo, have you ever wondered whether all the calories you ingest are actually absorbed? How many calories get flushed away? Maybe you're fat because you absorb more of the calories from the food you eat than other people? Maybe.

According to the American Society for Nutrition's consensus panel, the amount of calories a person absorbs from their food can vary. 'The net absorption of dietary energy components varies among individuals and is dependent on the specific foods eaten, how they are prepared, and intestinal factors.' On average, between 2 and 10 per cent of the calories people consume end up in the toilet.

So, yes, you may be pooing out some of your calories, but only about 5 per cent. And while it is possible some lucky people just happen to absorb less of their calories, this effect can only be small.

It's important to be aware that individual results can vary and our measurements are imprecise. According to Hall and his colleagues writing in *The Lancet*:

❝ The uncertainty of the baseline energy requirements translates to an expected inter-individual variability of weight loss, even if adherence to the prescribed diet is perfect. This is a fundamental limitation on our ability to precisely calculate the predicted bodyweight time course of an individual. **❞**

But that doesn't change the fact that every day your body has a certain energy requirement and you need to try to match it, or be under it, as best you can. Don't get downhearted if you don't see the results you initially expected. It is precisely because our methods for measuring your daily calorie allowance are less than perfect that you have to be patient. Keep at it, make necessary adjustments to your calculations and you will see results over time.

You should also be aware that there are feedback loops in the equation. Reducing energy in (eating less) affects some of the components of energy out, including energy burnt in digestion and incidental movement. If you reduce your calories too far you may feel lethargic and move less, burning fewer calories through incidental activity. Similarly, if you spend all day at the gym doing purposeful exercise, you may compensate by spending the rest of the week on the couch. It's a delicate balancing act which we'll consider more fully in part 3 of this book.

So, sure, there are measurement issues here. So too with gross domestic product—our main measure of economic growth. Does that mean we don't bother measuring economic output? No. We just know that it's an approximation—our best guess.

I've shown you the fundamental principles of how much energy your body needs. Now it's time to apply them to set your own goals for weight loss and build your own body budget. It's time to unleash your inner bookkeeper.

6

How to build your body budget

Every household has a person who takes care of the bills, every company has a chief financial officer and every government has a treasurer. Your body is crying out for a responsible bookkeeper too. You need to manage your body like you do your household budget, keeping a careful track of incomings and outgoings.

In chapter 5 we arrived at an estimate of your body's typical daily energy burn. You can think of this as your daily calorie allowance. If you're aiming for weight maintenance, this is the number of calories you get to consume guilt free each day without blowing your body budget. But if you go over your daily allowance, by consuming more calories than you expend, then the excess will be stored in your body as fat.

There are two ways you can start creating the calorie deficits you need to lose weight. First, you can reduce your calorie spending on food and drink and bring your intake to below your daily allowance. When you create a calorie gap like this, you force your body to start working off its accumulated fat storage to access the energy it needs. Second, you can stick to your daily food calorie allowance while doing extra chores—that is, purposeful exercise. If you do this and don't eat more to compensate, you will also create a calorie deficit and, hey presto! Bye bye, bottom. If you're really serious about it, you can do both—reduce your daily calorie intake and increase your calorie expenditure. Either way, you're going to need to learn how to keep track of your body budget.

One day at a time

Take it from me: there is no better feeling than going to bed at night knowing you have done everything within your power that day to lose weight and set yourself up for a healthier and happier future. You can have that feeling too, starting tomorrow if you like. Think of it this way. Every day you get a fresh sheet of paper to record your calories in and your calories out. And each day that you keep the number of calories coming in below the number of calories going out, you can go to bed knowing that your amazing body will start eating up your fat to get the energy it needs. All while you're asleep. Amazing. So here it is: your fresh sheet of paper. Feel free to photocopy the following page. It's your daily body budget. I want you to fill out a new one each day.

YOUR DAILY BODY BUDGET

DATE: _____	WEIGHT: _____

Energy in	
Breakfast	_____ cal
Lunch	_____ cal
Dinner	_____ cal
Snacks	_____ cal
Total energy in today	_____ cal

Energy out	
Basal metabolic rate	_____ cal
Incidental movement	_____ cal
Digestion	_____ cal
Purposeful exercise	_____ cal
Total energy out today	_____ cal

Today's energy balance (energy in *minus* energy out):	_____ cal

The aim of the body budget game is to produce a negative energy balance. You could do this, for example, by eating 2000 calories and burning 2500 calories in 'energy out'. The day's energy balance in that case would be –500. Success!

By now you should have a pretty good idea of how to fill in the 'energy out' part of your body budget. You may, however, be furrowing your brow at the 'energy in' part. How many calories did you consume today? No idea? Well, I reckon that might be a large part of your problem. We'll get it sorted in chapter 7. There are amazing new online counters and smart phone apps that can help you easily and quickly record your food and get an estimate of calories. There are even iPhone apps where you can take a picture of your food and get an immediate estimate of its calorie content.

Not a numbers person? Don't worry. I promise you won't have to count calories forever. But I'm convinced you do need to do it for a period of time to recalibrate your brain. You need to make time to stop and learn about what is in the food you're eating. The discoveries you make will stick with you for life. (Did you know there are about 165 calories in every 20 ml tablespoon of olive oil? More revelations in chapter 7.) Fill out a daily body budget for a while, and you'll start to make better decisions even when you're not counting calories religiously. And if you do binge, or if life goes off the rails generally for a while, you know you can always come back to the template. Pull out your body budget and get back on track. A large part of the success of people who lose weight and keep it off is having an action plan for when they go off the rails. This is your action plan. It will be there whenever you need it.

How do you lose 1 kilogram?

This is where things get really interesting. And contentious (as we'll see in chapter 9). We know that to lose weight you need to create an energy gap. But how big does that gap need to be before you start to see real results? I am so incredibly glad you asked.

Authorities in the United States have traditionally stated that for every 3500 calories you cut out of your diet you will lose 1 pound of body weight (or a 7700-calorie deficit to lose 1 kilogram). If you're a dedicated dieter, chances are you've heard this before. The 3500-calorie rule originated in a 1958 paper authored by researcher Max Wishnofsky. The number 3500 was his best guess of the number of calories stored in 1 pound of body weight and was based on several real-life studies which induced specific calorie restrictions in obese patients and measured how much weight they lost. Roughly, participants who experienced an energy deficit of 500 calories a day for seven days were found to lose 1 pound in body weight.

As we will see in chapter 9, where I'll introduce you to the advanced course in weight loss, there are some problems with the common application of this rule in terms of the time it takes for weight loss to be achieved. However, it gives us a useful—and for an overweight person a fairly accurate—starting point for the size of the cumulative calorie deficit you need to create to achieve your goal weight.

How do I know? Because I did it. From 1 January to 14 May 2013 I did exactly what I'm suggesting you do. I kept track each day of my calories eaten and calories burnt. I managed to create an average daily energy deficit of 250 calories. Over the eighteen weeks, I accumulated a total energy deficit of 31,000 calories. And guess what? I lost 4.8 kilograms—pretty close to what the Wishnofsky's equation predicted (31,000 divided by 7700 to predict a 4-kilogram weight loss). Turns out I had underestimated my daily calorie requirement slightly because I had failed to take into account calories burnt through digestion. This meant that I actually opened up a bigger calorie deficit than I had calculated and perhaps explains the slightly bigger than predicted loss. But as a rough rule of thumb, it appears that the 7700 calories per kilogram of body weight rule works. Once you build a cumulative calorie deficit of about 7700 calories you will have lost about 1 kilogram. What are you waiting for? Let's get cracking!

To get an idea of your own cumulative calorie deficit, you can start your own spreadsheet like I did, or transfer your daily results into the following table.

YOUR WEEKLY BODY BUDGET

DAY	ENERGY IN	− ENERGY OUT	= ENERGY BALANCE
1			
2			
3			
4			
5			
6			
7			
Total			

Add your daily energy balances to get your weekly energy
balance. If, like me, you managed to create a daily energy
balance of −250 calories, your cumulative energy balance
over seven days would be −1750. A weekly energy balance
like that could be expected to produce 1 kilogram of weight
loss every month (7700 ÷ 1750 = 4.4 weeks).

Remember, individual results will vary depending on
the exact mix of fat, muscle and water mass lost. Stick with
it and remember: the trend is your friend.

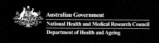

Australian Guide to **Healthy** Eating

Enjoy a wide variety of nutritious foods
from these five food groups every day.

Drink plenty of water.

Grain (cereal) foods,
mostly wholegrain
and/or high cereal
fibre varieties

Vegetables and
legumes/beans

Fruit

Lean meats and
poultry, fish, eggs,
tofu, nuts and seeds
and legumes/beans

Milk, yoghurt, cheese and/or
alternatives, mostly reduced fat

Use small amounts

Only sometimes and in small amounts

100 calories =
2 heads broccoli (550 g)

100 calories = ¼ of a large
(300 g, with stone) avocado

100 calories =
400 g strawberries

100 calories =
200 g blueberries

100 calories = 1 medium (16 cm)
banana (170 g) OR 1 large apple
(220 g)

100 calories =
½ cup baked beans (120 g)

100 calories =
½ cup cooked pasta (75 g)

100 calories =
1 thick slice wholemeal bread (45 g)

100 calories = 1.2 slices of tasty
cheddar cheese (25 g)

100 calories = 100 g raw skinless
chicken OR 65 g raw lean beef

100 calories = 125 g cooked
shelled prawns

100 calories = 50 g raw skinless
salmon OR 110 g raw white fish

100 calories =
1.5 medium (50 g) eggs

100 calories =
1 Tim Tam (original)

100 calories =
9 cashew nuts (16 g)

100 calories = 133 ml red or white
wine OR 46 ml whisky OR 265 ml beer

100 calories = 12 ml olive oil OR 75 g
tomato sauce OR 75 ml soy sauce

100 calories = 250 ml no fat milk
OR 200 ml low fat milk
OR 150 ml full fat milk

Setting your goal for weight loss

So you're all set with the paperwork. Time to decide on a goal.

JESS'S WEIGHT-LOSS GOAL
When I decided to lose weight using the body budget approach, I had a goal in mind.

Goal
I wanted to drop 10 kilograms in roughly eighteen weeks.

Calculations
If a 1-kilogram loss requires a deficit of 7700 calories, a 10-kilogram loss would require a deficit of 77,000 calories. I divided the 77,000-calorie deficit goal by the eighteen weeks, finding that I would need to aim for a daily deficit of around 600 calories. I had three choices on how to achieve the required daily deficit. First, I could simply eat 600 calories less than my daily energy allowance. Second, I could do an extra 600 calories of purposeful exercise a day. Or, I could use a combination of diet restriction and purposeful exercise. I decided to go for the latter. I set out to create a 300-calorie gap between my food intake and my base calorie requirement (excluding purposeful exercise) and to burn an average of 300 calories extra a day in purposeful exercise.

Result
At the end of the eighteen weeks I had met my target for exercise, but I ended up struggling to restrict my diet as much as I intended. As a result, my average daily deficit was only about 250 calories instead of my aim of 600 calories.

YOUR WEIGHT-LOSS GOAL

Goal
I want to drop _____ kilograms in _____ weeks.

Calculations
If a 1-kilogram loss requires a deficit of 7700 calories,
a ___kilogram loss will require a cumulative deficit of
_____ calories.

Cumulative calorie deficit required: _____
÷ days in which I want to lose the weight: _____
= a daily required deficit of _____ .

In deciding your own goal for weight loss, you must decide how you want to do it: through diet or exercise, or both? Many diet programs tell you to restrict energy in to 1200 calories a day for women and about 1500 calories for men. Please do not attempt to get by on anything less than these amounts. This isn't a race. The most important thing is that you make changes that can be sustained over many months and, eventually, for the rest of your life. You will be hungry on very low calories, and the hunger monster is hard to beat.

If you can stick to a very low-calorie diet, it will be dreadfully effective, in the short term at least. And there are immediate health benefits to rapid weight loss. But given my personal experience and the research I have done about how the body fights back against weight loss, I reckon there's a limit to how long you can keep up such a restrictive diet. You might try a low-calorie diet first, but ultimately choose to eat your full daily allowance and then create your deficit entirely through exercise.

If you are injured and cannot exercise, do not despair. You can still create a calorie deficit by restricting your food intake. It may take more self discipline and it may take longer, but it is absolutely still possible for you to lose weight.

It's up to you. You can play with the equation. It's your body; you don't need a permit to use it or to experiment with it to find out what works. You can decide how much to eat and how much to exercise, and determine the pace of your weight loss. There seems to be agreement that you can safely lose between 0.5 kilograms and 1 kilogram a week. Even that, I think, is pretty fast.

If you're up for it, I think it pays to set an ambitious goal at first. Why not start by aiming for a daily deficit of 500 calories? That would suggest a weight loss of around 0.5 kilograms a week. If life gets in the way, you can always relax your time frame a little. The aim is to balance your budget, on average, over the cycle. Realise there will be some weeks you'll be really into it and some when other things will distract you. The trick is not to blow out completely on the bad days and undo the good. Slow and steady wins the race.

Weighing in on weighing in

I choose to weigh myself every day. If you're going to go to
all this trouble, you're going to want to measure your results.
For the very brave, there's always the option of tweeting your
weight. In 2010 a tech writer called Drew Magary hit the
headlines with his 'Public Humiliation Diet'. Magary lost 27
kilograms in five months by tweeting his weight every day
(and eating less and moving more, of course). But I sometimes
notice a subtle shift in my mood after weighing myself. There
is a temptation to regard a weight-loss day as a success and a
weight-gain day as a failure. Don't fall into the trap.

Be aware that your weight can fluctuate on a daily basis. According to Kevin Hall and his colleagues writing in *The American Journal of Clinical Nutrition*, 'Body weight over a day, and between days, fluctuates unrelated to changes in energy stores because of changes in hydration and alimentary tract [digestive system] content, which are the primary contributors to the typical 1–2-lb day-to-day fluctuations in weight.'

The sting of failure can be a helpful motivator. But if you start to notice yourself having an excessively negative reaction to the scales every morning, scale it back. Weigh yourself every week instead. Don't leave it much longer though, or you'll miss out on the opportunity to fine-tune your diet and exercise regime and may need bigger remedial action later. Remember, it's the long run that counts. The trend is your friend. So accept your weight on any particular day as a data point and move on. Weighing in is worth doing, but beating yourself up about 100 grams here or there is definitely not.

The self-monitoring movement

Without my knowing it, my experiments with weight loss made me part of a worldwide movement of 'self-monitoring', which involves tracking indicators like exercise, food and even sleep in order to enable you to make better informed decisions about your health. According to a 2012 survey by the Pew Research Center, 60 per cent of Americans were tracking their weight, diet and exercise in some way. Half tracked it in their heads, one-third made notes on paper and about one-fifth used information technology. The study also found that one in five smartphone owners had downloaded a health app.

People living with a chronic illness like diabetes or heart disease are most likely to be tracking their health. But many do it just for their general health and to make well-informed decisions. Known as trackers (not trekkies, but closely related!), about half of the people surveyed as part of the Pew Research Center study agreed the information they had gleaned from their health tracking had changed the way they thought about their overall health, had led them to ask new questions of their doctor or had affected their health decisions.

Turns out there's a whole world of tools designed to help you track your energy expenditure and intake. There are pedometers and heart rate monitors that will sync to your bathroom scales and to smartphone apps that allow you to input your calories eaten and expended. Such gadgets are all the rage in the United States, but have yet to catch on in Australia. In the next two chapters, I'll mention a few of the major tools on the market. Turn to chapter 11 for review of my favourite weight-loss websites, gadgets and apps.

Some people have taken it even further. A movement called Quantified Self runs conferences and 'meet ups' around the world, including Australia, to share their self-monitoring results. Gary Wolf, a founder of the movement, puts it this way, 'If we want to act more effectively in the world, we have to get to know ourselves better.' I couldn't agree more.

It's exciting. Just as our need for more accurate information about our food and exercise has arisen, technology is helping us to obtain it. Technology may have led us to more sedentary lives, but it is also the weapon we need in the fight against the flab. Fitness geeks of the world, unite! You have nothing to lose but your love handles.

7

How to eat like an economist

How can I put this delicately? You are overweight because you eat too much. Sorry, probably failed on the delicate part there. But I say this from a place of love, understanding and experience. And I don't want to lie to you; to lose weight you're going to have to eat less. Or at least a lot less of the foods you're used to eating, and a lot more calorie-sparse foods like vegetables.

Mother Nature has given you a pretty strict calorie allowance to spend on food each day. But like any good mother, she's also trying to nudge you in the right direction by making nutritious foods low in calories so you can eat plenty of them. But it's up to you to learn how to spend your calories wisely, to make them go further to feel fuller for longer. You're probably shocked at how few calories you get to eat. But you'll be far more shocked when you see how many calories are in some of our most common foods.

CALORIE COUNTS THAT WILL SHOCK YOU

FOOD/DRINK	CALORIES	FOOD/DRINK	CALORIES
BBQ Meatlover's pizza, perfecto base	1600	Family block of milk chocolate	1325
McDonald's double Quarter Pounder burger	853	Six pack of beer (375 ml cans)	870
McDonald's Big Mac	493	A bottle of wine	560
McDonald's large fries	454	Meat pie	450
Hungry Jack's double Whopper with cheese	1025	Nachos with beans, sour cream and cheese	890
200 g packet of Shapes biscuits	980	Carbonara pasta	950
1 slice chocolate cake (200 g)	750	1 large bowl potato wedges	810
1 tablespoon peanut butter	120	Mi Goreng 2-minute noodles	390
Deep-fried fish and chips	930	Large packet of Doritos (230 g)	1195
Blueberry muffin	355	1 packet of Tim Tams (11 biscuits)	1050

Source: A Borushek, *Allan Borushek's Calorie, Fat & Carbohydrate Counter*, 2012; mcdonalds.com.au.

Hidden calories

STILL RECKON OILS AIN'T OILS?

If I could tell you only one thing about food, it would be this: there are 165 calories in every 20 ml tablespoon of cooking oil. I know what you're thinking: 'But olive oil is healthier, right?' Well, nutritionists will certainly steer you towards unsaturated oils like olive oil for heart health, but from a weight-loss point of view, every type of oil—including olive—has almost exactly the same amount of calories, including oil sold in bottles labelled 'light'. The 'light' just refers to a lighter colour or taste. It has exactly the same amount of calories as the others. Sneaky, huh? I'm not telling you not to eat oil, although I think you should minimise it in your diet. I am definitely warning you that takeaway and restaurant food is absolutely laced with the stuff.

Sugar too. An investigation by consumer group CHOICE in 2013 found that of 23 liquid breakfasts tested, ten contained more than 23 grams of sugar per serve—that's almost 6 teaspoons of sugar, about the same amount as in a chocolate bar. When it comes to pre-packaged food, it is wise to adopt a certain amount of paranoia.

Most of the devastation of weight gain arises from not understanding where it all came from. You think, But I haven't eaten that much! But if the food you eat is smothered in hidden calories then, yes, you did eat that much. Every day you walk into food traps that food retailers have set for you. Restaurants want you to keep coming back, so behind those kitchen doors they cover your food with oil, either deep-frying it or just being liberal with the liquid gold. Food manufacturing companies pump processed foods full of oil and sugar because they keep for longer on the shelves as a result, meaning more are sold before they go off.

Even at home, the way you cook your food matters. Chicken cooked with the skin on can have two to three times the calories of skinless chicken because the meat absorbs the fat as it cooks. For example, 100 grams of skinless chicken baked in your oven with no oil could have as few as 100 calories. A shop-bought barbecue chicken, on the other hand, will have at least 150 calories per 100 grams, and more if you eat the skin too.

Oil and sugar are the most common sources of hidden calories in our diets. Why? Because they make everything taste delicious! If something tastes delicious, it's probably because it's either soaked in oil or loaded with sugar. Every tablespoon is adding exorbitant amounts to your food calorie spending, and I'm here to tell you that you can't afford it.

MAYONNAISE WAS INVENTED BY THE DEVIL

I have met my enemy and it is mayonnaise. I love nothing better than a sandwich using soft bread with fried bacon and a liberal application of whole egg mayonnaise. I go weak at the knees for potato salad. But mayonnaise is one of the most calorific substances in the world. One tablespoon of whole egg mayonnaise packs a whopping 150 calories. It has about the same calories as a tablespoon of butter. Like I said, made by the devil.

By contrast, a mayonnaise that is 97 per cent fat free will set you back just 25 calories per tablespoon. Sure, it tastes like a distant cousin—twice removed—of the real thing. But for a calorie saving of 125, it might just be worth it. Or you could eat just one-sixth of a tablespoon of the good stuff. For me, I've gone cold turkey. I know my limits: I can't be trusted around mayonnaise.

BANANA BREAD IS NOT BREAD

Before I became calorie conscious, I often ate banana bread from my work canteen for breakfast. Toasted. With butter, please. Twenty-year-old Jess, if you can hear me, stop now. They're lying to you. Banana bread isn't bread. It's cake! You're eating cake for breakfast. The average slice of banana bread can hide about 500 calories. Don't fall for it like I did. Have two slices of bread instead (200 calories) with 2 teaspoons of butter (70 calories) if you must.

DRINKING YOUR CALORIES

It's no coincidence that fat people drink soda. Fizzy drinks are sugar-laden, calorie-dense, nutrition-free zones that you should avoid at all costs. Studies have shown that our bodies don't register the calories in them in the same way as they do food calories, and they don't reduce hunger. Processed fruit juice is little better, providing a few nutrients but a powerful hit of concentrated sugar. Eat an orange instead.

And trust me, alcohol is a dieter's worst friend. A 160 millilitre glass of wine contains around 120 calories. A stubbie or can of beer around 135 calories. Tastier than a tablespoon of oil, for sure, but almost as calorific. And, while one glass of wine may help you unwind from a stressful day, a bottle will set you back around 560 calories, not to mention making you want to eat a burger. And a pizza. And a big brekkie the next day. So a message to the big drinkers out there: drink less. Not only will it save you money up front, but, as you lose your tolerance for alcohol, it will be cheaper to get drunk in the future. Now you're beginning to think like an economist.

THE HEALTHY FOODS THAT ARE MAKING YOU FAT

Everyone has their own 'aha!' moments when it comes to the calorie content of their favourite foods. In addition to mayonnaise and banana bread, some of my other revelations have included the fact there's 180 calories in every slice of pepperoni pizza. Devour an entire pizza and, at more than 1500 calories, you've blown nearly a whole day's calorie allowance. And a medium portion of French fries will set you back around 400 calories—almost as much as a burger.

But it's not just the obvious foods that are blowing your budget. Nutritious foods are sometimes high in calories too. Nuts, for example, are an excellent source of protein and healthy fats, but there are 70 calories in just ten almonds, 100 calories in nine cashew nuts and 30 calories in each brazil nut.

Avocados, too, were sent to try us. Again, an excellent source of healthy fats, but high in calories. A large avocado contains around 400 calories. And beware the sushi roll. Traditionally seen as a healthier option, one sushi roll can contain around 350 calories. Salmon has twice the calories of white fish because of its oil content. Red meat—an excellent source of iron—has about double the amount of calories of white meats such as chicken and pork. And certain cuts are fattier than others. Here are some more facts about your food to get you started:

THE VEGETABLE SPECTRUM: CALORIES PER RAW CUP

VEGETABLE	CALORIES PER RAW CUP
Lettuce	8
Cucumber	16
Capsicum	30
Pumpkin	30
Broccoli	31
Tomato	32
Carrot	52
Sweet potato	114
Potato	116
Avocado	234

Source: USDA National Nutrient Database for Standard Reference, http://ndb.nal.usda.gov/.

THE MEAT SPECTRUM: CALORIES PER RAW 100 GRAMS

MEAT	CALORIES PER RAW 100 GRAMS
Prawns, without shell	85
Fish, white	90
Kangaroo fillet steak	100
Chicken breast, without skin	105
Goat	110
Pork loin medallion	120
Veal chop	120
Beef mince, heart smart	130
Beef, scotch fillet	145
Lamb mince	145

MEAT	CALORIES PER RAW 100 GRAMS
Fish, rainbow trout	150
Lamb loin chop	200
Fish, salmon	200
Beef mince, 10% fat	205
Pork sausage	235
Fish, white, battered	235
Beef sausage	260

Note: 100 grams of raw meat is approximately the size of a deck of cards.
Source: www.myfitnesspal.com.

MY FAVOURITE FOOD APP: MYFITNESSPAL

You've probably never heard of Michael Lee, though perhaps you've heard of MyFitnessPal, the calorie counter website and smartphone app he founded with his brother. In an interview with Rajiv Mehta of the Quantified Self website, he told the story of how he came to design it:

> In 2005 my wife and I wanted to lose weight before our wedding. We went to see a trainer at 24 Hour Fitness and he suggested that we count calories. He gave us a small book that had calorie counts for about 3000 foods in it, and told us to write down everything that we ate. Being a tech guy, there was no way I was going to do this on paper, so I immediately threw the book away and looked for an online solution. There were already tons of online calorie counters available— I had probably tried at least fifteen myself—but to my amazement, none of them worked the way I thought they should work. They were all incredibly hard to

use; I actually found it easier to track on paper than online. I was looking for a new project to work on, so I decided to write my own calorie counter—that's how MyFitnessPal was born.

In 2013 MyFitnessPal had more than 30 million registered users, 25 employees and a database of more than 2 million foods and drinks. If you use the app, it's like carrying a food dictionary and a food diary in your pocket. You can search for foods and choose from a list whichever one most closely matches your food. It works by having users adding to the database themselves. Often this leads to multiple and conflicting entries for the same food; you soon realise that there is wide variance in calorie counts even for similar foods. A takeaway Indian curry can top 1000 calories, while a homemade curry can have as few as 300.

Of course, you also need to have some idea of the quantity of the food you are about to eat. Most entries are in grams. Weighing out some foods at home with a kitchen scale can help until you get your eye in. 'The biggest benefit is education,' says Lee.

It's amazing how little most people know about what they eat or the activities they perform, and once they start using the app, it's eye-opening. They discover what they eat, how much, how often, the nutritional content of the food and the impact of physical activity. They build up a knowledge that stays with them even if they stop logging their food. With this knowledge they can make their own decisions about what to change in their lives, what trade-offs are best for them. It's not following some diet fad, but discovering what works for you.

How to eat like an economist

When it comes to eating, economics offers a few tips that can help you to make better decisions. According to the rational choice model in economics, humans make decisions that maximise their lifetime happiness. They do so with perfect information on all the costs and benefits of their actions, and after rationally considering all alternatives. Of course, real human beings fall woefully short of the rational choice mark. But we all have the capacity to make better choices about what food we put in our body to maximise our happiness in the long term. Here are my top ten tips for eating like an economist.

1. EAT WITH YOUR BRAIN, NOT YOUR EMOTIONS

Be aware that every mouthful is a choice. You can't choose not to eat, but you can choose what you eat. It's about finding what is right and sustainable for you. And you will fail to make better choices until you acknowledge that what you put in your body is, indeed, a choice. A choice made under difficult conditions and surrounded by temptations, sure. Your decisions are influenced by powerful hormonal and hunger signals. But you can—with effort—override them. Embrace hunger as a physical sensation and be aware of your emotional response to it. Ask yourself, What is the worst that can happen? It takes three minutes to die without air and it takes three days to die without water. But humans can, depending on their starting weight, survive three weeks without food. You are not going to die if you don't eat that biscuit.

The goal is to take the emotion out of your entire thinking about weight. Your excess weight is just the natural result of a fundamental energy imbalance. It's only numbers, and numbers don't care. Eating lots of calories doesn't make you a bad person. In fact, it makes you a very normal person—a person who is consuming more calories than they can burn in a day and is subsequently storing them as fat.

When I see a skinny person, I don't think (anymore), Gee whizz, that's unfair. I think, That person is not eating as much as I do. Or I see the hard work they've done to exercise and stay in shape. When I see an overweight person, I see someone who unknowingly eats too much. I also see a person who feeds their emotions with food. I see the person I used to be.

The first step to eating like an economist is to strip out all the emotion. If you eat more calories than you need on a certain day, you are not a failure. You are a person who has eaten more calories than they needed, either because you didn't know or because you couldn't help it. It's time to start helping it. It's time to eat to live, not to live to eat.

2. THINK AT THE MARGIN

Economists are a calculating bunch. They go about life constantly re-evaluating the potential costs and benefits of different courses of action. Most people who start a diet want to be given a strict set of rules to follow, like 'don't eat after 8 p.m.' or 'don't drink on weekdays'. But we're not very good at sticking to such arbitrary deadlines in the long term.

Turns out there's a little bit of the economist in all of us. As soon as we sense that there would be greater pleasure for us in sitting on the couch than in going to the gym, we ditch the arbitrary rule and opt for the pleasure. We are pleasure-seeking missiles. But what makes us happy can change, and quickly.

When it comes to food, you need to think at the margin—that is, consider the benefits and costs of every additional bite. With food indulgences, like cake, often the sweetest bite is the first. And while every bite has the same calorie count, there are diminishing returns from each additional bite, as you satiate the craving and then descend into guilt. At some point it becomes not worth it. You need to be conscious enough to know when that point is. Practise 'mindful eating' by not doing more than one thing while you eat. Eat more slowly. Chew more.

3. BE AWARE OF THE TRUE COST OF YOUR FOOD

According to a paper titled 'An economic framework for understanding physical activity and eating behaviors', written by John Cawley, an economist at Cornell University, a perfectly rational human being would make food decisions in the following way: 'Individuals will consume the foods within their budgets that provide the highest net benefit.' By 'net benefit' he means the total (or gross) benefits after subtracting any costs. 'Gross benefits include the momentary pleasure of taste plus any current and future health benefits. Gross costs include financial cost, discounted utility of any adverse health impact, and discounted utility of any resulting weight gain.' By 'discounted utility', he means the present value of any reduction in your future happiness—all that time you spend in front of the mirror feeling like you've got nothing to wear.

Humans are pretty good at sensing the instantaneous pleasure from food, but not so good at factoring in the losses from future ill health. If you eat a burger and it puts you over your daily calorie allowance, you must factor in the future costs of putting on weight. The costs of being overweight include the increased risk of heart disease and diabetes. These conditions can reduce your lifespan and also your out-of-pocket expenses if you need to spend money on drugs. Being overweight can also reduce your mental wellbeing if you worry about your appearance. Try to keep these costs in mind when you make your food decisions.

4. VIEW MONEY SPENT ON YOUR HEALTH AS AN INVESTMENT

Once you know the true cost of what you're eating, you may be prepared to spend more money on more nutritious, calorie-sparse foods. And given the research on how cheap some processed calories can be, it is entirely likely that to eat more healthily you will have to spend more on food. But remember, the health costs will catch you in the end if you don't.

See spending money on good food and exercise as an investment in your future, just like putting away money in a savings account. Don't view healthy food and exercise as burdens, but as gifts you give to your body. Spend on strawberries the money you would otherwise spend on getting a pair of jeans the next size up. Accept that you will need to forgo current pleasure in order to avoid future pain. This is a hard thing for humans. 'Individuals typically assign less importance to outcomes in the distant future than to those in the present,' Cawley says.

5. KEEP TO YOUR BUDGET

Remember that any pleasure you get from eating above your calorie allowance is only temporary—like going out to a store with a credit card and spending money you don't have. You might enjoy your purchase for a little while, but it's going to cause you pain when the bill arrives.

I find that writing a food diary is the only way to keep myself accountable and ward off calorie amnesia, in which I conveniently forget that I had that extra coffee or handful of nuts. If you also suffer from calorie amnesia, a food diary is your best bet. Usually when I can't be bothered or resent keeping track of my calories it's because I know, deep down, that I'm overeating. It's harder to lie to yourself on paper.

Try to find pleasurable things to do that don't involve food. Many of us eat because we're stressed or lonely. I get it. I've been there. Why can't I have just one snack to make me feel good? This is short-term thinking. In the long term that snack will only add to your unhappiness, catching you in a vicious cycle of weight gain and despondency. You need to break the cycle and start making investments in your future happiness.

Your goal must be to spend your limited calorie allowance on high-volume, filling, nutrient-dense foods. You have a strict budget to work with, and you must maximise its health and pleasure benefits. Ditch highly processed foods—you don't know what's in them. Learn to live within your calorie means first and then start paying more attention to the quality of your food decisions.

6. ACKNOWLEDGE THAT YOUR PREFERENCES ARE RELATIVELY FIXED

In an ideal world you would retrain your mind to love carrots more than chocolate. But this is one Jedi mind trick I haven't been able to pull off. What you *can* do is start sampling a wide variety of foods to see if you do like some that are nutritious and low in calories. Go to the fruit and vegetable section and buy everything you haven't tried. Stop eating the processed crap and your taste buds will adjust to enjoy the natural sugars in fruit.

But, ultimately, I think the human body is designed to crave fat and sugar. The best thing you can do is face up to this and realise you can eat what you want, but you must stay within the budget. Know also that there will be times when the benefit of eating delicious food will outweigh the negative effect of additional calories, such as birthdays and other special occasions. A cupcake won't make you put on a kilogram. And if you make it part of your daily allowance by forgoing something else, it can be guilt free. The most important thing is that you enjoy the calories when you consume them. No regrets. If you make the decision to eat the cupcake, enjoy the cupcake. The worst thing you could do is eat it, not enjoy it and then feel even worse. That is a lose–lose situation.

7. IGNORE SUNK COSTS

Don't eat everything in your pantry just because you bought it. You might think it's a waste, but the act of throwing out food may make you think twice about buying more than you need in the first place.

Humans are pretty good at ignoring some sunk costs, particularly when it comes to gym fees. Don't think that the act of buying a gym membership will be enough to keep you on the straight and narrow. It won't. We ignore sunk costs like gym fees when it suits us, but when it comes to food we insist on finishing everything on our plates.

Just because you bought it doesn't mean you should eat it. If you can't stand the waste, don't buy it next time.

8. WISE UP TO THE COMMERCIAL INCENTIVES OF PEOPLE WHO SELL YOU FOOD

Whenever I go out for a meal, I give myself an immediate 150-calorie penalty in anticipation of all the hidden calories. Even when something looks relatively healthy, you can be sure it has been smothered with delicious butter, oil or mayo.

There is what economists call a fundamental agency problem, or conflict of interests, when you eat out and someone else prepares your food. Their incentive is to sell you as much food as possible and keep you coming back. Your incentive is to eat nutritious, low-calorie food. There is an inevitable mismatch.

The solution is to try to prepare most of your meals yourself. As often as you can, cook at home, where you have control of the calories. I'm not much of a cook, but I have become a passable food assembler. I have learnt the basics of food and how much I need, and I go about assembling those foods with as few mixers, like condiments, spreads and oils, as possible. That's what cooking and preparing food should be about. It's not about smothering food with extra calories. Not every morsel you eat has to be the most delectable thing you're ever tasted. You're watching too much *MasterChef* if that's what you think. Try to eat like your grandma, not a master chef.

Another way to avoid the agency problem of people messing with your food is to eat whole foods. Try to eat your food in its natural form. Snack on fruit and vegetables and eat them whole—chopping only increases your time cost. Make your stomach do its job and burn more calories through digestion. There are better things you could be doing than chopping up fruit.

9.   MAKE REGULAR FOOD DEPOSITS

In theory, I don't care when you eat as long as you stick to your daily allowance. The number one rule is not to eat more calories than you need in a day, or to eat less than you need if you're aiming for weight loss. The template I've given you allows you the flexibility to change from day to day, week to week. But you should be striving to develop a new set of habits that do not require much thought.

I'm not a big fan of fasting. It would only lead to indecision on my part. When to fast? Which days? I make food an everyday habit, like taking a shower. Eating should recess into the background of your life, rather than being the centrepiece of it. I like to spread my calories out equally over the day. If I've given myself 1500 calories to spend, I'll split it up through the day so that I eat 400 calories for breakfast, lunch and dinner, which allows two snacks in between of 150 calories each.

10. REMEMBER, INFORMATION IS POWER

Finally, but most importantly, you need to educate yourself about what is in what you are putting in your mouth. Not everything you eat will come with a handy calorie label. But with information so increasingly freely available, it's getting harder to argue that you didn't know. Read labels. When in doubt, google it, or consult one of the many calorie-counting apps or websites that exist to help you.

Technology is revolutionising calorie counting. There are amazing online counters and smartphone apps that can help you easily and quickly record your food and get an estimate of calories. There are even apps that let you take a picture of your food and then give you an immediate estimate of its calorie content. It's so simple and easy to do; it doesn't have to take over your whole life.

Newton wasn't wrong, but he wasn't a nutrition expert, either

Don't be dumb. It's about how much you eat, but of course *what* you eat matters too. Your weight is only one measure of your health. Other measures are important, like nutrient sufficiency. Food is a vital source of essential micronutrients. There are vitamins and minerals that you need to live that your body can't generate, so you must ingest them. You must eat a diet full of vegetables and fruits of a variety of colours, plus leafy greens, lean meats and low-fat dairy. Eating these foods will give your body its best chance at health, according to nutritionist Joanna McMillan. McMillan also warns against getting too hung up on counting calories and forgetting the social aspects of eating. 'Calorie counting was what we did back when I was doing diets as a teenager. It was all about low-calorie diets. People become so completely obsessed with counting kilojoules that they lose sight of having a good relationship with food. I see so many women with body dysmorphia. They can't go out and enjoy a meal. Food is part of our family life, our social life, our culture. It's a form of communication. I do think it's good to have awareness of the energy content of food. But I don't personally advocate counting your calories. While the bottom line really is calories in and calories out, it also matters where those calories come from.'

In 2013 the Australian National Health and Medical Research Council released its latest guidelines, based on the most up-to-date scientific evidence about what and how we should be eating. Rule number one? Eat a diet that matches your energy needs. But there are other rules too:

AUSTRALIAN DIETARY GUIDELINES

1 To achieve and maintain a healthy weight, be physically active and choose amounts of nutritious food and drinks to meet your energy needs.
   - Children and adolescents should eat sufficient nutritious foods to grow and develop normally. They should be physically active every day and their growth should be checked regularly.
   - Older people should eat nutritious foods and keep physically active to help maintain muscle strength and a healthy weight.

2 Enjoy a wide variety of nutritious foods from these five food groups every day:
   - plenty of vegetables of different types and colours, and legumes/beans
   - fruit
   - grain (cereal) foods, mostly wholegrain and/or high cereal fibre varieties, such as breads, cereals, rice, pasta, noodles, polenta, couscous, oats, quinoa and barley
   - lean meats and poultry, fish, eggs, tofu, nuts and seeds, and legumes/beans
   - milk, yoghurt, cheese and/or their alternatives, mostly reduced fat.

   And drink plenty of water.

3 Limit intake of foods containing saturated fat, added salt, added sugars and alcohol.

a   Limit intake of foods high in saturated fat such as many biscuits, cakes, pastries, pies, processed meats, commercial burgers, pizza, fried foods, potato chips, crisps and other savoury snacks.

- Replace high-fat foods that contain predominately saturated fats, such as butter, cream, cooking margarine, coconut and palm oil, with foods that contain predominately polyunsaturated and monounsaturated fats, such as oils, spreads, nut butters/pastes and avocado.
- Low-fat diets are not suitable for children under the age of two years.

b   Limit intake of foods and drinks containing added salt.

- Read labels to choose lower-sodium options among similar foods.
- Do not add salt to foods in cooking or at the table.

c   Limit intake of foods and drinks containing added sugars, such as confectionary, sugar-sweetened soft drinks and cordials, fruit drinks, vitamin waters and energy and sports drinks.

d   If you choose to drink alcohol, limit intake. For women who are pregnant, planning a pregnancy or breastfeeding, not drinking alcohol is the safest option.

4   Encourage, support and promote breastfeeding.

5   Care for your food; prepare and store it safely.

Key performance indicators

Given that what you eat is important too, in the following table I've given you some key performance indicators—the number of recommended serves of each food group per day, with guideline serve sizes. These are based on the National Health and Medical Research Council's *Australian Dietary Guidelines* for men and women aged from 19 to 50 years. Every day you should be aiming to tick off the required number of serves of fruit, vegetables, grains, protein and dairy and you'll be on the right track for a nutritious diet.

Be aware that men are supposed to eat a half-serve of meat and dairy and a whole serve of vegetables more than women (lucky devils). Younger people need to eat a couple more serves of everything than indicated; older people a couple less. Find out more at www.eatforhealth.gov

In addition to proper nutrition, keeping properly hydrated is also important when trying to lose weight. Sometimes you eat when really you are just thirsty, so focusing on drinking plenty of water—eight glasses a day—will help you to stay on track with your eating.

Lack of sleep is also known to throw the body off whack, mess with your hunger signals and generally put you out of sorts. You need to give your body enough time to do all its maintenance and digging out of fat stores—you need to give it some downtime to do its work. Having trouble losing weight? You may need to hit the gym. Or you may need to hit the pillow.

YOUR KEY PERFORMANCE INDICATORS

	SERVES PER DAY	ONE SERVE	EXAMPLES OF ONE SERVE
Fruit		80 cal	1 apple, banana, orange or pear 2 small apricots, kiwis or plums 1 cup chopped or canned fruit
Vegetables		25–85 cal	½ cup cooked beans, legumes, green or orange vegetables 1 cup leafy vegetables or 1 medium tomato ½ medium potato or sweet potato
Grains		120 cal	1 slice bread, English muffin or crumpet ½ cup cooked rice, pasta, noodles or porridge
Protein		120–40 cal	65 g cooked beef, lamb, veal, pork or kangaroo 80 g cooked chicken or turkey 100 g cooked fish or 2 large eggs 1 cup legumes or beans or 170 g tofu
Dairy		120–40 cal	1 cup low-fat milk ¾ cup yoghurt or 2 slices cheese

Source: National Health and Medical Research Council, *Australian Dietary Guidelines*, 2013.

Can you be more specific, please?

The beauty of the Bottom Line Diet is that you really can eat anything you want, in moderation. Stick to your calorie goal for the day, and you're set. Some foods will make you feel fuller for longer, of course, like meat and beans. But it is entirely up to you what you decide to eat, once you are calorie aware. But I know it can be hard for beginners to know what to eat. To help you, I'll give you a peek at what I eat. A decade ago my cupboards were essentially bare—I subsisted on takeaway and restaurant food alone. But now I keep a few staples on hand.

IN MY FRIDGE
Eggs, tasty cheese slices, skim milk, haloumi, yoghurts, parmesan, olives, shaved turkey breast, carrots, zucchinis, broccoli, baby spinach in packets, strawberries, mint and basil.

IN MY FREEZER
Raspberries and blueberries (much cheaper than fresh), peas and corn, microwaveable fish fillets, wholegrain English muffins, individually wrapped chicken breasts and prawns.

IN MY PANTRY
Wholemeal bread, flatbread wraps (they come as low as 69 calories each), zesty wraps (for pizza bases), pasta, tins of salt-reduced diced or crushed tomato, canned tuna, cannellini beans, kidney beans, baked beans, peanut butter, spray oils, tomato sauce, soy sauce, potatoes, sweet potatoes, onions,

fresh garlic, chicken stock powder, curry powder and heaps of dried herbs.

IN MY FRUIT BOWL
Bananas, oranges, apples, lemons, limes, plus whatever is in season (mandarins, plums, peaches).

MY GO-TO MEALS
Breakfast
Eggs on toast (350 calories)
> 2 fried eggs (90 calories each or 70 if you poach them) on 2 slices wholemeal toast (100 calories each).

Quick oats with currants (358 calories)
> ½ cup quick oats (230 calories) and 10 grams currants (28 calories) microwaved in enough water to cover, served with 1 cup skim milk (100 calories).

Egg and cheese muffin (350 calories)
> 1 wholegrain English muffin (150 calories) with 1 slice tasty cheese slice (100 calories), 1 fried egg (90 calories) and 1 teaspoon tomato sauce.

Banana smoothie (305 calories)
> 1 banana (105 calories), ½ cup rolled oats (100 calories) and 1 cup skim milk (100 calories).

Lunch
Meat and salad sandwich (350 calories)
> 2 slices wholemeal bread (200 calories) or 1 brown bread roll, 1 serve meat (50 grams of turkey or chicken, 50 calories)

and as many salad ingredients as you can pack on there (tomato, roasted sweet potato, salad leaves, beetroot) plus a few sundried tomatoes, red onion or olives for flavour.

Turkey coleslaw wrap (320 calories)

1 low-calorie flatbread wrap (69 calories, available in the bread section), pre-mixed coleslaw from the salad section without the sauce (40 calories), 1 slice tasty cheese (100 calories), 100 grams fat-free sliced turkey (80 calories) and 10 grams dried cranberries (32 calories).

Vegetable soup (about 350 calories)

Chop up garlic, onion and fry. Add whatever vegetables you fancy. When soft, cover with water. Throw in beans (try four-bean mix in a tin) and a can or two of diced tomatoes. Add a cube of chicken stock. Simmer until it looks done.

Dinner

Fish and vegetables (300 calories)

Microwaveable frozen fish and frozen vegetables are your friends. The vegetables are snap frozen and just as nutritious as fresh. 1 cup of peas is 100 calories.

Meat and three vegetables (300 calories depending on meat)

Cook a 100-gram piece of meat (beef, lamb, pork, chicken) and steam as many vegetables as you can fit in a steamer. Really, it doesn't have to be that hard.

Vegetable pasta (300 calories)

Weigh out about 55 grams of dry pasta (equal to about 200 calories). Make a sauce with onion, garlic, a can of diced tomatoes and whatever vegetables you have in your fridge.

Stir-fry (300 calories) Weigh out a 200-calorie portion of any meat (around 250 grams of prawns or chicken or 130 grams of red meat). Throw in vegetables plus soy sauce and chilli.

Snacks

Banana (100 calories for a medium, 16 cm banana)

Apple (100 calories for a large apple)

Baked beans, mini can, salt reduced (140 calories)

Carrot (30 calories)

Strawberries, 250-gram punnet (63 calories)

Tasty cheese, 1 slice (85 calories)

Hot chocolate (100 calories for a cup of no-fat milk, 30 calories for 1 teaspoon hot chocolate powder)

Muesli bar, low sugar and low additives (150–200 calories)

TWENTY 'FOOD HACKS' YOU ABSOLUTELY MUST TRY

A 'life hack' is a techy term for any shortcut or trick that makes your life easier, like using your girlfriend's hair straighteners to iron your shirt collar or using old toilet paper rolls, cut down the side, to keep your Christmas wrapping paper rolls from unrolling. (You're welcome!) Throughout my journey of counting calories, I have also hit upon many tricks you can employ to drastically reduce your calories for little sacrifice of pleasure. I call them food hacks. Try them!

- Swap a glass of wine (120 calories) for a vodka and soda water (60 calories). *Save* 60 calories.

- Swap a glass of wine (120 calories) for sparkling water in a wine glass with a slice of fresh lemon or lime. *Save* 120 calories.

- Swap a full-fat milk latte (160 calories) for a skim latte (100 calories). *Save* 60 calories.

- Swap a skim latte (100 calories) for a skim piccolo latte (just 75 millilitres and 30 calories for the same coffee hit). *Save* 70 calories.

- Swap a skim piccolo (30 calories) for a green tea. *Save* 30 calories.

- Swap fruit juice for water. There's this amazing thing called water. It's pretty much free. It's good for you. It makes up about 70 per cent of your body weight and needs to be continually replenished. It's calorie free. Drink it. *Save* 110 calories on every glass of orange juice you swap for water.

- Swap coke for diet coke. *Save* 160 calories on every 375-millilitre can.

- Swap a Magnum ice-cream (283 calories) for a chocolate Paddle Pop ice-cream (79 calories). *Save* 204 calories.

- Swap a muesli bar (200 calories) for a banana (100 calories). *Save* 100 calories.

- Swap a chocolate bar (200 calories) for a cup of fat-free milk and hot chocolate powder (130 calories). *Save* 70 calories.

- Reverse your desserts. Swap chocolate cake with raspberries on top (400 calories) for a cup of raspberries (70 calories) with hot chocolate powder dusted on top (30 calories). *Save* 300 calories.

- Swap a tablespoon of sweet chilli sauce (40 calories) for little bit of fresh chopped chilli. *Save* 40 calories.
- Share your dessert with a friend. *Save* half the calories!
- Swap a full-fat cheese slice (85 calories) for a low-fat cheese slice (70 calories). *Save* 15 calories.
- Swap a tablespoon of whole egg mayonnaise (150 calories) for a tablespoon of low-fat mayonnaise (25 calories). *Save* 125 calories.
- Just say no to rice when you eat out. *Save* 250 calories per cup of cooked rice.
- Swap a side of fries for a side of broccoli. *Save* 300–400 calories, depending on size.
- Swap a tablespoon of barbecue sauce (40 calories) for a tablespoon of tomato sauce (25 calories). *Save* 15 calories.
- Swap a tablespoon of tomato sauce (25 calories) for a scraping of Dijon mustard (5 calories per 5 grams). *Save* 20 calories.
- Swap a sprinkling of parmesan on your pasta (40 calories) for fresh basil. *Save* 40 calories.

8

How to exercise
like an economist

I hate exercise. Sorry if you thought this was going to be a feel-good, 'exercise is awesome, I totally dig it, always want to do it and so should you' chapter. I would far rather pig out on the couch and watch television than go to the gym. I am that kid who always finished last on school sports day. For a long time, I was too scared to put my head underwater at swimming class. And diving? Don't get me started. There were tears.

I'm tall, though, so many people have, over the years, mistakenly assumed I'd be great at netball. I did once try out for my university netball team but never made it to the court because I couldn't keep up with the other girls running the kilometre or so to get there. Embarrassment has been the hallmark of my exercise career.

I blame my hatred of exercise on an excessive focus on competitive sports in school. I reckon we should just be focusing our kids on turning up. Rather than playing hockey or softball, or doing whatever particular torture the gym class teacher has dreamt up, I believe kids should be given the option to borrow a heart rate monitor and just run around the field at their own pace. They could soon figure out what level of activity is needed to get their heart rate up. We need to stop teaching kids that the point of physical activity is to win. The point of physical education should be to help kids form healthy habits they can stick with for the rest of their lives.

I spoke to a clinical exercise physiologist, William Sukala, who says he treats many obese patients who are still carrying the scars of school sports days. 'Some of those people are coming to you with a lot of baggage. Some people are in their fifties and they're still traumatised by what happened when they were ten years old.' The result is we spend most of our days sitting. And just as we underestimate our calorie intake, we also chronically overestimate the time we spend being active. 'People are notorious for underestimating how much time they spending sitting. People who are quite large spend more time sitting.'

We all hate exercise, right? So this is the point at which I unveil the miracle weight-loss secret for which you don't have to exercise.

Well, sorry, I can't. To lose weight and keep it off, you have to suck it up and get moving.

Technically, it is possible to lose weight just by eating less than your body needs. If you are injured and cannot exercise at all, eating less than your daily body allowance is the main option available to you. But as the science has shown, this is likely to induce a hunger reaction. The body fights back. Exercise can increase hunger in some people, but studies have also shown exercise can actually suppress appetite, at least in the short term. Humans are creatures of habit. We get used to eating a certain volume of food and find it hard to retrain ourselves to eat less. That is why creating an energy gap through exercise can be so effective. A major and ongoing study in the US conducted by James Hill and Rena Wing has shown that 90 per cent of people who successfully lose weight and keep it off do so through a combination of exercise and diet. And keeping it off is the important bit, which we'll learn about in the next chapter.

If you're like me and have never enjoyed or really done any exercise before, this can be a bit of an adjustment. If you're not a person who naturally enjoys getting all hot and sweaty, exercise will be a choice you have to make, weighing the pros and cons. On good days, I occasionally enjoy exercise. It's getting started that's my main problem. Like forgoing yummy food, choosing to exercise involves forgoing current pleasure (watching television) for future gain. Again, it's a decision to invest in your future wellbeing and not your current pleasure. It's hard to do.

The downside of exercise is that it takes considerable time and effort. Economists always like to think of the 'opportunity cost' of their actions—the cost of not doing something else you'd rather be doing. I can think of many other things I'd rather be doing than exercise, including, but not limited to, re-alphabetising my book collection. But I do make a conscious decision to exercise. Why? Because, ultimately, the pros outweigh the cons. So let me spell it out for you, if you need some convincing.

The benefits of exercise

The main benefit of exercise for weight loss is that it helps you build a calorie deficit much faster than you could by just restricting your calorie intake. The best way to burn calories is to get your heart rate up as high as you can for as long as you can. This is because it takes an enormous amount of energy to pump more blood around your body as you exercise. And the body has to get this energy from somewhere . . . you guessed it . . . your butt.

But there are other benefits to exercise beyond burning calories. According to James Hill, studies have suggested the body's natural systems of hunger regulation work better at higher volumes; that is, the hormones are more sensitised if you eat more and move more, rather than eat less and move less. This is known as being in a state of high-energy flux. One way to be in this state is to be obese, eating more and burning more. When you are no longer obese, the way to achieve this state is by exercising more. Purposeful exercise can also add to your daily calorie allowance. And that, my friends, means more food. Yep, one of the main reasons I exercise is so that I can eat more. Seems as good a reason as any.

In today's obesogenic environment, you simply can't eat perfectly all the time. It's too hard to deny yourself to that extent. It would require will power that most of us do not possess to manage a healthy weight without exercise. Ultimately, it's a lifestyle choice. Do you really think you can resist that sugary dessert at every turn? Or will you have your cake and exercise too? I choose the latter. And I know that every time I stop exercising, I become lethargic and put on weight.

A study published in 2008 by David R Broom and researchers at the School of Sport and Exercise Sciences at Loughborough University in the United Kingdom found evidence that exercise suppresses hunger for at least two hours after exercise. Not only do you get the benefit of calories burnt; you're less likely to eat that cake. The researchers took eleven healthy-weight males aged from 19 to 23 and submitted them to three separate trials: 90 minutes of weight lifting, 60 minutes of running (with an average heart rate of 169 beats per minute) and a control trial of complete rest. The men were given two meals, at two hours and five hours through each test. The researchers took blood samples to identify exercise-induced changes in gut hormones and measured reported hunger levels.

Both resistance (weights) and aerobic (running) exercise led to reduced levels of hunger during exercise and before and after the first meal compared to the control group. Both forms of exercise also led to lower levels of acylated ghrelin—the hunger hormone—during exercise compared to the control group. Aerobic exercise created a significant increase in peptide YY—a satiety hormone—compared to both the control trial and the resistance trial, and the increase lasted until after consumption of the first meal. 'Exercise is an effective method of increasing energy expenditure and it may, paradoxically, lead to a short-term hunger suppression,' the researchers concluded.

But were the effects lasting? Will you compensate by eating more later on? The researchers suggested that more studies were needed into the longer term effect of exercise on hunger hormones. They couldn't say how people moderate their food intake in response to these hormonal changes. However, other studies have found a transient increase in another satiety hormone, glucagon-like peptide-1, immediately after exercise and an increase in its response to feeding after five consecutive days of exercise. 'Collectively,' Broom and his colleagues said, 'these findings suggest that aerobic exercise exerts a transient, hormone-mediated, inhibition of appetite.'

Feeling hungry? Perhaps you should hit the gym. A good way to distinguish between true hunger and boredom hunger is to ask yourself, Could I sustain a workout? If not, perhaps you really do need food. If you could, acknowledge that you're probably just emotionally hungry.

I know exercise makes some people ravenously hungry. But I'm excited by this finding of a two-hour appetite-suppression window. I use it to my advantage by exercising after work and before dinner. I find this puts me in a less hungry state for dinner, and then I go to bed before I can get too hungry again. Works for me. You need to figure out what works for you so you stick to your daily calorie allowance and have the energy to exercise.

Exercise has other benefits too. It influences the distribution of your body fat away from dangerous visceral fat stored around your organs. A study by researchers in the Netherlands, published online by JT Jonker and colleagues in the journal *Radiology* in June 2013, found that people with type 2 diabetes who performed only moderate-intensity exercise were able to reduced the level of fat stored around their heart, liver and abdomen, even without changing their diet. The research was conducted using twelve participants with an average age of 46. Magnetic resonance imaging scans were taken of the participants before and after six months of moderate-intensity exercise of between 3.5 and 6 hours a week. The results were clear: less fat deposited around the heart, lungs and liver after the six months of exercise.

Exercise has also been shown to release endorphins—the feel-good hormones that can lift your mood and your spirit. Exercise also mops up cortisol, the stress hormone, from the blood. Together, these hormonal changes create a double whammy to help you deal with the stress in your life. Reckon you're too stressed to exercise? I reckon you're too stressed *not* to exercise.

Exercise helps you to breathe more deeply and more fully. It increases your bone density, making you stronger. Aerobic exercise increases capillerisation—delivering more oxygen to muscles. It helps the mitochondria, the powerhouse of cells, to oxidise fat more efficiently. It also increases the body's ability to take up blood sugar. Exercise helps to build muscle tissue, which is more metabolically active than fat, increasing your calorie burn even after exercise. And if none of that changes your mind, know this about exercise: it will make you look better naked. Phew.

The bottom line is you have to exercise. The good news is that the people who least want to exercise—overweight people—are the people who will get the biggest benefits from doing so. Fat people burn more calories. A wiry 60-kilogram runner will not burn calories at the same rate as a 100-kilogram first timer on a treadmill. Good news, first timer: you win! You burn more calories. It's almost like Mother Nature wants to give you a helping hand. She wants to nudge you towards equilibrium.

Don't know where to start? Let me tell you.

My favourite exercise gadget: a heart rate monitor

If I could only offer you one exercise tip, buying a heart rate monitor would be it. Buying a heart rate monitor will change the way you think about exercise. It is a way to listen in on your heart and find out how hard it's working—whether you can push yourself further or are overdoing it. It's an elastic strap that goes around your chest with a detachable sensor that communicates wirelessly with a watch you wear on your wrist. The watch displays a number showing how many times your heart is beating in a minute and an estimate based on that of how many calories you have burnt since you started your workout. A base model will cost you a bit over $100, although the fancy ones can cost hundreds more. You can buy them in sports stores or on the internet.

I love my heart rate monitor. It's always there for me. It never judges me. It never screams at me. I never feel intimidated by its well-developed pecs. It just silently and diligently helps me through my workouts, letting me know when my heart rate is up and when I could push harder. And it gives me a great big gold star at the end of every workout—a nice round number of how many calories I've burnt. Instant feedback.

Trying to exercise without a heart rate monitor is, for me, like trying to drive a car without a speedometer. How do you know if you're going too fast? Too slow? The speed limit for your heart is usually calculated as 220 beats per minute minus your age. So if you are 40, your heart can usually beat around 180 times a minute maximum. Of course, it varies with individuals. Pregnant women are advised to keep their heart rate much lower. I know my heart can go at a much higher rate than my age would suggest. Of course, don't be stupid. If you feel dizzy or faint, slow it down.

Once you know what your maximum heart rate is, you can start to play games with it and set challenges. People who are unfit will reach their heart rate maximum sooner than a fit person. But you may find it difficult to sustain exercise at that rate. One of my main fears when I started to exercise was of that uncomfortable feeling you're going too hard, that you're about to faint. A heart rate monitor allows you to push yourself, but at the same time reassure yourself that you're not about to keel over. It's your body. You don't need a licence to use it. Experiment, within reason.

The good news for overweight people is that even moderate levels of activity will push their heart rate sky high. It might feel a bit uncomfortable, but embrace the discomfort. Your red face, sweaty brow and racing heart are precisely the signs you need to tell you that you're doing it right. Remember, sweat is fat cells crying. (A technical note: while I love this expression, you actually breathe out and wee out fat after it has been broken down into carbon dioxide and water.)

Ten top exercise tips from a (somewhat) reformed exercise hater

Have you ever wondered what eyebrows are for? Me neither, until I figured it out. Turns out eyebrows are not there simply to elegantly frame the eyes, sell tweezers and support employment in those brow bars that keep popping up. Turns out eyebrows have a specific evolutionary purpose. They are there to divert sweat that would otherwise pour into your eyes when you are slogging it out on the treadmill. If you're not using your eyebrows when you exercise, you're not doing it right.

1. RUN; DON'T WALK

The body is designed to conserve calories. The movement of walking has evolved to use as little energy as possible so we can roam over the savannah at will. Unless you are walking very, very fast, it is hard to work up a sweat. If you want to burn calories for weight loss, you need to run. 'If there is no major medical reason that somebody shouldn't be running, then I don't see any reason why they shouldn't run,' advises William Sukala.

My best tip for running is to slow down. Most people try to run in the way they have seen fit people in movies run, i.e. FAST. But when it comes to running, form is more important than speed. What really kicks your body into gear from running is not speed, but height. Achieving height with your stride forces your muscles to work harder to defy gravity. It's about getting your heart rate up as far as you safely can, not your pace. Try to imagine you are Neil Armstrong bounding across the surface of the moon. Defy gravity.

If you don't believe me, try doing twenty squats or lunges and see what happens to your heart rate. Working the big muscle groups in your legs is the fastest way to get your heart rate up. Running achieves this too. You can think of running as a series of really fast lunges.

I run so slowly that I'm often overtaken by fast walkers. A dear friend of mine calls it the 'Jess shuffle'. The great thing about the Jess shuffle is you can do it anywhere—in the gym or outdoors. All you need to do is put on sneakers and a heart rate monitor and the world becomes your personal gym.

2. IGNORE THE FAT-BURNING ZONE

I'm a big fan of high-intensity exercise with maximum energy expenditure for weight loss. I have always been confused by gym machines suggesting there is a fat-burning zone which would require me to exercise at a low intensity. Is there any truth to the fat-burning zone?

According to Sukala, the fat-burning zone on cardio machines at the gym is a myth—an entertainment device invented by gym machine companies to sell ever-fancier machines. 'The cardio button is what you use to lose weight, and you push the fat-burning button to stay fat,' he tells me.

However, there is a kernel of truth to the fat-burning zone. During exercise at lower heart rates, the body draws a greater percentage of energy from fat stores. During high-intensity exercise, the body uses more of the readily accessible energy circulating in the blood. But the basic maths tells you that if you exercise at a lower intensity, you use less energy overall.

Better, says Sukala, to burn as much energy as possible, regardless of which energy source you happen to be using. If you use up your glucose during high-intensity exercise, later on—probably when you're sleeping— the body will turn to its fat stores for the rest of the energy it needs. And you still end up burning fat during a high-intensity workout, if you keep it up for long enough. Sukala again: 'I don't care what food source you're burning during exercise; what really matters is the cumulative energy deficit at the end of the day.' Bingo.

Don't overthink it. Just burn as many calories as you can, any which way you can.

3. REMEMBER, IT'S QUALITY, NOT QUANTITY, THAT COUNTS

You don't have to exercise for hours on end to get fit. And these days who has the time? National health recommendations advise a certain number of minutes of exercise each day. But they're not that helpful, in my view, because they don't tell you anything about the intensity of your workout. I often see women sitting in the gym on reclining bikes reading magazines. It takes all the strength I have not to go up to these women and tell them to stop wasting their time. When I use a reclining bike my heart rate reaches only about 140 beats per minute. For a person my age, that's not enough.

4. CLIMB EVERY MOUNTAIN

Remember what I was saying about gravity? If you don't feel like jogging some days, you can always try walking on an incline on the treadmill. Walking up hills is a great substitute for running for people who have injuries or other difficulties running. What matters is your heart rate. I find I get the same heart rate walking on an incline of 5 per cent and at a pace of 5 kilometres per hour as I do with a slow jog. This is because the muscles have to work harder to fight gravity. Another great way to turbo-charge your jog on a treadmill is to set the incline to 2 or 3 per cent. You won't really notice it, but it all adds up. If you are running outside, try to find stairs and hills to run up. As you get fitter, you will find it is harder to raise your heart rate, so using inclines is a great way to keep pushing yourself to achieve the same high heart rate. If you're using a monitor, you'll know when it's time to take it up a gear.

THE HILL-CLIMBER WORKOUT
1 Show up at the gym (always the most important part).
2 Start the machine on an easy walking pace, like 5 kilometres per hour. Set the incline to 1 per cent. Every minute or so, increase the incline by 1 per cent. Watch your heart rate climb a few beats per minute with every incline increase. Keep increasing the incline until you reach your target heart rate. If you feel fab, why not push a little harder? If not, stick at your target heart rate and watch television at the gym. Easy.

5. EXERCISE LIKE NOBODY'S WATCHING

I never exercise without music. Many's the time I've been about to give up on a workout when an awesome song comes on my iPod and I realise I've got that extra bit in me. There are websites you can go to for workout music to match your heart rate. Search for songs to get you going to 150 or 170 beats per minute.

I find what is really important is not the rhythm of the music (although a strong beat is a must—running in time with a beat is almost as good as dancing), but the emotional connection you have with it. Pick songs from your childhood.

For me, it's the 1980s. Often when I'm listening to these songs it's questionable whether I'm jogging or dancing. Choose songs that would get you out on the dance floor in a nightclub. In the box are my personal all-time favourite upbeat, awesome workout tunes. You're welcome.

Oh, and dancing is also great for burning calories, if you get the chance.

JESS'S TOP TWENTY WORKOUT SONGS
ABBA, 'Dancing Queen'
Avicii, 'Wake Me Up'
Black Eyed Peas, 'I Gotta Feeling'
Armin van Buuren, 'Alone' (feat. Lauren Evans)
Armin van Buuren, 'This Is What It Feels Like' (feat.
    Trevor Guthrie)
Kelly Clarkson, 'Since U Been Gone'
David Guetta, 'Play Hard' (feat. Ne-Yo and Akon)
David Guetta, 'She Wolf (Falling to Pieces)' (feat. Sia)
David Guetta, 'Titanium' (feat. Sia)
David Guetta, 'When Love Takes Over' (feat. Kelly Rowland)
David Guetta, 'Without You' (feat. Usher)
Icona Pop, 'I Love It' (feat. Charli XCX)
Maroon 5, 'Moves Like Jagger' (feat. Christina Aguilera)
John Parr, 'St Elmo's Fire (Man in Motion)'
Katy Perry, 'Firework'
Pink, 'Leave Me Alone (I'm Lonely)'
Rihanna, 'We Found Love' (feat. Calvin Harris)
Rock of Ages (Original Motion Picture), 'Don't Stop Believin''
Stafford Brothers, 'Hello' (feat. Lil Wayne and Christina Milian)
Starship, 'We Built This City'

6. RECLAIM THE WEIGHTS SECTION FROM THE BOOFHEADS

If you're tired of running, why not hit the weights section of your gym? Because it's populated by a bunch of rippled muscleheads? Well, yes, it is. But you have just as much right to be in there, pumping your 5-kilogram weights.

Not only do weight-bearing exercises help to build strength, they also maximise total daily calorie burn. While you may burn fewer calories during the weights workout itself, you build more muscle mass, and muscle tissue burns more calories than fat while at rest. According to William Sukala, 'Muscle is very metabolically active and pays a higher caloric "rent" to sustain itself (even at rest). Fat tissue, on the other hand, is nothing more than a metabolic freeloader which burns comparatively fewer calories.' Severe calorie restriction diets can result in a high proportion of muscle loss as well as fat loss. That's why it's best to lose weight slowly and to do some weight-bearing exercise to keep your muscle intact.

And remember, you don't necessarily have to pick up weights to build muscle. The best dumbbell in the world is you. I don't mean that in an unkind way, but your muscles are working hard all the time just to lug you around. Squats, lunges and push-ups all work the muscles using your own weight. All these movements spike my heart rate massively. They also have a compound effect because they use multiple muscle groups. Push-ups don't use only your arms, but your abs too. In your time-poor life, you multitask all the time. It's the same for your muscles. Speaking of which . . .

7. GET UP OFF THE FLOOR!

What on earth are you doing down there? Stop! Get up! Never do another sit-up. Why? In part because I hate them and it pains me to see you like that. But there is a better reason.

The best way to get those rippling abs you so desire is not through endless sit-ups but through removing the blanket of fat they're hiding under. We all have abs. The reason you can't see yours is because they're covered in a layer of fat. No matter how big you build the muscles, if they're buried in fat, you won't see them.

So never do another sit-up. Plank if you must or do rollouts on a fitness ball because these are compound movements, using your arm muscles as well as your abs. Building core strength is important, but you can do that running. Your heart rate drops as soon as you sit down. Seriously. Get off the floor.

8. DO AN EXERCISE YOU ENJOY

Exercise, for me, has become a form of meditation. I like to repeat the same workouts time and time again. When I run outdoors, I like running the same route every time. Personal trainers will tell you to chop and change, mix it up for maximum effect. But I enjoy the predictability of doing the same workout. Do you brush your teeth a different way every day? Are you constantly coming up with innovative new ways to shower?

Just like eating, it's best if exercise recesses into your daily life and becomes part of a routine. In an ideal world (with no deadlines, friends or dinners to go to) you should exercise every day. It takes away the dilemma of 'will I go to the gym today or not?' A day without exercise should be an oddity.

I used to see exercise as a penalty. Now I see it as a reward. Time is the most precious commodity you can give yourself. So put some time aside to take your engine out for a whirl.

Think of your body like a pet dog. It would be cruel not to take your dog out for a walk each day, right? Well, it's cruel for your body too.

Exercise is a gift you give your body. Tune out. Meditate. It's the half-hour of the day in which you put your health first. And this knowledge will help you to make better choices at other times of the day, by relieving stress. And you're not about to undo that hour in the gym with a piece of banana bread, are you?

9. FIDGET MORE

So far in this chapter I've focused on the purposeful exercise part of the body budget equation. But there are opportunities to maximise your incidental calorie burn at all times of the day. You need to fight inertia at every turn. As I was writing this bit of the book, I happened to be at the New York Public Library—yes, where they filmed *Ghostbusters*—and a woman sitting next to me tapped her foot for four hours straight. It was driving me mad, but then I realised she was burning extra calories. So I tapped a bit too, and got on with it.

10. CREATE A VIRTUOUS CYCLE OF EXERCISE

But don't imagine fidgeting can get you off the hook for real exercise. Walking for ten minutes rather than sitting on a bus may earn you an extra 30 calories or so. That is nowhere near enough to make up for a lost gym session.

Actually, when you start exercising regularly, it helps you to fidget even more during the day. You decide to take the stairs because your leg muscles no longer burn with the fire of a thousand suns when you do. You walk faster because your muscles can cope. I believe it is possible to create both virtuous and vicious cycles of physical activity. The more you exercise, the more you want to exercise, because the easier it gets—a virtuous cycle. The less you exercise, the harder it is, and so the less you do. I can tell you that it's a lot more fun to be active than inactive, and it's the only way to lose weight. Yes, it's hard work. And yes, you still have to do it.

You will need to give up something to find the time to exercise. For me, it's television. I really don't need to watch that much television. So I'll go to the gym rather than watch an hour at night. Also, you can watch television in a lot of gyms, either in the machine or on the screen. You may not be able to have your cake and eat it too, but you can have your television and exercise too.

Can you be more specific, please?

My standard workout is to keep going until I hit 500 calories. I don't think about leaving until I get to that number and I get enormous satisfaction from knowing I have done enough to get the job done. And, of course, if you go harder you can get it done quicker and get out of there. Here are my three favourite no-fuss, go-to workouts.

1. THE ANYWHERE, ANY TIME WORKOUT

Put on your sneakers, your heart rate monitor and your headphones. Jog around your neighbourhood or on the treadmill until you burn 500 calories. It should take between half an hour and an hour, depending on how hard you go. You're done.

2. THE TEN-MINUTE CARDIO BURST CIRCUIT

Go to the gym. Spend ten minutes on different pieces of cardio equipment until you reach 500 calories. This should take about four ten-minute bursts. If you fall short, do another ten-minute cycle. But always finish the full ten minutes, even if it means burning more than 500 calories.

GYM MACHINES I AUTHORISE YOU TO USE

The treadmill

Find your Jess shuffle speed—the magic speed at which you have to start running, not walking. For me, it's about 7 kilometres per hour. Crank it up half a notch and stay there for ten minutes. Don't try to go any faster. Watch your heart rate monitor. You may feel like you're dying, but your monitor will tell you otherwise. (Of course, if it's off the chart, reduce the speed.) What is important is knocking your body out of its natural walking rhythm. But once you've forced yourself into a running motion, there are diminishing returns from increasing the speed. I know that, for me, walking will only get my heart rate to about 110 beats per minute. Even a slow jog will soon send me to 160 or 170 beats per minute. And that is plenty.

The cross trainer
Turn it to at least level 5. I always exercise on level 7. The cross trainer makes you use your biggest muscles in your thighs and calves. It's a real heart rate cranker. My top tip with the cross trainer is a strange one, and you should do it only if you're comfortable: don't hold on. I find that holding on to the arm bars slows me down without really working my arm muscles. My heart rate certainly falls. If you don't hold on, it forces you to engage your abs and core muscles more, enables you to go faster, increases the calories burnt and has the added benefit of meaning you don't have to touch grubby, sweaty gym machines.

The rower
I hardly ever use the rower because it doesn't get my heart rate up very far. You are using the smaller muscle groups in your arms, as well as your abs and core. Remember, it's all about picking exercises that use multiple muscle groups to get your heart rate up. If you do use the rower, use strong fluid movements and go hell for leather. Your heart rate monitor will tell you if you're doing it right.

The upright bike
There's something dangerous about the bike for me—it reminds me too much of sitting. But it does use the big muscle groups in your legs, so if you can keep your heart rate up to a decent level, do it. Once again, I don't hold on.

I think I'm a germophobe. I sit up straight and cross my arms or hold the seat at the back. It forces the power down into your legs rather than through your arms and seems to get the heart rate up more. Make sure you have the resistance set on at least level 5, or you're just paddling air.

THE GYM MACHINE I FORBID YOU TO USE

The reclining bike

Fancy jumping on the bike and catching up on the latest edition of *Cleo* or *Men's Health*? Are you kidding me? The best way to use the reclining bike is to get off it and go sit on the couch. Seriously.

3. THE 'RECLAIM THE GYM FROM THE BOOFHEADS' WORKOUT

(*Jargon alert:* 'Reps' is short for repetitions—the number of times in a row you do a certain movement. 'Fifteen reps of squats' means fifteen squats. 'Sets' is the number of times you repeat a group of reps. 'Two sets of fifteen reps of squats' means 30 squats in total.)

First, do ten minutes on a cardio machine of your choice to really get your heart rate up. Then follow this routine:

Wide squats (15 reps)

Take a wide stance, with your toes pointing slightly outwards. Pull in your tummy and sit back like you're sitting on a seat. Aim to get your legs to form a 90-degree angle at the knee. Don't worry if you can't go that low immediately. Remember to pull in your core and stick out your chest, shoulders down.

Push-ups (10 reps)

I do push-ups on my knees. Get on the floor like a puppy dog. Shuffle your hands forwards a bit so that your bum is in a straight line with your shoulders and knees (not up in the air). Have your hands set a little wider than your shoulders. Pivot on your knees. Drop down until your arms get to 90 degrees at the elbow, then push back up. Again, don't worry if you can't get down that far immediately. Do another set of wide squats and push-ups.

TRX pull-ups (15 reps)

If your gym has TRX ropes, grab one in each hand and stand with your legs hip-width apart. Slowly lean back until your arms are fully outstretched. Pull your elbows to your sides, bringing you more upright. Slowly lower and pull back up. That's one rep. Shuffle your feet forwards a step or so to adjust the strength of your lift. If you can't find TRX ropes, do more push-ups.

Lateral raises (10 reps, with at least 2.5-kilogram weights)

Stand in front of the mirror. Bend your knees slightly. Pull in your abs, shoulders down. Have the weights in your hands down by your sides. Keeping your arms straight, lift directly out from your sides until the weights are at the same level as your shoulders. Ouch! Yep, that's not a move your body does every day. It'll really shape things up (and give you awesome shoulders). Do another set of pull-ups and lateral raises.

Bicep curls and lifts (15 reps)

Stand in front of a mirror with feet shoulder-width apart and a dumbbell in each hand (you decide the weight). Lift your hands up to your shoulders, keeping your elbows in the same spot. Now lift your hands above your head until your arms are fully extended. Bring your hands back down to your shoulders, then to your sides. That's one rep.

Tricep dips (15 reps)

Sit on a bench with your hands gripping the seat either side of your legs. Lift your body up and then dip your bum in front of the seat and back up. That's one rep. Do another set of bicep curls and lifts and tricep dips.

And that's a wrap. Get back on the treadmill for a ten-minute blast, and if you've got the time and energy, repeat the workout.

•

At the end of the day, I don't care what you do, only that you do it. If you want to do 500 squats a day, that'll get your heart rate up, so go for it. Similarly, I don't care what time of day you exercise. It's all the same from a calorie point of view. Find out what best suits you. Then do it. And keep doing it.

The important thing is that once you start exercising each day you don't stop. The most common problem with diet and exercise regimes is that people stop them. Even when you get to your goal weight, you still have to exercise or you'll start putting it back on. Now you've figured out how to lose weight, keeping it off is the next step. And that's where the real work begins.

PART 3
HOW TO KEEP IT OFF

9

Why losing weight becomes more difficult

So, you're eating less, moving more and the weight has been peeling off. But recently you've found you're not getting the results you expected. Your weight loss each week has slowed. Perhaps you've hit the dreaded plateau.

You start beating yourself up about it. In a fit of frustration you think, Oh bother it, I'm not going to the gym and I *will* have that side of chippies, thank you very much. Plus, you reason, you're looking pretty good now. Perhaps you can finally throw in this boring weight-loss thing. Problem solved. Back to business as usual.

For a couple of weeks, you get away with it. The scales don't head any lower, but nor do they really shoot upwards. Great, you think, I'm eating like I used to and I'm not putting on weight. I won't bother counting my calories anymore. To be honest, I never really did like the gym. And I don't see why I should continue to weigh myself every morning—what a drag.

A few more weeks pass and, having noticed some changes to your body shape, you tentatively step back on the scales. Boom! You've put on 3 kilograms. What the . . . ? All that hard work undone. You ask yourself, Do I really have the energy to get back on the weight-loss wagon? Work's busy at the moment. I'll start my diet again later. Maybe next month. Maybe on my next holiday.

A year goes by and you regain 10 kilograms of the 20 kilograms you originally lost. Those skinny jeans and short shorts you bought at your lightest are now languishing at the back of your wardrobe . . .

Oh no, wait. I'm not talking about you. I'm talking about me.

Anyone can lose weight. It's keeping it off that's hard. It is no coincidence that an estimated 95 per cent of us stumble, slowly but surely putting our weight back on. Having lived through it myself—the elation of weight loss and the frustration of weight regain—I think I get it now. The key is to better understand the way your body changes in response to weight loss and what this means about how you must care for your new body.

Let's drill down on how your body changes, the lighter you become.

BASIC BODY FUNCTIONS

When you lose weight your basal metabolic rate tends to fall. Several factors cause this decrease. Because your body is smaller after weight loss, there is less stress on it and it takes less energy to power basic body functions. For example, there is less pressure on the heart, meaning it can pump blood around the body with less effort. You may find it easier to breathe. You may sweat less.

As you get thinner and have less fatty tissue, your body is also more likely to burn muscle rather than fat. If you start losing muscle mass, because muscle is metabolically demanding, it will reduce your basal metabolic rate.

Scientists are not entirely sure, but they also suspect changes are happening at a deeper level. In 'Modeling Metabolic Adaptations and Energy Regulation in Humans', weight-loss expert Kevin Hall says that during weight loss, the body may undergo a process of 'adaptive thermogenesis', in which the organs slow down, requiring less energy to do the same tasks. The body may also experience decreased levels of leptin—the satiety hormone—or decreased thyroid activity.

So we burn fewer calories at rest the lighter we become. And it gets worse.

INCIDENTAL MOVEMENT

As we learnt earlier, your incidental movement burn is calculated as a multiple of your basal metabolic rate. If your basal metabolic rate falls, so does your calorie burn from incidental movement, even if you keep doing exactly the same movements.

It makes sense, of course. The muscles in a lighter person don't have to work as hard to move the body around as the muscles in a heavier person. As you lose weight, it takes less effort to do the same activities, and you consequently burn fewer calories doing them. Walking up the stairs just doesn't floor you like it used to.

If you are losing weight by building substantial calorie deficits, say of 500 to 1000 calories a day—a rate that would produce a weight loss of around 1 kilogram every one to two weeks, initially at least—you may start to feel you don't have as much energy as you used to. This is because you don't. People on low-calorie diets may begin to compensate for less incoming energy by generally slowing down their everyday activities. You may walk more slowly, sit down more or even breathe more slowly. Maybe you fidget less. Or perhaps, now you're going to the gym regularly, you feel less guilty about sitting down at other times. I've done my exercise today, thank you. I'm taking the elevator. Little by little, you slow down your incidental movement, reducing your calorie burn.

DIGESTION

The third and often overlooked part of the equation is the thermogenic effect of food. This is the energy that is used as your body starts to break down food, sorting it into junk and useable stuff, sending the former down the chute and the latter around the body to the organs and fat cells. Now that you're eating smaller portions, there's less digesting work for the body to do. This digestion energy expenditure makes up only a small part of the energy equation—about 10 per cent of calorie intake—but it all adds up.

PURPOSEFUL EXERCISE

And finally, when you do hit the gym, you're fitter. I say that like it's a bad thing. It's not. But getting fitter does mean it takes less effort to do the same gym routine. It is harder to spike your heart rate. It takes longer to burn the same amount of calories.

ENERGY IN

On the calories in side of the equation, you are dealing with the human tendency to underestimate the calories in your food. Calories have a funny way of sneaking up on you. If you let your guard down even just a little, it is easy to mistakenly consume a couple of hundred calories unawares. Eating is such a habitual thing. We've been doing it three times a day, seven days a week, 52 weeks a year for as many years as we've been on this earth. We have developed certain tastes and expectations about how much food we should eat. And of course, our environment puts us into constant contact with temptation. Is it any wonder that we tend to revert, slowly but surely, to the dietary patterns we have become accustomed to?

Perhaps you're eating healthier foods, but you're eating more of them. Maybe you give in to temptations, grazing here and there, and don't realise how it's all adding up. Having lost some weight, you relax and start to eat more. Studies of rapid weight-loss diets with low calories that afterwards allowed participants to go back to eating in the real world have shown that weight loss tends to plateau after about six months. After a year, it's a process of steady regain. Even when given advice on how to eat better, people fail to adhere to the prescribed diet. 'An energy imbalance resulting in transient weight loss leads to an eventual adaptation of behavior to return to the original lifestyle,' says Kevin Hall. Old habits die hard.

Together with Holly Wyatt, George Reed and John Peters, in 2003 James Hill developed the idea of the energy gap: the gap between what you could consume to maintain your old weight and what you can consume now, to maintain your new, lower weight. The difference can be as big as 500 calories a day—that's an entire Big Mac a day you don't get to eat. And then, you're always getting just that little bit older, and that will work against you too, as your daily energy needs decline with age, by about 5 calories each year.

The sting in the tail of weight loss

I realise I have been the harbinger of a lot of bad news lately. I'm telling you that to lose weight you have to eat less. I'm also asking you to move more. And here's the double whammy. To keep weight off, you need to keep doing both of those things. Forever. Rinse and repeat. Every day. The reward from weight loss is not that you get to eat more or go back to your old habits; in fact, you get to eat less. Increasingly less. Hard? You betcha. 'It is no surprise that few people can consistently fight their biology and their environment to sustain energy restriction. When they fail, they rapidly regain their weight,' says James Hill.

Kevin Hall and his colleagues writing in *The American Journal of Clinical Nutrition* recommended that the 3500-calorie rule should no longer be used in the way it has been in the past. Overweight people, they said, must be counselled that it will take longer to reach their goals than they think.

Why does weight loss slow down?

Are you ready for the advanced course on the weight-loss equation? First, a quick recap of what we know. Weight loss can occur only when you consume less energy than you expend. We also know there are four component parts to the energy out side of the equation: basic body functions, incidental movement, digestion and purposeful exercise.

The good news for overweight people, as we have also learnt, is that being bigger tends to increase the energy expended in each part of this energy out side of the equation. If you are bigger, you require more energy to perform basic body functions, leading to a higher basal metabolic rate. Overweight people eat relatively more than skinny people to sustain their higher weights, meaning more energy is used in digestion. It also takes more energy to move around in daily life, increasing the calorie burn from incidental movement. And when bigger people exercise, the excess fat acts as an inbuilt weights system, forcing the muscles to work harder to do each exercise. That is great news for people looking to lose weight.

But as you lose weight things soon begin to change. You soon discover you can keep to the same food and exercise routine, but the weight loss slows down. Why?

In his paper 'Modeling metabolic adaptations and energy regulation in humans', Kevin Hall takes to task the common '3500-calories-per-pound' rule that states every 3500 calories you cut out from your diet will lead to a kilogram of weight loss. That rule of thumb contains a hidden assumption that whatever a person's weight, their energy expenditure remains static as they lose weight. But, in fact, a person's energy expenditure and rate of weight loss will vary, depending on a person's starting weight and the magnitude of their total weight loss. A person with more fat to start with will use proportionately more of it to fuel their daily activities than a leaner person, who will access more stored energy from lean muscle mass. Not only is it easier for an overweight person to create an energy deficit, when that energy deficit is created, the larger person will draw more energy from stored fat than stored muscle. Larger people also initially lose more water mass, leading to more rapid weight loss. As a person becomes leaner, their calorie need falls, meaning they must eat ever less to create the same energy gap. And even if they do manage to create the same energy gap, a lean person will access proportionately more of the required energy from their stores of lean muscle tissue than fat stores. This means that even if they maintain the same energy deficit, their weight loss will slow down. So, according to Hall, while the 3500-calorie rule's claim that a deficit of 500 calories per day will lead to 1 pound of weight loss per week is a 'reasonable approximation' for overweight and obese people, it is not as correct for leaner people. As a result, Hall and his team writing for *The Lancet* caution against relying too heavily on the 3500-calorie rule. 'Because this static weight-loss rule does not account for dynamic physiological adaptations that occur with decreased bodyweight, its widespread use at both the individual and population levels has led to drastically overestimated expectations for weight loss.'

One way to ensure you are creating the required energy deficit is to recalculate your daily calorie allowance every day, based on your new lower weight. If you take that into account and still managed to create a deficit, the equation will still hold true. It's not that the 3500 number itself is wrong, just the assumption that your energy needs won't fall as you lose weight, making it harder to create the same energy deficit over time.

After I had finished my experiment, I sent Hall my eighteen-week body budget spreadsheet that showed I had lost the amount of weight in the period predicted by the rule. 'Look, see,' I said, 'the rule works!' Hall was encouraging, but not entirely impressed by my sample size of one. He pointed out an error in my assumptions (I hadn't taken into account energy burnt through digestion) that meant I had underestimated my calorie allowance, creating a slightly bigger deficit than I had intended. This would explain the slightly bigger weight loss I achieved than would have been predicted by the equation. But in general, yes, I was right, the equation works.

The lesson I've drawn from all this is that measurement issues abound when it comes to the weight-loss equation. You should be conservative in your estimates of how many calories you are burning a day. And the energy required to fuel your basic body functions and the energy cost of physical exercise change as your body composition—the amount of fat you have—changes.

When the typical weight-loss pattern is tracked on a graph, rather than a straight downward line, it forms a curve like a skateboard ramp, with bigger weight losses at the top, or the beginning of weight loss, and a gradually flattening path of weight loss over time. (You still lose weight; it just takes longer for the same change of diet.) 'It might help explain why even the most diligent followers of diet programs often fail to reach weight-loss goals that were set by use of the static weight-loss rule,' says Hall and colleagues in *The Lancet*. If you stick to cutting out a certain number of calories from your diet each day, the weight-loss returns from that diet will reduce over time as your daily calorie need falls.

But despite the weight-loss plateau and the shortcomings of the 3500-calorie rule, it is important not to throw the baby out with the bathwater. It's important to realise that a plateau, or slowing down, in your weight loss is not your fault. It is, in fact, an entirely natural and predictable part of weight loss. You can overcome it by eating less and less over time to build the same size of calorie deficit. It may be hard to predict exactly how long it will take you to reach your goal. The bottom line, though, is that if you keep creating energy deficits, you will lose weight.

And there is help at hand.

'Mathematical modeling of human energy regulation and body weight change has recently reached the level of sophistication required for accurate predictions,' Hall says in 'Modeling Metabolic Adaptations and Energy Regulation in Humans'. As mentioned in chapter 6, Hall and his team have developed an online tool called the Body Weight Simulator (http://bwsimulator.niddk.nih.gov), which allows you to do many of the calculations we've already done, but online; importantly, it also takes into account the changes that occur in energy expenditure as you lose weight. You put in your height, age and weight, and it will calculate your calorie allowance. It then lets you play with variables like how much you will eat in a day and what type of exercise you will do, to see what your path of weight loss is likely to be. You can set goals and it will tell you whether they can be met and how much you need to eat and exercise to achieve them. It's super nifty. Check it out.

The bottom line on any diet is that adherence is key. Hang in there. Weight loss happens, but over a slower time frame than you might think. And your body's reaction to the weight loss may be different from somebody else's.

What is clear is that to keep losing weight, you have to keep eating less and less or keep moving more and more.

The former route means you're likely to be quite hungry. The latter takes time and effort. You will need to constantly fight the environment you live in.

It seems our bodies have evolved to protect us more against weight loss than weight gain. According to Hill:

❝ It is clear that humans have a preference for sweet tastes and perhaps for high-energy dense foods. There does not seem to be a strong biological drive to promote energy restriction or to promote physical activity. Our biology is strongly aimed at promoting energy intake and protecting against weight loss. Environmental factors that facilitate energy intake and discourage physical activity do not appear to be biologically opposed. The reason why the entire population is not obese is probably because some people are able to oppose these environmental factors with conscious efforts to avoid overeating and engage in regular physical activity. ❞

Yes, this is going to take some effort on your part. When I see skinny people these days, I no longer feel jealous. I see the embodiment of a different set of choices. A skinny person is a person who has chosen to go to the gym and to eat better. It is true that some skinny people are lucky—gifted somehow with small appetites. But for many, it's just that they're actually working hard at the gym while you're watching television.

Getting skinny and staying skinny these days is no easy feat. It requires a lot of hard work behind the scenes. If you want to become a successful loser, you need to act like a successful loser. So, how do they do it?

10
How successful losers keep weight off

So you've lost weight. Congratulations! You are a successful loser. But for how long? It's time to shift from weight-loss mode to weight-maintenance mode. These are two distinct processes, according to nutrition and obesity researcher James Hill. 'Our work suggests that a big reason for the high failure rate in obesity treatment is the failure to see weight-loss maintenance as a separate process from weight loss,' he writes. 'From an energy balance point of view, weight loss involves a temporary period of negative energy balance, whereas weight-loss maintenance involves a permanent period of achieving energy balance at a new level.'

Most weight-loss programs focus on the weight-loss part and then set you free into the world, struggling to keep up the strict weight-loss regime and unsure what to do next. As Hill explains:

" Negative energy balance is a temporary state that cannot be easily maintained for long periods of time. Weight-loss maintenance is about achieving energy balance, but at a new, lower body weight. It requires diet and physical activity patterns that can be maintained indefinitely. The challenge is not just achieving energy balance, but achieving it at a lower body weight. This is a challenge because energy requirements decline with weight loss. **"**

We all know it's hard to keep weight off. But it is far from impossible. I, and many others, have managed it. What's the secret?

The secrets of successful losers

Perhaps because successful losers—people who have lost weight and kept it off—are something of a rarity, few studies have been conducted into them. But there is one. The National Weight Control Registry, founded by James Hill and behavioural psychologist Rena Wing, is a database about people who have successfully maintained a 13.5-kilogram weight loss for one year or longer. Established in 1994, the register of successful losers had 4000 members by 2003, and the number has since grown to more than 10,000. Members of the registry join through self-selection and voluntarily report information about their lifestyle, diet and exercise habits to help the researchers glean the common traits of successful losers. The researchers wrote up some of the survey's key findings when it had 4000 participants. Their message is one of hope:

❝ Although the popular media encourage the perception that almost no one succeeds at long-term weight loss—a 99% failure rate is the figure perpetuated most commonly—we are getting better at helping people achieve weight loss sufficient to greatly improve their health. We have come a long way in using protocols—structured, skill-based, group, and individual—to produce lifestyle change. **❞**

Hill and Wing stress that even a 7 per cent weight loss in overweight or obese people who are at high risk of diabetes produces more than a 50 per cent reduction in this risk.

In participants' successful attempts to lose weight, there was no single pattern of eating that stood out, though most participants had tried one or more of the popular diet programs on the market.

❝ The only common characteristic was that 89% of registry participants used both diet and physical activity to lose weight: only 10% used diet alone, and 1% used exercise alone. This finding is very important because most weight-loss programs focus primarily on dietary restriction. We could not identify any successful diet common to these people: Many reported that they restricted their intake of certain foods; some participants stated that they restricted the amount of food consumed; some participants counted calories or grams of fat consumed; some used prepackaged liquid formulas; and some used different kinds of exchange diets. **"**

However, the researchers found significant similarities in the participants' methods of keeping the weight off. 'This difference in commonality suggests that the two processes—losing weight and maintaining weight loss—may have important differences,' said Hill and Wing.

" We found four types of behavior common to the National Weight Control Registry participants: 1) eating a low-fat, high-carbohydrate diet; 2) eating breakfast almost every day; 3) frequent self-monitoring of weight; and 4) participation in a high level of physical activity. **"**

Let's look at those in turn, starting with food intake. According to the information provided by participants, and keeping in mind people's tendency to underestimate their calorie intake, they consumed between 1300 and 1500 calories per day, of which about 23 per cent came from fat. (That's pretty low compared to the average intake, of about 35 per cent.) Eating a diet lower in fat by definition means eating more calorie-sparse carbohydrates or protein. Participants said they ate between four and five times per day and ate out at fast-food restaurants about once a week. So if you want to eat like a successful loser, limit your calories and fat intake, eat regular meals and eat out only occasionally.

Second, while overall calorie intake is what matters, the results point to a special role for breakfast in helping people keep the weight off. 'Starting the day with breakfast may therefore be even more important for weight maintenance than previously thought,' the researchers concluded.

Third, three-quarters of the successful losers said they weighed themselves at least once a week, and many weighed themselves daily.

" Frequent weighing may therefore serve as an 'early warning system' for these people. I suspect that when they have gained a few pounds, they implement strategies to prevent further weight gain. Although this possibility represents speculation, many participants told us that they have a plan for what to do if the scales reach a certain number. Other studies have found that self-monitoring predicts success in long-term maintenance of weight loss. **"**

And finally, the average weekly energy expenditure through purposeful exercise was 2500 calories for women and 3300 for men. 'This level of physical activity is very high and equates to about 60 to 90 minutes of moderate-intensity physical activity per day.' Only 9 per cent of participants reported keeping their weight off with no purposeful physical activity. Walking was the most popular form of exercise, but only 28 per cent used walking alone; most also engaged in planned exercise sessions, and half combined walking with another form of exercise, for example aerobics classes, biking or swimming.

When the researchers put pedometers on a sample of the participants, they found they walked, on average, between 11,000 and 12,000 steps per day—about 9 kilometres. This is almost double the norm. 'We can confidently state that a great deal of physical activity is necessary to maintain substantial weight loss,' said Hill and Wing.

So, in case you missed it, the four common traits of successful losers are:

- eating a low-fat diet
- eating breakfast every day
- weighing regularly
- exercising vigorously every day.

If you think it all sounds a bit like hard work, you're right. But there really doesn't seem to be a substitute. There is little point in trying to kid yourself.

Why you need to keep exercising

Perhaps the most daunting part of those findings for me is the focus on physical activity in weight maintenance. Who has an hour a day to exercise? But the failure to continue exercising regularly after weight loss seems to be one of the most common contributors to weight regain. I know it is for me. 'We focus too much on diet and not enough on physical activity; and we focus too much on losing weight and not enough on keeping it off,' say Hill and Wing.

Drawing on the 1950s work of hunger and nutrition expert Jean Mayer, specifically his suggestion of a minimum threshold of physical activity needed to keep the body's natural processes of energy regulation working well, Hill has suggested that 'biological regulation of energy balance is optimum at a high level of energy flux (i.e., achieving energy balance at a high level of intake and expenditure)'. As we have seen, there are two things that produce high energy flux: high physical activity and obesity. So if you're used to high energy flux due to obesity, in order to stick to the body budget to maintain your new, lighter weight you may need to continue your high energy flux through high levels of activity. 'The only way to reduce obesity and maintain a high energy flux is to substitute increased physical activity for the lost body weight.' You may find that in order to maintain balance between energy in and energy out, you need to eat more and move more rather than eat less and move less.

Some studies have suggested low-calorie diets are associated with increased longevity. So perhaps it is better if you can retrain yourself to eat less. I believe this is possible. But in the shorter term, if you are finding it hard to restrict your diet because of hunger, you may need to keep exercising, potentially quite a lot, to bring your body into energy balance. As Hill says:

ff There is very strong epidemiological data suggesting that moderate to high levels of physical activity protect against weight gain and obesity . . . Our work suggests that very small increases in physical activity may prevent weight gain, whereas very large increases are necessary to avoid weight regain after weight loss. **JJ**

Remember that the body doesn't want you to lose too much weight. Indeed, it has evolved several mechanisms to stop you from doing that, including a raging appetite. But there is good evidence that it does like it when you are more physically active.

Having realised that you need to permanently eat less or move more, it's up to you how you choose to adopt this new lifestyle. I find it nearly impossible to resist some of the temptations of modern life. Indeed, I don't want to resist them. So I rely on exercise to maintain my energy balance. And Hill ultimately agrees: 'We believe that those who rely more on increasing physical activity than food restriction to address the energy gap will be more successful in long-term weight-loss maintenance.'

My top ten tips for weight maintenance

1. EXERCISE EVERY DAY

Take the thinking out of the issue by telling yourself that you are a person who exercises every day. Put an end to the mind tricks: Will I do exercise today or tomorrow? Is this a rest day or a move day? Every day is a move day.

I believe there are virtuous and vicious cycles of exercise. The more you jog, the easier it is to jog, and you are much more likely to take the stairs when your muscles don't feel like jelly. Similarly, if you don't exercise for a while, it starts to hurt again and you feel less motivated to move. Being in a virtuous exercise cycle feels awesome. Being in a vicious exercise cycle sucks and makes you feel like crap. I know there will be days when you just can't get to it. But, as I said earlier, you need to make days when you don't exercise the exception rather than the norm. If you start out with the idea that you must exercise every day rather than three or four times a week, you will always be ahead at the end of the week. So stop the mind games. Make exercise a daily habit and you will reap the rewards.

2. EAT TO LIVE; DON'T LIVE TO EAT

If you need more joy and happiness in your life, buy a puppy. Food is not the answer. Food is not why we live but simply the means by which we live so that we can do other fun stuff. Modern advertising would have you believe that food should be a miraculous journey of discovery, taste and delight. It's not. It's just eating. You should eat to satisfy the energy needs of your body, not the emotional needs of your mind. If you do find yourself looking for comfort in food, chances are you are lacking joy in other areas of your life. Better to identify what those things are and try to change them than to numb yourself with food.

3. WRITE IT DOWN

Make sure you have a system of accounting. When I feel myself going off the rails, I start to keep the body budget I described in chapter 6, recording all my food and exercise calories. The process of writing things down helps identify your behaviours and keeps you accountable. Sometimes writing everything down is such a hassle, I decide not to eat something simply to avoid having to log it. Counting calories burnt, on the other hand, is a joy.

4. PREPARE AS MANY MEALS YOURSELF AS YOU CAN

I hope I have managed to instil in you enough paranoia to believe the world is, genuinely, out to get you. They saw you coming, and when you weren't looking they laced that salad or pasta with enough oil to sink a battleship. No one has a greater interest in your health than you do. So why would you trust anyone else to prepare you fresh and healthy food? Any meal you cook at home will be healthier than a meal you eat in a restaurant. I'm no chef. But I know the building blocks of a healthy meal—a modest serving of protein and plenty of colourful vegetables—and I go about assembling them. People tell me this is boring. I tell them I used to like eating exciting food, until it made me fat.

5.   EAT BREAKFAST

Eating breakfast is a great way to tell your body that today is not a starvation day. Get your metabolism firing with a protein-packed meal of eggs or oats. Your body has spent the night fasting (hopefully) and needs energy to get going. When I was fat, I often skipped breakfast. Now I never do. Of course, technically it doesn't matter what time of day you get your calories, only how many you get. But I consider breakfast a sacrifice to the hunger monster, and if I don't placate the beast it tends to be out of control for the rest of the day, driving me to consume too many calories. One of the clearest findings from the National Weight Control Registry is that successful losers eat breakfast. So do it.

6.   INVEST TIME IN YOUR HEALTH

I know what you're thinking: Jess, I don't have time to do all this stuff. You want me to exercise for an hour each day *and* cook all my meals? Fine, I say, be overweight. But if you want to keep the weight off, you need to make time in your day for your health. You need to decide what you will give up to make time for food and exercise. For me, it has been television. It is hard to justify watching as much television as we do, especially when we can watch it at the gym. For you, it may be less time with family, making sure you leave work on time or not catching up with friends. Life is all about juggling competing priorities. It's time to prioritise your health. Make exercise and cooking your hobbies. Yes, it takes effort. But the time you invest in improving your health will pay dividends for the rest of your life.

7. WEIGH YOURSELF REGULARLY

I weigh myself every morning and I'm rarely surprised by what I see. If I have eaten too much the day before, it shows up on the scales immediately. It is a reminder that what you put in your mouth has lasting consequences. If I am eating well and exercising, I see the positive outcome of that on the scales.

Remember the scales measure both fat and muscle. If you are exercising a lot, it could be that you are gaining muscle and losing fat, so your weight may remain constant. Conversely, if you stop exercising and start eating more at the same time, you will be gaining fat but losing muscle, so it may take a while for the true result to show up on your scales. It's a trap for people who have lost weight and think they can revert to eating more and moving less. You can try it, but eventually the scales will catch you out.

8. HAVE FAITH IN THE EQUATION

You may be thinking that what I'm telling you to do to maintain weight is remarkably similar to what I told you to do to lose weight. That is very astute of you. It is. Except, instead of aiming for calorie deficits, you're aiming for energy balance. Remember, weight loss involves creating an energy deficit.

Weight maintenance is about balancing energy intake with energy expenditure. Both processes require careful attention to how much you are eating and how much you are exercising. If you are failing to keep your weight off, it is highly likely that you are simply eating more or not moving as much as you think you are. It is also possible you are getting your calculations wrong. Perhaps your daily calorie allowance is a bit smaller than you have estimated. Perhaps you're not as expert as you think on proper portion sizes. Just remember that everyone has a number—the number of calories they can consume in a day without putting on weight. If you are putting on weight, you are exceeding your number. You are special and unique, but not so special that you can defy the laws of physics. It may be a process of experimentation for you to find out what your correct weight-maintenance number is. But trust me that you do have a number and that, if you find it and stick to it, you can maintain your weight.

9.   DON'T BEAT YOURSELF UP

Trust me, there will be times when a delicious dessert is simply too good to pass up. The trick is to really enjoy it. If you're going to consume the calories, savour every bite. Don't beat yourself up about it. The typical yo-yo dieter swings constantly from perfectionism to guilt-induced blowouts. Their weight goes up and down, with each spree bigger than the last. They end up worse off than if they'd never tried.

Accept what you have done. Accept that you are an imperfect human living in an obesogenic world. Move on.

Get out your body budget. Analyse the situation. Where are you wandering off track? What are you going to do to get back on track?

Chances are, some of your weight is going to creep back on. The aim should not be to eat and exercise perfectly all of the time, just most of the time. Aim for two steps forwards, one step back.

10.   TAKE IT ONE DAY AT A TIME

Every day of your life is a fresh sheet of paper, a chance to do over and do better. Forget what happened yesterday and think of what you can do today to improve your health. Accept that there will be days when the distractions are too great and you can't set aside the time needed to exercise and eat well. Seize the days when you really do have enough time to put in the work required. If you find there are too many distraction days and not enough health days, you may need to look at your work and personal life and make some decisions about priorities. When you decide to give your health the priority it deserves, you will know exactly what to do, and it will work. Treat every day as a new day and a fresh chance to balance the books.

11
How to find help

O nce upon a time losing weight meant parting with hard-earnt cash and turning up in person for weekly group counselling sessions. The two big weight-loss companies, Weight Watchers and Jenny Craig, had a near duopoly on the weight-loss assistance industry. The rest of the market was saturated with a lot of fluff. Think miracle weight-loss pills, abdominators and meal replacement shakes.

But increasing demand for weight-loss advice and support, combined with new technologies, has opened up a new front in the fight against the flab. It is now possible to lose weight safely and cheaply from the comfort of your own home. The internet has democratised access to information about what to eat. New gadgets have made it possible to track your calorie expenditure without expensive gym memberships. It is no longer necessary to pay for access to good-quality information and tools to support and inform your weight-loss journey.

Twitter can help you lose weight

Just ten years ago, I would not have felt comfortable writing a book recommending people count the calories in every bite. To follow a calorie-counting program would have required a huge effort, endless flipping through calorie-counting books and recording each number and calculation by hand. Of course, it is still possible to do it this way. But a range of new websites and smartphone apps has revolutionised the ways in which we can access and record information about our diets and exercise routines. The internet has also provided social media and online forums that are rapidly replacing the traditional support groups of the established diet industry. It is now possible to share details of your recent run with friends on Facebook, tweet pictures of what you eat and crowd source calorie counts. New communities and support groups are springing up every day. People with the common goal of weight loss are finding each other over the internet and providing support and advice. There is no longer any reason to feel alone in your weight-loss attempts. You can jump online to share experiences, keep yourself accountable and even start new friendships.

People who use the microblogging site Twitter lose more weight than those who don't. Researchers led by Gabrielle Turner-McGrievy at the University of South Carolina's Arnold School of Public Health followed 96 overweight or obese people for six months as they attempted to lose weight. Half of the study's participants received a biweekly podcast with health tips. The other half received the same podcasts and were also required to follow each other on Twitter, reading each other's posts and posting daily themselves. The Twitter participants shared useful information about their discoveries in losing weight and provided their fellow participants with emotional support, praise and compliments. At the end of the study, the people who used Twitter had lost more weight than those who did not. Every ten posts on Twitter correlated with an extra 0.5 per cent drop in body weight.

When I began my go-it-alone spreadsheet diet to shed my regained kilograms, I created a Twitter account called @dietonomics, which I checked regularly. I would tweet pictures of my meals (with calorie counts) and of my heart rate monitor when I had done a workout. It turned out to be a great way of recording and sharing my achievements, receiving support and accessing a lot of freely available information from other tweeters. I was lucky to have several hundred followers, who, even though they probably didn't realise it, kept me going to the gym when I didn't feel like it. I once confessed on Twitter that I was torn between watching a show on television and going to the gym. 'Why not go to the gym and watch the show there?' one of my Twitter followers—a complete stranger—responded, immediately breaking my mental deadlock. Why not, indeed? And off I went.

I have found Twitter to be a great source of inspiration and information. There are many health organisations, publications and experts who are keen tweeters and who share tips and links to articles. Checking in regularly throughout the day to read a Twitter feed packed with health-related tweets is a great way to crowd out the otherwise constant stream of bad health messages that bombard us. If you're bored and feel like eating, why not jump on Twitter and read some articles about the latest advances in weight loss instead? I have found even the act of reading something informative about my health can help curb a craving.

Of course, it always pays to have your bullshit-o-meter turned on in the Twittersphere. There are questions you should always ask: Who stands to gain—and what will they gain—from giving me this advice? Is this just another program that wants my money and will then spit me out? Look for Twitter accounts that promote a healthy, balanced diet and exercise and that are not pressuring you to sign up to their programs. And be aware that some health 'experts' endorse certain products for money. Even government bodies aren't immune to conflicts of interest, because they often appease big businesses and employers, including those in the sugar, grain, dairy and meat industries. But you're an adult. Make up your own mind. Having read this book, you should know that any weight-loss advice that does not include either increasing your exercise or reducing your calorie intake is unlikely to get you very far.

Why not start today by creating a Twitter account and following some of the tweeters I've listed on the following pages?

USEFUL TWITTER ACCOUNTS TO FOLLOW

Here are some Twitter accounts to follow for helpful weight-loss information:

People

Me!

My official twitter is @Jess_Irvine and I also tweet as @dietonomics

Michelle Bridges

personal trainer and co-creator of the 12 Week Body Transformation

@MishBridges

Susie Burrell

health and wellbeing expert

@SusieBDiet

Amelia Burton

health and fitness coach

@AmeliaBurton

Natalie Corcoran

dietitian at University of Canberra

@ncnutrition1

Edwina Griffin

health and happiness expert

@FIT_EDDY

David L Katz

director of the Yale-Griffin Prevention Research Center

@DrDavidKatz

Joanna McMillan

Australian nutritionist

@joannanutrition

Marion Nestle
    author of *Why Calories Count*
    @marionnestle
Matt O'Neill
    Australian nutritionist
    @MatthewONeill
Michael Pollan
    author of *In Defense of Food*
    @michaelpollan
Amanda Salis
    obesity researcher at the University of Sydney
    @dramanda_salis
Nicole Senior
    Australian nutritionist
    @NicoleMSenior
William Sukala
    exercise physiologist
    @drbillsukala
Sarah Wilson
    author of *I Quit Sugar*
    @_sarahwilson_

Organisations
8700 Find Your Ideal Figure
    NSW government weight advice
    @8700kj
Better Health
    Victorian government health advice
    @BetterHealthGov
Deakin Nutrition
    nutrition and dietetics information from

Deakin University
@DeakinNutrition
Dietitian Connection
industry links for nutritionists
@DNconnection
Eat Right
food and nutrition information from the US Academy
of Nutrition and Dietetics
@EatRight
Get Lean
health advice by Joanna McMillan
@GetLean4Life
Harvard Health
health information from Harvard Medical School
@HarvardHealth
Jean Hailes for Women's Health
Australian not-for-profit women's health organisation
@JeanHailes
Michelle Bridges 12 Week Body Transformation
weight-loss advice and programs
@12WBT
Nutrition Australia
healthy eating and nutrition information
@NutritionAust
Obesity Australia
foundation for research into obesity
@ObesityAus
Sports Dietitians Australia
information about sports nutrition
@SportsDietAust

Publications

Healthy Recipes OW
    recipes from health website Organised Wisdom
    @Recipe_Healthy

HFGAustralia
    Australian Healthy Food Guide magazine
    @HFGAustralia

Men's Health
    men's health guide
    @menshealthAU

Men's Health Mag
    US *Men's Health* magazine
    @MensHealthMag

MNT Nutrition News
    nutrition and diet news
    @mnt_nutrition

NYTimes Well
    New York Times medical reporter Tara Parker-Pope
    on medical news for healthy living
    @nytimeswell

Prevention Australia
    Prevention Australia magazine
    @PreventionMagOz

Runner's World
    Runner's World magazine, Australia and New Zealand
    @RunnersWorldmag

Science Daily
    news about science and health discoveries
    @ScienceDaily

TIME Healthland
    health news from *Time* magazine
    @TIMEHealthland

Today's Dietitian
    Today's Dietitian magazine
    @TodaysDietitian
Women's Health Aus
    Australian Women's Health magazine
    @womenshealthaus
Women's Health Mag
    US *Women's Health* magazine
    @WomensHealthMag

Bloggers
Cooking Healthy Food
    healthy cooking recipes and tips
    @CookHealthyFood
Health Habits
    avid blogger and personal trainer from Canada
    @HealthHabits
Judy Davie
    healthy food tips and recipes
    @TheFoodCoach

My favourite weight-loss gadgets

You may have noticed that I am something of a geek when it comes to fitness (and I'm sure my friends might argue when it comes to life more broadly). For me, the word geek just means the ability to hyper-focus on one hobby or on solving a particular problem, and my particular problem has been weight. There is a wonderful world of geek fitness out there waiting to help you solve the same problem, and devices to assist you in learning about your body and how you are using it. Essential, I think, if you want to start using it better. Here are my favourite weight-loss gadgets:

BATHROOM SCALES

Digital scales are a must when it comes to weight loss. They allow you to track your weight to one decimal point and pick up small changes over time. Many scales also come with sensors that send a small electrical current through your body to give an estimate of your body fat percentage. I own a set of Tanita Body Composition Scales, for which I paid around $150. There are also scales on the market, including Withings models and the Fitbit Aria Wi-fi Smart Scale, that will sync with your smartphone to record your weight changes over time. These will also set you back about $150.

HEART RATE MONITOR

There are many brands of heart rate monitors on the market. All of the most credible models involve an elastic strap worn around your chest with a sensor that transmits information to a watch. You can get heart rate monitors with inbuilt GPS, which you can plug into a computer to show you the route of your run, the incline and so on. The major brands include Garmin and Polar. You can buy them through online retailers, in fitness or electronics stores, or secondhand through eBay. I use a Polar FT4, which cost me about $140. You can pay anything up to a couple of hundred dollars if you want extra features, but the FT4 has served me well.

KITCHEN SCALES

Becoming calorie aware requires you to become measurement aware. There's no point in knowing how many calories are in 100 grams of pasta if you don't know what 100 grams of pasta looks like. (Hint: it is much, much less than you think!) I promise you won't have to weigh your food forever, but you probably do need to do it initially, and it helps to check in sometimes to make sure you're not getting too liberal with the oatmeal. You can buy cheap digital kitchen scales in supermarkets and homeware stores for around $20.

MEASURING SPOONS

Ah, measuring spoons—the original and best geek gadget. Make sure you have them in your kitchen. A set of measuring spoons is the best weapon you have against the insidious calorie enemy: oil. Remember: 165 calories in every 20 ml tablespoon. Invest in a set (they don't cost much!) to make sure you're not loading up with more calories than you thought.

MUSIC PLAYER

A reluctant gym goer's best friend. An iPod or other music player is an essential tool in any weight-loss regime.

A PEDOMETER OR ACTIVITY TRACKER

If you've tried pedometers before, look again. There has been a proliferation of new models with LED displays that sync with your smartphone and a web-based account. My favourite new breed is the activity tracker. We know we are not walking nearly as much as we used to, or nearly enough to hit our daily fitness requirements. According to an article published in *The Journal of the American Medical Society* in November 2007, people using pedometers walked nearly 2500 more steps a day than those who did not, in 26 separate studies reviewed. 'The results suggest that the use of a pedometer is associated with significant increases in physical activity and significant decreases in body mass index and blood pressure,' the article found. Worth a try, then.

It is possible to purchase pedometers for as little as $15. But some are more accurate than others. A new breed of activity trackers by Fitbit, Nike and Jawbone have reinvented the pedometer, allowing you to sync information with wristbands and smartphones. Fitbit activity trackers currently come in three levels. The base level, called the Zip, costs $70 and measures steps taken and provides an estimate of calories burnt. The One, at $120, fits into your pocket or can be attached to a wristband to track sleep patterns. The Flex, also around $120, is a permanent wristband. I have a One, and while I don't use it every day it is fun to see sometimes how I'm tracking. The tracker's estimates of calories burnt are not as accurate as a heart rate monitor, however, so I use my heart rate monitor more often.

Sports shoe company Nike was an early adopter of the activity-tracking technology. The Nike+ FuelBand is, like other activity trackers, essentially a glorified pedometer, showing you calories burnt and steps taken. It syncs via Bluetooth to your smartphone. It is a little more expensive, costing around $150.

Jawbone was one of the first-generation producers of new pedometers. The Jawbone UP is another wristband that can be worn all day and night to track what you eat and how much you move and sleep. It also syncs to a dedicated smartphone app and to other health and fitness apps like MyFitnessPal and RunKeeper. It costs about $150. Its slogan is 'Know yourself, live better.'

My top ten weight-loss smartphone apps

Perhaps the king of all fitness equipment these days is the smartphone. Given we're permanently glued to the things, why not use yours to enhance your health? It's a music player, calorie counter, calculator and notepad all in one. I never exercise without my smartphone. Here are my favourite apps for weight-loss support, advice and monitoring:

8700

This free NSW government app allows you to 'find your ideal figure' by providing an estimate of your daily kilojoule allowance. It also provides information on the kilojoule content of popular foods and tells you how many kilojoules you burn doing different exercises. There's a handy calories-to-kilojoules calculator and a website packed with information: 'If we consume more kilojoules than our body uses, the spare energy is stored as fat and we will put on weight. So it's important to know your ideal daily kilojoule figure.' Amen to that.

CALORIEKING

The CalorieKing app is an Australian-made calorie counter with an accompanying database of food calories. You can search the database for free, or, if you register your name and email address, you can also access an online diary for logging meals and exercise. It's a useful resource and fairly user friendly. It's also free.

CRUISE CONTROL AND PACEDJ

Both apps sync with your own music collection and select songs that match your running pace. They will slow down or speed up your songs, depending on how fast you are going. You can also pick a certain number of beats per minute and stick to it. PaceDJ is $2.99, while Cruise Control costs $5.49.

ENDOMONDO

This is another running app that uses the GPS in your smartphone to track your run. It allows you to see where you have been (using Google Maps) and share results with friends. It can be linked to certain heart rate monitors and used for a variety of sports, including cycling and walking. It shows distance, duration and an estimate of calories burnt. It's free.

FITBIT

This app syncs to the Fitbit activity trackers. In addition to logging your movements, you can add foods eaten to calculate calories and build a path to weight loss, tracking your results over time. You earn badges for hitting your goals, like walking a certain number of steps or stairs in a day. The app is free after purchase of a Fitbit activity tracker.

FOODSWITCH

Created by health insurance company Bupa and the George Institute for Global Health, FoodSwitch uses the camera in your smartphone to scan barcodes on food. It then gives you a green, red or amber light based on the food's concentration of fat, saturated fat, sugar, salt and energy, along with options for healthier choices.

MEAL SNAP

Meal Snap allows you to take a picture of your meal and 'magically' estimates its calorie content. Pros: any guess is better than no guess at all and the latest version allows you to keep a visual food diary of what you have eaten. Cons: calorie estimates can be wildly wrong on foods that are out of the ordinary. It's hardly perfect, but it's a bit of fun and worth a play. It costs $2.99.

MYFITNESSPAL

This is the ultimate calorie-tracking app. Users have access to a database of calorie information about millions of foods. You can also input exercise calories burnt and receive estimates of how long it will take to lose weight, based on the 3500-calories-per-pound rule. It's so clever you can even use the camera in your smartphone to scan barcodes and get an instant breakdown of the calorie and nutrient composition of what you're about to eat. Free.

RUNKEEPER

This is an easy-to-use app for tracking your runs. You press 'Start' when you're jogging outside and the GPS in your smartphone tracks how far you run. You can set goals for weight loss, log workout reminders and share your jogging information on social media. The app is free.

SUNSMART

My favourite smartphone app for running is the Australian government's SunSmart app. It shows you throughout the year what times of day it is safe to run outdoors without getting sunburnt. In winter, the danger zone can be as short as between 11 a.m. and 1 p.m. In summer, the ultraviolet rays are elevated from as early as 9 a.m. to as late as 4 p.m. I love running outdoors but don't love smothering myself in sunscreen, so the first thing I do before a jog is check SunSmart.

My top ten weight-loss websites

BODY WEIGHT SIMULATOR

http://bwsimulator.niddk.nih.gov

As we saw earlier, the Body Weight Simulator, designed by Kevin Hall and his colleagues, enables you to set your own goal for weight loss and tells you how long it will take to get there. You input your age, height and weight and then play with how much exercise you're prepared to do to see how fast you can realistically reach your target weight.

CALORIEKING

www.calorieking.com.au

CalorieKing is a great source of calorie information for common foods. The idea can be traced back to a 1973 calorie-counting book published by Australian dietitian Allan Borushek. Since going digital it has become one of the biggest databases of calorie counts you will find.

FITOCRACY

www.fitocracy.com

In this social fitness game you compete with other users to complete quests. You can join group challenges such as 'Getting fit for the zombie apocalypse' or just doing 100 push-ups. The site integrates with Twitter, Facebook and RunKeeper. Essentially, it's a game that allows you to earn badges for good behaviour and compete with friends to meet goals.

JOGTUNES

www.jogtunes.com

'Music at your speed.' Search an online database of songs that are categorised by beats per minute, so you can exercise to music that matches your step rate. Find new songs to ramp up your workout.

MICHELLE BRIDGES 12 WEEK BODY TRANSFORMATION

www.12wbt.com

The 12 Week Body Transformation was Australia's first entirely online weight-loss program, run by celebrity fitness trainer Michelle Bridges. It costs $199 upfront or twelve payments of $19.99, which gives you access to the site for one round, consisting of twelve weeks of meal plans, calorie-controlled recipes, workout instructions, online forums, weekly videos and live web chats with Bridges herself. The basic plan is pretty simple: consume 1200 calories a day and exercise six days a week. As Bridges told me, 'Despite comments to the contrary, the mathematics of weight loss do work. I know because it's my job and I see it happen every day. Yes, calories get burnt at different rates and, yes, our bio-individuality dictates that it won't be the same for all of us. But when it comes down to it, outside of extraordinary medical conditions, increasing our energy output and decreasing our energy intake to a state of calorie deficit will result in weight loss. End of story. That's what our bodies are designed to do and they do it very well.' What can I say? The woman talks a lot of sense.

MYFITNESSPAL

www.myfitnesspal.com

I really don't understand how anyone counted calories before MyFitnessPal was invented. It makes it so easy. On a smartphone or on a computer, just use it. Often. There are also forums to discuss your weight loss.

REDDIT

www.reddit.com/r/progresspics

Reddit is a website where people can start forums to discuss a particular topic. This particular forum, where people share before and after pics of their weight loss, has been going for some time. Before/after pictures of people changing their body are incredibly inspirational. But beware, content is user generated and not regulated, so I can't guarantee what you'll see!

STICKK

www.stickk.com

This website allows you to make a pre-commitment to donate money to a friend, charity or organisation you hate if you miss a goal. For example, you could make a donation to the National Rifle Association or your least preferred political party every time you fail to take 10,000 steps in a day.

SUPERTRACKER

www.supertracker.usda.gov

This is a weight-loss tracking tool designed by the US Department of Agriculture. It includes a database of foods called Food-A-Pedia and allows you to track your food and exercise.

USDA NATIONAL NUTRIENT DATABASE

http://ndb.nal.usda.gov/

This is another website designed by the US Department of Agriculture, containing calorie counts of 8000 foods. It is an easy-to-search and authoritative source of calorie and other nutritional information.

Final thoughts

Health researchers are quite pessimistic about people's ability to take individual control of their weight. 'Although in principle a simple energy imbalance problem, the factors leading to obesity are complex,' according to Arne Astrup, the lead author of the Diogenes study.

" Whilst susceptibility to obesity is determined largely by genetic and intrauterine factors, the current obesity epidemic is heavily influenced by adverse lifestyle factors. Given our genetic background, it is essentially infeasible for humans to self-regulate food intake under current environmental circumstances. **"**

Researchers have debated the role of environment and personal responsibility in finding a solution to our obesity epidemic. 'It is certainly possible in our current environment for people to choose to eat a healthy diet and to engage in regular physical activity,' writes James Hill.

" However, in an environment where high-energy dense foods are readily available and vigorously marketed, and where physical activity is not necessary for most people to get through their daily lives, it is hard to maintain a healthy lifestyle. For these reasons, we cannot approach obesity solely as an issue of personal responsibility . . . We have to do this together as a society; if we remain as individuals struggling with the problem, environmental change will not likely occur. **"**

It's neither the environment nor individuals alone that need to change; it's both, according to Hill:

" To get back to the obesity rates that existed [before 1980], individuals are going to have to make a greater conscious effort to manage their weight than they did then. These efforts won't be sustainable unless we can lessen the environmental pressures toward weight gain . . . It will not be easy, but we have dealt with other hard social issues such as tobacco smoking, recycling, and seat belt use. It can be done, but it needs to be done quickly. **"**

I believe you can beat the system. You can retrain your brain to make better decisions. It will require extraordinary effort and constant vigilance. Every hour of every day you will be tested with choices between calorie-dense foods and calorie-sparse foods, between being inactive and being active. To go with the flow these days is to get fat. To get skinny you must swim against the tide. Constantly.

But wouldn't it be good if our society as a whole made it a bit easier for people? Economics says that people will always respond to the incentives on offer. At the moment, lifestyle incentives are pointing us in the wrong direction—towards cheap, calorie-laden food and the couch. The system needs to change, and that comes down to governments. How should public policy respond to the obesity crisis?

Bring in the economists

When we want to influence human behaviour at a social level, it is time to turn to economics. The goal of economics is to maximise societal happiness. If your overeating was affecting only you, perhaps we could overlook it. But the negative health consequences of obesity are borne by everyone. We're all in this together. We'd all be better off if we could work together to reduce the costs of obesity.

Economists have a broad range of tools available to guide us in the right direction. They range from blunt instruments like fat taxes to bans on junk-food advertising, amending competition laws to end the dominance of major food companies, removing subsidies on unhealthy foods and providing subsidies on healthy foods, and even providing subsidies on gym memberships and sporting equipment like heart rate monitors.

If I were the prime minister, I would provide a heart rate monitor to every Australian who is overweight or obese. With two-thirds of Australia's 23 million people in this category, and assuming we could get a pretty big group discount so the monitors cost $100 each, I would conservatively cost this policy at $1.5 billion. Compared to the federal government's total spend of $65 billion on health policies in 2013–14, that's small bickies.

I'm only half kidding. But let's look at some of the more mainstream ideas on offer.

FAT TAXES

Economists have long admired the idea of 'sin taxes'. When you tax an activity, the activity occurs less often. If people are engaging in an activity that we don't want them to engage in, like consuming fatty foods, we could apply a sin tax to the food, just as we do to alcohol and cigarettes.

Studies suggest consumers are price sensitive when it comes to food. Indeed, calorie counting can be undone by pricing strategies. At Hungry Jack's, for example, in 2013 a Sausage & Egg Muffin cost $3.70 and a coffee $3.95—altogether, $7.65. But if you opted for the Sausage & Egg Muffin Meal Deal, which added a hash brown to the muffin and coffee, you paid just $5.95. How do you fight that logic?

A study published in June 2013 titled 'Food prices and body fatness among youths', by researchers Michael Grossman, Erdal Tekin and Roy Wada, found a link between higher fast-food prices and lower body fat percentages. And guess what? They also found that higher prices on fruit and vegetables led to higher body fat percentages. 'Our results . . . do suggest that a tax on meals purchased in fast-food restaurants or a subsidy to the consumption of fruits and vegetables would lead to better obesity outcomes among adolescents,' they wrote. Economists do not usually support subsidies for particular industries, believing governments should not be in the business of 'picking winners'. But if increased consumption of healthy foods like fresh fruit and meat leads to reduced health costs associated with obesity, such subsidies may well save money for governments.

Denmark introduced a fat tax in 2011, but abandoned it after just a year because of widespread confusion over how the tax should apply. You see, it's hard to know what the real enemy is. In its article 'Fat chance', *The Economist* concluded that fat taxes would not work as well as the tax on cigarettes because fatty foods are not uniformly unhealthy. All foods, including fat and sugar, are healthy if consumed in moderation.

Fat taxes are also highly regressive, meaning they hurt poor people proportionately harder than rich people, because people with lower incomes spend a higher proportion of their income on food. And they're an administrative nightmare. Unfortunately, we're back to square one.

ADVERTISING BANS

Even the most determined of dieters can be thrown into disarray by the sight of a juicy Big Mac. (Trust me.) Studies have shown that humans are highly susceptible to framing—the way information is presented. There's a reason why advertising exists: it works.

Children, with less knowledge about the world to give their experiences context, are particularly susceptible to advertising. David Katz, the director of Yale-Griffin Prevention Research Center, says it's time to eradicate not only junk-food advertising to children, but children's junk food altogether. As Katz points out, humans are the only species in nature that feeds its children special food:

" Imagine if baby whales, weaned from milk, didn't learn to eat krill; they were indulged with sugar-frosted flukes or some such thing. Imagine the fussy eaters among the lion cubs who turned up their noses at wildebeest and held out for mac and cheese. Imagine mama and papa dolphin talking themselves into the need to indulge junior's apparent aversion to fish. Crackers shaped like fish—fine, but actual fish? Fuhgeddaboudit! **"**

The solution, says Katz, is to eradicate special kids' food altogether.

According to groundbreaking work by economist Richard Thaler, an advisor to the UK government, policy 'nudges' can steer people in the right direction to serving their long-term interests. Humans, argues Thaler, are imperfect and need protection against people who would deliberately exploit their weaknesses. Governments are making progress in this, says Daniel Kahneman, a Nobel Prize winner in economics:

" The US government has introduced a new version of the dietary guidelines that replaces the incomprehensible Food Pyramid with the powerful image of a Food Plate loaded with a balanced diet, and a rule formulated by the USDA [US Department of Agriculture] that permits the inclusion of messages such as '90% fat-free' on the label of meat products, provided the statement '10% fat' is also displayed 'contiguous to, in lettering of the same color, size, and type as, and on the same color background as, the statement of lean percentage'. Humans . . . need help to make good decisions, and there are informed and unintrusive ways to provide that help. **"**

Banning junk-food advertising to children would seem to be the most obvious way. I can't believe we haven't done it yet.

EDUCATION AND CALORIE LABELLING

This is where the rubber hits the road for me. According to economist John Cawley's paper, 'An economic framework for understanding physical activity and eating behaviors', information is a public good. Health information, then, is something governments should produce for all individuals.

❝ Once someone produces information, it can be distributed among consumers beyond the control of the producer. For this reason, objective information tends to be under-provided by private markets, and there is a role for governments to sponsor the production and dissemination of information. **❞**

The figures are old, but Cawley reports that the 1996 advertising budget for McDonald's was US$599 million, and just US$1 million was made available for the National Cancer Institute's '5-A-Day' campaign promoting fruit and vegetables. It's time to level the field a little, either by banning some advertising or by countering it with better health information.

In particular, I would like to see more widespread calorie or kilojoule labelling. The NSW government has been something of a pioneer in this area. All of the state's chain fast-food stores are required to display kilojoule counts on their price boards. Supermarkets, too, must put kilojoule counts on those delicious ready-roasted chickens. Is the strategy working? International evidence for the effectiveness of calorie counts is pretty sketchy so far. Proper food labelling is important. Reading food labels can be time-consuming, so labels should be as quick and easy to read as possible. I would like to see less emphasis on macronutrient breakdown and greater prominence given to energy content. Food labelling should help consumers think through the consequences of their eating actions in the real world. For example, a label might read, 'If you eat this muffin every day in addition to your daily calorie allowance, you will need to do 60 minutes' brisk walking every day, or in a year's time you'll be roughly 5 kilograms heavier.'

I would also like to see calorie or kilojoule counts on alcoholic drinks. For some reason, alcohol manufacturers have been able to fly under the radar on calorie labelling. But with a bottle of wine containing 560 calories or more, consumers need to know.

In education, greater focus should be given to portion sizes—*how much* you're supposed to eat—rather than teaching children just *what* to eat. We have to be careful not to make our kids too obsessed by food, but we shouldn't hide the truth from them. If you eat too much, you'll get fat. Better to know now. Habits are formed at a very young age. That's okay if you're living at home and eating healthy food prepared by your parents. But kids need to know about food to be able to navigate their way in our calorie-dense world.

THE FREE MARKET

'For consumers who want to decrease calorie intake, raise energy expenditure, and/or reduce their weight, private industry, seeking profit, will try to help them achieve it,' according to economist John Cawley.

Tough Mudder is a US company founded in 2009 that runs competitive obstacle courses, usually involving a lot of mud. 'We are in explosive growth mode right now,' co-founder Guy Livingstone told Julie Satow of *The New York Times* in July 2013. Tough Mudder was on course for US$120 million revenue that year and was hoping to reach US$200 million in 2014.

There has been an explosion of gyms in our cities as people seek a healthier lifestyle. Fitness clothing and equipment have never been easier to come by. Food companies, too, have begun taking baby steps towards making their food healthier. Soft drink manufacturers have removed their vending machines from schools. It's possible that we are seeing the beginnings of a health revolution in which consumers will demand healthier products and the market will supply them. But it is also possible that the economics of food production will be too overwhelming for governments to wind back.

The bottom line

Small changes are happening in our environment that may eventually nudge us in the right direction. 'In the absence of a single big solution to obesity, the state must try many small measures,' says *The Economist*. The bottom line, though, is that control of your bottom line is down to you.

" There is a limit . . . to what the state can or should do. In the end, the responsibility and power to change lie primarily with individuals. Whether people go on eating till they pop, or whether they opt for the healthier, slimmer life, will have a bigger effect on the future of the species than most of the weighty decisions that governments make. **"**

Will we, as a society, be divided between a high-income elite who can muster the strength and resources to fight against obesity while the rest continue to get fat on cheap, calorie-rich foods? If healthy living is going to be anything more than a niche industry, it is clear that we will need better education, bans on junk-food advertising, subsidies of fresh whole foods and better and more meaningful food labelling. If you want to wait for the government to solve this problem, fine. But, just as a warning, you may spend the rest of your life fat.

It's time to take back control of your body. Beat the system. Get cynical. Stop believing the lies. I hope this book will get you started on a lifelong journey of discovery. There is plenty more to find out about how to nourish and care for your body.

Good luck out there.

Acknowledgements

This book would not have been possible if not for the generosity of the obesity experts who donated their time and patience to answer my questions. In particular, I would like to thank Stephen Simpson, Joseph Proietto, Jennie Brand-Miller, Amanda Salis, William Sukala, Joanna McMillan and Kevin Hall. Any errors are mine alone. Many thanks also to the wonderful team at Allen & Unwin. To my loving parents and brothers, who have hardly seen or heard from me this past year. And to my amazing husband, Ashley: my gym buddy, part-time personal chef and the love of my life. My love for you is beyond measure.

For more tips, online tools or to get in touch,
go to **www.thebottomlinediet.com**

References

American Heart Foundation, 'Dietary sugars intake and cardiovascular health: A scientific statement from the American Heart Foundation', *Circulation: Journal of the American Heart Foundation*, vol. 120, 2009, pp. 1011–20

Astrup, A, 'Diet, obesity and genes', DioGenes, n.d. (viewed August 2013), www.diogenes-eu.org/news/DioGenes%20Unilever%20 Satellite%20Astrup%202.1.pdf

Australian Bureau of Statistics, *Australian Health Survey: First Results, 2011–12*, cat. no. 4364.0.55.001, ABS, Canberra, 2011

——*Australian Health Survey: Physical Activity, 2011–12*, cat. no. 4364.0.55.004, ABS, Canberra, 2011

——*Motor Vehicle Census, Australia, 31 Jan 2013*, cat. no. 9309.0, ABS, Canberra, 2013

——*Retail Trade, Australia, July 2013*, cat. no. 8501.0, ABS, Canberra, 2013

——'We're spending less time playing, sleeping and eating but working longer: ABS', media release, ABS, 21 February 2008, www.abs.gov.au/ausstats/abs@.nsf/Latestproducts/ 4153.0Media%20Release12006

Bassett, DR, Schneider, PL, and Huntington, GE, 'Physical activity in an Old Order Amish community', *Medicine & Science in Sports & Exercise*, vol. 36, no. 1, January 2004, pp. 79–85

Borushek, A, *Allan Borushek's Calorie, Fat & Carbohydrate Counter*, Family Health Publications, 2012

Broom, DR, Batterham, RL, King, JA, and Stensel, DJ, 'Influence of resistance and aerobic exercise on hunger, circulating levels of acylated ghrelin and peptide YY in healthy males', *American Journal of Physiology—Regulatory, Integrative and Comparative Physiology*, vol. 296, no. R29–R35, 1 January 2009, http://ajpregu. physiology.org/content/296/1/R29

Bureau of Home Economics, United States Department of Agriculture, '100-calorie portions of a few familiar foods', [1927–31], copy at ARC no. 5838434, US National Archives, College Park, Md

Cawley, J, 'An economic framework for understanding physical activity and eating behaviors', *American Journal of Preventive Medicine*, vol. 27, no. 3S, 2004, pp. 117–25

——'The impact of obesity on wages', *Journal of Human Resources*, vol. 39, no. 2, spring 2004, pp. 451–74

Dalley, E, 'Liquid breakfasts: 02. A sugary start', *Choice*, 24 June 2013, www.choice.com.au/reviews-and-tests/food-and-health/food-and-drink/groceries/liquid-breakfasts/page/sugary-start.aspx

de Souza, R, Swain, J, Appel, L, and Sacks, F, 'Alternatives for macronutrient intake and chronic disease: A comparison of the OmniHeart diets with popular diets and with dietary recommendations', *American Journal of Clinical Nutrition*, vol. 88, no. 1, July 2008, pp. 1–11

Dunstan, DW, Barr, ELM, Healy, GN, Salmon, J, Shaw, JE, et al., 'Television viewing time and mortality: The Australian Diabetes, Obesity and Lifestyle Study (AusDiab)', *Circulation*, vol. 121, 2010, pp. 384–91

'Fat chance', *Economist*, 15 December 2012, www.economist.com/news/leaders/21568389-state-can-do-some-things-encourage-people-eat-less-not-lot-fat-chance

'Food search', CalorieKing, n.d. (viewed August 2013), www.calorie king.com/foods/

Foresight, *Tackling Obesities: Future Choices—Obesity System Atlas*, Department of Innovation, Universities and Skills, London, 2007

Fox, S, and Duggan, M, 'Tracking for Health', Pew Research Center,

28 January 2013, http://pewinternet.org/Reports/2013/
Tracking-for-Health.aspx

Gosby, AK, Conigrave, AD, Lau, NS, Iglesias, MA, Hall, RM, et al.,
'Testing protein leverage in lean humans: A randomised
controlled experimental study', *PLoS ONE*, vol. 6, no. 10, e25929,
2011, www.plosone.org/article/info%3Adoi%2F10.1371%2
Fjournal.pone.0025929

Grossman, M, Tekin, E, and Wada, R, *Food Prices and Body Fatness
Among Youths*, NBER Working Paper 19143, National Bureau of
Economic Research, Cambridge, Mass., June 2013

Hall, KD, 'Modeling metabolic adaptations and energy regulation in
humans', *Annual Review of Nutrition*, vol. 32, 21 August 2012,
pp. 35–54

——'What is the required energy deficit per unit weight loss?',
International Journal of Obesity, vol. 32, no. 3, March 2008,
pp. 573–6

Hall, KD, Heymsfield, SB, Kemnitz, JW, Klein, S, Schoeller, DA, et al.,
'Energy balance and its components: Implications for body
weight regulation', *American Journal of Clinical Nutrition*, vol. 95,
no. 4, April 2012, pp. 989–94

Hall, KD, Sacks, G, Chandramohan, D, Chow, CC, Wang, YC, et al.,
'Quantification of the effect of energy imbalance on bodyweight',
The Lancet, vol. 378, 27 August 2011, pp. 826–37

Harrar, V, and Spence, C, 'The taste of cutlery: How the taste of food
is affected by the weight, size, shape, and colour of the cutlery
used to eat it', *Flavour*, vol. 2, no. 21, 2013, www.flavourjournal.
com/content/pdf/2044-7248-2-21.pdf

Harris, JA, and Benedict, FG, *A Biometric Study of Basal Metabolism in
Man*, Carnegie Institution of Washington, Washington, DC, 1919

Hill, JO, 'Understanding and addressing the epidemic of obesity: An
energy balance perspective', *Endocrine Reviews*, vol. 27, no. 7,
1 December 2006, pp. 750–61

Hill, JO, and Wing, R, 'The National Weight Control Registry',
Permanente Journal, vol. 7, no. 3, summer 2003, pp. 34–7

Hill, JO, Wyatt, HR, Reed, GW, and Peters, JC, 'Obesity and the
environment: Where do we go from here?', *Science*, vol. 299,
2003, pp. 853–5

Jonker, JT, de Mol, P, de Vries, ST, Widya, RL, Hammer, S, et al.,

'Exercise and type 2 diabetes mellitus: Changes in tissue-specific fat distribution and cardiac function', *Radiology*, 25 June 2013, http://radiology.rsna.org/content/early/2013/06/04/radiol.13121631.abstract

Kahneman, D, *Thinking, Fast and Slow*, Farrar, Straus and Giroux, New York, 2011

Katz, D, 'We must be kidding! The case for eradicating "kid" food', *U.S. News & World Report*, 17 June 2013, http://health.usnews.com/health-news/blogs/eat-run/2013/06/17/we-must-be-kidding-the-case-for-eradicating-kid-food

Kish, S, 'Healthy, low calorie foods cost more on average', Cooperative State Research, Education, and Extension Service, United States Department of Agriculture, 19 March 2008, www.csrees.usda.gov/newsroom/impact/2008/nri/03191_food_prices.html

'[Losing] battle against obesity', *Nordstjernan*, n.d. (viewed August 2013), www.nordstjernan.com/news/sweden/3866/

Lustig, R, 'Sugar: The bitter truth', lecture at Osher Center for Integrative Medicine, University of California, San Francisco, 2009, video, YouTube, uploaded 30 July 2009, www.youtube.com/watch?v=dBnniua6-oM

Magary, D, 'The Public Humiliation Diet: A how-to', *Deadspin*, 25 May 2010, www.deadspin.com/5545674/the-public-humiliation-diet-a-how+to

Major Cities Unit, *State of Australian Cities 2012*, Department of Infrastructure and Transport, Canberra, 2012

Mehta, R, 'Toolmaker talk: Mike Lee (MyFitnessPal)', *Quantified Self*, 15 February 2012, http://quantifiedself.com/2012/02/toolmaker-talk-mike-lee-myfitnesspal/

Monsivais, P, and Drewnowski, A, 'The rising cost of low-energy-density foods', *Journal of the American Dietetic Association*, vol. 107, no. 12, December 2007, pp. 2071–6

Nahal, S, Lucas-Leclin, V, and King, J, *Globesity: The global fight against obesity*, Bank of America Merrill Lynch, New York, 21 June 2012

National Health and Medical Research Council, *Australian Dietary Guidelines*, NHMRC, Canberra, 2013

Newton, I, 'Fitzwilliam Notebook', cat. no. ALCH00069, Fitzwilliam Museum, Cambridge

'Reversing the obesity epidemic', executive summary, *The Lancet*,
    26 August 2011, http://download.thelancet.com/
    flatcontentassets/series/obesity-summary2.pdf

Rutter, H, 'Where next for obesity?', *The Lancet*, vol. 378, no. 9793,
    27 August 2011, pp. 746–7

Sacks, FM, Bray, GA, Carey, VJ, Smith, SR, Ryan, DH, et al.,
    'Comparison of weight-loss diets with different compositions of
    fat, protein and carbohydrates', *New England Journal of Medicine*,
    vol. 360, no. 9, 26 February 2009, pp. 859–73

Satow, J, 'Even boutique gyms need back offices as they grow', *New
    York Times*, 2 July 2013, www.nytimes.com/2013/07/03/
    realestate/commercial/even-boutique-gyms-need-back-offices-
    as-they-grow.html?pagewanted=all&_r=0

Simpson, SJ, and Raubenheimer, D, 'Obesity: The protein leverage
    hypothesis', *Obesity Reviews*, vol. 6, no. 2, May 2005, pp. 133–42

Sumithran, P, Prendergast, LA, Delbridge, E, Purcell, K, Shulkes, A,
    et al., 'Long-term persistence of hormonal adaptations to weight
    loss', *New England Journal of Medicine*, vol. 365, 27 October 2011,
    pp. 1597–604

Swinburn, BA, Sacks, G, Hall, KD, McPherson, K, Finegood, DT, et
    al., 'The global obesity pandemic: Shaped by global drivers and
    local environments', *The Lancet*, vol. 378, no. 9793, 27 August
    2011, pp. 804–14

Thaler, RH, and Sunstein, CR, *Nudge: Improving Decisions about
    Health, Wealth, and Happiness*, Yale University Press, 2008

Turner-McGrievy, GM, and Tate, DF, 'Weight loss social support in
    140 characters or less: Use of an online social network in a
    remotely delivered weight loss intervention', *Translational
    Behavioral Medicine*, January 2013, http://link.springer.com/
    article/10.1007/s13142-012-0183-y

UK Metric Association, 'Adult weight and height', UK Metric
    Association, 2013, www.metric.org.uk/bmi

Wansink, B, *Mindless Eating: Why we eat more than we think*,
    Bantam-Dell, New York, 2006

Wishnofsky, M, 'Caloric equivalents of gained or lost weight',
    American Journal of Clinical Nutrition, vol. 6, no. 5, September
    1958, pp. 542–6

Wolf, G, 'Gary Wolf: The quantified self', speech at TED@Cannes,

June 2010, video, TED, www.ted.com/talks/gary_wolf_the_quantified_self.html

Wycherley, TP, Moran, LJ, Clifton, PM, Noakes, M, and Brinkworth, GD, 'Effects of energy-restricted high-protein, low-fat compared with standard-protein, low-fat diets: A meta-analysis of randomized controlled diets', *American Journal of Clinical Nutrition*, vol. 96, 2012, pp. 1281–91.